Channeling the Past

Channeling the Past

Politicizing History
in Postwar America

Erik Christiansen

THE UNIVERSITY OF WISCONSIN PRESS

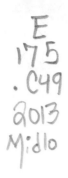

E
175
.C49
2013
Midlo

Publication of this volume has been made possible,
in part, through support from
Rhode Island College.

The University of Wisconsin Press
1930 Monroe Street, 3rd Floor
Madison, Wisconsin 53711-2059
uwpress.wisc.edu

3 Henrietta Street
London WC2E 8LU, England
eurospanbookstore.com

Printed in the United States of America

Library of Congress Cataloging-in-Publication Data

Christiansen, Erik, 1974–
Channeling the past: politicizing history in postwar America /
Erik Christiansen.
p.   cm. — (Studies in American thought and culture)
Includes bibliographical references and index.
ISBN 978-0-299-28904-1 (pbk.: alk. paper)
ISBN 978-0-299-28903-4 (e-book)
1. Public history — Political aspects — United States — History — 20th century.
2. History in popular culture — United States.
3. Mass media and history — United States.
I. Title.   II. Series: Studies in American thought and culture.
E175.C49   2013
302.2309 — dc23
2012011999

To
my teachers,
especially my parents

The American Clio has been placed in the role of a sacred oracle from whom the meaning of events and the pathway of the future are periodically sought. The answers the oracle has given have been in the form of reinterpretations of American history. And the interpreters of the Oracle have not always belonged to Clio's ordained priesthood of historians.

C. Vann Woodward, *American Attitudes toward History*

Contents

Illustrations

Preface

This is a history of the usable past in the postwar United States. Or rather, it is a collection of five interrelated histories of sometimes conflicting, sometimes overlapping usable pasts. In each story, a particular group of Americans purported to teach their rendering of the vital lessons of history to the public. The large number of popular historical productions in this period, the unique ways in which they competed for the public's attention, and the range of *contemporary* subjects that they addressed make in-depth study of the postwar usable pasts critical. Their stories also describe the challenges faced by various individuals who have nobly attempted to bridge divisions between academic, popular, and public history.

Somewhat paradoxically, these constructed pasts reveal a high degree of consensus as well as significant cracks in the nation's public, though unofficial, history. On the one hand, postwar Americans generally drew upon a broadly shared and familiar heritage, a usable past that was then reinterpreted to fit particular agendas. On the other, as early as the late 1940s some of the histories examined in this book came from well beyond the limited, narrow mainstream perspective, and included ignored or forgotten episodes of black or Native American struggles against white oppression. However, even when the more obscure counternarratives were brought to mainstream (white) America's attention, they still relied on a basic foundational understanding of the national past and were rooted in recognizable values and traditions; they just struggled for inclusion.

The postwar pasts designed for consumption by the American public originated within one or another community of elites who were able, through new and emerging media, to effectively disseminate their political and historical interpretations to a surprisingly large audience. This public apparently accepted the premise that mass education in history, however defined and interpreted, was relevant, or even necessary, to any attempt to deal with the issues of the day. These facts make the postwar relationship between contemporary Americans and the past very different from that of other periods, particularly today.

For example, throughout the spring of 2010, the *New York Times* ran a series of articles about the Texas school board's review of the state's public school history curriculum. The *Times* bemoaned the conservative tenor of the proposed amendments to American history textbooks, as well as the decision-making process itself. The affair mattered because the importance of the giant Texas market elevates the significance of its school board's choices. The board itself was dominated by outspoken conservatives, none of whom was a historian. Some amendments, like a directive to emphasize the leading actors in the late twentieth-century conservative movement, may make sense historiographically, though the *Times* did not approve. Others, like the erasure of Thomas Jefferson because he too clearly advocated for a separation of church and state, appeared indefensible.

The *Times* reporter who covered the story, James P. McKinley Jr., wrote of the underlying change that the process made manifest: namely, the utter lack of agreement in America today about the national past.[1] Not only do liberals and conservatives interpret history differently, he said, but they also no longer share a common past at all. Whereas liberals might want students to study Thomas Jefferson and to learn about the reasons for establishing a "wall of separation" between church and state, conservatives wish for schools that emphasize the Christian principles on which, they say, the nation was founded. There are, of course, elements of truth in both interpretations, but, in part because of the democratic nature of education in the United States, history has become so politicized that any part of it that some group finds offensive to their ideological sensibilities is in danger of being erased. Equally disturbing is the result that Americans no longer feel connected to each other through a common heritage: I have my past, and you have yours, and never the twain shall meet. Liberals might read Howard Zinn's *People's History of the United States* while conservatives have made the more recent *Patriot's History of the United States* into a best-selling counterargument; most historians would say that neither book deserves kudos for objectivity or nuance. For a public less than deeply educated in the discipline of history, it is increasingly difficult to make sense out of political debates that reference wildly divergent accounts of the past. We are left with a situation in which not just polarized opinion but polarized *knowledge* means there is no consensus on where America came from, let alone where it should be going.

To a certain extent, this has always been true: people draw on elements of an invented past capacious enough to support their current worldview. In fact,

Texas saw a similar fight play out in the late 1950s.[2] What has changed is the loss of a shared store of historical knowledge, widely known and more or less taken for granted. At midcentury, consensus about a shared past could, ironically, support a particular political position. A founding father like Jefferson could not be erased from history, but he could be used for different ends. However, the beginning of a transition to a society of more divergent pasts began to intrude upon this accepted narrative, and rightly so. Groups long oppressed began to discover their own previously marginalized or unknown histories. Their challenges to the dominant strain encouraged the disintegration of a history in common. More important, perhaps, the new communication technologies of the postwar era that allowed the subjects of this book to reach broad audiences have been improved or replaced, so that a clearly defined audience for interpretations of history is difficult to find. Thus, in the late 1940s historians thought that they might guide the public through a new history book club run like a reading seminar. Today, however, Internet-based discount book clubs offer tens of thousands of titles that appeal to every niche interest. Likewise, the early days of television provided a medium with very limited choices and substantial historical and other educational programming. Today that medium offers hundreds of channels, nearly all of them for entertainment. While the actors, objectives, historical approaches, and media vary, the stories told in each chapter share a similar denouement when it comes to the eventual loss of a captive audience for historical productions.

This is not to suggest that the examples discussed within these pages were ideal. Each of these methods of representing the past massaged historical fact until it became malleable enough to answer any objection raised against its producer's usage. People and events were cherry-picked to support arguments, while contradictory evidence remained buried in the silt of history. But these were all ultimately unifying projects in intention; as such, they may have something to offer in our current age of historical and political polarization. If some kind of relationship with the past is presumed to be good for society, perhaps some answers—and warnings—can be found in these historical examples.

Many people have helped me with this book, starting with my wife, Shanna, and my parents. Students at Rhode Island College and the University of Maryland provided thoughtful feedback, and both of those institutions supported this project in numerous ways, including research time and funding. A special thank you to Dean Earl Simson for his generous support. Innumerable friends, mentors, and colleagues have critiqued drafts along the way; Kate Keane in particular spent more time on this than she should have. Without David

Glassberg's critical suggestions for improvement, this book would not exist. I hope that my writing reflects something of David Grimsted's inimitable influence and that my deep gratitude to Jim Gilbert is known to him. I also must thank David Sicilia, Saverio Giovacchini, Claire Goldstene, and Jeremy Sullivan for their early guidance and support. The Hagley Foundation generously supported weeks of fruitful research at the Hagley Library in Delaware. The University of Pennsylvania Humanities Forum, the Freie Universität Berlin, the University of Maryland, and the American Historical Association's Annual Meeting provided opportunities to present portions of my work to critical audiences. I am also grateful to the many librarians and archivists who assisted my research at the National Archives; the Library of Congress; the libraries at Stanford University, the University of Maryland, and the University of Virginia; the New York Public Library at Lincoln Center; the Wisconsin Historical Society; the Paley Center; and the Hagley Library. Finally, it has been a pleasure to work with Gwen Walker, Sheila McMahon, Paul Boyer, and everyone else at the University of Wisconsin Press, and I greatly appreciate their tremendous efforts on behalf of this book.

Channeling the Past

Introduction

History's Past Presence

In the spring of 1947, President Harry Truman formally launched the domestic Cold War by issuing Executive Order 9835, which established the federal government's employee loyalty program. In November, the House Committee on Un-American Activities launched its investigation of the motion picture industry with public hearings into the activities of the "Hollywood Ten," and names soon began to appear on an entertainment industry blacklist. In an unambiguous response to the nation's darkening mood that aired just over a month later, millions of radio listeners heard a staged news report from the Salem witch trials of 1692, in which "anxiety and unrest" led the people of Salem to *wrongly* believe that scores of their friends and neighbors were "plotting the destruction of our government." That same year, over the same medium, the Greek philosopher Plato also spoke from the past to the present—and directly to Americans, chastising them for irrational paranoia and explaining that "a fever of fear runs high among us. We're confused, desperate, and so we seek someone to blame and sacrifice." Then Plato pleaded with listeners to resist succumbing to fearmongers. These dramatized historical protests against the rising tide of anticommunism continued in a varied form on the CBS News series *You Are There*, while simultaneously, and in the months leading up to the 1948 presidential election, listeners of the Du Pont Company's *Cavalcade of America* series heard Thomas Jefferson speak of the debt of gratitude all Americans owed the Du Pont family, and by extension other business leaders, past and present, and of the need to keep American businesses free of cumbersome government regulation. As the mass media delivered these antipathetic messages from the past to tens of millions of radio listeners, a group of prominent historians launched the History Book Club (HBC) in an effort to bring intellectual guidance to what they hoped would be an emerging public dialogue with history. And on Pennsylvania Avenue and Wall Street, political and corporate leaders organized the Freedom Train, which during the years 1947–49 would carry the documents declared to be most vital to American history all over the country, ostensibly so that Americans could commune with history directly, but actually for purposes of propaganda. Meanwhile, in the pointed shadow of the Washington Monument, planning began for a national museum dedicated to celebrating, through icons and commemoration, the history of the nation's development and its modern triumph as world superpower and global champion of freedom.

The early postwar era was inundated by a wide variety of projects focused on connecting contemporaries with particular perspectives on the past. This book focuses on several of the most important of these in order to examine why and how Americans interacted with history in this period, and what that interaction reveals, both about postwar society and about the continuing evolution of historical consciousness in the United States. The contemporary state of the development of radio, television, and other technologies, and the challenging political climate of the period, encouraged efforts to mine the past and affected both the style and substance of popular historical representations.

Using the past to argue for the appropriateness of a particular agenda depended upon a successful and persuasive effort to define and claim the nation's heritage and traditions. The individuals discussed in the following chapters found means, of varying effectiveness, for doing this. Their media of communication ranged from traditional sites of historical interpretation, such as books and museum exhibits, to the latest technologies, including radio and television. Their messages represented a startling diversity of political opinion in the United States, even at the height of McCarthyism.[1] Liberal academics, communist television writers, and right-wing corporate leaders all espoused their politics through popular historical reconstructions. Their methods involved an extensive interpretation, revision, and explanation of history for a public that they all thought lacked sufficient historical knowledge—that is, knowledge enough to meet the considerable challenges of the age. They all believed in the power of history, and they intended to wield it.

Sources of Anxiety and Reassurance

In 1949, George Orwell wrote, "Who controls the past controls the future."[2] The actors in this study certainly subscribed to that contemporary aphorism, believing history to be centrally important to their political agendas. Orwell also suggested that control of the present allows for control of the past; in open societies like the United States, the past has remained contested terrain. Public battles over history suggest how control of that narrative has been, and continues to be, important to major interests in American society, however difficult it is to achieve that goal with any precision.

The popular success of these historical productions makes them all the more important to understanding midcentury social thought. Individuals may think about the past, but the origins of one's historical ideas are found in society's collective memory, a point made long ago by Maurice Halbwachs.[3] That public memory, rooted in symbols, structures, and shared knowledge, possesses socially cohesive and explanatory power. According to Warren Susman, "The idea of history itself . . . and various attitudes toward history always play—whether intelligently conceived or not—a major role within a culture. . . . Attitudes toward the past frequently become facts of profound consequence for the culture itself."[4] Barbara Misztal's recent and comprehensive work on memory further substantiates how collective memory of the past functions as society's foundation.[5]

In the early 1950s, following their own contemporary observations and historical work, C. Vann Woodward and Daniel J. Boorstin separately posited that Americans have "made more exorbitant demands upon history than have other peoples." As much as any historian, Boorstin represents 1950s consensus, and his analysis of postwar historical consciousness deserves more attention. He argued that Americans "use their history not only as a source of myth and an object of filial piety, but as a substitute for political theory." By this he meant that while postwar Americans generally looked upon political or economic theory with suspicion, they actually approached the nation's past as if it were a coherent theory in its own right—which needed only to be properly deciphered. Americans, Woodward explained to an audience at Oxford, "sought their values, the meaning of their experience, and a chart for their future in their history." And the historical "American Way of Life," wrote Boorstin, "harbors an 'American Way of Thought' which can do us for a political theory, even if we never make it explicit." For Americans, "political theory never appears in its nakedness but always clothed in the peculiar American experience. We like to think that . . . we can guess what lies underneath and that such a guess is good enough—perhaps actually better than any naked theory."[6] Historical understanding thus shapes and limits American politics.

In an essay published a decade later, the English historian J. R. Pole wrote of the "peculiarly American version of the space-time continuum" and its "triangle of space, time, and political ideology" that apparently conflated politics and popular historical understanding. Pole described how American citizens, political leaders, and even historians spoke of historical figures as if they inhabited the present and thus could participate in current debates. In his work on how Americans remember Lincoln, Barry Schwartz finds revealing parallels— and differences—between this practice and the "What Would Jesus Do?" tendencies of recent years.[7] When public discourse relies on precedent rather than creative argument, intricate and objective history seems less vital to society than immediately usable history. Recognizing this as problematic, Boorstin suggested that while "citizen's history" carries more weight in the real world, academic history remained important to the extent that it influenced more popular conceptions of the past. He noted in the introduction to his *American Primer* that while historians seek the original meaning of a document or event, others want to know, "What do they mean to us?" Historians may endlessly debate the finer points, but citizens must act immediately. Authors who refuse to draw conclusions may be fine historians, but they fail to serve the citizen who must vote today, and who must take what the past has left and make something with it now.[8]

Within this paradigm, specific interpretations of history directed toward the public took on great importance; elites who similarly understood history's utility worked to ensure that their preferred interpretation gained broad acceptance. The Great Depression and World War II altered American life in myriad ways and contributed to postwar feelings of general apprehension.[9] After the war, many Americans felt compelled to reestablish or establish basic tenets that may have been thrown into confusion by the crises of the 1930s and 1940s.[10] The atmosphere in which such attempted revisions took place after World War II was characterized not only by anxieties about the postwar situation and fears of nuclear annihilation, but also by hope and the promise of "better living," which created another type of anxiety. Even school history textbooks of the 1950s, with their depictions of an American past completely devoid of conflicts, concluded with "many grim warnings" about the present: "the most difficult and challenging period in American history."[11] The groups below expressed the same attitude when they referenced the past specifically because of presumed present dangers.

The mixture of anticipation and angst created a sense of urgency regarding history: specifically, what was the past's essential meaning and how did it now apply? The same fears, needs, and possibilities that contributed to the rise of social scientists and other experts who answered fundamental questions about society and offered solutions for confronting new challenges also presented a moment of opportunity for elites to provide guidance through usable pasts.[12] A 1948 survey revealed that the average book reader apparently was "unconcerned about international affairs, the atom bomb, or the recent war." Fiction and nonfiction books on these topics proved surprisingly unpopular. But while readers shied away from these important subjects, "the classics," historical fiction, and nonfiction history surged in popularity.[13] The interest in history did not necessarily mean a retreat from contemporary issues; rather, postwar Americans often dealt with these new challenges through the prism of the past. In the contemporary culture, history had authority. Significantly, all of the popular "historians" studied in this book also possessed a certain authority in American society, whether derived from academic credentials, corporate dominance, the prestige of network news, the cultural capital possessed by museums, or apparent consensus.

In the 1950s, "Space Age" discourse offered another, contrapuntal attitude toward the present, which perhaps increased the determination of those who believed that answers lay in the past. Certainly it presented Americans with another alternative reality through which present concerns might be addressed, in that sense functioning in much the same way as history. This is most obvious in contemporary science fiction, but both past and future offered limitless settings for analogies rife with present meanings. Indeed Du Pont, as well as other corporations, advertised futuristic visions and products while simultaneously engaging in historical revisionism through *Cavalcade of America*.

Exciting new possibilities for mass communication further encouraged efforts to mine the past for commercial and propaganda purposes. History has long existed partly in the abstract, accessible over the airwaves of mass media. The spread of radio and then television offered ways of directly communicating carefully crafted messages to the public, and the emphasis on educational and enlightening programming in the early years of both media further galvanized the growth of popular history as a tool for advertising and persuasion. Limited choices also meant that a high percentage of Americans watched or listened to the same broadcasts—a situation unique to the middle decades of the twentieth century. Increased secondary school and college attendance also presented new reasons to focus on history: more students were obliged to study the discipline and absorb the lessons taught. Besides textbooks, postwar schools made use of audio and visual materials to teach history, much of which came from the commercial sources discussed in chapters 3 and 4.

The academic discipline may remain the province of professional historians, but of course many other actors affect public memory. As C. Vann Woodward put it more than sixty years ago, "The interpreters of the Oracle have not always belonged to Clio's ordained priesthood of historians."[14] The public, or collective, memory differs from academic history in its ultimate reliance on apparent consensus instead of scholarly authority or evidence, its overwhelming emphasis on only the most memorable ("historic") events and people rather than broad attempts to depict societies of the past, and also, I would say, in its greater relevance to the political culture of a democracy. David Glassberg's work on historical memory calls attention to how "various versions of the past are communicated in a society through a multiplicity of institutions and media," and John Bodnar's work on the politics of collective memory shows that even well-established "official" versions of the past must compete with the "vernacular" memories of groups and individuals.[15] Thus, any attempt to comprehensively describe and locate history in society must grapple with the "complexity of the overlapping sites where history is produced" and reveal "the concrete production of specific narratives."[16] A number of recent works illustrate how historians have begun to incorporate interpretations generated beyond the ivory tower into their narratives in order to study how interactions between personal experience, commemoration, and academic history produce the remembered past.[17] These volumes persuasively argue for greater attention to the creation of popular attitudes toward history and the often dubious "uses to which it is put outside the academy," in order to better understand the construction of cultural hegemony.[18]

For the sake of being able to look in depth at particular cases that elucidate how and why history was used in postwar American society, this book focuses on popular sources that specifically sought recognition as reliable history and deliberately created usable "citizen's history," tailored to the age. The approach differs from existing work on collective memory in its tight focus on a few key sources in a fairly short period of time as well as its broad inclusion of many historical subjects (rather than examining a single event or person in American memory).[19] Hollywood movies and theme parks like Disneyland are not discussed in detail here, even though both produced similar contending versions of the past—especially in this period, the "Golden Age of the Western."[20] The line between serious history and historically themed entertainment may be very fine in some cases, but the projects in this study all strove for credibility in ways that Disney and Hollywood generally did not. Each of the following chapters evaluates a different source of purposely politicized history, demonstrating why the historical trope particularly suited the sponsor's needs and objectives and how they managed to convey ideas through representations of the past. They also reveal what messages were entwined with these representations of the past, how the messages were transmitted, and how these messages were received.

Interest in history surged during this period. Initially, demand for both popular and academic history grew in tandem in the early postwar era, but the popularity of academic history declined, while the public's interest in popular history (and nostalgia) continued to rise.[21] The reasons for this divergence had to do with contrary expectations of history on the part of academics and non-academics, including both the "great mutation" in academia away from narrative and toward histories that confronted accepted interpretations by critically examining issues of race, class, and gender, and also the politics of education. Historians have complained that "although the diversified and de-mocratized academics produced a cornucopia of studies that looked at neglected chapters of history, they exercised only limited influence upon the history that was taught in the schools" or was read by a broad public.[22] As academic histo-rians increasingly interrogated the foundations of the state and society, the public preferred more conventional history.[23] In *Historians in Public* Ian Tyrrell tells the almost tragic story of professional historians' attempts to engage with secondary education in this period. Tyrrell argues that rather than a deliberate withdrawal from the public sphere, complex developments resulting from a perhaps misguided wartime and early Cold War alliance between historians and the state, in which utilitarian American history courses and programs helped mobilize public opinion, plus resistance to new academic proposals from entrenched educators and interest groups, and the unfortunate hostility of recently professionalized historians toward local practitioners, all acted to isolate professional historians. In turn, this drove the wedge deeper between scholarly work and popular historical understanding.[24]

In the early 1950s, popular history boomed. Some at the Smithsonian specu-lated that global travel in the armed forces, higher education levels resulting from the GI Bill and other federal funding, and increased leisure time following near universal adoption of the forty-hour work week contributed to a widespread hunger for knowledge and accounted for the dramatic increase in museum visitors.[25] Likely the golden age of middlebrow culture correlated with the rela-tively short work week and high salaries of the postwar era. Engaging with history, whether through a book club, a television program, or a museum visit, is certainly easier if one has leisure time.

Chapter 1 uses the rapidly developing story of the early History Book Club to illustrate first how professional historians attempted to bridge the gap between academe and the public in order to increase the diffusion of applicable

historical knowledge; and second, why they failed. The first chapter also estab-
lishes a paradigm that the trajectories of each of the other popular history
enterprises approximated. The charter group of historians at the club conceived
of their task as educative. They selected and taught, in the form of lengthy
explanatory reviews, history books that offered particular lessons to HBC
members, using the past as a sort of critical commentary on present issues that
concerned them. Their business model performed poorly, however, as the
imperative to educate conflicted with the underlying profit motive and mere
survival. The resolution of this conflict led the first editorial board to resign.
The club changed its mission and operation, attempting to respond to a market
that they struggled to define instead of pedagogically directing the public to
required readings in history. In the other cases examined in this book the tension
between principle or ideology and commercial or popular success resolved
itself differently, since those "historians" possessed the ability to write or revise
history, which, ironically, was a power the professional historians lacked in
their particular role with the HBC. But each ultimately confronted its own
restrictive conditions.

The choice of media always resulted in particular restrictions. The medium
most associated with the 1950s, television, offered a premier venue for battles
between competing narratives.[26] Two distinctive series achieved unparalleled
success in distributing politicized histories to the American public. *You Are There*
served as a forum for the Left during the years of the film and television blacklist. On a different channel, in every sense, viewers watched *Cavalcade of America*'s
history by and for big business. Both series dealt with a wide range of contemporary political, social, and economic subjects through the medium of history.
Additionally, both series were so highly acclaimed by critics that educators across
the nation utilized their productions as educational materials for teaching history
in their classrooms.

Chapter 2 reconstructs the efforts of the Du Pont Company to mold the
past into usable propaganda that naturalized and legitimized modern corporations: a dominant theme found throughout this book. Restoring the reputation
of business in the 1940s, following widespread anticorporate animosity during
the Depression years, required a past in which business played a predominant
and overwhelmingly beneficial role. Following Woodward's and Boorstin's
contemporary analyses, this historical reformulation substituted for more overt
ideological argument. Revisions in both academic and popular histories of
American business helped legitimate the massive corporations that have since
dominated economic life.[27] Consensus historians, who unlike their progressive
school forebears found little class or other conflict in American history, also

Private sponsorship contributed to the success of the Freedom Train (1947–49) and other popular history productions but also delimited historical interpretations to suit corporate objectives. (Courtesy of National Archives and Records Administration.)

reacted against earlier "feminine idealism," as historian Allan Nevins put it, in histories that wrote too critically of the captains of industry who made the United States into a world power.[28] Epitomizing this group, David M. Potter, in *People of Plenty* (1954), echoed contemporary business leaders who heralded "abundance" and material wealth as the most significant, though for Potter not necessarily best, American characteristics.[29]

Beginning as an anti–New Deal radio series, and remaining on television into Eisenhower's second term, Du Pont's *Cavalcade of America* brought the past to life in order to identify the fundamental values that heralded free-market capitalism. It created an exemplary past, proclaiming model heroes who possessed or, more accurately, were given the character traits that Du Pont either wished upon the public or claimed for itself. Emulation, not contemplation, was the goal. In the process of its dramatization, history became mythologized, a result perfectly in keeping with Du Pont's conservative objectives. Eventually however, changes in the television industry, including the proliferation of channels and viewing options, the diffusion of set ownership, and the move from prestigious single-sponsor anthology programs to formulaic network-produced series, all forced Du Pont into an attempt to appeal more directly to popular tastes.[30]

Chapter 3 closely examines the foremost alternative to *Cavalcade*'s historical interpretation, *You Are There*. CBS News produced *You Are There*, which started on radio in 1948 and moved to television in 1952. Where Du Pont controlled the content and message of *Cavalcade*, the series' sponsors and CBS generally left *You Are There* to producer Charles Russell and director Sidney Lumet or second director John Frankenheimer. The involvement of leftist writers, actors, and directors, including prominent figures from the Hollywood blacklist, as well as the series' presence on the airwaves during anticommunism's most intensive period, practically guaranteed that the history reported by Walter Cronkite and his team radiated politics. Yet, much of the story is surprising. At the height of anticommunist hysteria, a network news division reported from the past, "interviewing" historical figures long deceased, according to scripts prepared by communists and fellow travelers. In a way very similar to *Cavalcade*, the *You Are There* writers submerged ideology just below the surface of their historical dramatizations, which allowed them to continue to participate in a political culture from which they might otherwise be excluded. History here generally resembled a blueprint past, a new plan for the present and future that boldly challenged postwar society by demonstrating its errors. *You Are There* also influenced the style of network television news during its crucial formative years; it introduced new themes, approaches, and people into popular historical memory; and it brought a radical alternative perspective into American homes and classrooms at a time when such viewpoints seldom heard expression in mainstream society. The series' historical interpretations contrasted not only with *Cavalcade* but also with school textbooks that presented American history as the continuing saga of conflict-free progress and manifest destiny. School boards were careful to adopt textbooks that were "not objectionable to anyone," and publishers, wrote Frank Dobie of the History Book Club, would rather "print the texts in Hindu" than offend potential buyers.[31] Like *Cavalcade*, *You Are There* disappeared as television abandoned the diversity of programming that characterized its early years. At CBS this meant both an increased emphasis on shows with more clearly popular appeal and the distancing of its News Division from infotainment programs like *You Are There*.

Both *You Are There* and *Cavalcade of America* molded the past into propaganda. The subject of chapter 4, the Freedom Train of 1947–49, also used the past for propaganda and, in so doing, helped transform history into civil religious iconography, or a kind of commemorative past. The transcontinental, diesel-powered train carried ten dozen carefully selected historical documents to help make the case for "free enterprise" to the American people. Historical consultant Frank Monaghan described the train as a "dramatic device" that would unswervingly "focus the attention of the American people on their heritage."[32] To define that tradition, the American Heritage Foundation, the organization behind the Freedom Train, drew authority from an unparalleled collaboration between leaders in business, government, and, to a lesser extent, religious organizations, the military, labor unions, and the educational system. Dominated by corporate America's message of the inviolability of laissez-faire capitalism, the Freedom Train exhibits also limited history, and thus ideology, to a narrow focus on great leaders and well-known historic events. Moreover, and as the foreseeable result of how the train's organizers selected, displayed, and promoted the documents, this opportunity for Americans to engage with history became an almost obligatory ritual of a revived and reconfigured civil religion, with its sacred objects preserved and protected in reinforced railcars. Yet, because of the extraordinary range of participants, the meaning of "freedom" was challenged by segments of the population unwilling to accept the imposed definition. Despite these rebellions, the train managed to drive through a unified propaganda campaign that experienced an attendance rate and breadth of participation that would be unimaginable only several years later. It thus encapsulates the broader story, evident throughout these chapters, of a brief postwar moment in which elites instructed a relatively willing public in history.

The final chapter examines another case where history became iconography. The Smithsonian Institution's postwar American history exhibits also suggest a time-capsule past, a preservation-focused approach to history that grew in importance during the atomic age, with its attendant uncertainties regarding the future of American civilization. The Smithsonian's exhibits also reveal the particular role of corporations at the nation's semiofficial repository of collective memory. New exhibits and eventually a new museum didactically presented the nation's past as a series of business and military triumphs in the form of persistent technological and material progress. This history also melded together the state, the armed forces, and the nation's largest corporations, while fostering patriotic reverence for a past, and a present, in which these institutions dominated American society. However, the same impulse that first drove the Smithsonian to make its exhibits more informative, accessible, and entertaining eventually led the institution to largely abandon its effort to put forth grand narrative, rife with meaning, in favor of an increasingly segmented and popular approach to American history. As in the other cases, the necessity of popular appeal eventually trumped pedagogic considerations. The Museum of American History later managed to combine aspects of both popular memory and academic history, incorporating recent historiographic developments into the exhibits. However, the *Enola Gay* controversy, and the Smithsonian's failure to uphold scholarly standards in the face of hostile resistance to even modest revision of sacred parts of the national story, illustrates the challenge of making public history in such a conspicuous place.

Each of these efforts to remake the past encountered certain restrictions beyond accommodating popular taste and memory. For example, Du Pont's historical dramas needed to balance the company's propaganda requirements, historical accuracy, and the need to generate popular appeal. Similarly, the Smithsonian's refurbished exhibits, including the innovation of educative panels that explained the displays' meanings, deliberately attempted to instruct *and engage* a public that often desired entertainment. Above all, these singular views of the past were themselves restricted by their chosen media—a paradox, since each project's communicative capabilities depended on the new technologies. On *You Are There*, to fit within the confines of the format, the "authentic" re-creations usually had to compress several days' events into one day—and into one twenty-eight-minute broadcast.[33] The news-report format of the show allowed at least for concise explanations; on *Cavalcade* the format included little to no contextual narration, which meant that the brief histories had even less time to develop their subjects. Despite the intentions of the historians, the books offered by the History Book Club were not accessible to great numbers of people. The Smithsonian's reliance on objects and the Freedom Train's deployment of documents also ran into trouble, particularly with their lack of contextualization. The medium of a three-car train that seldom stayed at rest for even twenty-four hours before its diesel locomotive hauled it to another town or another state may have been the most restrictive space of all. Walking down the train's narrow aisle, literally and figuratively prevented from veering too much to the right or left, and hurried along by Marine Corps guards, visitors stole only the most fleeting glimpses of the selected documents said to represent all that was important in American history. Thus, each case offered a kind of history—but severely limited.

Whither the Past?

These popular representations of the past appeared in an era in which history seemed poised to play a key role. Historians like Woodward and Boorstin offered their explanations, but the popular and influential historical works of nonhistorians, including theologian Reinhold Niebuhr and sociologist David Riesman, more definitively suggest the strong presence of the past in postwar society. And when Oxford Press published an abridgement of Arnold Toynbee's *Study of History* in 1947, it quickly became a best seller in the United States.[34] To explain such success, the author suggested that many people, harboring feelings of "anxiety," turned with him to the "scriptures of the past to find out whether they contain a lesson that we can decipher."[35] This turn to the oracle of History was a common one to make in the years just after World War II and, not coincidentally, simultaneous with an intellectual debate over history's practical utility. How many of the book's purchasers actually read Toynbee's difficult and often confusing text is of course unknown, but the great number who bought it at the time undoubtedly felt that this grand historical explanation of the rise and fall of civilizations was a book they *should* read. W. H. Auden read and borrowed from the work for his poem "Age of Anxiety," which won a Pulitzer Prize in 1948 and was transfigured into music as Leonard Bernstein's Symphony No. 2.[36] Yet many historians found Toynbee's broad generalizations vexing, if not inappropriate. Criticisms usually centered on his very large units of history—civilizations—and the inherent inevitability of civilizations' "life" cycles.[37]

The critique connoted a more fundamental disagreement about the uses of the past. In particular, how should people access and assess the rich store of knowledge that presumably reposes in history? A surprisingly public discussion of this question took place in 1948, the year in which Toynbee also published his more clearly contemporary work, *Civilization on Trial*. Toynbee debated the merits of his approach with Pieter Geyl on BBC radio. Geyl was a Dutch historian who would later author *Use and Abuse of History* (1955), a work that argued that the past was generally "ransacked for material that might support the case of one side."[38] Some months before, Geyl had denounced Toynbee's approach—essentially the approach followed in all but one of the case studies in this book. Not only did Toynbee offer generalizations based on insufficient examples, but he also selected only the "instances which will support his theses" and deliberately excised contradictory evidence. Geyl recognized the need to generalize based on limited evidence, but he criticized Toynbee for too narrowly restricting his readers' views and making his conclusions seem inevitable.[39] The past, Geyl said, is not so easily usable.

"The fate of the world—the destiny of mankind," Toynbee responded, "*is* involved in the issue between us about the nature of history." He claimed that preparing his readers for what lay ahead necessitated limiting their horizons to the key lessons of the past. Historians and society were confronted with the choice of trying to "chart" the past in order to navigate the present, or else sailing ahead with the blank map offered by those who said that history is too complex to use effectively. For Toynbee, these options represented, respectively, the traditional view that "history is a revelation of God's providence" and the "nonsense view of history" espoused by his opponents.[40] Either it all means something, he said, or none of it means anything.

The conversation between Geyl and Toynbee presented the two poles of contemporary debate concerning history's utility. Herbert J. Muller's *The Uses of the Past* tried to find a middle ground. Like Toynbee's work it was "designed to give perspectives on the crisis of our own society." However, Muller, like the early History Book Club historians, argued that attempts to use history were almost always so oversimplified that they failed not only to capture the real meaning of historical events but also to elucidate whatever contemporary problem it was that led to their invocation. In the beautifully written introduction, titled "Hagia Sophia, or the 'Holy Wisdom,'" Muller describes how the great Istanbul cathedral/mosque had been used repeatedly for the lessons that its history supposedly revealed. He was particularly concerned with Toynbee's use of the Hagia Sophia as a symbol for his schematic depiction of history. Referring to the moment of the Turkish conquest in 1453, Toynbee argued that the cathedral represented the moment in every civilization when its people lose their faith, and the civilization therefore dies. Muller refutes this by pointing out that most of Constantinople's population was inside the church praying for salvation when the Ottomans took control of their city—hardly a sign of lost faith.[41] But Muller reveals his larger point through an extended metaphor that counters Toynbee's use of the past with a "close inspection" of the impressive edifice. Like history, Hagia Sophia is an "everlasting wonder in its anomalies. . . . Everything stands; but everything is wavering, bulging, or askew." The past is too messy to use so grandly—unless one ignores the contradictions and exceptions present in almost any historical event. "We cannot afford to spare the past its troubles," Muller concludes, since whitewashing history precludes any chance of learning from it. He acknowledges the need for every age including his own to create its own usable past, "yet this admission of relativity does not permit us to . . . make over the past to suit ourselves."[42] Toynbee and his adherents went too far in this direction.

Muller joined many historians in praising instead the historical perspective introduced by theologian Reinhold Niebuhr. Niebuhr's *The Irony of American History* influenced more than a few contemporary American historians (among others), encouraging a "cult of complexity" within postwar historiography. Historian Peter Novick argues that the Niebuhrian terms *complexity, irony*, and *ambiguity* "became the most highly valued qualities in postwar intellectual life." Certainly this was true of some leading academics like Richard Hofstadter, whose 1948 work *The American Political Tradition* revealed key paradoxes of major historical figures and events. But this stance distinguished the historians in Niebuhr's camp from contemporaries on the left and right, including many writers who were much more interested in discovering accessible meanings than hesitations and ambiguities.[43] It also distinguished them from important trends in history that generally have been ignored by historians focused on postwar academic history. If elite intellectuals embraced the irony of the past, the rest of the nation did not seem inclined to follow them. On the one hand, as several historians have argued, Americans of the late 1940s longed for a generally unhistorical and reassuringly nostalgic version of the past.[44] On the other, there was in fact a revival of popular historical interest, but it usually resembled Toynbee's neat system of historical lessons more than Neibuhr's paradoxes. If we look beyond the ivory tower, at some of the more popular narrative reconstructions of the past, we see that the lessons of history remained simple, comprehensible, and, most importantly, usable.

Some scholars also sought a greater civic role for history, or for its supposed lessons. The story of the History Book Club illustrates something of the scope of the more public-minded academics' ambition. So does the rapid postwar growth of American civilization and American studies programs in the late 1940s, which were largely interested in the past as cultural foundation—another varietal of the usable past prominent in this period.[45] Excavating this cultural foundation was a defining subgenre of the emerging American studies discipline and also related to efforts to establish an American canon, in history as much as in literature.[46] American studies introduced new approaches to the study of the nation and its people, including the incorporation of a greater variety of sources and a range of topics not yet thought of as legitimate in the field of history. The diversity of the interdisciplinary approach was anchored by the unity, geographically *as well as temporally*, of the subject. The discipline in effect merged history and contemporary analysis in the effort to describe American society and in the process created new usable pasts.

Beginning in 1949, the field's periodical, *American Quarterly*, sought to provide a "sense of direction to the studies of the culture of America, past and present."[47] Like the History Book Club of Bernard DeVoto and Arthur M. Schlesinger Jr., the *Quarterly*, launched by a group of American studies founding fathers that included Henry Nash Smith, William Van O'Connor, and Merle Curti, was for the "lay reader who wishes to avoid the thinness of much popularization" and the "excesses" of overspecialization.[48] It offered a "common area of interest in which specialists of various kinds and the aware reader might meet."[49] The two projects also shared a goal of mingling historical understanding with contemporary policy making, in an essentially democratic way. That is, the "small town intelligentsia," to use DeVoto's phrase, would learn from these experts in order to apply historical knowledge to the great political questions of the postwar era: elitist perhaps, but also geared toward improving participatory democracy. This is one key characteristic of the uses of the past in the decade after 1945 — the early postwar efforts sought to affect social thought at the grassroots level, through an informed (elite-led) dialogue with ordinary American citizens.

The emphasis on the past's utility and connectedness pervades Tremaine McDowell's *American Studies* (1948), which provided the discipline's foundation by stressing the goal of reconciling "all three tenses" of American civilization: "past, present, and future." This could be done by forging a "'synthesis' of past and present" that "deduces diversity to some degree of unity" in American culture throughout the nation's history.[50] Or to put it another way, a "single entity" that we may call the "American Mind" has persisted through time.[51] The postwar situation demanded greater attention to and better understanding of the American experience, and the emerging discipline sought to fill the void by elucidating and in a sense inventing American culture.[52]

In the postwar era, the necessity of making sense of American history sometimes led to opportunities of communication with a wide audience — even if, as it turned out, *American Quarterly* settled into a quiet existence by the mid-1950s as a journal by and for academics, rather than a journal by academics for a lay readership. Non-academic individuals, groups, and corporations more directly determined the role that the past would play in postwar America, as they delivered didactic histories to Americans in a variety of packages. As Warren Susman suggested, American society allows for considerable flexibility in approaches to the past. History flows from many founts, and citizens absorb the lessons of the past through a number of currents — often deliberately channeled toward a particular political or ideological destination.[53] As the midcentury architects of new historical constructions attempted to affect the collective memory, they often fought against crosscurrents — competing interests — for an audience. The following chapters reveal how these varied groups maneuvered in an effort to dominate discourse.

While some Americans may have doubted the relevance of history, many others recognized both its utility and its malleability and sought to harness the "powers of the past" — particularly history's sanctioning power.[54] In a period characterized by rapid and dramatic changes, actively rooting new proposals in the American past functioned as an effective substitute for more overt communication of ideology.[55] Jan Vansina writes that "performances [of oral tradition] are not produced at random times"; they appear only when appropriate and necessary.[56] The same can be said of these popular and public histories, which materialized precisely when their creators believed society required their particular lessons. The confluence of major historical developments and influential new technologies encouraged elite efforts to reconfigure popular historical memory. The "tools of the reproduction of collective memory" had changed.[57] Increasingly, Americans interacted with the past through electronic media that claimed to accurately represent the world, both past and present.[58] In modern literate societies historical knowledge is "fragmented" by and for specialists, while the majority generally relate to the past through mass media filters.[59] American society possessed characteristics of both literate and oral societies, but the way that these popular histories blurred past and present also demonstrates that the majority of Americans approached the past in ways more similar to those of oral cultures.[60] Barbara A. Misztal suggests that in oral societies people retain only the "memories which have present relevance and which articulate inconsistent cultural inheritance."[61] Similarly, she argues that oral societies remember the past "only as long as it serves present needs," and they orient collective memory toward origins and mythical heroes: "In an oral culture, the past refers essentially to a mythical creation or Golden Age, with personal genealogies claiming to run to the beginning of time."[62] This echoes the first part of Daniel Boorstin's still-useful concept of American "givenness," the "notion that we have received our values as a gift from the *past*; that the earliest settlers or Founding Fathers equipped our nation at its birth with a perfect and complete political theory, adequate to all our future needs."[63] At midcentury, the individuals and organizations that presented history to the American public, particularly Du Pont and other conservative groups, tended to frame the past in precisely these terms, and blended mythology, genealogy, and history into a smooth narrative for a public that, for a time, seemed interested in how the past related to "present needs."

As the Cold War made challenges to the definition of the United States as anything other than capitalistic increasingly unacceptable, fewer of the ideological battles that had played out in historical guises took place. Appeals to founding principles or the "real" American heritage lost relevance once major economic questions had been settled by the widespread acceptance of powerful corporations and a relaxed New Deal state by the late 1950s, though this would prove to be only temporary. Meanwhile, without discounting some major flare-ups in the later Cold War, the crisis feelings of the 1940s and early 1950s faded. The situation also changed as available sources of information and entertainment increased during the 1950s; the growing diversity of mass media since then has meant less of a common experience across the vast American space. The notion of broadly shared historical knowledge has become more difficult to imagine. Moreover, a citizenry growing accustomed to or still pushing for wider participation and expanding opportunity could not use these pasts, which, despite important differences, all represented a limited tradition. As these attempts to control Americans' views of the past thus began to break down, popular history was less confined to perspectives carefully chosen by a particular group of elites.

1

The History Book Club
Offers the Past as
an "Image of Ourselves"

In the short span of one lifetime, the personal contribution of the individual scholar to the great and growing stream of knowledge can't be more than a tiny pailful. But if he could inspire—or provoke—other scholars to pour in their pailfuls too, well, then he could feel that he had really done his job. And this job of making sense of history is one of the crying needs of our day—I beg of you, believe me.

> Arnold J. Toynbee, in *The Pattern of the Past: Can We Determine It?*,
> by Pieter Geyl, Arnold J. Toynbee, and Pitirum A. Sorokin

The future is just a pool that ideologies go a-fishing in. It is only by the most vigorous effort that we can make of the past anything but a similar fishing pool.

> Bernard DeVoto, "Notes on the American Way"

The moment seemed propitious. In 1947 historian Bernard DeVoto sensed that there was an awakening of a "growing national consciousness about the American past. Not only readers but writers are turning to it in increasing numbers," which meant a "vast production of books about our past."[1] A contemporary referred to a postwar "boom in American history."[2] Together with the new abundance arose the question of how interested Americans could figure out which histories should be read, and which could be ignored. Once they decided that history might have something important to say, to them and to their age, where should they begin? If it were possible for concerned historians to guide the general public, DeVoto thought, perhaps history might realize its potential as a source of knowledge that would help to create an informed citizenry, something many Americans believed was vital as the nation took on greater global responsibilities. Perhaps readers in every part of the country, of various backgrounds and education levels, could learn from the same educative texts, in turn leading toward a broadly shared *and sophisticated* consciousness of the past. The promise of the History Book Club (HBC) was that it would allow a select group of historians, actively engaged in contemporary affairs, to show thousands of other Americans how the past, as they knew it, informed the present. The HBC advertised the promise of historical answers to these questions: "How did we get this way? What are we? And can our way of living survive?"[3]

For a while, the club operated along these lines: like a purpose-driven course in directed readings rather than a discount bookseller. But a tension existed between education and profit, and the charter group of historian-editors quickly concluded that, at the HBC, the profit motive superseded their goals for history education. The first year of the club's existence thus stands separate from its later years when a new cohort took over the duties but not the attitude or objectives of editor Bernard DeVoto and his like-minded colleagues. For several years the club continued to function as DeVoto hoped it would, but by the end of the 1950s it lost its coherent philosophy. The selective history, meant to convey some specific relevance to the contemporary situation, fell by the wayside and was replaced by history selected for its promise of high sales.[4] Moreover, almost unlimited choice replaced the limited selection of expert-chosen books. Where the early club editors hoped to establish new connections across time in order to foster new ideas in the present, the later HBC built a booklist that, by design, would be dependent on established historical memories. Historian Roy Rosenzweig revealed how a similar story occurred at *American Heritage* in the early 1950s, with the key difference that the "newsmagazine of the past" had already abandoned Allan Nevins's original goal of educating Americans "in the historical backgrounds of many a world problem of today" even before the first glossy, full-color issue went to press.[5] At the HBC the objectives of the undertaking were debated and revised over several years, a process that is revealing of postwar historians' approach to history and the public.

The clearly liberal ideology professed through the HBC's first-year selections also disappeared during that transition. The changes in the editorial board took place in 1948, the same year as the Wallace Progressives' last stand. Soon after that, the kind of progressive politics associated with the New Deal, which were also manifest in the HBC history book selections, declined rapidly—at the club, in the historical profession, and in society. The HBC change was also contemporaneous with what Joan Shelley Rubin identified as a slowly diminishing middlebrow culture that, as it disappeared, claimed other ventures similarly designed to educate and uplift a public that had earlier expressed interest in the sort of self-improvement they offered.[6] Thus, the beginning of the HBC corresponded to the end of a political age, and the transition at the club reflected the broader shifts in contemporary American culture.

The History Book Club's story in some ways encapsulates the history of all of the educative efforts elucidated in the following chapters. Each of the groups discussed attempted, in some sense, to write real "history" for the public. As happened with the HBC, these attempts inevitably faced commercial or political realities that forced them to modify their approaches and replace "history" with "memory." In place of history's critical distance, and its pursuit of an objective evaluation of the past, memory tends toward mythologization, which denies the past its complicated realities in favor of reassuring, popular remembrances and obliterates its "pastness" as well.[7] Based on their internal discussions, of history in general and the selection of books in particular, the HBC's original group of historians apparently reconciled themselves to a presentist approach; but in choosing books and topics that they knew would be unfamiliar to subscribers, they demonstrated an unwavering faith in the benefits of historical inquiry. The successor board led by Dumas Malone professed no such faith, instead preferring greater commercial success based on catering to what people already knew. *American Heritage* took this same approach. The groups profiled in the following chapters dealt with the pedagogic/profit conflict in varied and critically different ways, ranging from the resignations proffered by the original HBC editors to the full embrace of history's mythologization by Du Pont. However, at some point, all of the attempts at creating new popular history were forced to acknowledge the increasing commercialization of American culture and the rapid expansion of individual choices and individual claims to authority in leisure and mass culture. Ultimately, the public would strongly influence, if not determine, how the past was remembered. The history of the HBC succinctly chronicles this pervasive pattern.

Founding the Club

> Subway riders and Rotarians have their rights as readers, [and] they
> are the people whom we would like to have reading U.S. history.
>
> Randolph Adams, BDV M0001, Box 6, Folder 109, Circular No. 9
> from Randolph G. Adams (RGA), March 17, 1947

In 1947 Bernard DeVoto nominated his friend and protégé, Arthur M. Schlesinger Jr., for two positions, both rather surprising for someone just twenty-eight years old. One nomination was for Schlesinger Jr.'s admittance into the Century Association, an elite social club in New York, generally reserved for much older men of professional distinction. The other was for the young historian to be included on the first board of editors of the HBC. Both nominations succeeded, a testament to DeVoto's perseverance and influence as well as Schlesinger Jr.'s already substantial reputation following the publication of *The Age of Jackson* in 1945.[8]

DeVoto himself had recently published *The Year of Decision: 1846*, which at the time received at least as much praise as Schlesinger Jr.'s work.[9] While DeVoto was with the HBC, his next work, *Across the Wide Missouri*, won the Pulitzer and Bancroft prizes in 1948. By then, he had already had a long career writing history, historical fiction, essays, and articles. He authored a regular column in *Harper's* called "The Easy Chair," a perch from which he wrote about contemporary issues that concerned him, particularly conservation, civil liberties, and political corruption. Very much interwoven with his work and the book choices he made for the HBC were DeVoto's critical writings about growing corporate power and the resurgence of conservatism.

DeVoto's writing career had brought him into contact with a number of people in the world of publishing, many of whom became friends. One of these was Charles P. Everitt, publisher and almost legendary book dealer, and a few years later the author of the idiosyncratic *The Adventures of a Treasure Hunter: A Rare Bookman in Search of American History*.[10] In January 1946, a friend of Everitt's named Ray Dovell approached him with the idea of starting a new book club. At the time, Dovell worked as the director of public relations at a "large chain-store organization" and had worked previously in the newspaper business.[11] The new club would be modeled on the successful Book-of-the-Month Club but would restrict itself to nonfiction works of history. A panel of experts—historians—would select from the numerous new titles in the field a monthly offering for club members. This selection would be sold at a 20 percent discount, and club members would also receive "dividend" books as rewards for purchasing three of the monthly selections. Upon signing up for the club, new members also received a "premium"—a free book specially selected by the historians. Members had to purchase four books within a twelve-month period to fulfill their obligation.[12] Everitt would publish the dividend books, which were to be out-of-print older works that the board believed would be valuable to readers and also cheap to reprint. In exchange, Everitt's recognized name might benefit the as yet unknown HBC in negotiations with publishers.

It would be difficult to imagine a more suitable historian than Bernard DeVoto for the job of chief editor/judge. DeVoto had been laboring for years to bridge the gap between academe and non-academic Americans. In general, however, he elicited little sympathy from academics and never managed to secure a permanent position at Harvard. When he put together the board of editors for the HBC, he wrote to Dovell, "the best thing I know about the board as it stands is that it contains no academic historians." Though "young Schlesinger" would soon move to Harvard, DeVoto confidently proclaimed, "they will never make him an academic."[13] Schlesinger Jr. had been closely mentored by DeVoto and subscribed to his belief that history served little purpose if confined to the all but enclosed community of professional historians. Both men held in low regard those historians who seemed, to them, to be inclined to write for an exclusive audience. "Damn if the academic aren't horrible asses," wrote DeVoto. "I've watched the contagion spread from the literary profs to the historians in my own lifetime . . . and it has certainly made them gangrenous."[14]

The other historians on the new HBC board—Randolph Adams, Stewart Holbrook, and Frank Dobie, all friends with both Everitt and DeVoto—held similar views. Adams headed the Clement Library at the University of Michigan, but he interacted often with people in that school's history department and would sometimes solicit their advice for selections. But, as he wrote DeVoto,

> I get mighty little help from the History Faculty at Ann Arbor. They are, after reading a book, more anxious to prove how bright they are than to criticize what they have just read. Besides which, they are jealous as hell at the fact that the History Book Club did not pick one of them in the first instance. But among some of the instructors, and the members of my own staff, the books submitted get a lot of reading, roasting and reflective appreciation. That is why I'm glad Li'l Arthur [Schlesinger Jr.] was retained. I have three or four [like him].[15]

In Portland, Oregon, "lowbrow" historian Stewart Holbrook worried that the "real history boys" would scrutinize their selections and think them "flighty" when they offered something too "popular." Holbrook's background as a logger and amateur historian of the working class was perhaps reason to fear the judgment of the professional elite of the 1940s. In fact, the HBC editorial board expressed excitement when they could offer the club's subscribers something "abstract" or something with "intellectual distinction," rather than a mere "easy read." Often it may have been subconscious, but these men clearly had the reactions of academic historians on their minds, and they worried that their books would not appear intellectual enough to maintain their own professional reputations.[16] In addition, as DeVoto frequently said to Dovell, the historians' purpose—the reason they joined with the HBC—was to guide the public to the better contemporary works of history. It would not be long before conflicts over this central objective arose.

At the University of Texas at Austin, Charles Everitt's close friend and fellow self-identified "storyteller," J. Frank Dobie, rounded out the board so that East, West, Midwest, and South were all represented. This deliberate geographical dispersal would be matched by an effort to alternately select histories from each section of the country. The club's first regular selection focused on the Confederacy, the second on Concord, Massachusetts, the first premium studied the West, and so on. The historians recognized a special need to represent the South, however, since they anticipated more subscribers there—partly due to traditional interest in the Civil War period, but also because of the dearth of booksellers in that underdeveloped region.[17]

As they read through piles of historical books and galley proofs, trying to find the right works with which to launch their enterprise, the board wrote each other frequently to share their thoughts about history, historical writing, and historians. They also, piecemeal, began to articulate a vision for the club. They agreed that, somehow, they would attempt to "distribute important books about America without trying to 'educate' Americans." From the very beginning, Dovell, Everitt, DeVoto, and the rest consciously avoided any talk of uplift or even guidance.[18] Fighting against the notion of hierarchy in matters academic, they believed themselves true democrats. They would provide a service by winnowing down the great number of new historical titles, but they would not seek "the best that has been thought and said." That was not the point. They hoped to be a better sort of educator than those who insisted they knew who and what should be canonized: for example, Robert Hutchins's board that selected the "Great Books of the Western World" series that debuted in 1952. Great Books pointedly did not include new or even recent works and did not acknowledge the fact of revision within any field.[19]

However, since the point of the club was to choose for Americans at least some of the right things to read, an element of uplift certainly existed. Their mission diverged, though, from that of their model, the Book-of-the-Month Club, which, according to Joan Shelley Rubin, was summarized by their slogan, "Why is it you disappoint yourself?" That is, instead of the larger club's emphasis on self-improvement and the avoidance of personal failure, the HBC's goals were closely connected to ideas of nation, service, and an internationalist, progressive politics. The postwar situation demanded something more from citizens than self-absorbed attention to their own deficiencies during cocktail party conversations about the latest novels. It was time for Americans to understand themselves as Americans, proclaimed Randolph Adams, and the HBC seemed to him to offer the best chance of doing that. Through careful selection and direction, the editorial board could help to ensure that Americans interested in such an endeavor of *national* self-discovery would not be misled or simply bored by poor history.[20]

The board's approach also reflected a desire they shared with other contemporary historians to "mobilize" history for the struggle against totalitarianism. As Peter Novick has shown, wartime service in the Office of Strategic Services, the State Department, or the armed forces led many historians in the early postwar period, including Schlesinger Jr., to link their historical work with service to the nation. Samuel Eliot Morison wrote that "the historian who knows, or thinks he knows, an unmistakable lesson of the past, has the right and the duty to point it out." However, where calls for the past to serve the present were made too explicitly, historians tended to back away from such an obvious danger to objectivity.[21] The Geyl-Toynbee debate described in the introduction replayed itself many times throughout the 1940s and 1950s.

During the postwar period, historians often critiqued their colleagues' work in terms of Cold War concerns. For example, in his review of Allan Nevins's Civil War history *Ordeal of the Union* in 1947, Schlesinger Jr. wrote: "The issue here posed—what policy would have averted war—goes down to the question we formulate today in terms of appeasement or resistance." "In essence, [Nevins's position] is Mr. Wallace's current thesis about the Russians."[22] DeVoto wrote often against Civil War historical "revisionism" and shared Schlesinger Jr.'s belief that "the vogue of revisionism is connected with the modern tendency to seek in optimistic sentimentalism an escape from the severe demands of moral decision; . . . it is the offspring of our modern sentimentality which at once evades the essential moral problems in the name of a superficial objectivity and asserts their unimportance in the name of an invincible progress." DeVoto's critiques of Avery O. Craven and James G. Randall followed this line, though DeVoto argued even more broadly for moral judgments in history. If slavery was excused from moral condemnation, he asked, where would society ever be able to draw a line? He would not permit revisionists to argue that the issue of slavery in the territories was tangential and might have been resolved politically. His response was, so what? What was it then that prevented Americans from facing the problem "squarely, . . . with the soberest realism"? "That is the question that historians must answer—the more necessarily, I submit, because in an answer to it there may be light or forecast, some judgment whether we are capable of squarely meeting the fundamentals of inescapable questions hereafter, perhaps even some wisdom that would help us prepare to do so."[23] Only by asking and answering the really significant historical questions could historians perform their professional and civic duty.

The two historians' demand for judgments in history ultimately was a demand that history speak to the present. These arguments did not go unchallenged; John Higham responded to Schlesinger Jr.'s writing on the Civil War with a comment that it represented "an obvious exercise in historical rearmament for World War III." With each side charging the other with fostering another war through either appeasement or militarism, the "consensus" age historians seem to have had tremendous difficulty divorcing their academic work from contemporary politics.[24]

Ray Dovell and DeVoto discussed their approaches to history on many occasions during the club's first year. They appeared to have agreed for a time at least, though in retrospect their later split was presaged in their respective formulations of their merely superficially similar philosophies. DeVoto's group of historians may have scoffed at any creed of uplift through great books, but they were not ready to abandon the idea that history had educational value. On the other hand, Dovell occasionally summarized for DeVoto the results of their consultations on the HBC's mission as an understanding between them to "[sell] the thrill and romance of history, not its educational value."[25] The advertisements for the club that Dovell crafted with Carl Jones, chairman of the HBC Board of Directors, reflected this view: "Men and women in every community are fascinated by the vitality, the romance, and the spectacle of what to them is 'incomparably the greatest story on earth'—the story of the United States of America."[26] Seven years later, *American Heritage* would be launched with a similar claim that American history "is as exciting, as flamboyant, as filled with actions and thought and daring (and true purpose) as any citizens ever had." In that case, Allan Nevins apparently made peace with the admen, just as he accepted the magazine's emphasis on nostalgia and "things to smile at," despite his stated preference for the vocabulary of uplift, duty, and civic responsibility.[27] But in 1947 DeVoto objected strongly and frequently to such overblown language and complained to Dovell and Jones that they misrepresented or misunderstood the historians' participation. Randolph Adams called the advertisements "some of the God damnedest tripe I ever read"; DeVoto thought Jones "quite incapable of writing copy that does not make us all vomit." And he worried that the business office failed to "understand that there is a difference between a man who wants to buy a life of Jefferson and one who wants to buy some black lace step-ins for his secretary." More important, DeVoto thought playing up *romance, grandeur,* and *heart* risked history's integrity. "The

This advertisement featuring the Freedom Train reflects a glorification of America's past that the historians objected to frequently in communications with the History Book Club office. (Advertisement in the *New York Times*, October 19, 1947.)

point about our history is not its grandeur, for only fragments of it have any." Rather, DeVoto believed they offered subscribers the "substance out of which contemporary American life has been formed." He felt even stronger about the term *heart*, writing Dovell, "I don't know what the heart of the U.S. is, either historically or today. I don't like this kind of pepping up. We aren't going to make a movie serial out of history and we aren't going to sentimentalize it, either."[28]

This represented the key conflict between DeVoto and Dovell, and between history and memory. The original HBC editors set out to provide their conception of the essence of history—new research and new interpretations written in comprehensible narrative form—to the public. To succeed commercially, the club eventually aborted this mission in favor of a business plan that tried to provide the public with books on popular subjects. In other words, the later club sought to profit from subscribers' existing historical memories. DeVoto believed in strong writing in a narrative style that made for enjoyable reading, but he also believed in the integrity of historical work. Dovell never showed much interest in the history and seemed to be concerned exclusively with selling more books. Where the historians, particularly DeVoto, agreed with Dovell was on style. DeVoto despised "academic historians" for their failure to understand that "history is not only knowledge, not only knowledge and wisdom even, but is also an art." He tried to write his own books using the "methods and techniques of literature" so that their "form is used to reveal meaning." Auguring Hayden White's later analysis in *Tropics of Discourse*, DeVoto suggested that "[history] books are like novels—they are constructed and written like novels, to exactly the same end as novels."[29]

The problem was that they often were not. DeVoto believed that too many historians wrote without consideration for their readers or for the writing itself, with the result that American readers shied away from serious historical works. Not only that; far too many historians refrained from making meaningful judgments, a failure that vexed DeVoto. After reading an early draft of Henry Nash Smith's *Virgin Land* in 1948, he strongly urged Smith to rewrite the book and submit some real value judgments to his readers. "What we want from a man who has done all this work is not a report on the work he has done but, always and foremost, judgments on what the content meant in our culture and means to it now." For DeVoto, the historian had an "obligation" to make historical judgments and thereby contribute to contemporary discourse. As he said to Smith, "society is supporting you in order that you shall do just that."[30]

People wanted history "appraised, judged, interpreted, and converted to an explanation of the present," wrote DeVoto. The past could not be fully recovered; rather, "what we recover from the past is an image of ourselves."[31] Therefore, if a historical work failed to connect past and present, if it contained nothing useful for readers who, like DeVoto, thought of themselves not as scholars "but as workers with ideas to the end of affecting society or culture in the United States," then it failed to do much of anything.[32]

DeVoto's books, particularly those written during the 1940s (*The Year of Decision: 1846*; *Across the Wide Missouri*; and *The Course of Empire*), illustrated both his vision for historical writing and his objectives for history's uses. Intended as a "form of art for all Americans," and for the "common reader" more than his fellow academics, DeVoto's histories, like his many essays and articles, grew directly out of his deep involvement in contemporary affairs. In turn, he hoped they might influence the public's understanding of the major issues of the day, from intervention in World War II, which was a specific goal of *Year of Decision*, to protection of the environment, perhaps the unifying theme of most of his historical work. In 1942 the *Atlantic Monthly* serialized *Year of Decision*, and the Book-of-the-Month Club offered it to its subscribers, an experience that DeVoto apparently appreciated enough to seize the opportunity when asked to help build a new book club devoted to the promulgation of new works of history.[33]

DeVoto wrote that he desired to "have some effect on the writing of history," to the end of making it more novelistic and thus ultimately more meaningful. The success of his own works might do that, he thought, if academic historians really paid attention and followed his example, but the position with the HBC offered, potentially, far greater influence. In that role he could reward historians who wrote as he liked, and punish, through nonselection, those who ignored his prescriptions—perhaps changing the writing of history in the process.[34] As Toynbee remarked the year after the club's founding, no one historian, alone, could accomplish much in the way of affecting society, but if he could inspire other historians to "pour in their pailfuls too" then he might really achieve something.[35]

Unfortunately, from his stance on narrative history, Ray Dovell seems to have understood that DeVoto would suggest for the club some sort of historical romances, and this became a source of tension between the historian and the publisher. "Certainly some of the stuff is going to be heroic, picturesque, fantastic," wrote DeVoto, but "some of it is also going to be brutal as all hell, and a lot of Americans are going to look awfully sad stuff in some of it." Furthermore, "whether or not [lay readers want romantic history], I don't think we can afford that particular kind of inflated writing. I favor sticking to the concrete and letting the oratorical, or radio-commercial, slide." One can easily imagine— even sympathize with—Dovell's apparent difficulty in understanding what it was exactly that DeVoto did want. For DeVoto, the misunderstandings would quickly become intolerable.

The Books

DeVoto wrote apocalyptically in his column in *Harper's*, "We must accept that the barbaric horde has won and must join together in a resistance movement and hold our lines fast till the sun shines again. Our duty is to become a fellowship of the good life and, in known and trusted places and in the privacy of our living room, to tend the flame of civilization during the dark age." He is referring, of course, to the majority of drinking Americans, "so little worthy of [liquor]." Alcohol was a serious subject; Schlesinger Jr. recalled that, growing up, he assumed DeVoto was his family's bootlegger, so often did the older historian supply his parents' home with liquor. But the sentiment expressed here is also indicative of DeVoto's urgent attitude toward history and intellectual life in general. Through the HBC, he would have an opportunity to send out books to aspiring middlebrows who in the privacy of their own living rooms might help him to "tend the flame of civilization."[36]

The five historians selected books for the club ostensibly for their historiographical value, but often due to other considerations as well. Altogether they compose a particular perspective, one that we can identify as, largely, DeVoto's. The books met his explicit criteria for good narrative history, but they also seem to represent a consistently progressive interpretation and a recognizably liberal political agenda. And in general they are presentist in their approach to the past, sometimes including long discourses on the relationship of the history to the present. All were historical, but they also, from the historians' perspective, spoke directly to issues of concern to contemporary Americans. Because of this, and unlike the selections made by the later club, American history was the only area considered by DeVoto's team.

By design they were new works, preferably published no more than a month or two before their distribution to subscribers. Particularly in the club's first year, the publishers and historians thought that the club would best serve the public by sorting through new titles to discover which texts should be read and which could be ignored. Moreover, the only way the editors might hope to influence historical writing would be through the selection or rejection of new works. "Every generation ought to, and will, re-write history," wrote Adams to the other editors. The board believed they now had a wonderful opportunity to judge their contemporaries' revisions.[37]

Both the texts themselves and the historians' discourse about each new book underscore the issues and concerns of 1947 as well as the logic behind the assumption that history offered solutions, or at least guidance. The first three monthly selections, and the first premium, warrant especially close examination because the editors selected them with the greatest care and consideration of both their own objectives and the potential for influencing social thought. After that, the system began to fail, and even though they continued in their task, the book choices often followed practical considerations first and scholarly judgments second.

The group made its first choice for a monthly selection in December 1946. Because of a delay in financing it would not ship to subscribers for four more months, though at the time they thought February would see the start of club operations. Because the first and second books at least would be "less than current," DeVoto felt "as strongly as possible [that] we must be absolutely current for several months," an indication of how seriously the board took their responsibility to subscribers.[38] All agreed that Clifford Dowdey's *Experiment in Rebellion* was "good stuff" and a brilliant book for launching the new venture. In concurring, DeVoto reminded the group of a conclusion he had earlier shared with them: that it might be "exceedingly cagey to discover the virtues of a book about the South in our earliest months," ideally as their first monthly selection.[39] Not only would a book from the "Southern perspective" appeal to potential club members in the South, but it would demonstrate to those who cared that the historians, especially DeVoto and Schlesinger Jr., who had both written "pretty acidulous things about slavery and the Confederacy," acted objectively. Moreover, wrote DeVoto, "all other things being equal, I think we would do well to spread our selections geographically and chronologically."[40]

Dowdey writes critically of the Confederacy, but with the affection of a native son raised on stories of the Lost Cause. In addition to the usual archival sources, he relies on a personal and hereditary knowledge of the land and its people. In this, his work closely resembled DeVoto's scholarship, and it is not surprising to learn that the two men respected each other's historical writing *and* their respective works of fiction.[41] As someone who disparaged historians who wrote about territory they had never traversed, DeVoto must have been delighted to read Dowdey's descriptions of southern topography. The many pages devoted to social history read almost like folklore—like Carl Carmer perhaps, or Carl Sandburg, whom Dowdey credits along with Henry Adams and the progressive historian Charles Beard with the formation of his general outlook on history. Before *Experiment*, Dowdey had written five novels over ten years, and this work reflects his background in fiction. Even the political history deals mainly in personalities, psychological explanations, tragic faults, and heavy consciences. Despite the historians' statements, it is not really pro-South.

Dowdey never suggests the antebellum South possessed any real merit, nor that it seceded constitutionally. And while he devotes comparatively little space to discussing southern blacks, when he does he writes of their mistreatment. At 432 pages of readable but dense text, it was an ambitious choice with which to launch the club.

The group selected as its first "premium" Jeannette Mirsky's *The Westward Crossings*, first published by Knopf in late 1946. The decision reveals several important considerations. First, Mirsky did not hold an academic position. She wrote history from outside academe, so the audience she had in mind while writing was already the audience the HBC hoped to reach. But, like all of the "popular" histories the historian-judges accepted, Mirsky also met their standards for quality. Contemporary reviewers in the leading professional journals of history agreed with this assessment, praising Mirsky's style and mastery of the subject and her ability to create a work of literary as well as scholarly merit.[42] In other words, Mirsky had produced precisely the sort of work the group sought to promote. They loved her vividly descriptive writing; Adams told the others, "I can feel the heat of that Central American jungle, get the horrible taste of pemmican and wonder how Sacajawea changed her baby's diapers."[43]

The selection of a female author did not seem to be of the slightest concern to anyone in the group. None of them raised the issue in their correspondence, though Adams wondered if the name Mirsky might cause "sub-conscious unfavorable reaction among potential clientele in hinterland." And yet, in an era of very few female academic historians, highlighting a female historian's work at the moment of the club's genesis seems at the very least to have been another bold declaration of difference: a further rebuke to the history departments of which none of these historians was really a part. And, in fact, the group had considered both the work of Mirsky and another female author, Marion Starkey (*The Cherokee Nation*), for the first month's selection before deciding in favor of Dowdey's southern history.[44]

The content of Mirsky's text surprises again, especially in its emphasis on hemispheric rather than national (much less eastern seaboard) colonial history. A very recent and much celebrated trend in contemporary American historiography of the conquest/colonial period has expanded the field to include New France, New Spain, and the West Indies.[45] In 1946's *Westward Crossings*, Mirsky writes, "Considering North America as a whole gives unity to elements that are commonly separated into preludes to Latin American history, or Canadian history, or the history of the United States." And, "For us here in the United States it would be well if we learned to think of Spanish America as one of our own antecedents." She further argues against any idea of American exceptionalism by emphasizing that the "ennobling idea of freedom—the right to life, liberty, and the pursuit of happiness—was, like so much else, brought to North America from many parts of Europe." Mirsky's tale of three westward explorations—Balboa, Mackenzie, and Lewis and Clark—unified the histories of Mexico, Canada, and the United States. She further relates how America's first democratic assembly actually took shape in New Spain, following from a tradition of local assemblies in Castile and Aragon, and suggests the need for more transnational historical studies. This "one world" philosophy is not exactly surprising given the historical context, yet it complicates the common assumption that the emphasis placed on the national and exceptional history of the United States by some prominent historians was followed by everyone in the field. Instead, many early postwar historians, including DeVoto, called for and wrote both broader and more inclusive colonial histories—though not for the same multicultural purposes as in the 1990s. Peter Novick shows that there was an emphasis on the Atlantic community—at the expense of an American exceptionalism paradigm—in the work of many early postwar American historians who subscribed to an internationalist political philosophy. Additionally, for DeVoto at least, incorporating western history into U.S. history was as elemental to his explanation of America as it was to Frederick Jackson Turner's.[46]

DeVoto often complained that narrative histories faced unfair and increasing criticism from academics. He believed narrative history—history written with literary quality in mind—to be superior to overly analytical texts that failed to create a storyline out of past people and events. Mirsky offers a perfect example of why DeVoto subscribed to this belief. Her sources are, not surprisingly, few. But she uses the narrative form to discuss this problem openly with her reader rather than blanket it with academic prose, extensive footnotes, and an analysis based on too little evidence. When she has two or more sources that contradict each other, Mirsky submits each story to the reader's judgment.[47] This is more than the author's prerogative: it is a result of writing in the open, conversive, narrative style that DeVoto and his colleagues promoted. The author's authority derived from the skill with which she related the story rather than from her credentials.

In that sense, the reader accepts the authority of the author in much the same way that a television viewer acknowledges the authority of a particular program only after the narrative has been successfully put across. The HBC offered the authority of its historian-editors, but the selected texts stood on their own once subscribers began to read. Thus, even during the club's first year, when the educative program remained intact, the public held considerable but at that point only potential power to determine the direction of popular history.

The second month's book, Thomas Scudder's *Concord: An American Town,* pleased the historians because it had just been published, which satisfied their need to find a brand new book for subscribers, and because it brought New England history to the club, which countered both the southern history of *Experiment in Rebellion* and the mostly western history of *Westward Crossings.* DeVoto, Adams, and Holbrook also thought Scudder had written a solid work of history—unusual in form but highly effective. The book offers the whole of American history through the experiences of the town of Concord, a "more human approach to America's story" than would be possible without that geographic limitation. Scudder emphasizes how history touched the lives of Concord's citizens, from its most famous sons to the lowliest town drunks. In so doing, he thought that "history" would move "closer to the reader's own experience" of American life. Making the people of one town's past seem like the people of any town's present offered a fascinating solution to the problem of how to make history tangible.

Schlesinger Jr. objected to the book, thinking it "hasn't got a whole lot of history in it." But Adams and DeVoto both insisted that it did—"history of the kind which I think important," wrote DeVoto. Adams thought that Schlesinger Jr. suffered from the "delusion that history is made by the Big Names, such as Jackson and Roosevelt, and now Robert Taft." The others apparently convinced Schlesinger Jr. to at least abstain from voting, arguing that Concord had not only contributed more to the United States than had the White House but also was "a goddam sight more interesting to read about."[48]

Another concern was that subscribers might not possess the intellectual background to appreciate a book that paid a significant amount of attention to Ralph Waldo Emerson (as much as it focused on any one figure). In the end, the editors decided that, regardless, readers should enjoy becoming acquainted with the man and his transcendentalist circle. At any rate, the whole point of their involvement with the HBC was to expand subscribers' knowledge by directing them to meaningful people and events in the past, particularly those that were less familiar to a non-academic audience.[49] Again, at this stage the club still valued the potential for education more than selling merely entertainment to perhaps more people.

Like most of the books selected during the HBC's inaugural year, Scudder discusses the present as well as the past. The book concludes with young World War II veterans, some of whom had joined organizations such as the American Veterans' Committee and the Student Federalists, returning to Concord and organizing a conference promoting world government. Most of the delegates had served in the armed forces or in Washington, and several delegates had been in San Francisco for the United Nations Charter Conference. They had concluded from these experiences that people over thirty, clearly more interested in holding onto oil fields or strategic bases than in achieving peace, should not be welcomed into the movement. The "Concord Charter" advanced the idea of world citizenship, pushed for an end to power politics, and advocated a strong, federal world government. To the delegates and to Scudder, it was the logical conclusion to World War II and to two centuries of Concord/American history.[50] Scudder's work reflected the contemporary liberal understanding of internationalism as a movement for weakening both nationalism and the potential for future military conflict. With tension growing between the United States and the Soviet Union, this liberal internationalist ideology rapidly faded from view. It is hard to imagine a book like *Concord* being published, not to mention selected by a book club, even a year later.

However, the politics inherent in Scudder's conclusion paled in comparison to the radical arguments presented in the HBC's third monthly selection, by William Harlan Hale. A reporter and author, and a progressive Democrat, Hale wrote for the *New Republic* under Henry Wallace's brief editorship and contributed to *Harper's* several times during DeVoto's "Easy Chair" tenure there. He also introduced The Voice of America to the world in 1942 with the words, "The news may be good. The news may be bad. We shall tell you the truth."[51] Hale's *The March of Freedom: A Layman's History of the American People* opens with two quotes. The first, from Samuel Adams, announces, "It is the common people who must, under God, finally save us." The second, from Henry Wallace, reads, "The march of freedom of the past 150 years has been a long-drawn-out people's revolution."[52] Together, Adams and Wallace announce the progressive tenor of Hale's work: in his words, a "personal history" that looks to the past for a "manageable body of facts and feelings about our heritage to take along with me into this new age." He intends a history as transportable and as useful as a compass. "You may gather that this book is not 'objective,'" he writes, but he certainly does not apologize, for objectivity is a false hope in Hale's "new age."[53] Similar to Reinhold Niebuhr's *Irony of American History*, Daniel J. Boorstin's *Genius of American Politics*, or David M. Potter's *People of Plenty* in the early 1950s, Hale's work explores the past to discover just what it is that postwar Americans desire the rest of the world to emulate. His contemporaries needed, he wrote, to "set promise against reality" in American history before asking other nations to follow "our ways."[54]

Hale almost seems to be appealing directly to DeVoto, disingenuously apologizing for the book lacking the "impedimenta of good scholarship." In a rather moving introductory recollection, he explains his immediate motivation for this "people's history" in a way that, I think, explicates not only how Hale approached history but also how DeVoto and the other historians on the board approached it: personally, emotionally, and with a strong connection to their contemporary world. After serving as head of various psychological warfare operations in Europe, Hale arrived at Dachau, Germany, on May 1, 1945, to see ex-prisoners of the concentration camp collecting rags to create their own national flags to fly. When American soldiers brought out the U.S. flag, they marched it toward the tall flagpole from which the German flag had flown, then sharply turned and placed it in line with the other, ragged banners. "And at this there arose a shout," wrote Hale, "a general shout of brotherhood and joy. . . . I thought as I came away: This is what we mean, this is what we are. Should we seem to be less than this—should we stand apart from the lowly, from the people oppressed for faith, from those who will not be bound—then, in spite of all our riches and our power, we are not what we set out to be."[55] It is Wallace's "century of the common man" brought to life.

Hale focuses on the "people" rather than the usual "stuffed heads"—from whom he sarcastically begs forgiveness for their absence. He wrote elsewhere that while "the times surely call for holding our past heroes high . . . there is still room for thinking critical thoughts about non-heroes, or even about heroes if we happen to disagree with them."[56] Instead of conventional figures from American history, the book tells of the clashes between, on the one hand, the people and their allies who would expand their opportunities and, on the other, those men of wealth who feared them and wanted to "restrict privilege." Hale sees "no law of inevitable progress" and no evidence that the people necessarily retained the gains they had won in any given struggle. American history holds no pattern save the people's constant struggle for greater democracy.

This history begins not in colonial Massachusetts or Virginia but in Main Street, USA, in 1947: "in the beginning, which is here and now." He continues, "You start your day as a few big companies show you how to do it," and just like everyone else, you end it listening to the "same jokes that are bringing the same laughs from people slouched in the same way by their sets in every town and hamlet of America."[57] His extended opening salvo continues from there to offer as sharp a critique of contemporary America as any historian has ever written. He explores regional differences, though he thinks this mostly means having to watch what you say as you venture into a new area, particularly the South—where, if you happen to be black, you have no rights. He also condemns not just the doctrine of states' rights but also the idea of political representation based on states.

Corporate power appears everywhere in Hale's work, though it is never welcomed. Defining the Northeast, he notes it is "bounded on the west by the Mellon Family's Pittsburgh and on the south by the Du Pont family's Delaware." "Class war" occurs throughout American history, though it is often, Hale says, disguised as sectional conflict.[58] Where the great progressive tome, Charles and Mary Beard's *Rise of American Civilization*, concentrated attention on "vertical divisions" in American society—economic classes existing in separate regions— Hale concerns himself with what Beard called "horizontal divisions": the "antagonism of classes dwelling together."[59] Hale explains the relative peace between classes in the past as Turner did, noting that the frontier "had the effect of a gigantic WPA," postponing the "rigors of the system." Now, however, "you are likely to be a landless, tool-less tenant or laborer or white-collar worker" who serves and depends on a giant corporation, which, despite advertising to the contrary, is not owned by "countless widows and orphans" holding a few shares each. Freedom had developed into enslavement by "private bosses," and the road to true emancipation ran through a large federal government that could counterbalance the power of the corporation.[60]

This history contains little romance. Hale ridicules greedy colonial explorers and financiers who headed early efforts at exploitation. The Salem witch trials showcased a battle between Christianity and emergent capitalism, in which admirable resistance to the latter led to unfortunate accusations of witchcraft. Hale's chapter on the American Revolution draws attention to the impressive political organizing of the "radicals" and offers a narrative of two revolutions, one against England and another, more radical social revolution at home.[61] After the Revolution came Constitution, and Hale here traces the development of anti–big government sentiment from the Jeffersonian radicals who erred in thinking small government would best preserve liberty, to later states' rights southerners who desired small government to preserve slavery, to later capitalists who made cruel use of Jefferson's arguments in order to exploit the people. And then, Civil War, where "big business takes over," and the freedman gets "kicked back practically to the place where he came from" once the victorious capitalists have no more use for him. The ultimate effect of the "uncontrolled business corporation" had been to "disembody evil and make it anonymous."[62]

Hale ends his book where he began, in 1947. Contemporary Americans feared the "threadbare Soviets" not because of their strength but because of the "uncertainty" of America's position and the fact that many Europeans seemed disinclined to follow "our capitalist cause."[63] He closes with the promise of men like Henry Wallace, who, for a new generation, revive the vital belief in the

American people to improve their society through the "instrument of self-government." It should be noted though that in the following year Hale wrote of Wallace's presidential campaign as a mistake.[64]

With Hale's book and most of the other club selections, DeVoto expressed fury at his colleagues' noncommittal voting and indecisive critiques. Sometimes one man voted for multiple books under consideration or voted with an explanation that seemed to negate his vote. Debate dragged on for weeks. Unsurprisingly, the historians were not unanimous in the selection of Hale. The book presents a left-wing, anticapitalist interpretation, makes no pretense of objectivity, and enters much more directly into contemporary political debates than any other selection. For just the third month of the club's existence it made for a bold choice. Seeing nothing there but criticisms of America, Stewart Holbrook declared himself against it, but the rest of the group outvoted him (though DeVoto would later express some ambivalence about the work). Coincidentally, but also revealingly, several years later Hale would publicly criticize Holbrook, specifically his stated reluctance in his latest book, *The Age of Moguls*, to "pass judgment."[65] To pass judgment or not was apparently a central question, but of course to Hale the answer was obvious. To Randolph Adams, Hale's writing represented the best of the "by the fire side with a couple of highballs" style — just fine since, "dammit, that's where decisions are made in this America of ours." For Adams and Schlesinger Jr., Hale's book seemed perfectly suited to their purpose of reaching a lay audience. In particular, they thought this all-encompassing text met the demand for an American history accessible to the waves of veterans washing over university campuses.[66]

It rendered history relevant to contemporary readers, a case Adams made as he argued with increasing passion for Hale over several weeks. Responding to criticism from Holbrook of Hale's bias, he retorted that the book was "as objective as I can conceive a humanly written book on such a subject to be." Moreover, he appealed to the others as men who wanted history that spoke to the present: why object when an author gives them exactly what they want? "If history should 'tell something'—this book certainly tells it."[67] DeVoto, more attentive to the business of publishing, gave his blessing once the Book-of-the-Month Club had passed on Hale.[68] But given DeVoto's concurrent attacks on corporate and American Medical Association obstructions to universal healthcare, as well as what he saw as business's effort to rob Americans of their public lands, the selection of a book with such a strong anticorporate message seems perfectly in line with his political objectives.[69] Here again the original HBC contrasts sharply with *American Heritage*, where editor Bruce Catton insisted that "this publication will reflect no left wing tendencies whatever." And while the magazine intentionally spoke in "a politically bland tone" and avoided discussing the "contemporary implications of U.S. history," the HBC meant to draw readers' attention to "the historical backgrounds of many a world problem of today."[70]

Politics sometimes confronted the club more directly than through the book selections. Shortly *before* they selected Hale, Adams received a warning to disassociate himself from this "red" book club. He apparently found it highly amusing to be labeled a communist in 1947 and proudly informed the others, "Boys! We are made! We are being attacked!" He joked, "Of course, it may be that Frank carries a bomb under that big Stetson he wears—and yes, Schlesinger is writing a book on that Dreadful Man. Of course Bennie writes books about psychiatrists (they must be communists) and once I saw him wear a red necktie. As for Stewart, everyone knows the Northwest is full of communists and that even the sunset is red way out there."[71] To this, Holbrook replied, "I'm happy to learn from Adams that the Judges have been smeared with red." Given their bold book selections, this lighthearted exchange suggests a determined willingness to risk criticism, censure, or even the failure of their enterprise, so long as they could choose the history they thought was best: specifically a progressive interpretation that lingered into the age of consensus history.

The book that precipitated the conflict that led to the board's resignation in spring 1948, John C. Miller's *Triumph of Freedom: 1775–1783*, like Hale's book, began with an explanation of how this history of the American Revolution would "profit" contemporary American society. Targeting a broader audience than in much of his other work, Miller substitutes a bibliography for the footnotes that he feared would distract the lay reader. Nevertheless, as he himself suggests, Miller's work follows the "canons of historical scholarship," reviewing historiography and discussing problems of evidence and interpretation.

Predictably, Miller writes extremely well, weaving battles and campaigns together with politics and economics on both sides of the Atlantic. Through almost seven hundred pages, again illustrating the HBC's ambitious agenda, the pace remains quick and the story exciting. For those "many citizens" who wonder where the country is going, or why its progress seems so "rough and jolting," Miller offers the tumultuous but ultimately successful revolutionary period. One of the most interesting chapters, "Inflation and Its Consequences," describes the failure of richer Americans to sacrifice for the cause of freedom, which destroys the morale among those who were sacrificing. The lesson is for the reader's generation: all Americans need to contribute to the defense of freedom, and all need to be protected by a government that cares as much about the well-being of the poor soldier or farmer as it does about the financial state of the union.[72]

Although the editors took book selection very seriously, they made some choices for practical reasons. When the club suddenly needed the October selection ahead of schedule, DeVoto picked *Pontiac and the Indian Uprising*, written by a former student of Adams's, Howard H. Peckham. The book had "real 'news value,'" according to Adams's review, as it attempted to uncover just what sort of man had been able to inspire twelve tribes to revolt against the English.[73] But *Pontiac* contains almost nothing besides a military history of the Indian-European conflicts of the eighteenth century—there is hardly any social, economic, or even political history. In other circumstances it seems unlikely that DeVoto would have agreed to the choice.

DeVoto's group selected a "damn good book," Thomas Jefferson Wertenbaker's *The Puritan Oligarchy*, for December.[74] In contrast to the HBC authors without strong academic ties, Wertenbaker served for fifty-six years as professor of colonial history at Princeton University. He taught the history of material culture, which likewise differentiated him from many of his colleagues. His emphasis on barn architecture, tools, agricultural methods, and other aspects of everyday life shared the focus of Dixon Ryan Fox, Arthur M. Schlesinger Sr., and the other new social historians of the 1930s; in fact, Wertenbaker had contributed volume two of the series edited by Fox and Schlesinger Sr., *A History of American Life*, in 1927. *The Puritan Oligarchy* completed Wertenbaker's trilogy, *The Founding of American Civilization*, following *The Old South* (1942) and *The Middle Colonies* (1938).[75]

Wertenbaker paints a bleak picture of seventeenth-century Massachusetts, which he refers to as the "Bible State." The book fits the 1930s–1940s model of critical histories of the Puritans, soon to be countered by Perry Miller.[76] In this historiography, and in this book, the Puritans are undemocratic, authoritarian, superstitious, and morose. Only persecuted dissenters like Anne Hutchinson and Roger Williams offer positive examples for the present; to Wertenbaker, these outcasts are the wellspring of democratic thought. He finds the Puritan leaders to be a power-obsessed group intent on enhancing their own status through the persecution of others. Distributed by the club the month after the Hollywood Ten hearings, the judgment bore contemporary weight.

Like the HBC editorial board, Wertenbaker had no intention of "divorcing [himself] from the twentieth century." Whether past or present, he wrote, he "disliked the fettering of men's minds and the denial of the right of the people to rule themselves," a sentiment he hoped was "apparent in these pages." He thought it impossible to write "impersonal" or bias-free history in any case. Consequently, his work resembles many of the uses of the past explored in later chapters of this book, particularly several of the *You Are There* episodes that examine twentieth-century tendencies toward totalitarianism through historical reenactments.[77] As that contemporary radio series did, Wertenbaker devotes considerable space to the Salem witch trials, describing the context as a battle between conservative clergy and "rationalism."

The people had begun to "revolt against mental fetters," educating themselves with new ideas at the predawn of the Enlightenment, and reactionary leaders feared for their own authority. As the "invisible world fades," conservatives exploit feelings of uncertainty in order to demonstrate their usefulness and power. In 1681, a decade before the trials, eminent clergymen decided to combat the growing rationalism that threatened their religion and their power by making a coordinated effort to publish examples of "divine judgments, tempests, floods, earthquakes, thunders as are unusual, strange apparitions, or whatever else shall happen that is prodigious, witchcrafts, diabolical possessions, remarkable judgments upon noted sinners, eminent deliverances and answers to prayer." They plotted to reintroduce a frightening "invisible world" to people who seemed to be maturing past the point of believing in such things—past the point of needing leaders who promised to defend them against Evil. The most popular of these works was Increase Mather's *An Essay for the Recording of Illustrious Providences*, a book still credited with providing the intellectual foundations for the witch hunts. Nothing explicitly suggests that the HBC historians linked this with the anticommunist atmosphere of late 1947, though it is peculiarly coincidental. Nor is there evidence that DeVoto made a connection between Wertenbaker's Bible State and his own scathing history of the Mormon state, his own home state of Utah; nevertheless, the same theme of a manipulative, exploitative, and authoritarian clergy elite permeates both histories.[78] DeVoto seems to have relished subjecting founding myths to critical scrutiny.

In the March 1948 letter that informed Dovell of his resignation due to irreconcilable differences with the club's increasingly profit-oriented philosophy, DeVoto authorized one last monthly selection. Again he chose a progressive history. Deciding to make a clear political statement, even if Dovell ended up rejecting the recommendation, he selected *The Great Forest* by Richard Lillard—to DeVoto a long, historical argument in favor of environmental protection and a book undoubtedly recommended by Holbrook.

DeVoto had been crusading for conservation for many years by this point. In the late 1940s he was extremely vocal in denouncing the efforts of western corporations and their allies in the Republican Congress to turn over vast expanses of public lands to industry. At the time of the Lillard selection, DeVoto recorded that he was promoting three books wherever he went: Lillard's *Great Forest*, Fairfield Osborn's *Our Plundered Planet*, and William Vogt's *Road to Survival*. He felt very strongly the urgency of the situation given the likelihood of Republican victory in November 1948, in which case "we are all going to be called on for harder and more urgent work" if public lands were to be protected.[79]

The Great Forest itself offered a modified frontier thesis, with the North American forest providing for the nation in ways similar to those of Turner's frontier. It was the immense supply of wood that made America great, ran the argument, and as the forest disappears, so does the country's future. The "reputable lawbreaking" of corporations threatened to obliterate this resource, but progressive legislation managed to at least slow them down. Lillard's book also provides a rich social history of lumber camps and backwoods life—Holbrook's bread and butter—and relates the long history of labor struggles in the timber industry. It is unflinchingly pro-union and anticapitalist, concluding with dire warnings for the future if the forests are not protected and replenished.

Lillard also argues that culturally the forest served a key function in collective memory and consciousness. "Backwoods life survives as a pervasive national memory," he writes. Losing this "refuge from mechanized life and mass neurosis" would be catastrophic to America's conception of itself, which, Lillard believes, included important group memories of backwoodsmen, log cabins, lumberjacks, Indians, and transcendentalists in their New England woods.[80] In truth, these memories probably *have* faded since the time of Lillard's writing—superseded by the West and more recent frontiers, as Americans put greater geographical, temporal, and cultural distance between themselves and the "great forest."

Each HBC book challenged readers to apply newfound historical insight and engage in some way with contemporary issues. They also challenged popular memory by revealing less familiar episodes from American history and suggesting alternative interpretations of better-known people and events. As DeVoto said, they pointedly refrained from romanticizing or mythologizing the past and instead hoped to foster appreciation of rigorously researched and effectively written history. After the first year, it remained to be seen whether any significant part of the American public would accept that approach.

Troubled Waters . . .

Problems with publishers, the lack of subscribers, and conflict between the editors and the business office plagued the HBC's first year of operation. Publishers failed to mail books as promised, and some objected to the club selling their books at lower prices. Tellingly, DeVoto, rather than Dovell, fought the club's battles with Alfred A. Knopf, despite his protestations to the publisher that he had nothing to do with the business side of things. But DeVoto, frankly, had more publishing experience than Dovell, and Knopf and several other publishers knew him well.[81]

Little, Brown accepted the club's arrangement whereby subscribers would purchase their books for about 20 percent less than the cover price. Profits remained slight with the club's initially low membership of a few thousand, but once the club grew to twenty thousand or more, the 20 percent discount would easily be offset by higher sales. Knopf meanwhile led a revolt against not only the HBC but all book clubs save the entrenched Book-of-the-Month Club and the Literary Guild. Those two clubs seemed untouchable, but publishers thought they might limit the proliferation of discount clubs by "squeezing" the smaller ones. At the very least this would mollify the booksellers that made up most of their customer base. DeVoto tried to convince Alfred Knopf that the HBC opened a new market for him: the "small-town intelligentsia" that lacked easy access to many new books. But Knopf decreed that he would only sell his books to the club three months after their initial publication date. By July 1947, DeVoto had decided the publishers could not be relied upon to assist their enterprise; therefore, the historians would need to create a backlog of selections that could be ordered quickly in case of trouble with a publisher. When he left for vacation the following month, he mused ruefully that agreeing with his colleagues on four book possibilities would probably still leave them scrambling to come up with more once it "develops that we cannot get any of these books."[82]

Meanwhile, internal organization proved difficult at a time when, "God damn it, the mail service is disorganized at the moment because, God damn it, the railroad service is disorganized." As the editors saw it, postwar labor troubles threatened to derail their nascent enterprise before it could gather sufficient steam. DeVoto's colleagues expected books or galley proofs in a timely fashion, but more often than not books arrived too late or not at all—sometimes because of the U.S. Postal Service and sometimes because of the dysfunctional HBC office. To meet a deadline, Adams reviewed *Pontiac* for the club newsletter without having seen the book! As their go-between, DeVoto bore the brunt of the complaints from the other historians. He protested that he was doing everything he could short of riding around to each of them on his bicycle to hand them their own copies and accused them of acting like "a bunch of prima donnas." In fact, DeVoto tried for weeks to make the club's distribution system functional, but to no avail. Remarkably, during the first board's tenure, the HBC never standardized any method of getting manuscripts or books to each of the five editors. The difficulties in distributing books—rather an important part of operating a book club—continued to frustrate everyone on the editorial board.[83]

The incompetence of the business office infuriated DeVoto, who felt like he constantly acted as their tutor. The office still had no telephone in late spring 1947, which meant all communication had to be by wire, through the mail, or in person.[84] In addition to his reluctant visits to New York to help straighten things out in the office, DeVoto wrote Dovell many times explaining through step-by-step instructions how to complete particular tasks. After such interactions, DeVoto would write to his colleagues of the many "vagaries, annoyances, and inefficiencies" of the HBC that plagued him.[85] He complained that the office knew nothing about publishing; they were fixated on getting subscribers to the point that they ignored normal business operations; deadlines became meaningless since the office would suddenly and unexpectedly demand selections; and most important, the office failed to distribute the books.

DeVoto held a high-minded view of both the club and the historians' role in it, and he apparently created a set of principles that he considered inviolable. Most vital, the historians' professional opinions were sacrosanct, and business considerations could not be brought to bear on their decision making. Ray Dovell once asked DeVoto to edit a review by Frank Dobie that criticized the American Legion. In refusing, DeVoto protested first on principle but also suggested that the "appearance of such talk in the bulletin of a book club is a considerable novelty very favorable to us. . . . We will always have to let the boys say what they want to—and I think that in the end we'll profit from doing so." The judges had to remain independent: from the club and from him. He thought it inappropriate to try to persuade anyone to accept a book they had already rejected on merit. "We're telling our subscribers that one of the unique distinctions of the Club is the expert opinion of its board of editors. I don't want to depreciate that uniqueness in the minds of either the editors or the subscribers." To DeVoto, the club existed as a way for independent experts in the field to communicate with interested readers, and any hint of compromise for reasons of profit or politics would disillusion subscribers.[86]

By August 1947, DeVoto realized that the club would have to be reorganized if it was to succeed. After a meeting with Carl Jones, he understood that fundamental disagreements existed between them. Jones told DeVoto that his selections to date had not been popular enough, and the historians would have to find some way of selecting books that would sell well. DeVoto countered that the reputations of the expert editors were the sole business assets of the club, and that jeopardizing those reputations in any way would undermine the club's claims. He admitted that Jones might be right about the need to change things, but he argued that "you cannot advertise the Club as one thing and run it as another thing." If Jones and Dovell insisted on choosing books for commercial reasons, DeVoto informed them that he and his colleagues would resign. "We began by saying that we would distribute the books which the board of editors regarded as the best American history being currently written. I still think that that is a sound idea commercially and also that it embodies something of a public service. Whether or not I'm right about that, I am not interested in doing something else."[87]

In fact, as DeVoto himself admitted, he had always "flexibly interpreted" this position. On occasion he had supported books that he thought more likely "than equally eligible ones" to appeal to the potential audience. Adams and Schlesinger Jr. did so too, he thought, but Holbrook and Dobie were always "for the best book regardless of all other considerations." DeVoto would never, he told Dovell, select a book that did not satisfy his standards. Nor would he "consent to negotiate" with anyone in the business office about which book might prove popular. That would "break our contract with the subscribers" and "falsify" the very basis for the club's existence.[88]

The crisis that led to this last declaration had been provoked by the business office resisting the selection of *Lions under the Throne*, a history of the Supreme Court that seemed to them destined for low sales. After Jones told him that a book on the Supreme Court was a mistake, DeVoto threatened immediate resignation if the book was not adopted. If the club limited the choice of topics or anything else, if it tried to "pick winners" and "pick the Americana" that would generate the most sales, it could find a new board that would "work within the limits set but it can't get me and I doubt if it can get any of the other four."[89]

In December, to cut costs, the office asked DeVoto to fire two of the editors. He selected Dobie without hesitation but had a more difficult time choosing between Schlesinger Jr. and Holbrook, both close friends. In the end, communicating with Holbrook through the mail often took too long, and so Schlesinger Jr. remained by default. After their abrupt termination, the business office never contacted Holbrook or Dobie, a snub that infuriated them and DeVoto too.[90]

The final straw came in March 1948, when the editors chose Miller's *Triumph of Freedom* and Dovell declined their suggestion. The issue was cost—the book would cost subscribers $4 or more, and club selections were supposed to be $3. DeVoto thought the difference negligible for what the board considered to be one of the best history books of the year. The two men worked out a deal whereby the club would offer the low-cost Dixon Wecter, *The Age of the Great Depression, 1929–1941*, in June to offset the "expensive" Miller in August. When

DeVoto later discovered that Dovell had reneged, he quit. The fundamental basis of the club had been destroyed, and DeVoto divined no further advantage in his continued participation. If he and his colleagues could not determine the content of the history that subscribers would read, and that content instead would be determined by business considerations, the endeavor was from DeVoto's perspective utterly worthless.

On March 30, DeVoto sent the club his last review (*The Great Forest*), copy for his HBC newsletter column, "Editorially Speaking," and his letter of resignation. It seemed apparent to him that the business office would not always accept the recommendations of the editors, and that made the enterprise unacceptable. "The Miller book clinches it: the Club has rejected a unanimous choice of the editors. . . . I can't go along with you any farther." The loss must have hit the New York office especially hard when DeVoto accepted the Pulitzer Prize less than a month later.

. . . And a New Crew

> If Dovell asks me for suggestions about possible successors, I will tell him to use his own judgment but to consider Louis Hacker, whose last name has one more syllable than it needs.
>
> Bernard DeVoto to Randolph Adams, March 29, 1948

> Arthur has suggested that you might get Louis Hacker to take charge.
>
> Bernard DeVoto to Ray Dovell, March 30, 1948

Despite the above sardonic suggestion, when DeVoto, Schlesinger Jr., and Adams resigned, the club turned to Dumas Malone to build a new board of editors. Like DeVoto, Malone had already had a long career as a historian engaged with the world outside academia and was thus another natural fit for the venture. At the time, Malone was working on the second volume of his nearly endless work on Jefferson, which would take the rest of his life to complete. He had been on the faculty at Columbia and would soon become "biographer-in-residence" at the University of Virginia, but in 1948, researching full-time, Malone survived solely on a Rockefeller Foundation grant before the addition of the HBC's monthly check for $150, soon reduced to $100.

Malone and DeVoto knew and respected each other, and DeVoto expressed considerable surprise when he learned that the club had managed to enlist Malone's services; he seems to have hoped the club would fail without his leadership.[91] Writing Malone, DeVoto explained why he and the others had resigned, arguing again that the club violated "its explicit contract with its subscribers" by disregarding the judges' decision. He appealed to Malone to "stand on the same platform."[92] The other new board members were Louis B. Wright and Walter Millis. Wright served as director of the Folger Shakespeare Library, as a historian at the National Geographic Society, and as secretary of the American Historical Association. Millis was on staff at the Center for the Study of Democratic Institutions. All three men resided in the same part of the country—a situation that apparently concerned no one at the club but one that represented a significant departure from the charter board's careful geographic distribution.

In the 1920s, Malone had edited the *Dictionary of American Biography* and had asked DeVoto (and Randolph Adams) to write entries. That experience reveals quite a lot about the two men's approaches to writing history for the public. When DeVoto submitted his entries on Brigham Young and Joseph Smith, Malone asked him to "tone down" his critical perspective so that Mormons would not protest. Characteristically, DeVoto refused, and the Mormons complained. According to Malone, DeVoto said, "You've got to face it. Either he was a faker or he wasn't." The historian must judge. Malone later noted that many of the entries for the *Dictionary* had to be edited for content that might prove offensive to one group or another, though he evidently saw nothing objectionable in that. Furthermore, he deliberately asked Presbyterians to write about Presbyterians, southerners to write about the Confederacy, and so on.[93] In other words, no entry would be permitted to disturb any group's cherished heritage. This approach contrasted very sharply with DeVoto's; it would contribute to the success of Malone's long tenure at the HBC.

Malone proved much more willing to consider the commercial merits of a book. In his correspondence with his fellow editors, Wright and Millis, Malone often remarked on particular books that would be unlikely to sell well and therefore should not be considered for selection by the club. This attitude extended to controversy as well. If one of the editors considered a book controversial, Malone agreed to drop it to avoid the possibility of complaints or low sales. Around the beginning of the 1970s, the editors rejected at least three books on John Brown because they thought him too radical a subject to be treated mostly favorably in a biography. After Wright objected to Richard Hofstadter's *American Violence*, Malone accepted his opinion that they probably should try to avoid works by recognized "academic liberals."[94] This was a far cry from the heavy progressive tenor of the postwar DeVoto board.

The *History Book Club Review* reflected the club's changing philosophy, from edifying and boldly progressive to conservative and commercial. The HBC had from inception sent its readers reviews, written by the editorial board, of the books offered. In the beginning, when the club offered only one book each month, the reviews were long and educative. The historians "taught" the book as they might teach it in the classroom. This fit with their understanding of the club's mission to help Americans to comprehend their world through the history books they selected. In the early 1950s, the *Review* grew in overall length, offering more books at discounted rates, but the reviews shriveled and lost the lecturing tone. By 1957 the *Review* contained dozens of book choices, and though the featured selection still warranted a longer write-up, it bore no resemblance to the critical reviews of a decade earlier. Just two or three promotional sentences accompanied each of the many other books on offer.[95]

This followed the change in emphasis from education to popular appeal, but perhaps too, these later books required less substantive reviews since the topics were largely familiar to subscribers. Coincidental with these changes, the HBC began to offer books on topics other than American history. By the mid-1950s subjects ranged from the Dead Sea scrolls to the Notre Dame cathedral. However, rather than revealing greater cosmopolitanism or engagement with contemporary foreign affairs, this change reflected a retreat into the safer territory of established collective memory. The move to world history offered more prominent historical subjects — more major battles, more great leaders, more conventional national histories — that subscribers would recognize at first sight. This approach contrasted with, for example, the earlier selection of *Concord*, which, while superficially more provincial, considered all sorts of cultural, social, political, and international issues from an unusual and challenging perspective.

By the end of the 1950s the goals of the club had changed from instruction and guidance to sales. In correspondence with Malone, Dovell sought in vain to discover some pattern visible in the kind of history that sold well. In 1958, he and Malone analyzed the books sold through the club during 1955-57, hoping to find a topic or theme that would appeal to readers, but, as far as they could tell, no form of logic determined a book's popularity. Thus it would be impossible to predict which new books would sell well and which would not. Ten years earlier, DeVoto had warned Dovell that if he attempted such a wrong-minded enterprise, this would most certainly be the case — otherwise publishers would have developed and stuck with a successful formula long before then.[96]

For the publishers and the rest of the business office, this shift to focus primarily on salability may not have been a significant change at all. But for the historians, who through their selection process determined the club's philosophy, the shift in emphasis meant the abandonment of loftier objectives to the profit motive. Partly this resulted from the change in personnel, but through the first ten years of the new board's tenure Malone and company continued to use rhetoric similar to that of DeVoto's group when discussing the club's purpose. Only later did they abandon language that connected the contemporary world with the history they selected. In an advertisement for the club in the mid-1950s, Malone assured subscribers that the historians were all "close observers of the contemporary scene," interested in the "story of their country" as it pertained to American engagement with "problems in the modern world." Whether this attitude had somehow carried over from the DeVoto period, or whether Malone for a time shared these sentiments, by the 1960s the club had retreated fully into the past and reversed the founding principle that history should confront the present.[97]

Like the purveyors of the past described in the other chapters, postwar historians also selected from the overabundance of recorded history only a few gems they judged worthy of the public's attention. In many respects, the HBC business model rested on the same shaky foundation as that of *Cavalcade of America*, which is profiled in the next chapter. Both chose episodes from history that not only served their agendas but would also, they hoped, appeal to a wide audience. Similar to the demise of Du Pont's television program, the HBC devolved into an enterprise that relinquished its educative goal in order to appeal more directly to presumed consumer tastes.

This shift also had a deeper significance for the role of history in society. DeVoto's board believed that history should challenge the reader's conception of the past. Consequently, they selected only those works that offered some new information, interpretation, or perspective on historical events, and often on contemporary events as well. The whole point of the enterprise, as far as they were concerned, was to affect the way that Americans thought. That could only be achieved through books that provoked and stimulated new ideas. In contrast, in their selections, Malone's board tried to appeal to America's collective memory. By choosing books that they hoped would sell well, the later editors showed less interest in confronting Americans with a challenging past than in helping readers to access a past that they already knew. Rather than following the earlier editors' example, and further deconstructing the narrative of American history into its rougher components, showing confrontations between "elites" and the "people," or exploring the conflict between patriotic collective memory and more critical history, they suggested works like Malone's own biography of Jefferson: history that, while very well done, nevertheless reinforced the idea of a national heritage comprised mainly of founding fathers and later president-monuments. In other words, they offered a kind of history unlikely to challenge collective memory or affect contemporary social thought in any meaningful way. Instead they constructed a past that was usable in only the limited sense that it reassured the history buff and the patriot—and also generated some income for the historians and publishers.

By 1955 William Harlan Hale observed that while "adults are now being offered a galaxy of instructive series about our past," very little contemporary history writing offered critical perspectives on the past. For Hale this was problematic since "suspension of criticism equals uncritical acceptance," though he also understood the prevailing wisdom that "the times surely call for holding our past heroes high."[98] Increasingly, the HBC resembled its younger relation, *American Heritage*, merely "holding past heroes high" for easier consumption. The story of the HBC thus offers a paradigm of how history, when attempting to appeal to a broad audience, becomes subjugated to memory. The subsequent chapters follow this basic outline in their own unique ways as other popular "historians" attempted to create and disseminate their own historical interpretations. Instead, confronted by the public's assumptions and desires, their histories took on characteristics of memory, mythology, and iconography, and their educative missions devolved into catering to every recognized part of an increasingly segmented audience.

The next two chapters examine how two competing radio and television history programs, *Cavalcade of America* and *You Are There*, attempted to balance educational or propaganda objectives with the need to appeal to a large audience. Despite very significant differences, in both cases the interaction of history and popular culture yielded similar and now familiar results. Each series began as an effort to influence social thought, transformed into merely popular entertainment, and finally disappeared altogether as television matured during the later 1950s into a medium that made no pretensions of offering the public anything other than that which the majority seemed likely to watch.

2

Mythologizing History
on Du Pont's *Cavalcade of America*

Tucked away in a pleasant corner of space, away where Time has no
meaning—there's a part of the Promised Land reserved for Americans,
where all comers are allowed to wander anywhere they want . . .

> Hagley Museum and Library, Pictorial Collections,
> *Cavalcade of America* Transcripts,
> "Davy Crockett," no. 227

So began a 1941 *Cavalcade of America* radio play about Davy Crockett. These
words also serve as an introduction to the *Cavalcade* itself. Blending together history and myth, accentuating nationalism and patriotism, and defining
who and what belongs in the American story, the Du Pont Company's two-
decade-long public lesson in American history achieved all this while reshaping
the past into a consistent argument against government regulation. History was
molded into something useful, both for the sponsor and for many other Americans, who saw the series as an educational opportunity that might encourage
civic renewal through greater knowledge of the nation's history. Educators,
historians, and community leaders looked to Du Pont to provide what that they
felt lacking—first on radio, later on television: the educational programming
that had largely failed to flow forth as expected from these new technologies.
Following the endorsement of prominent historians, schoolteachers across the

country used *Cavalcade* films and phonograph records to instruct their students in American history. Additionally, millions of Americans tuned in to the series on their own radio and television sets. The popularity of the program raises questions about how a carefully calculated advertising campaign by one of the largest and most visible corporations in the United States was so widely accepted as an educational tool for teaching American history—or even accepted *as* history in itself—and how Du Pont could reach millions with its interpretations while the professional historical associations struggled to communicate with the public.

This mythic history retold tales from America's past, especially stories that celebrated individualism, the benevolence of big business, and a traditional America where men and women possessed "the consoling knowledge that no government taboos would interfere with their progress."[1] The program emphasized Du Pont's "contributions to people's welfare and happiness" and also elucidated the "fundamental religious, social, ethical, political and economic principles" that fostered the past, present, and future environment wherein the corporation thrived.[2] *Cavalcade* generally used familiar historical moments but reconfigured the stories into usable fables. Through this process, history lost context, chronology, and any sense of distance. *Cavalcade of America*'s highly selective picking and choosing from the past to find the desired lessons for the present bears close resemblance, in both act and consequence, to combing the Bible for a single verse that supports or refutes a particular argument. The failure to consider how the anecdote fits into the larger "text," including contradictory passages of both verse and time, determines that any discovered meaning must have come from the one doing the choosing rather than from the broader text itself.

"Men do not actually search history to avoid the mistakes of the past," wrote Thurman Arnold in 1937. Rather, said the unusually literary head of the Justice Department's Antitrust Division, "they seek convenient analogies to show the dangers in failing to adopt the creed which they advocate."[3] Arnold's words in *Folklore of Capitalism* could almost have been instructions for Du Pont's *Cavalcade* instead of the critique of such kinds of "history" that he meant it to be, so closely did the series follow this agenda. David Lowenthal's explication of the differences between history and heritage provides another useful way to think about this series, which was billed as history but better resembled Lowenthal's definition of heritage. Heritage works with "exclusive myths of origin and continuance," he writes, "endowing a select group with prestige and common purpose."[4] Certainly this was both the objective and the function of *Cavalcade of America*, which identified suitable heroes and legends and then linked them to both its corporate sponsor and its national radio and television audience. In fact, some episodes dealt quite openly with the question of admittance *into* the "cavalcade of American history"—who belonged, who had to be left outside the imagined boundary, and what behaviors made the difference. In the age of the House Un-American Activities Committee (HUAC), such definition was not merely an academic exercise.

Other historians have written about *Cavalcade* in terms of corporate advertising efforts. In particular, the works of Elizabeth Fones-Wolf, Roland Marchand, William L. Bird Jr., and Howell John Harris have situated the Du Pont series within the larger pre- and postwar public relations campaigns against the New Deal regulatory state and for "free enterprise."[5] Bird also traces the development of increasingly sophisticated corporate advertising strategies that eventually allowed Du Pont president Lammot du Pont and other corporate executives to grasp the bottom-line value of indirect campaigns and seemingly unfocused programs like *Cavalcade*. Michael Kammen argues that a democratization of tradition and a renewed emphasis on referencing the past occurred during the 1920s and 1930s. Other works agree with this assessment, noting the proliferation of popular historically themed parks such as Colonial Williamsburg and Ford's Greenfield Village in the former decade and attempts to position the New Deal and even the radical left in the American tradition during the latter. *Cavalcade* also paralleled Ford's village in its attempt to situate a corporation that radically transformed work and life patterns within a traditional and familiar context. Following an emphasis in the 1930s on more accessible theater and other forms of performance, the decade also saw a broader focus on theatricality as a way of making the past more appealing to the general public.[6] The *Cavalcade* that began in the thirties in a way exemplifies that accessibility and "democratization." Although it hired "experts" (historians) to check scripts for inaccuracies, the show's creators and its audience hailed from outside of the historical profession. However, due to the resources needed to effectively utilize largely unregulated mass media, capital dominated this ostensibly more democratic approach to the past.

Du Pont concerned itself with public opinion despite the fact that the company sold few products directly to the public because of a growing recognition that politics—and voters—could greatly affect their business.[7] Sponsored solely by Du Pont and produced by the advertising firm of Batton, Barton, Durstine and Osborne (BBDO)—a typical arrangement in early radio and television— *Cavalcade* represented a significant part of a larger project to redefine America in terms that suited business. According to Bird, the series was the "foremost popular expression of business leadership to survive the election of 1936."[8]

These efforts at persuasion largely failed during the 1930s, a decade during which Du Pont faced one public humiliation after another and New Deal agencies contributed historical productions that offered nearly opposite lessons from history. The format of the show changed several times before firmly settling down in dramatized American history just before World War II, and the series' steady persistence prepared the way for greater success in the postwar years— when, incidentally, no New Deal programs offered contrary presentations of the past. The fundamental concerns that motivated Du Pont's campaign never really changed, and therefore the basic philosophy, apparent in episodes from across the decades, remained fairly consistent from 1935 through 1957, even if immediate crises sometimes necessitated specific responses.

Exemplary heroes that the series identified as worthy of remembering also stayed the same: historic Americans whose individual efforts introduced some measure of progress—usually material. Unsurprisingly, the series drew many of its protagonists from the business world, but prominent scientific and political figures also appeared regularly. One type of hero *Cavalcade* generally *avoided* was the man or woman who questioned authority—generally, but not always. Though both Lincoln and Lee condemned John Brown and prevented his inclusion *in* the cavalcade, he did appear as a protagonist on the series. So did many women who questioned their inferior positions in society.[9] But there was a fine line between doing one's part to advance the grand march of the *Cavalcade of America* and gumming up the works with protest. Overall, things moved in the right direction—as they naturally should, this being America—with just a little nudge here or there by some responsible, well-mannered citizen. But any social issues left unresolved in America in 1940 or 1950 could not be addressed, even historically, on *Cavalcade*. With rare exception, African American history was avoided at least partly for this reason. Political action could be celebrated in the past, but only if Du Pont would also welcome similar actions in the present. Patriotic service and political engagement such as supporting Cold War policy could be reinforced by lessons from the past, but historical subjects that suggested controversy or disruption in the present were excluded.

Cavalcade of America debuted in the fall of 1935, as the New Deal seemed poised to dramatically change the economic climate and as the Communist Party opened itself up to cooperation with liberals as part of a Popular Front opposed to fascism and its supporters. At the time, Du Pont faced an actively angry and hostile public. The Great Depression had turned opinion very much against big business—a group that certainly included Du Pont. Further sinking Du Pont's reputation, the company became known as a "sinister symbol of war-making" following the publication of *Merchant of Death*, a Book-of-the-Month

Club selection in 1934 that also appeared in abridgments in *Fortune* and *Reader's Digest*. In 1935 the Nye Committee on World War I profiteering held Senate hearings to interrogate Du Pont executives.[10]

World War I transformed Du Pont from a large corporation into a global economic force. Gross revenue increased to ten times its prewar amount.[11] The war also enriched the du Pont clan while hundreds of their non-union employees suffered horrible illnesses and painful deaths caused by working with hazardous chemicals in unsafe conditions. More irksome to the Nye Committee, however, was that Du Pont drove hard bargains for its gunpowder, first with the Allies and later with the U.S. government. The company also managed to secure public funding for its wartime factory expansions yet kept all of the extraordinary profits in the family. Most troubling of all, the du Ponts allegedly used their money and influence to push the United States toward a declaration of war.[12]

The du Pont family announced their antipathy toward President Roosevelt through the creation and funding of the American Liberty League and a number of more radical right-wing groups like the KKK-dominated Southern Committee to Uphold the Constitution.[13] Several leading du Ponts voted for Roosevelt in 1932, including the brothers Pierre, Irénée, and Lammot du Pont, who were then the former president, chairman, and president of the company, respectively. Ending prohibition (in order to replace the income tax with a liquor tax) and the lure of a partnership between business and government, which offered both stability and control to the nation's largest corporations, drew the usually reliable Republicans into the Democratic camp—but only for a moment. The New Deal favored workers too much. Pierre du Pont, who served on the National Labor Board, dissented when the board ruled in favor of collective bargaining and then resigned from that appointment as well as his position on the National Recovery Administration's Industrial Advisory Board in early 1934. By then, his brothers had already rejected Roosevelt.[14]

In 1935–36, the du Ponts offered the most visible business opposition to the president. Irénée set to building the Liberty League, and the family contributed more than $855,000 to the 1936 campaign of Republican Alf Landon. Both the league and the election were disasters for the du Ponts, and Roosevelt's easy victory was also their own crushing defeat. Even Delaware, the family's virtual fiefdom, voted for Roosevelt.[15] In the aftermath, emboldened autoworkers led a successful sit-down strike at General Motors, then a vital part of Du Pont's empire, representing about a quarter of its income.[16] By then, only 20 percent of the public held a favorable opinion of Du Pont.[17]

Having failed in traditional politics, yet realizing that public opinion mattered more than ever, Du Pont sought an alternative approach. Bruce

Barton, already famous as a genius of advertising, as a Republican Party activist, and as author of the books *A Young Man's Jesus*, *The Man Nobody Knows*, and hundreds of articles, wrote to Lammot du Pont in the spring of 1935 about the obvious image problem the company faced. Public opinion, whether due to "hysteria" or "decadence," had turned almost 100 percent against war, and that same public strongly associated Du Pont with not only war but war-mongering. Barton compared the negative opinion to "infected tonsils," and BBDO to the doctor who advised removing those tonsils before they "hurt you"—in Roosevelt's America, one never knew "when or how it might hurt."[18] For a remedy, BBDO proposed to change Du Pont from "merchants of death" to the people who brought you "Better Things for Better Living . . . Through Chemistry," the slogan devised by Barton and adopted by Du Pont for the first *Cavalcade* broadcast. Barton convinced Du Pont that he could "create a vast constituency . . . willing to accept readily anything that bears the Du Pont name."[19]

The trick would be to do these things without seeming to engage in self-promotion. By employing the historical trope and presenting "educational" programming rather than propaganda, Du Pont might avoid the trap. In 1938, Lammot explained how, through *Cavalcade*'s historical productions, the company minimized the suggestion of "paid self-advertising" or "tooting one's own horn" and, most importantly, any hint that, as he put it, the "'economic royalists' were ganging up." Learning from Du Pont's earlier public relations disasters, in the late 1930s Lammot refused all requests for more overt coopera-tion and coordination from the National Association of Manufacturers (NAM) and other organizations, which might have exposed *Cavalcade* as propaganda.[20] For the same reason, his head of advertising, William A. Hart, agreed that indi-vidual corporations had better stick to their own advertising but also keep "in mind all the time the main objectives, to help industry be better understood and appreciated."[21]

The series opened on October 9, 1935, with "No Turning Back." The first lesson fittingly dealt with the Pilgrims. Establishing a pattern, the broadcast explicitly linked the Pilgrims' refusal to return with their ship to England with, in the second half, present-day descendants refusing to leave their midwestern farm after brutal dust storms and a plague of grasshoppers of biblical scale had devastated their crops. Thus, perseverance and self-reliance, two defined traits of Americans, were as necessary in 1935 as three hundred years before. In the hundreds of subsequent broadcasts, Du Pont and BBDO interpreted the past to emphasize these and other desirable traits, as well as those aspects of American history deemed suitable to their contemporary objectives of deregulation, lower taxes, weaker labor unions, and a reversal of the New Deal tide. In so doing, they worked to shape collective memory and redraw the boundaries of acceptable political, social, and economic activity.[22]

BBDO used the word *cavalcade* to mean a "moving panorama of the historical characters and episodes entering into the formation of the American character."[23] The program title had originated with NBC's Stanley Hoflund High, who proposed to NAM the sponsorship of a program called *American Cavalcade* in early 1935 (the word *cavalcade* had recently become well known from Noël Coward's play *Cavalcade*, the movie version of which won Best Picture for 1932). This countered the sponsor's proposal for a series called *The Men Who Made American Industry*. High understood that the public in 1935 was antipathetic to such overtly pro-capital propaganda and thus suggested "an 'epic of America' sort of thing" that would offer "just as good a chance there for propaganda and a whale of a lot better chance that the public will swallow it." As High explained to Lammot du Pont, *American Cavalcade* would not dwell on opposition to the New Deal; rather, "the material will be historical." But instead of dramatizing "events, as such," it would "dramatize those American qualities which dominated the events." High's vision of those qualities proved to be too moderate for both Du Pont and NAM, and he soon departed the network to write speeches for FDR, coining the phrase "economic royalists" in reference to his former clients for the 1936 campaign. Interestingly, as written by High, Samuel Rosenbaum, and Thomas Corcoran, FDR's national convention speech in Philadelphia inverted the whiggish *Cavalcade* story so that American history devolved toward "new kingdoms built upon concentration of control," where the people struggled to "remain free" instead of being "impressed into this royal service."[24] NAM sponsored the program eventually titled *American Adventure*, which ran on NBC for three months in the summer of 1935, but it was the Du Pont series that started in October (on CBS) that followed, or perhaps plagiarized, High's plan.[25] High was among the critics who expressed dissatisfaction when the first *Cavalcade* program aired. "I thought it was terrible," he wrote, adding, "the action was slow and the climax sounded like a page out of Horatio Alger—and a poor page at that."[26]

The series, designed to be educational as well as entertaining, ran on radio from 1935 to 1953 and on television from 1952 to 1957. It suffered cancellation by Du Pont's Executive Committee twice in the late 1930s, for one season airing as a musical hour, before the build-up to World War II called out for the kind of patriotic historical memories that Du Pont wanted to offer the public. As soon as CBS started broadcasting, NBC sought to win the Du Pont account back; after 1939 the show aired on NBC radio. Much about this program was unique in the world of commercial media, including the high level of control and responsibility over content exercised by the sponsor, the involvement of prominent historians, and the distribution of episode soundtracks and films to schoolchildren. Du Pont wanted a program that would stand apart from the crowd and earn the company critical praise. The company never considered this to be merely a sponsorship; Du Pont wanted the public to associate the company with an admired *institution* in the world of broadcasting.[27]

BBDO publicists assured that *Cavalcade* advertisements and hundreds of newspaper columns around the country asserted the series' allegiance to historical fact. Critics responded to this effort with praise and awards for the radio series and later declared *Cavalcade* to be among the "best of TV."[28] The claim of disinterested education and history was bolstered by the prominent historians brought in to consult on the show, beginning with Arthur M. Schlesinger Sr. and Dixon Ryan Fox, and continuing with Frank Monaghan, James Truslow Adams, Marquis James, Julian Boyd, Francis Ronalds, and folklorist Carl Carmer. Moreover, Bruce Barton was enough of a historian himself to have been offered a fellowship by Frederick Jackson Turner, and his father had been an amateur historian of Abraham Lincoln's early adulthood—a subject of several *Cavalcade* episodes. Barton nearly became a professional historian, but the emerging field of advertising proved more alluring. His famous speech, "They Knew Not Joseph,"—based, like much of his writing, on his own or his father's interpretations of the Bible—argued the necessity of constantly re-educating the ever-changing public. If people today knew not the "truth," as his clients defined it, Barton would steer them toward it. Since new consumers and voters emerged every day, affecting public thought and behavior meant a consistent, long-term, educative approach to advertising. Barton influenced the series as he oversaw the whole project, but he left the details to others.[29] Ideas for episodes generally came from within BBDO or Du Pont's Advertising Department, and the scripts came from professional writers; the historians served mainly as fact-checkers, but their association with the series was still mutually beneficial. All shared an interest in the wider diffusion of historical knowledge and a revitalization of civic engagement. Fox and Schlesinger Sr. edited and presumably profited from two book versions of the early *Cavalcade*; Carmer edited a longer, full-color edition in 1955; Monoghan, who joined following four years as research director and historian of the New York World's Fair of 1939, linked his work on the *Cavalcade* with his other postwar public history project, the Freedom Train of 1948.

Fox's foreword to the first *Cavalcade* book reveals something of the historians' hopes for the *Cavalcade* series and their reasons for collaborating. Wrote Fox,

"We thought that one of the best uses [the public] could make of a half hour once a week would be to listen to a series of spoken dramas which revealed the spirit of America." Schlesinger Sr., a supporter of the New Deal, had reservations, writing Fox, "The connection with the Du Pont company bothers me somewhat." Specifically, he worried about becoming "involved in an undesirable type of propaganda," that is, the "glorification of the employer who maintains the 'American system' of the open shop against the labor unions." He also objected to the characterization of the show as "true stories" and instead described it as "telling stories about true incidents"—all a historian could hope to do. In communications with his colleague, Schlesinger Sr. often downplayed both their roles and the series' importance. In contrast, Fox said they were doing real historical work, important "for the American tradition and particularly for the DuPont Company as an American institution."[30]

Fox's declaration that *Cavalcade* was "what people ought to want" reflects the attitude of the historians associated with the show: history, generally speaking, was something the public could use a bit more of.[31] Whereas Du Pont looked at *Cavalcade* as the right kind of education, ideologically, for the listening public, Fox and the other consultants—as well as countless other educators who admired the program—seem to have been excited by the mere fact of *any* educational history program. Monaghan later explained his role, saying, "In those days of world chaos it was increasingly important that every student become better acquainted with the colorful and sturdy traditions of America's past. That was the basic concept of *Cavalcade of America*." The possibilities for history education on the radio ultimately won Schlesinger Sr. over, as they would the other historians hired as consultants. He still thought it was propaganda, but "not in any objectionable sense."[32]

BBDO initially promoted the series as the "new social history" that Fox and Schlesinger Sr. had fostered with their coeditorship of the twelve-volume *A History of American Life*.[33] When the two historians signed on with Du Pont, the American Historical Association (AHA) was seeking its own radio program. Fox thought the *Cavalcade* would be just what the AHA desired, "though, of course, the Association is not being brought into it." In fact, the AHA as well as other prominent historians continued to try (and fail) to mount historical series on the radio; interestingly, one of the biggest obstacles was *Cavalcade*'s success.[34] When Allan Nevins, then president of the Society of American Historians, launched his own series in 1954, critics pointed out that it was "not an original series." There had been "others of this general type, and of these, Du Pont's 'Cavalcade of America' is probably the most outstanding." Nevins insisted that "to comprehend their responsibilities, their national ideals, their capacities under stress, Americans need a better knowledge of their past."[35] But Du Pont had already said the same thing, even if its objectives differed.

Du Pont and Education

> To students in schools and colleges and to all thoughtful persons who would grasp the meaning of our troubled times, the program [*Cavalcade*] offers complete authenticity for illuminating material of absorbing interest.
>
> Dr. James R. Angell, president emeritus, Yale University, testimonial,
> reprinted in Martin Grams Jr., *History of the Cavalcade of America*

While the historians appreciated the opportunity to spread the gospel, history for history's sake was hardly what Du Pont had in mind. Beyond *Cavalcade*, Lammot du Pont involved the company with other educational and historical activities that served similar purposes to that of the series. Education, he said, was the "only preventive, or cure, for attacks on industry" perpetrated during the 1930s by the "horde of alphabetical organizations."[36] As chairman of NAM's Educational Cooperation Committee, Lammot oversaw business efforts to weed out negative depictions of advertising and business from the nation's schools. This coincided with a wider textbook controversy and fears of "subversion" in schools and elsewhere in the 1930s, but Lammot's interest also derived from his concern about public opinion toward Du Pont. His *Cavalcade* consultant, Dixon Ryan Fox, warned Lammot of the hostility directed specifically at the company by college professors who taught students to hate the du Ponts.[37]

Under Lammot's leadership, the education committee attempted to walk a thin line between censoring free speech and allowing perceived attacks on capitalism to go unchecked in the schools. Rather than create a textbook blacklist, as the American Federation of Advertisers had done, the committee drew up guidelines for distribution to educators that included the stipulation that the community rather than individual teachers should decide instructional content. The questions with which the committee concerned themselves were both timeless and particular to the Age of Roosevelt: Should a "factual foundation" be present before children are exposed to controversial interpretations of history? Is some "understanding of traditions behind American institutions" necessary before students can grapple with current issues concerning those institutions? How does society balance fostering "healthy skepticism" against the creation of "morbid cynicism"? Is it necessary to first root oneself in the past? Du Pont knew the answers, and *Cavalcade* represents the company's effort to prepare that foundation, establish that sense of tradition, and explain what it all meant to an uneducated yet increasingly powerful public.[38]

A confidential memorandum prepared by Lammot's committee offered explicit suggestions for how to transform students into "citizens" of the sort preferred by the association's membership. The program's stated objectives are strikingly similar to those of *Cavalcade* and suggest even more specifically some solutions to the problems they had identified in public history education. As such, they help to explicate Du Pont's grander vision of how history related to the economic and political climate of the present. Principally, since the educational system had failed to cultivate the "American Way," manufacturers needed to assume greater responsibility for public education. The report suggested, first, a "revival" of history that explained the "historical and spiritual foundations of the American system" in such a way that unequivocally encouraged "patriotic pride in our institutions," including major corporations. Second, the nation's teachers needed a better historical perspective of social and economic issues, which business would provide. The gospel of capitalism must replace alleged advocacy of leftist economic theories. "Academic freedom ends" before criticism of "free private enterprise" begins. In fact, free enterprise should be taught as the foundation of representative democracy and religious freedom. Schools should also begin to maintain thorough reports on "character attributes, intelligence and aptitude tests and personal conduct," which, when provided to potential employers, would help to expose subversives. Recommendations also included specialized vocational training of disabled children, higher teacher pay (perhaps to make them more solidly bourgeoisie), and time for students to participate in religious activities, which was seen as essential to good citizenship.[39] While working with educators—particularly with a recently harassed and newly chastened Teachers College at Columbia University—to instigate these proposals in the curriculum, NAM also distributed millions of propaganda booklets directly to high schools.[40] And, of course, Du Pont had an even straighter line to students and the public through *Cavalcade*. Additionally, offensive textbooks could be removed, teachers could be accused of disloyalty, or educators could be brought to Wilmington for reeducation.

After World War II, an expanding horde of research and public relations firms encouraged the belief that "left-wingers" taught "false" history in schools and colleges so that companies like Du Pont would engage their services. Their reports suggested that university courses "tend[ed] toward critical evaluation" of capitalism and taught only its shortcomings.[41] Du Pont responded to these reports by increasing its educational advertising during the 1950s. Besides the continued allotment of *Cavalcade of America* films and records, the company distributed informational pamphlets in high schools and colleges, produced motion pictures in the fields of science and economics, and donated large sums of grant money that would link academic communities to the company. In the mid-1950s the company also increased its philanthropic activities, giving about $300,000 in 1954, over a million dollars in 1957, and two million by 1964.[42] Other corporations made similar efforts, contributing fifty million dollars in printed material and other media annually by 1954, half the amount spent nationally by public schools on textbooks. After World War II, the Du Pont Educators Conference brought faculty from across the nation to Delaware to learn the "philosophical basis of free enterprise," convincing at least some skeptics that, after all, "du Pont was O.K." Through the Junior Achievement program in the 1950s, which also involved other leading corporations, thousands of students partook of the same fruit.[43]

During *Cavalcade*'s final season in 1957, as if to illustrate how Du Pont had used history education to promote conservative, business-friendly politics, Emile F. du Pont, director of the Employee Relations Department, spoke at the dedication of the Hagley Museum and Library in Delaware. The museum and research library would be built on the site of the abandoned Du Pont powder works on the Brandywine River. Its dedication culminated two decades of intensive historical work sponsored by Du Pont, primarily but not exclusively in the form of the *Cavalcade of America*. Emile told the assembled guests that "we derive from history maximum benefit only if we learn from it, only if we derive from it truths that we can apply to our own times and our own problems." Here, as on *Cavalcade*, the history sponsored by Du Pont would be functional.

"History is like a mine," he continued. "It serves no useful purpose until the ore is extracted and refined into metal." Yet, converting the idle powder works into a museum would "produce no physical wealth." Extricating himself from this convoluted metaphorical paradox, du Pont explained to his audience that using the site to demonstrate how the free enterprise system had benefited all Americans would, in fact, be profitable, both for the company and the country. Too many Americans supported regulations that would soon "cripple" corporations, and the public "will pay the price for that sort of blunder." The penalties for violation of "natural" economic laws were "inevitable and inescapable"; if the United States continued down the road of regulation, nothing could save it. Speaking amid the ruins of the original powder works, du Pont closed by noting, "The ruins of Greece and Rome, among others, are stark, if beautiful, reminders that these laws of which I speak should not be trifled with, unless one is prepared to pay the penalty." A grim picture of the country's future if Americans failed to learn from Du Pont's history lessons.[44]

Defining the *Cavalcade*, Defining America

There is much to recommend in *Cavalcade*, both as history and as public service. Historical consultants made it as "accurate" as possible, and many saw the program as an effective method of teaching history. The identifiable lessons for the present included such unobjectionable themes as community and national service, the equality of women, and the inalienable right of free speech. On the other hand, despite the somewhat surprising presence of actors and writers from Group Theatre and other leftist backgrounds, the politics never strayed into even vaguely anticapitalist territory. Contrary to the reasoning of the anti-communist forces behind the postwar entertainment industry blacklists, *Cavalcade*'s content was never much affected by the left-wing talent that occasionally worked on the show, which included performers such as Carl Sandburg and Orson Welles and frequent scriptwriter Arthur Miller. As Miller explained, the subjects and themes came from above; writers were well paid but restricted in their work by the sponsor's objectives. Scores of different writers worked on the series, but none of them influenced the show as much as BBDO and Du Pont's Advertising Department. *Cavalcade* could have Ethel Barrymore read Stephen Vincent Benet's "Listen to the People" and simply delete the lines about "apple-sellers in the streets . . . the empty shops, the hungry men," and change Benet's fascist character's speech promoting "home grown" American fascism "wrapped in cellophane" (a well-known Du Pont product) to fascism "wrapped in tissue." Arthur Miller could write a script about Rockefeller seizing the rights to an iron ore deposit discovered by two unheralded brothers that Du Pont then presented as a story of a large corporation able to manage what a small business could not handle—in the best interests of the nation.[45] At any rate, if individual scripts, characters, or lines ever deviated from the conservative Du Pont political philosophy, assessing the overall effects of two decades of calculated history as presented by Du Pont remains more important.

During the first season the show was divided into fifteen-minute halves, with two distinct yet related stories separated by a brief commercial. Martin Grams, *Cavalcade*'s chronicler, perceives correctly that in these episodes the theme was put forth rather "didactically," a practice eventually replaced by more entertaining fables. For example, the debut explicitly linked the refusal of the "Pilgrims" to return with their ship to England with present-day descendants refusing to leave their midwestern farm. *Variety* thought this show a bit obvious in its concern "with what America is thinking"; it may "help galvanize the already conservative thinking" into firmer resistance to the New Deal, but it was "hard to believe" the average listener would take heed.[46] These early broadcasts also began and ended with the company's new slogan, "Better Things for Better Living . . . Through Chemistry," and a summation of the main point that Du Pont hoped to get across (a technique later abandoned). In the third broadcast, "The Spirit of Competition," the lead-in neatly expressed the point of the whole series, which was to identify Du Pont with America, and to define America in terms acceptable to Du Pont: "Just as traditions of American character grew up with our nation—so did the Du Pont company grow up with the nation to occupy an increasingly useful place in our economic life. And Du Pont presents 'The *Cavalcade of America*' in the belief that the stories of faith and courage you will hear on this program represent an heritage too precious to be forgotten. . . . What trait is more American than the spirit of healthy competition? Friendly rivalry has done much to advance our nation's progress."[47]

At the close of the program, listeners were asked to give thanks "that this inherent quality remains an essential element in our country's lifeblood." Indeed, competition, of a very specific kind, was one of the key American traits identified throughout *Cavalcade*'s two decades: competition free of government involvement, historic competition in which the victor always deserved to win, and competition that resulted in better and especially bigger business enterprises. This theme gained greater prominence during the 1949 antitrust suit brought by the Justice Department against Du Pont. A later television ad that appeared after a 1954 teleplay in the guise of an educational film covered the "benefits of free competition" in the nation's fabric industry, noting that Du Pont had "plenty" of competition, a situation somehow maintained by the distinct *absence* of regulation.[48]

Another key *Cavalcade* trait was perseverance, or self-reliance, which meant the refusal of "outside" aid and, often, an unwillingness to migrate—an important point for a family that voiced concern about the revolutionary potential of millions of displaced workers.[49] Several early episodes suggested that struggling families stay on their farms instead of leaving for the city. "We're the sticking kind," says one father. "That's our heritage." And, added the announcer, the fundamental belief in sticking it out, no matter what, is "one of America's real riches."[50] More to the point, the first *Cavalcade* "Thanksgiving" episode revealed that, "from the early days of our country, America and her communities have been solving their own problems without asking for outside aid." As the *Mayflower* made landfall and the Pilgrims established their colony, the first Americans did for themselves. Of course, help received from Indians does not count—nor do Indians count as "Americans" in this series. The condescending morals of these early episodes were almost irrelevant given the circumstances facing many Americans in 1935; how could families "stick it out" on foreclosed farms?[51]

Cavalcade often segued seamlessly into the closing advertisement. The above farming episode led into a story about how Du Pont first began to produce "fixed nitrogen" to improve the soil of American farms. Episode 13, the first of several about the Declaration of Independence, concluded with this statement: "The *spirit of independence* is well exercised by the American housewife as she does her daily shopping. A good example of Mrs. Housewife's firm intention to get the things she buys in first class condition, fresh, clean and sanitary, and to *see* exactly what she's buying—is shown by the *revolutionary* improvements in packaging during recent years, particularly transparent wrapping."[52] Later television advertisements often offered short histories of Du Pont products that were somehow connected to the evening's broadcast.

The frequently aired "willingness to share" parable similarly supported the notion that "outside aid"—that is, government assistance—was un-American. The first of these, broadcast in 1935, recounted disasters during which *individual* Americans donated money, clothes, and food to help those in need. Clara Barton appeared in a few of these stories, probably so that BBDO could use the Red Cross to cross-publicize—a common technique over the two-decade run. The episode closed with Du Pont's articulation of the promise of American life: "the naked will always be clothed, the hungry fed, new homes spring up, crops revived, business resumed"—not because of an expansive role for government, but due to self-reliance and individual efforts.[53]

Cavalcade also strove to personalize the corporation—to put a specific historical face on the faceless corporate giants of contemporary America. For a half hour, multinationals again became one-man operations. A similar goal motivated the creation of a relatively large number of female lead roles and women's history episodes, since BBDO and Du Pont recognized the need to present a flattering self-portrait to both female and male consumers and voters. The sixth broadcast, "Women's Emancipation," celebrated the fact that "American women have taken the lead in assuming women's proper place in the affairs of the world." Moreover, as the "purchasing agents of America's homes," they play a vital role, "not only politically but economically." Because of the suffragists heard on that evening's *Cavalcade*, "today we find women successfully competing with men in every walk of human endeavor," including literature, the arts, industry, and politics. Now "welcomed as an equal—admitted to her place in the *Cavalcade of America!*"[54]

While more men figured as protagonists, women made significant contributions to American progress. Time and again on the program, female pioneers prove they are made of tougher stuff than their male counterparts. They are quite often widows, that traditionally safe position from which women could engage in activity otherwise reserved for men, but even married women with all-consuming careers were celebrated. Rebecca Lukens, widow and owner of Lukens Steel, and Nell Donelly, wife and founder-owner of a huge garment factory in Kansas City, featured in two similar stories of businesswomen defying sexist stereotypes. Donelly's rise in the garment industry in the 1930s probably generated far less controversy than Lukens's mid-nineteenth-century rise in steel, but the broadcasts of their stories both occurred in the 1949–50 season, years during which we might expect to find programs advocating that women "return" to the home. Yet rather than increasing our confusion, the Nell Donelly episode helps to pinpoint the politics behind *Cavalcade*. This broadcast drew the ire of the International Ladies' Garment Workers' Union because Donelly was one of the last holdouts in the industry still resisting unionization. The seemingly liberal point of view about women thus contrasts starkly with the episode's anti-union message. The series' politics were not particularly interested in gender and were in fact generally supportive of women active in the professional and political world, but they were without question concerned with economics. The series featured women entrepreneurs, women scientists and doctors, and even women activists, but never would these female characters engage in economically radical activity. Rather, they generously added their previously unwanted talents to the system and helped to maintain the status quo.[55] Radicals such as Margaret Fuller and Anne Hutchinson appeared on the program too, but their presence only served to elucidate a part of what was great about America. In her identifiably American quest "to think and write what I believe," Fuller rises quickly, becoming editor of the *Dial*, then literary critic for Horace Greeley's *Tribune*, and finally the first American female foreign correspondent.[56] Similarly, Hutchinson represents an early manifestation of American freedom, even though things end badly for her personally.[57]

In the postwar era, probably in order to present Du Pont as in step with contemporary mores, the historical dramas more frequently emphasized the wives of successful men admitted to the *Cavalcade*. "The Justice and the Lady," about Oliver Wendell Holmes and his wife, "Fanny," exemplified this change. An earlier *Cavalcade* that dealt with Holmes barely mentioned a wife; in the postwar version, the wife makes the man. As they aged, Fanny "continued quietly to make his home his castle," but, as she complains, "Sometimes it's a bitter fact for a woman to face that the great man in her life would be just as great without her." Fanny is wrong, of course. On his eightieth birthday, the judge toasts "the lady without whom I should never have survived" or found "the power to write the words." By staying home and taking care of him, Fanny made her man into the great justice Oliver Wendell Holmes.

Cavalcade treated Abigail Adams similarly in a 1947 story, "Abigail Opens the White House," starring the well-known left-wing actress Ida Lupino. Mrs. Adams understood the strain on her husband and "determined to spare him every needless worry." Though short on money and nice things, she managed to make an attractive home. She "discovered that the success or failure of her counsel rested upon her own capabilities as a hostess." Rather than acting as an "aloof and dignified First Lady," or demanding female suffrage, Abigail performs as a "loving wife who inspired her husband's achievements, comforted him in despair and renewed his courage. Then, as now, the resolute faith of American wives and mothers helped our country weather its most trying times."[58] Other postwar episodes reinforced the theme of wifely support.[59]

Part of mythologizing history is the creation of leading roles, with all of the glamour that entails. While the series aired on the radio, the narrator had to explain to listeners that women's rights activist Susan B. Anthony was not a "repulsive-looking female," but rather beautiful and "becomingly-garbed."[60] Once the series moved to television in 1952, fans could see for themselves just how attractive these feminists were. While not surprising—mostly beautiful people appear on American television—it is still important to recognize that *Cavalcade* transformed almost all of its historical characters, but especially women, into dazzlingly attractive heroes.[61] The much-publicized authenticity did not prohibit this idealization through casting and makeup.

The television series also emphasized marital teamwork, which was thought to particularly interest female viewers. Many episodes featured the "triumphant husband and wife team" that overcame obstacles together to achieve greatness— for the husband.[62] "Toward Tomorrow," the Ralph Bunche story, presented a variation on this theme. As usual, the "woman has been consumed to produce a man," but in this case the woman is Bunche's grandmother. Still, the expectation was that female viewers would appreciate and identify with the grandmother's role in sacrificing for "her man."[63]

This episode was a rare exception: African Americans seldom appeared on the television *Cavalcade* and were heard from only infrequently on radio. Rejecting anything that might embroil the company in controversy, Du Pont steered clear of African American subjects. Native American characters appeared in many radio scripts before nearly vanishing when the show moved to television. They were a safer group to caricature than African Americans, but shots of Hollywood Indians would hardly distinguish *Cavalcade* from the low-brow television programs that Du Pont wanted to stay a class above. Cowboys and Indians did not offer "prestige."

In the radio shows, Indians fulfilled roles as either obliging friends or vicious savages. *Cavalcade* featured an amicable Sacajawea on several broadcasts, beginning with "Courageous Curiosity or the Will to Explore," in fall 1935. True to its early form, the show's opening linked Lewis and Clark exploring the unknown continent with Du Pont "exploring unknown realms of science and industry"—both were "bright pages in the history of the nation" and "good evidence of the finest traits of American character." Sacajawea proves herself braver than anyone else in the party and receives due credit for assisting *Cavalcade*'s westward march. In the spring of 1936 the program presented its first male Indian character. After greeting us with "Ugh. How," Squanto teaches a white family how to farm corn. Though even less developed than Sacajawea, his role is the same: to assist as best he can the great American expansion.[64]

In the months leading up to American entry into World War II, Indians appeared with their greatest frequency on *Cavalcade*, usually as violent enemies. For a series that historians have described as deliberately pacifistic, these and many other 1940–41 *Cavalcade* broadcasts sound an unmistakably martial tone.[65] The utter inaccuracy of that interpretation, as well as the related claim that Du Pont worked to avoid war, explains the dissonance. In fact, the du Ponts welcomed the massive global rearmament at the end of the 1930s and, as in World War I, profited enormously from World War II.[66] The pre- and early wartime Indian episodes, which depict Americans at war with a savage adversary that must be beaten and tamed, and eventually must accept American civilization, support the conclusion made by the less hagiographic studies of Du Pont that the company actively sought to capitalize on the deteriorating international situation by rearming not only the Allies but also, to some extent, Germany.[67]

Additionally, these episodes articulate, dramatically, the vision of Henry Luce's "American Century," also offered in 1941. During that year on *Cavalcade*, Americans defeated the bloodthirsty "Geronimo" and imposed their civilization on his people. During the episode the white hero modifies his original view that "the only good Indian is a dead Indian" and accepts instead that he has an obligation to govern and civilize the Indians. As Geronimo is promised a fair trial, we hear not only that Geronimo's "land and liberty will be protected" but also that whites and Indians would be "at peace with each other, from this moment on, for all time."[68] And so it happened, on *Cavalcade of America* at least. A 1941 iteration of the Sacajawea story brought the Indian Wars to a similarly idealized conclusion. After Sacajawea threatens to kill Clark and harangues him for failing to protect her people, Clark, and by extension white America, refutes the charge and promises that "these wrongs you speak of will be made right. They must be." Fortunately, as the narrator explains, "the Great White Father" established a "council of white chiefs" to assuage the Indians' "sorrows" and make everything all right. For a program that prided itself on and was praised for its attention to historical detail, the vague conclusion wrapped things up a little too neatly. But continuing the story in specificity would surely have complicated the happy ending, rooted as it were in contemporary notions of *Pax Americana* more than in history.

In November 1941 Henry Fonda and Errol Flynn both performed *Cavalcade* adaptations of their just-released Warner Bros. productions, *Drums along the Mohawk* and *They Died with Their Boots On*, respectively. The drums of approaching war are indeed audible in Fonda's portrayal of an ordinary farmer, forced by savage Indians into fighting, killing, and nearly dying in order to bring about "a better world for our son to live in." Flynn played a most courageous, just, and almost prophetic George Armstrong Custer. His oddest lines, though, came in a wrap-up interview in which he revealed a bizarre conflation of past and present, reality and fiction:

> ERROL FLYNN: You know it made me kind of nervous working with those
> Indians. You see they were real Sioux from the Dakota reservation—the
> actual descendants of the braves who fought the original battle. I kept
> remembering I was dressed like General Custer, and had my fingers
> crossed hoping they'd remember I wasn't really Custer.
> BUD COLLYER: Well, Errol, it's good you did or you'd probably be wearing a
> wig right now.
> FLYNN: Yeah, a bald one.

In both episodes, whites were outnumbered and attacked by a more powerful enemy.[69] As historian Tom Engelhardt explains, Hollywood films about Indians in this period used the ambush, or "last stand" narrative, to turn "history on its head, making the intruder exchange places with the intruded upon." Thus, he argues, by December 1941 tales like these had prepared Americans to understand the Japanese attack on Pearl Harbor as another in a long series of unprovoked attacks by darker-skinned peoples.[70]

Several other episodes in 1941 also prepared the nation for war, which again seems counterproductive to Du Pont's propaganda objectives.[71] One motivation behind *Cavalcade* was to demonstrate that Du Pont would never push the country into another war. Yet the content of these episodes and the ubiquity of the theme of necessary wars indicate that the company's objectives had changed by 1940.

Assertions by several pro–Du Pont historians to the contrary, the company and the family actively supported Roosevelt's increasing involvement in World War II at the end of the 1930s.[72] Rapprochement between the elite families had already been helped along by the 1937 marriage between Franklin Roosevelt Jr. and Ethel du Pont. In July 1940, a month after the company signed munitions deals with France and Britain, Roosevelt ordered $20 million worth of Du Pont's smokeless powder, the first of many profitable wartime transactions for Du Pont. Lammot led the cheers for the return of the "seller's market." He lectured a NAM meeting: "They [the government] want what we've got. Good. Make them pay the right price for it." During the war, Du Pont built 54 new plants, with $1 billion contributed by taxpayers. In addition to explosives, the war demanded unheard of quantities of the company's nylon, paints, dyes, cellophane, insecticide, and many other products.[73] As in World War I, Du Pont took advantage of opportunities to expand rapidly and inexpensively. The final frontier was nuclear energy, and Du Pont's successful management of the Manhattan Project brought the company invaluable knowledge, influence, power, and later profit. Du Pont's Crawford Greenewalt oversaw the massive operation, the success of which launched him into the company's presidency.[74]

Unlike the 1930s, the World War II years saw the interests of Du Pont and the U.S. government overlap. Beginning in 1940, and then with increasing frequency in 1941, *Cavalcade* aired the historical "reasons" for American involvement in the war. However, during the conflict, many *Cavalcade* episodes featured dramatizations of current or very recent events, something that occurred only rarely afterward, and never before. For once, contemporary events were as safely devoid of controversy as was the past. Few would object to pro-war propaganda after December 1941, even with Du Pont's self-serving imprimatur, but most of the historical episodes also referred in some way to the war. On more than one occasion *Cavalcade* dramatized the "dark days" at Valley Forge to encourage American resolve. It also invoked Thomas Paine to rally another generation of patriots. Claude Rains and Basil Rathbone both played Tom Paine very effectively on the wartime *Cavalcade*: Rains in the spring of 1942 and Rathbone in the fall of 1943. The stories are very different, but the uses of Paine are the same. Both actors quote from "Crisis": "These are the times that try men's souls . . . Tyranny, like hell, is not easily conquered, yet . . . the harder the conflict the more glorious the triumph." And as might be said by a truly dedicated GI, "Where freedom is *not*, there is my home." At the end of his show, Basil Rathbone explicitly connected the history to 1943, noting, "Our problems today in waging war are much the same as in the days of Tom Paine and the need for working together are [*sic*] greater than ever." "Buy war bonds," adds the announcer.[75]

When Claude Rains and Agnes Moorehead portrayed Benedict Arnold and his wife, "Peggy," the story revealed the vital necessity of patriotism. This wartime story stressed Arnold's failure to remain patriotic over the specifics of his treason. Arnold dies wearing his old Continental Army uniform, but outside the borders of the country that he belatedly realized he both loved and needed. Consequently, "for Benedict Arnold there is no place in the *Cavalcade* of America." Historian Frank Monaghan introduced this episode by revealing some just-finished archival research that resulted in this new history of Arnold—so new, said Monaghan, that it was more up to date than any historian's understanding. Apparently, *Cavalcade* provided listeners with cutting-edge history as well as quality drama. Rains, who performed lead roles on the series quite often in the 1940s, reminded the audience at the end of the show that "a man without honor or love of country has no place with other men." One must choose patriotism or exile.[76]

Sophistication in advertising and propaganda grew along with budgets. Patriotic duty may have inspired the increasing number of stars who appeared on *Cavalcade* during the war years, but *Cavalcade*'s increased production value also helped to draw bigger names. Wartime tax policies that allowed corporations to deduct all advertising expenses led to increased radio budgets for Du Pont and many other companies, as well as the associations, such as the War Advertising Council, that they funded. Corporate advertising of all kinds increased many times over during the war years.[77] By 1945 Du Pont and other major corporations had advertising and public relations departments of several thousand employees.

After the war, Du Pont continued to emphasize patriotic service and preparedness on *Cavalcade*. In 1948, Basil Rathbone starred as Thomas Jefferson in Erik Barnouw's adaptation of Paul Green's play *The Common Glory*, then about to open in Williamsburg, Virginia. "Colonial Williamsburg" had itself become a useful historical site for the Cold War. Each of these performances—the play, the radio series, and the colonial city—adapted the past for the latest battle for freedom. In sponsoring Williamsburg's redevelopment, John D. Rockefeller III claimed, in words similar to those heard on *Cavalcade*, that it demonstrated how "freedom, self-government, and sovereignty of the individual have been the well-springs of our greatness." A grateful visitor suggested that the setting acted as a "stimulus for the preservation of our National Security."[78] As Rathbone's Jefferson said in the play, "The struggle, for what we believe . . . the common glory . . . that has to go on, without rest."[79] The Rockefeller Foundation's purchase and distribution of several *Cavalcade* episodes to the nation's public schools likely followed the same line of reasoning that led to the re-creation of Williamsburg.[80]

Fittingly, given Du Pont's expanding global empire, several postwar episodes encouraged international engagement and expansion through stories of Americans making the wider world a better place. "Ordeal in Burma" (1954) related the history of American missionaries in 1820s Burma, specifically their "struggles to bring enlightenment to a backward country." With the action set abroad, this was an unusual episode—a story of the "men and women who made America great" . . . overseas. After several ordeals, the missionary couple struggles to keep faith that the pitiable natives really do want their help to bring them out of darkness. They succeed through the power of their medical science and their ability to mediate between the British and the Burmese, who cannot understand each other. Only the American missionary can end the war because only he "understands" both sides impartially. Thus, America brings peace to the region. In another example, "The Gentle Conqueror," Father Junipero Serra's eighteenth-century mission to the Californian Indians recalls contemporary American objectives overseas. As he works to improve the Indians, he pleads, "We want to help you, not harm you . . . teach you, not beat you. If only you could understand."[81]

In the space where history meant to serve Du Pont's interests and history made to support the war and other forms of civic engagement overlapped, many people, including educators, historians, businessmen, and government officials, heard something they liked. But the commendations lose their gleam once we see how Du Pont attempted to benefit from *Cavalcade*'s manipulation of historical memory. The series' core conceptual framework always remained American history as individual achievement. One of the repeat lessons of this strain was affirmation of the Horatio Alger–style myth. A 1941 episode used Alger himself to promote the ideology of individualism: "Against the charge that his rags-to-riches formula was not true-to-life, there stands a scroll of immortal biographies in the American scene. For while Horatio Alger wrote, Thomas A. Edison was selling newspapers, Charles M. Schwab was driving a hack, and the late great John D. Rockefeller was out of a job. Yes, Horatio Alger was simply telling the old American story that is forever new."[82]

Du Pont continued to regurgitate the "old American story": any individual can become wealthy through hard work. Of course, even in Alger's stories hard work alone never achieves much of anything—some lucky happenstance turns the tide instead, though luck rewards diligence. Rags-to-riches biographies appeared on *Cavalcade* frequently, usually connecting an individual's modest origins to a well-known corporation and thereby legitimizing the success and growth of that company. In 1947, for example, Don Ameche starred as Amadeo Obici, founder of Planter's Peanuts. More than a story about peanuts, it was billed as "a tribute to a truly American system of free enterprise that made the rapid growth and success of such an industry possible."[83]

Episodes that featured the long history of Du Pont found ample evidence of hard times successfully overcome through the selfless dedication of various generations of du Ponts. From the beginning, *Cavalcade* linked Du Pont and the United States through their shared history; the company had "grown with the nation."[84] For a time, Lammot du Pont resisted an episode explicitly dedicated to family history, but for a company so interested in history and its uses, it was too much to resist. "At the request of many listeners," they eventually presented their own story.

The episodes dealing with Jefferson and the Louisiana Purchase offered the most direct route to locating Du Pont in American history. In response to the "merchant of death" charge, *Cavalcade* dramatized Jefferson's request, or order, to company founder Eleuthere Irénée (E. I.) du Pont de Nemours that he build a powder works for the benefit of the American nation. Who would dare to call Jefferson a merchant of death? That very same Du Pont powder used for weapons also helped farmers grow their crops, as demonstrated in episodes that related the history of American agriculture.[85] In another repeated story, Jefferson's friend Lafayette visited E. I. du Pont's struggling factory on the Brandywine River in 1824, which offered du Pont an opportunity to share with his compatriot and the audience the hardships he and his family had endured, as well as demonstrate the du Ponts' benevolence to their employees. His wife explained that du Pont "felt he should take care of our people here. So he built homes for them and gave them pensions." As his father had taught him in the episode's opening scene, "No privilege exists that is not inseparably bound to duty."[86]

Such benevolence historically obviated any need for labor unions presently. Du Pont fought as hard as any corporation to prevent unionization except within the company's Du Pont Council, yet also vigorously sought public approval of its industrial relations.[87] One of the questions asked as part of almost every survey that attempted to gauge how *Cavalcade* affected public opinion toward Du Pont dealt with how the company treated its employees. The surveys consistently reported that regular listeners believed Du Pont treated employees well, and much better than most large corporations.[88] Of course, that would be expected of a family with such a strong, historic sense of duty. While Du Pont determinedly undermined unionization efforts within the company, the du Pont family also worked to reverse the broader twentieth-century trend toward unionization, through political contributions and propaganda campaigns, *Cavalcade* included.

According to *Cavalcade*, the single greatest contribution of the du Ponts to America in the time of Jefferson was the Louisiana Purchase. For this land, which more than doubled the area of the United States, listeners learned they owed a special debt of gratitude to Du Pont. Evidently, Pierre du Pont first suggested to Jefferson that the United States might gain not just New Orleans but the entire Louisiana Territory. Later, when negotiations broke down in Paris, and Talleyrand schemed to deprive America of its manifest destiny, Pierre intervened to restore the natural course of American history. *Cavalcade* related these events on the series' final radio broadcast, on March 31, 1953.[89]

Henry Adams's extensive history of the negotiations treats du Pont's role in Paris similarly. These episodes' assertions never strayed far from fact. Yet the emphasis and repetition of this version meant the exclusion of other parts of American history, including segments bearing directly on Louisiana. And, of course, the purpose of portraying Du Pont's historical contributions was the promotion of the contemporary corporation, rather than elucidation of the history or even memorialization of Pierre du Pont.

Other companies' histories, likewise featured on *Cavalcade*, often used this device: the "just doing what was asked," for the good of the country, or "God's will" explanations for their existence. For example, in "The Forge," Eliphalet Remington reluctantly enters the gun business only after his fellow Americans demand it of him (just as Jefferson demanded that Du Pont manufacture gunpowder). Afterward, he reflects, "Maybe it's almost like I've got a . . . well . . . duty—do you know what I mean?" The announcer knew just what he meant: "Firearms for the pioneers who were to transform a vast wilderness into a land where millions of Americans could live in freedom and plenty."[90] The fact that Remington Arms had become a Du Pont subsidiary went unmentioned in the story.

These episodes reflected the lingering perception at Du Pont and BBDO of the need to defend the company against the old "merchant of death" charge. But perhaps they also reflect a climactic change, when, by the early Cold War, the notion that guns had been necessary to American success seemed pretty reasonable. *Cavalcade* had subtly promoted this message since the mid-1930s, even while Du Pont professed a disinclination for war in other arenas. The experiences of World War II, the nascent Cold War, and Korea certainly lent support to the idea that America's gun and powder manufacturers had played a key role in the nation's history. In this new environment, the voice of Du Pont's *Cavalcade* grew more confident.[91]

DU PONT
CAVALCADE OF AMERICA

Presents

RONALD REAGAN

in

"The Forge"

MONDAY, OCTOBER 13, 1947

NATIONAL BROADCASTING COMPANY

Coast to Coast Network

| 8.00-8.30 | E.T. | 9.30-10.00 | M.T. |
| 7.00-7.30 | C.T. | 8.30- 9.00 | P.T. |

BETTER THINGS *for* BETTER LIVING . . . THROUGH CHEMISTRY

One week before appearing as a friendly witness before the House Committee on Un-American Activities, Ronald Reagan, in *Cavalcade of America* (1947), portrayed an entrepreneur who strengthened America both economically and militarily in his role as the founder of Remington Arms (a Du Pont subsidiary). (Courtesy of Hagley Museum and Library.)

New Medium

Soon after the war, BBDO and Du Pont began to consider broadcasting *Caval-cade* on television. In 1946 Du Pont aired an experimental television simulcast of a radio broadcast of *Cavalcade of America*, the first time a radio series had been aired on television. In a 1947 report, Du Pont's Film Steering Committee (an exploratory group made up of Public Relations and Advertising Department executives) drew on the educative and propaganda successes of World War II military films to conclude that film would be a more "effective media" for Du Pont's purposes. Unlike radio, movies and television "command undivided audience attention."[92] An idea discussed at this time was to make 16mm films of *Cavalcade* for schools, clubs, patriotic societies, and "welfare agencies, particularly those working among the foreign-born." The decision to shoot the television series on film allowed this vision to be fulfilled. BBDO created the first made-for-television film of *Cavalcade* in September 1951, broadcast only to a limited audience in New York and Los Angeles.[93] Not long afterward, Du Pont and BBDO, excited about the rapid growth of television viewers, prepared for a televised 1952–53 season.[94]

At BBDO, questions persisted about the wisdom of continuing with the historical format. Du Pont stayed with *Cavalcade* because, for one thing, residual rights to *Cavalcade* would be more valuable than for any other program yet made for television, according to a BBDO analysis. History programming never became more outdated than it was to begin with, and *Cavalcade* episodes, whether first-runs or repeats, could be shown in any sequence, since each episode stood on its own. This was important for distribution to schools and clubs as well as for rebroadcasts.

BBDO considered recommending instead sponsorship of a political-forum-type show such as *Meet the Press* or *American Forum*. This would meet Du Pont's "prestige" requirement, but Du Pont would be identified with controversy and perhaps even controversial stances on major issues of the day—precisely what Du Pont had tried to avoid by using the past. Similarly, newscasts (and newsreels) had to be rejected because of the "lack of sponsor approval of content." BBDO thought about recommending Edward R. Murrow's critically acclaimed *See It Now*, but content control was again a problem—though not as much as its abysmally low ratings.[95] Du Pont's insistence on full creative control, as well as all residual rights, meant that other interesting proposals, including a partial sponsorship of the science films made by Frank Capra for AT&T such as "Our Mr. Sun" and "The Moon," had to be rejected. The "tense" atmosphere of sporting events would not provide the proper mood for reflection about Du

Pont's contributions to America, and musical programs would be either too light for the serious Du Pont message or, if the programs could be limited to art music, ratings would be too low to justify the change.[96]

In the end, BBDO and Du Pont agreed to continue with their half-hour program of historical dramatization. Both parties believed that the investment in *Cavalcade* had generated tremendous "dividends" in "favorable public attitude" toward Du Pont. Public opinion had improved, from 20 percent favorable in 1935 to 82 percent in 1952.[97] Continuing to monitor each proposed television episode, Du Pont executives maintained total control of the show's content, vetoing controversial subjects such as African Americans and the atomic bomb, and approving each script individually. One Advertising Department executive wrote, "One of the unique things about *Cavalcade* is the control that we (the agency and ourselves) have exercised over story suggestions."[98] Under such scrutiny, the message sent over the airwaves remained notably consistent.

The show's reach was impressive. BBDO claimed that 7.5 million people heard *Cavalcade* each week over the radio. Estimates for the television audience varied considerably, but audiences of 10 to 15 million tuned in during the mid-1950s, though this number declined by the 1956–57 season. Still, four out of ten adults reported viewing at least one episode in one three-month period in 1956.[99] Additionally, about 6 million students regularly watched *Cavalcade* films distributed free of charge, as did men and women of the armed services, members of various clubs and societies, and millions of Du Pont's clients, workers, and their families. BBDO research suggested whole families watched *Cavalcade* together more than almost any other program.[100] Mothers wrote Du Pont that they modified dinnertime once a week so the family could watch together.[101] One mother invited the superintendent of schools and her child's history teacher to watch the show so that they could see for themselves what a wonderful educational tool Du Pont provided.[102] Many teachers told Du Pont that they required their students to listen to or watch the show as homework, while others had their classes learn history from Du Pont collectively.[103] A California schoolteacher wrote that she considered *Cavalcade* "a special part of our history curriculum," and a Santa Ana school administrator thanked Du Pont for making "our jobs easier and more effective." An Illinois teacher who required at-home viewing wrote in to express her students' condolences when Pierre du Pont passed away in 1954. They had come to think of the du Ponts as dear friends.[104]

Assessing how teachers used *Cavalcade* in the classroom is difficult, but *English Journal* articles from the 1940s and 1950s offer evidence that at least some educators integrated episodes into lesson plans on a regular basis. Concerned that the great number of programs on television and radio overwhelmed viewers with choice, one writer suggested "pupil monitoring groups" assigned to keep tabs on selected series, including *Cavalcade of America, You Are There, Omnibus,* and *US Steel Theatre,* and then report on promising upcoming programs. Classes were encouraged to keep a card index of the series for analysis at the end of the year. The underlying discourse revolves around the question of what kind of medium television would become. One article suggested, "Here is our opportunity to develop a wise, appreciative, discriminating audience for television—now and in the future." Another made the point that listening skills had to be taught; this teacher offered colleagues directed listening assignments that his students completed each week while listening to *Cavalcade.* Most interesting, another teacher-author related how she used *Cavalcade* episodes as examples of biographical writing (by listening to radio episodes and reading complimentary scripts sent by Du Pont) and then had her high school students write their own *Cavalcade*-style biographical dramatizations.[105] Likely other teachers used *Cavalcade* similarly, especially after publication of these articles.

Besides schools, particular episodes targeted specific groups using a web of public history organizations. Regional history allowed for concentrated promotion through historical and patriotic societies, state boards of education, and business associations.[106] For episodes with heroes of a particular ethnicity BBDO worked with organizations active in that community. For example, "Breakfast at Nancy's," which told the story of a Revolutionary War heroine in Georgia, led BBDO to contact the state boards of education in Georgia and in surrounding states, all local and regional newspapers, and the many patriotic and historical organizations that focused their attentions on the revolutionary period or the South. Releases for the Ralph Bunche film were sent to two hundred "Negro publications whose circulation is around 2 millions," and the NAACP promoted it through its 1,200 branch offices.[107]

BBDO activated all sorts of promotional networks as part of their "Total Exploitation" package for Du Pont. Unlike many contemporary programs, the months of planning and back-and-forth communications between sponsor and agency for each episode of *Cavalcade* meant that late changes were rare. This enabled long-term "exploitation." The "big monthlies with their three-month deadlines" could (and would) write stories that coincided with the broadcast. Editorials, photos, long Sunday features, "home-town" stories on cast members in their regional papers, fact sheets, and other material were distributed to newspapers and magazines across the country. Syndicated columnists included *Cavalcade* information written by BBDO in their columns, presumably in exchange for money or some other consideration. Additionally, BBDO developed a campaign to distribute free "booklets" in listening areas, to give school news-papers "specially angled stories," to list the program in a series, "Listenables and Lookables," which was distributed to 2,500 schools and libraries, and to offer slides from still photo shots to high schools for viewing during auditorium assemblies. Occasionally, films that seemed particularly important were screened for select critics at BBDO offices in New York. This was true, for example, of the Bunche film and of "Sunset at Appomattox," a copy of which Du Pont presented to the War Library and Museum of the Military Order of the Loyal Legion of the United States, where it apparently became "one of the museum's prized possessions."[108]

The frequent focus on business history allowed for additional exploitation, as featured companies could be relied upon to distribute publicity material to dealers, employees, local chambers of commerce, and publications that Du Pont would not normally use.[109] Sometimes this worked well, as with "The Melody Man," the story of the Magnus Harmonica Company, which advertised for the program in music stores nationwide. For "Sam and the Whale," on the other hand, an effort to engage the American whaling industry, which BBDO discovered no longer existed, failed.[110] And when BBDO proposed to AT&T that they demand signage promoting "The Great Experiment" (the first trans-atlantic cable) in every stockbroker office nationwide that sold AT&T stock, the telecommunications giant declined the advice.[111] Trade associations also publi-cized episodes. When "Spindletop" (about the discovery of oil in Texas) aired each October during "Oil Progress Week," the American Petroleum Institute made and distributed prints of the film. A Milwaukee television station reported back to BBDO during the 1954 "crude" celebration that "we were able to incor-porate promotion for 'Oil Progress Week' and 'Spindletop' into our *news programs* for the week preceding" (emphasis added). A *New York Times* article on Oil Progress Week similarly worked in the *Cavalcade* program. History, institutional advertising, news, and petroleum had been successfully blended into a consum-able commodity.[112]

Local television stations did quite a bit of their own publicity, airing adver-tisements and drafting releases for local organizations, schools, and libraries. BBDO ensured they always had *Cavalcade* material on hand and prepared historical teasers to be read on air with still photo slides in advance of each episode.[113] NBC radio had also promoted the show to educators, inviting state and local superintendents of education to the New York studio to watch *Cavalcade* performances.[114] ABC, *Cavalcade*'s television network after its first season on NBC, created promotional kits, distributed in the fall of 1953 to 1,050 newspapers with a combined circulation of over 44 million, 40 magazines with combined circulation of over 60 million, and affiliates, which then distributed material to additional local publications.[115]

Cavalcade's audience was broad and enthusiastic. Educators, from elementary school teachers to law school professors, requested records and films; various clubs, associations, and fraternal societies gathered to watch films they had a particular interest in; and the public tuned in each week in consistently high numbers. *Cavalcade* made history enjoyable. "I remembered having that in history but it was more interesting and well brought out on TV," said one viewer. "They tell you more than history books tell you. It's an easy way to learn," declared another. Although the programs found their way into schools across the nation, the majority of home viewers were adults, nearly 50 percent between the ages of thirty and forty-nine. Half of *Cavalcade* viewers had not graduated from high school, so their interest in history may have been in part a quest for knowledge they felt they lacked. Some noted that the history classes they took would have been more effective if they had adopted *Cavalcade*'s method of instruction. Law schools too suggested that certain episodes might profitably replace lectures by their professors. For many viewers, the significant difference between history in school and history on *Cavalcade* was that they enjoyed the latter.[116]

Du Pont invested almost as much in measuring the effectiveness of its program as in producing it. Advertising Director William Hart first hired the Psychological Corporation, a business and advertising research firm, for *Cavalcade* studies beginning in 1938.[117] According to its 1939 study of the program, attitudes toward Du Pont varied according to whether, and how much, one listened to *Cavalcade*. Listeners were three times as likely as nonlisteners to positively change their impression of the company. Even among listeners who could not remember consciously the name of the sponsor, attitudes toward Du Pont were significantly more positive than among nonlisteners.[118]

Over the years the company used several research firms to determine who watched the program, what they liked and did not like, what they remembered, and, most importantly, how *Cavalcade* affected their opinions on economic issues.[119] The results are striking in several ways. First, they tell us a lot about how viewers understood history and its relation to their lives. Second, they offer at least some insight into the impact of television and advertising on the public. Third, and most clearly, they reveal exactly what Du Pont and BBDO attempted to achieve through their historical drama.

One reason fans enjoyed *Cavalcade* was its allegiance to convention. Publicity material emphasized the complete *absence* of interpretation, and viewers knew it was "based on actual facts." Fans appreciated reinforcement of their own historical memories. One father told an interviewer, "I like my children to see the events of American history as they always remember it." Another noted, "It is good . . . I know what they're talking about."[120] Many identified themselves as history buffs, teachers, and struggling college students, pleased with the educational content. The authenticity of the costumes, the attention to obscure details, and the interesting minutiae appealed to *Cavalcade* viewers and appreciative critics. Even a museum curator noted he used *Cavalcade* to brush up on "details." Critics loved the attention to dress and scenery especially, which for them meant they could tell readers to consider the program to be authentic historically. The authenticity of uniforms and southern accents in "Sunset at Appomattox" so impressed a Virginian that General Lee and General Longstreet "seemed as though they had stepped out of the pages of history."[121]

Clearly a willingness to believe was at work here—a desire to be fooled into thinking that what is on the screen was real; nevertheless, attention to detail invited suspension of skepticism. David Glassberg's analysis of Ken Burns's *Civil War* (1990) found that most viewers approached that series similarly, with an understanding that onscreen images represented "facts and experiences that cannot be changed and that offer a stable anchor for personal, family, and national identity."[122] When television presents well-made historical re-creations, viewers looking for casual entertainment and enlightenment might understandably assume not just the factual nature of what they see on airwaves but even the unassailable truth of events that they have now personally witnessed. Emphasizing authentic details created an aura of believability about the series, but the obsession that some dedicated viewers had with details drove the "harassed" *Cavalcade* historical consultants crazy, according to Francis Ronalds. Besieged by complaints of what he thought minor errors, Ronalds tried to explain to his bosses that viewers confused "source" with "fact." When sources used for *Cavalcade* scripts contradicted conventional wisdom, letters poured in from people intent on displaying their "superior erudition." Occasionally, disgruntled interest groups and individuals voiced discontent too, like the irate Daughters of the American Revolution member who declared it inconceivable that Jefferson Davis's daughter would have "demeaned herself" by contemplating marriage to a Yankee.[123] Self-identified patriots especially enjoyed the program, and organizations like the American Legion awarded the show on dozens of occasions over the years.[124] More than critics, educators, and perhaps even BBDO, the fans of *Cavalcade* understood the politics behind the history. One fan, New Mexico state legislator Ervin W. Mitchell, wrote in several times to express his appreciation for the conservative message. "Every schoolchild should see it," of course, but "it also makes one . . . feel that there is only one part of the anatomy by which traitors to this country should be hung."[125]

Critics seemed unaware of this particular subtext in the *Cavalcade* dramas, but Mitchell was hardly the only fan who understood the series in political terms. Many thought that the show "[would] help to defeat Communism," "shake evil out of our country," "help mankind," and "[inspire] people that consider themselves 100 percent Americans." The inspirational aspect of the program appealed to many Americans, including Dr. Norman Vincent Peale, author of *The Power of Positive Thinking*, who believed it to be "one of the most constructive programs on the air."[126] Many fans opined that this "intelligence pill" would benefit children most of all since *Cavalcade* gave young children "reasons for their love of America, and [planted] faith before traitors [could] place doubts."[127] Du Pont won praise for working to "sell America to this generation," something many viewers thought necessary and urgent after several decades spent "forgetting American history and traditions, debunking the great men who built this nation"—that is, progressive history. As one woman declared, "*This* is the material with which American young ones should be subjected."[128] With luck *Cavalcade* might act as a "powerful antidote for juvenile delinquency" in postwar America.[129]

Most pleasing to Du Pont, warranting little hand-drawn smiley faces on Public Relations Department reports, were unsolicited comments that linked the patriotism of the program to the company. One episode made a Clinton, Michigan, viewer so "proud to be an American" that she wrote in to inform the sponsor that "the Du Pont company stands for our American ideals." A New Orleans man thanked the company for the "reenactment of the famous figures of our Nation in years past, who like Du Pont, have helped to make our Country strong and great."[130] Fans unconsciously blended patriotism and consumption in letters that included references to Du Pont as surrogate for the United States. Mrs. Beatrice Swartz of Detroit wrote, "You cannot realize how important you are to the country as you create desire and interest for new things for a fuller and richer life." Another viewer thought an episode's "simplified portrayal of our capitalistic system" "excellent" and greatly appreciated Du Pont's efforts to "inform" the public on economics. A Middletown, Ohio, viewer wrote, "Continue to talk about free enterprise and pro-Americanism—it can't help but do good!" In their letters, viewers consistently demonstrated an excellent understanding of Du Pont's mission. If some Americans remained ignorant of the show's politics, too many fans mentioned the conservative nature of the program for it to have gone unnoticed by most regular viewers. Over time, one could hardly have missed the repeated lessons.

These lessons came from both the evening's teleplay and the subsequent three-minute commercial. Often related to the episode's theme, these films usually told a "brief story of chemistry," that is, some successful Du Pont research, or linked the company's industrial products to consumer goods, showing how Du Pont "contribute[d] to everyone's better living." Polled viewers generally saw these spots as "educational." But after the lesson, "No one needs to say, 'Buy Du Pont products!' We couldn't be kept from it, once we understand." "You don't even realize it's a commercial," said one man. "All selling is on an educational basis," noted another, yet it was "not a program trying to sell you something." For most of its run, the radio version also followed this format, airing commercials that aspired toward education. Many of them taught listeners/ viewers about the American economic system and their roles in that system. Two of the most common roles described were consumer and stockholder. As consumers, the American people determined which products and thus which companies succeeded; as stockholders, they acted as business owners. "YOU may own Du Pont stock too without knowing it as your insurance policies or fraternal organizations or banks may own stock using your money." So, "anything that hurts business—hurts you. And anything that helps business—helps you."[131] Here is the attempt to portray a "people's capitalism," in which "countless widows and orphans" collectively own the Du Pont Company, that so galled William Hale in his History Book Club offering.

Other companies appreciated what *Cavalcade* did for business. Irving Olds, chairman of the board of U.S. Steel, wrote that the program demonstrated "the benefits from our American system of free private enterprise."[132] Robert Brown of Minute Maid especially liked a Christmas program that explained that "American business is based on the fundamentally Christian principle of the sacredness of the individual and his enterprise."[133] After an episode that portrayed the early years of the Dennison Company, H. E. Dennison wrote, "It is one of the landmarks in our history to have had the Dennison story placed before so high an audience."[134] In thanking President Crawford Greenewalt for the *Cavalcade* story of his World War II heroism, Eddie Rickenbacker, then president of Eastern Air Lines, wrote, "If we had more programs like it on radio and television, it would help eliminate the crimes blamed on youth delinquency, as well as to help recreate in the youth of this country the true American spirit of our forefathers."[135]

Analyzing Television in the 1950s

"While people as we know them are never wholly good or bad, posterity demands of historians that they label their leading characters either one extreme or the other."[136] This approach, voiced by consultant Frank Monaghan, describes how *Cavalcade* transformed historical figures into a "real symbol of evil" to hate or a real hero to love. For dramatic and didactic purposes, this method worked well. Every listener knew for whom to root and whom to disdain in these myths made from history.

Research conducted on Du Pont's behalf by John Dollard Associates attempted to formulize the mythic history in order to maximize an episode's impact—in terms of both popular appeal and the effectiveness of Du Pont's message. The reports reveal surprisingly complex calculations behind 1950s television. Using advance copies of scripts, Dollard and his researchers predicted how men and women would respond to each character, each scene, the overall plot, storyline, and subject. With revealing exceptions, the focus groups and surveys used to test the predictions affirmed Dollard's analyses. The analyses were insightful and creative, and they reveal overwhelming concerns about gender in the 1950s. They also indicate the types of heroes Du Pont emphasized. Much to Dollard's disappointment (as someone interested in maximizing the show's effect), the protagonists were a varied group of men and women, doctors, scientists, statesmen, lawyers, artists, lawmen, and poets. On the other hand, nearly all were white, all were American, and, more often than not, they were businessmen. The key purposes of the reward scale studies were to

> predict the reward value of a play from its script and to test the prediction; to derive a new index of audience size, so the audience of one show can be compared to that of another; to combine index of audience size with reward score of play, so as to derive a new statistic which measures reward to sponsor; to invent a reward scale for commercials and learn to predict their reward value; to study man-woman differences in reaction to play and commercial; to test program innovations as an aid to policy formation; cautiously to derive "marks and guide posts" for creative people.[137]

Dollard's research suggested that foreign villains contrasted best with American heroes. Sometimes a good villain made up for an overly intellectual story, as in "Mr. Peale's Dinosaur." In this case, Dollard suggested that the "mass audience" would enjoy hating the condescending and "effeminate Frenchmen" so much that they would endure the unfortunately less-than-masculine artist-scientist subject of the episode. American heroes could be women as well as men, as in "Breakfast at Nancy's," a Revolutionary War story. In that play, men could identify positively with a woman "capable of masculine hatred, determination, and courage," and they could easily hate the male Tory villain, "disloyal to both his marriage and his country," for what could be more evil than that in 1950s America? Nevertheless, a male hero with Nancy's qualities would have been "more satisfying."[138]

Some episodes showed greater character complexity. "Betrayal," a television version of "Benedict Arnold," examined the psychological reasons behind the decision to betray one's country. Unaccepted by his peers, his honor insulted, Arnold looked elsewhere for status.[139] Dollard recommended more stories like this one, which capitalized on Cold War interest in spies. In fact, spies were among the most celebrated group of patriots on the program, whether they served the Continental Army, the Union, or the Confederacy.[140] Patriotism, *Cavalcade* style, followed something of a southern model that emphasized honor and duty above justice or idealism. "My Country, Right or Wrong," the title of *Cavalcade*'s Stephan Decatur story, sums up this meaning perfectly. The stories about Confederates further illustrate the sort of patriotism advocated by Du Pont. In tenor and substance they appealed to Americans who found something in the extinct Confederacy that they found wanting in the contemporary United States. Many viewers appreciated the frequently pro-Southern viewpoint. As a typical example, a Marylander wrote, "It is most gratifying to know that there is [*sic*] still those who recognize the good and outstanding qualities of the leaders of the Confederacy."[141]

Those "qualities" shone best through Robert E. Lee, the protagonist of several episodes, including "Sunset at Appomattox." The 1953 "Sunset" television premiere was a major historical event. The Reverend Richard Henry Lee, a last-minute replacement for Rear Admiral Fitzhugh Lee, attended for the Confederates, and Major General U.S. Grant III attended for the Union. After speeches by Du Pont representatives and the screening of the movie, the print was solemnly carried to Appomattox Historical National Monument and presented to the director of the National Park Service. Simultaneously, the battle flag of the Sixty-First Infantry Regiment of the Army of Northern Virginia, taken by a Union soldier at the surrender and discovered just in time for the premiere, was also presented to the monument as an artifact equal in stature to the reel of film.[142] *Cavalcade* films premiered at sites of special interest a number of times, but production always took place in the studio. Only a few times on radio did *Cavalcade* broadcast from a location associated with the events depicted.

Confederates appeared first on the radio show and remained a part of the *Cavalcade* until the end. Du Pont and BBDO always took pains to make sure their portrayals would not offend southerners, perhaps because new Du Pont plants were increasingly located in the South, a "place of increasing opportunity" as a result of its non-union workforce. So, for instance, the 1940 episode on

Robert E. Lee, who "symbolized all that was noblest in a struggle that was . . . a proud last stand of a great culture and a vanishing way of life," was approved by Richmond's Douglass S. Freeman, author of the pro-South, Pulitzer Prize–winning biography *R. E. Lee*. That broadcast was performed live in front of a Richmond audience that presumably "remembered" the general rather favorably.[143] The introduction to this episode noted the affection that all Americans had for Robert E. Lee and the Old South but then focused on the South as a region of economic opportunity. The series also twice "salute[d]" Sam Davis, spy for the Confederacy. "The ideals for which he gave his life are principles of American character—loyalty to a promise, devotion to a cause, and unselfish and sacred honor."[144] The 1950 radio play, broadcast from Nashville, centered on the romance between Sam and "his girl," Connie Hardison (Joan Caulfield). Not even mentioned in the prewar version of this story, Connie stands steadfastly by her man in this postwar production, but the end result is the same: he hangs. The Confederate spy he protected tells Connie that Sam "will always be remembered whenever men, in the North as well as in the South, speak of loyalty and sacrifice . . . honor and virtue." The fact that Sam Davis spied *against* the United States did not disqualify him from *Cavalcade*.

Cavalcade featured the popular Stonewall Jackson in an emotional 1951 story about an old man who remembers, and still suffers from, watching Jackson die. Jackson developed over the years into a Christ figure for many Southern Christians (especially the Christian Reconstructionists, whose project of revising American history to discover its Christian significance commenced in the 1950s). The Du Pont show reflected their interpretation of the "martyred" general. In the episode, Jackson prays almost constantly. He uses Joshua 10:8 to form his battle plan at Chancellorsville, and because of his faith and, it is implied, the justness of the South, the plan works. But Jackson is killed by friendly fire. The old man telling the story to his grandson weeps as he tells him of how, on his deathbed, Jackson asks to be read the psalms. The granddad cries out, "Why did he have to die, boy? Why did it have to happen that way?" It is an oddly disconsolate ending for a *Cavalcade* program. As William Boddy argues in *Fifties Television*, institutional advertisers like Du Pont, General Electric, and U.S. Steel always provided an upbeat story to make sure audiences associated them with happy feelings instead of sad. Perhaps the sadder memorial-type broadcast made it on air because it was Jackson's birthday.[145]

Producing these pro-South episodes apparently did not seem controversial to Du Pont. Another 1950 Civil War lesson starred Lee Bowman as the Confederate spy Beasley Nichol, an underling of General Nathan Bedford Forrest, an early leader of the Ku Klux Klan. After the same interpretation of Civil

War history heard in every related *Cavalcade* broadcast—"Confederate brains licked the Yankees, but they'll lick us in the end because there are more of them"—Bowman returned to the mike to relate past to present, advising listeners to "attend conscientiously to your duties of citizenship" and "stand by to do whatever is asked."[146] The direction sounds strange coming from the man who gladly took orders from Nathan Bedford Forrest.

A solemn consideration of gendered interpretations permeated the research conducted on *Cavalcade* in the 1950s. The Dollard reports and correspondence with BBDO and the Du Pont Advertising Department analyzed the appeal of each episode in terms of separate male and female "reward scales." Before production, scripts were deconstructed in an attempt to measure how each sex would respond. For example, Samuel Morse is "not a true man's hero" (since he needs help), but he partly redeems this by persevering, and then he fully transforms from the "effeminate occupation of artist" to the "masculine occupation of inventor." Dollard warned that opening the episode in the artist's studio might cause men to change the channel immediately. On the other hand, "women consider artistic things worthwhile" and they also like a man who, like Morse, needs their "comfort and care." Unfortunately, the many "gadgets" will repulse women. Gadgetry and technology appeal to men, however; such things inherently interest them. Guns, particularly, held high value in this regard, since "a gun is a fascinating object for men."[147] So in "Spindletop," the anyone-can-strike-it-rich favorite reprised on television for Oil Progress Week in October 1954, the "technical talk of oil diggers [would be] unfamiliar to women," but men, presumably, would understand oil industry jargon instinctively. Men also enjoyed watching and rooting for tough male characters, including convicts who take bold chances.[148] On the other hand, scientific and medical research stories, almost the bread and butter for Du Pont's show, were not the "very highest man's stuff" in any case. Health is "one of women's highs"—they respond favorably to "the sight of ill people." So, paradoxically, episodes that treated advanced medical research received higher reward scores for women than for men. Yet both men and women "experienced relief" to watch and cheer for the rare Jewish or African American protagonist, regardless of their occupation, because of a strong "guilt factor." The "Spindletop" episode also contained a love story—a danger for the male audience, which disliked "love stuff"—but a bonus for females, usually. In this case the plot is problematic because "nothing happens"—the female lead has her husband and child at the beginning, so it hardly mattered to her whether he struck oil or not! "Actually her problems may lie in the future when his newly gained wealth will make him more sought after by other women."[149]

Dollard tested his predictions for the scripts, and focus groups responded more or less as predicted. The discrepancies usually came with women's higher than expected interest in, and responses to, violence—they did not show the revulsion that Dollard predicted—nor did they always appreciate the characters who preached nonviolence and the element of forgiveness. For example, women unpredictably enjoyed and remembered a violent scene in which British soldiers battered American patriot James Otis in a bar fight. Dollard suggested that they must have been overcome with maternal feeling for Otis. However, Dollard predicted that sometimes women would enjoy violent scenes. In "Breakfast at Nancy's," a female character shoots and kills an ex-lover, a Tory and attempted rapist. Most women would appreciate this violence because she had no alternative, and "as a good woman should, she stands stunned after the gun explodes."[150]

Men, on the other hand, were thought to require violence in order to stay focused. Violence also had real meaning on *Cavalcade*. Timid statesmen were often contrasted negatively with courageous military men of action, and indecisive thinkers usually lost out to inventive doers. "Man-against-nature" themes held high appeal, but man-against-man promised even higher ratings.[151] A good brawl kept men watching intently, while the absence of physical assault ruined entire episodes. Full annihilation was best. Young Abe Lincoln fights his rival for Ann Rutledge's affections in "New Salem Story," but the scene fails for men because Lincoln "doesn't really clobber his rival," and he "forgives the bully at the moment when he should have been resonating with angry excitement." Unlike unfulfilled male viewers, women would love the "New Salem Story" presentation of young Abe Lincoln's "painful" love affair with Ann Rutledge. But because "it brings anguish to see the hero depressed and despondent," men will "steel" themselves against identification with Lincoln and would "avoid remembering the story"—the worst possible outcome for the sponsor.[152]

While violence played well to all men according to Dollard, some men did possess more refined tastes, and the reports addressed this discrepancy by explaining the presence of distinct divisions of intellect and class within the viewership. Two legal histories generated concern about how to appeal to an audience of both educated and uneducated viewers. In "John Yankee," young John Adams makes an unpopular decision to represent British soldiers on trial for murder. While "liberal and intellectual" viewers would "identify" with Adams for defending the right to due process and a fair trial, and would appreciate his "going against the crowd," less educated (and less liberal?) men would be confused by seeing a founding father defend the enemy. They would not be "permitted to 'enjoy'" the massacre at the beginning, nor would they be allowed by the film to support the American mob, even though the mob expressed popular historical opinion that the British soldiers committed an atrocity. Thus the "average" man would be left unfulfilled by this story, despite the violence; *all* women would be left confused by this story, since "the courtroom is no place for a woman, and legal technicalities mean little to them." However, "because of the patriotic taboo," women would be unable to express boredom with this film. As Dollard casually remarked, "any TV play about 'our country' cannot be disapproved"—a nice unstated principle for Du Pont to work from.[153] The intellectual audience for *Cavalcade* was not large, but as Dollard explained, "it may be of value to hit them hard once in a while" anyway, even though the "lack of overt action and physical aggression" would undoubtedly lose countless male viewers—non-intellectuals at any rate.[154] *Cavalcade* had a reputation to uphold, and episodes lacking "educational" information or enough history for the history buffs might disappoint important audiences. "Gunfight at the OK Corral," though "true" historically, exemplified this danger.[155] Indeed Dollard worried that women especially would actively resent Du Pont for airing such a "trivial" episode. More important, teachers could not use that in their classrooms.

While the Dollard reports suggest how some contemporaries may have viewed *Cavalcade*, there is little to suggest that Du Pont or BBDO significantly altered the series in response to the firm's suggestions. However, the great number of these reports paid for by Du Pont indicates that these analyses were taken very seriously. At the very least, they suggest something of the thought and planning process behind this and probably other contemporary television series. These episodes, and consequently the way that history was constructed and presented to the public, were shaped by advanced calculations that tried, as much as possible, to predict how particular segments of the audience would respond to specific scenes—even specific lines. Imagine history written that way.

Selling Bigness

The Depression-era radio shows may have been didactic, but they expressed a cautious approach to politics. In contrast, the postwar radio and television broadcasts more boldly announced the supremacy of business and not just the fallacy of the New Deal. Even during the 1949 antitrust suit, Bruce Barton informed his client, "I think the public is getting about to the point of being willing to support a vigorous stand on the part of industry in defense of its constitutional rights and in defense of the future of our economic system on which depends our national prosperity and security."[156] Public opinion had turned enough in favor of business by the end of the war that, despite lingering fears, large corporations argued assuredly for their interests. The 1949 recession that led Du Pont to lay off thousands of plant workers caused less of a decline in confidence than a renewed sense of urgency in the fight to change the political balance in favor of large corporations.

Hoping to maintain gains in strength and popularity made during the war, corporate America initially feared a postwar economic downturn and a return to the antibusiness sentiments of the Depression years. Historians such as Elizabeth Fones-Wolf and Roland Marchand have documented these changes in focus and strategy, mainly in terms of advertising and public relations work, demonstrating the great and in retrospect surprising extent to which corporate America feared for its future. Capitalism, many business leaders thought, would soon "face the greatest challenge in its history." This challenge required a massive propaganda effort to convince people in Washington and across the country that their interests lay with business.[157]

Continued discussion about what types of advertising benefited Du Pont reveals more about why the company preferred to sponsor a series derived from history. Conservative publications from the *Wall Street Journal* to *American Mercury* aggressively sought Du Pont's advertising money, but to no avail. Du Pont executives repeatedly explained that the company had no interest in general advertising because it sold few products directly to the public. Institutional advertising made the public aware of Du Pont's contributions to the American economy and also attempted to positively influence public opinion toward large corporations. Advertising in trade publications helped Du Pont establish contacts throughout industries that used its products. However, the company would not spend money for general advertising, even for the sake of supporting friends like the *Wall Street Journal*, whose politics were "right."[158] The same logic underpinned Du Pont's sponsorship of *Cavalcade*, which presented a broad picture of the company's principles. Similarly, for the 1939 World's Fair in New York, Du Pont used the company's exhibit space to highlight the "superiority of private ownership and management versus government owner-ship," rather than to showcase new Du Pont products.[159]

The advertising industry also made great strides during the war; in the peace that followed, admen envisioned an expanded role for themselves in the economic and political life of the nation.[160] Four days before Hiroshima, Du Pont's J. W. McCoy spoke to his Advertising Department, one of the largest, "most imaginative," and most revered corporate advertising sections in the country, about creating "new demands and desires." "A satisfied people is a stagnant people," and the department bore the responsibility of making sure that "Americans are never satisfied."[161] By 1946, the Advertising Department under McCoy and William Hart began to look positively at cooperative, industry-wide advertising campaigns. The war had taught industry the "value" and "power" of a "united effort by all advertisers using the same or coordinated types of appeals." Du Pont would not abandon its own institutional advertising, but it would increasingly support campaigns by organizations such as NAM, the United States Chamber of Commerce, and the Advertising Council (discussed in chapter 4).

Beginning in 1950, NAM's television series *Industry on Parade* in particular paralleled the work of *Cavalcade*. *Industry* profiled the histories of over 1,400 U.S. businesses by 1957. These histories lacked the drama of *Cavalcade*, but they followed Du Pont's lead with a focus on business history as central to the "natural" growth of America, as well as an emphasis on the "contributions of American industry" to the national defense, "higher standards of living," and the "civic, religious, and social life of American communities." NAM operated its program on a nonprofit basis, not charging broadcasters for the use of their films. In fact, NAM's Public Relations Department followed television guidelines for "public service" time, which meant they also paid nothing for airtime on over 250 television stations. Like the *Cavalcade* films, *Industry on Parade* films were given free of charge to schools. Exact numbers cannot be found, but one state-level affiliate of NAM in Utah reported that 75 percent of the state's high schools used the series in 1957. Educators enthusiastically used the films, and thanks to Voice of America and the Armed Forces Information Service, *Industry* films appeared all over the world by the mid-1950s, in English and in many other languages. In addition to several awards from the Freedom Foundation and the National Citizens Committee for Educational Television, the program won the 1954 Peabody Award for "Outstanding National Public Service by Television" and received high critical praise from the New York Film Council.[162]

Du Pont joined with NAM and other businesses to fight against labor unions and, in the later 1950s, the growing threat of "left-wing censorship by taxation," their words for what the IRS referred to as an appropriate tax on corporate advertising campaigns for "free enterprise."[163] In 1958, in a "scandalous violation of free speech," the IRS ruled that institutional advertising was in fact propaganda.[164] In their reading of changing social and political conditions, the heads of Du Pont's Advertising and Public Relations Departments thought that "increasing pressures and intensities of the 'cold war' have developed a certain amount of hysteria among many people, leading them to accept as the lesser of evils any penalization of large companies, through taxes or otherwise." As in 1935, public "hysteria" threatened Du Pont. By the late

1950s, however, the concern was high taxes rather than New Deal regulatory programs or socialism.[165]

Worried about public opinion toward big business, one persistent theme Du Pont tried to communicate through *Cavalcade* was the "interdependence" of "small" and "big" business. The answers given to the ubiquitous question of the respondents' attitudes toward large corporations permeate the piles of research reports on *Cavalcade*. As it had faced the war profiteering charge in the 1930s, Du Pont faced several antitrust suits in the early postwar period. According to *Newsweek*, at the end of the 1940s the company was in a "neck-and-neck race with General Electric for the dubious honor of being the Justice Department's No. 1 target." At times like these, history had to be summoned to service quickly. To fight the 1949 antitrust suit in the public relations arena, BBDO moved *Cavalcade* further in the direction of propaganda and presented historical episodes that explicitly argued the benefits of trusts. The opening show of the fall 1949 season, "Wire to the West," revealed the true story of Western Union. With the "telegraph industry in utter confusion because so many small companies were in the field," founder Hiram Sibley bought everyone out, increased efficiency, and reduced costs: "a place where big business greatly improved a bad situation." The rest of September's shows followed this script for other sectors where big business had served consumers' interests. Emphasizing the contributions of business was not new of course, but the intensity of the pitch during that fall season marked a change in approach. And BBDO executives figured to "use a good many more of this kind of shows [*sic*] than we have in the past" in an attempt to naturalize big business in American history. Company presidents Lammot du Pont and Crawford Greenewalt also wrote and spoke publicly about how large companies actually fostered the growth of the smaller businesses that contracted with them. In a 1949 interview, Greenewalt explained that the condition of "bigness" directly results from "usefulness." If a company serves the public well, it grows large. The larger it is, the more useful it must be.[166]

Du Pont's forays into and uses of the past extended well beyond *Cavalcade*. It is remarkable how much of Du Pont's postwar propaganda took the form of public history lessons of some kind. To commemorate Benjamin Franklin's 250th birthday, company headquarters housed an exhibit for the public on the man labeled the "best example of free enterprise in action."[167] For its twenty-fifth anniversary cover, *La Revista Du Pont*, a Spanish-language magazine for clients and employees in Latin America, featured the famous scene of E. I. du Pont and Jefferson discussing plans for the new company in 1802.[168] Most ambitiously, in 1951 the company produced a motion picture called, simply,

The Du Pont Story. The Technicolor production used 225 "Hollywood actors" and 91 different sets. According to a publicity release, the highlight of the film occurs when Jefferson, at the White House, "gave his support" to E. I. du Pont. During this 1801 meeting, Jefferson first mentions America's debt to Irénée's father, Pierre, who "was of great service in our peace negotiations with England." Then the president becomes agitated about America's economic dependence and excitedly tells the younger du Pont, "We *need* that powder—not only for defense, but for blasting—clearing farm lands—building roads": all of the uses for Du Pont's powder that had been demonstrated throughout American history on *Cavalcade.* Concerning funding, Jefferson explained that in America, rather than government-funded projects, "we believe our citizens should take the risks of industry—and reap the rewards." Later scenes emphasized how the du Ponts insisted on using the company's great size to do expensive research that smaller firms could not afford. Unsurprisingly, this history never mentioned controversial wartime profits or the resulting investigations.[169]

Du Pont intended the film to be seen by employees, their families and friends, and locals in plant communities. This population was not insignificant; within two years of the release, 6 million people, including 1.1 million high school students, had viewed it. *Scholastic Teacher's Magazine* helped publicize the film by recognizing it with an "Award for Outstanding Merit" and recommending it for use in the classroom. Du Pont also advertised to schools directly, putting the Jefferson scene from *The Du Pont Story* on the cover of a new full-color pamphlet, "Du Pont Motion Pictures for Colleges, Schools and Clubs."[170] The motivation behind this motion picture history of Du Pont did not differ from that which drove twenty years of *Cavalcade.* The film would "create a vivid and lasting impression on the minds of today's younger generation" and would demonstrate that Du Pont "GAVE to America and grew WITH America, as distinguished from the mere exploitation of America's opportunities." Viewers watched as Du Pont answered Jefferson's call to "meet a national need," played a "vital part" in the "winning of the west," improved American research so as to gain economic independence from Europe, and created new products for consumers. Du Pont produced another very successful film in the 1950s called *It's Everybody's Business,* which received the top motion picture award from the Freedom Foundation and great praise from the United States Chamber of Commerce. This animated film told the success story of America's system of free enterprise and was shown to junior and senior high school students, adult education classes, and clubs and organizations of various stripes; it was also broadcast on some 266 television stations. By 1955, the U.S. Chamber of Commerce estimated more than 30 million people had seen it.[171]

The year 1952 not only saw the debut of the *Cavalcade* television series but also marked Du Pont's 150th anniversary; a fact advertised every week on the *Cavalcade* program. As with history in general, but even more so, Du Pont viewed the anniversary as an "unparalleled opportunity for selling economic ideas of value to Du Pont specifically and business and industry in general."[172] The company released its feature film as part of the publicity and also considered such devices as a rail- or road-traveling company history exhibit modeled on the Freedom Train of 1947, but in the end the celebrations fell along more traditional lines: a long day of festivities at Eleutherian Mills, including a historical play and several speeches. The play told the familiar story of E. I. du Pont's origins and his strong principles of "duty." Of the speeches, President Crawford Greenewalt's stands out for its bold rejection of the Four Freedoms as such. Business had begun to advertise a fifth freedom, free enterprise, almost immediately after Roosevelt enumerated his four.[173] However, in this 1952 address, Du Pont's president expressed the idea, increasingly popular among corporate advertisers, that freedom could not be subdivided "into convenient piles, like so much laundry." American freedom was "indivisible." That said, freedom meant first and foremost the right to economic "self-determination." As proved by history, E. I. Du Pont succeeded because he was free to "deal with his employees as individuals, with his customers and shareholders as they and he saw fit." Perhaps freedom cannot be subdivided, but its meaning can be restricted. In closing, Greenewalt declared that today the "torch of freedom burns less brightly." Lest anyone think this meant something grandly idealistic, he explained that this dimming of the sacred light followed from corporate taxes, "penalties so severe as to discourage both the desire and the ability to progress."[174]

President Greenewalt, who married into the du Pont family but also worked his way up the company ladder from his first position as a chemist, showed at least as much personal interest in the *Cavalcade of America* as had Lammot du Pont. He not only screened the films before broadcast but also listened to tapes of telephone interviews with viewers and read the reports prepared by John Dollard and other research firms. However, his family would not have been able to view the program at home since the Greenewalts did not buy a television until after *Cavalcade* left the air.[175]

The Long March Comes to an End

By 1957, pressure on Du Pont to end or dramatically change *Cavalcade of America* came from several quarters. Its research firms became convinced that audience share would increase if Du Pont abandoned the historical format or altered factual evidence to make stories more dramatic.[176] The fact that Du Pont resisted such appeals, which also came from the networks, suggests that the company did retain some allegiance to history. Another source of pressure came from the changing nature of the television industry. When the show first aired on TV, about a third of American households owned televisions, and most viewers had only one or two channels to choose from. But by then the cost per thousand viewers on television had stabilized at about $1.68, down from $6.29 in 1947 and $2.95 in 1949; sales of television sets were rapidly rising; radio use was falling; and the trend was clear enough to warrant the switch in media.[177] The move to TV initially went well, and ratings increased in both the second and third seasons. By 1954–55 *Cavalcade* averaged a 26 percent share.[178] Habitual viewing increased at an even greater pace. Nationally, two-thirds of this was "spot" coverage rather than network, since ABC lacked affiliates. The combined network and spot coverage reached an average per broadcast of eleven million homes in the 1953–54 season and almost seventeen million homes during the 1954–55 season. By the end of that season, two-thirds of American families owned a television set, and in major markets the number was almost 90 percent.[179]

The number of channels available in all markets increased along with set ownership. Two-thirds of Americans received four or more channels by December 1954, compared to just one-third when *Cavalcade* began in September 1952, and half could watch five or more.[180] This meant more competition for viewers' attention. A historical program attracted viewers when nothing else was on, but could it attract viewers who had other choices? The answer was mixed and depended on the local market competition, but overall *Cavalcade*'s audience share declined after 1955. Still, the series performed well compared to both other dramatic programs and programs sponsored by institutional advertisers. At the end of the 1956 season, of the institutional sponsors' programs only *GE Theater* and *You Are There* reached more men-per-set and more homes overall than *Cavalcade*. Other institutional programs (e.g., *Meet the Press, Omnibus, Person to Person, U.S. Steel Hour, Voice of Firestone*) sometimes reached more viewers per set *or* reached more viewers total, but BBDO worked to maximize both numbers with *Cavalcade*.[181]

ABC never fully satisfied Du Pont, and the feeling was mutual. The third network had limited coverage, which meant that Du Pont had to pay for spot coverage on independent local stations. ABC hoped Du Pont would change *Cavalcade* into an hour-long entertainment program similar to *Disneyland*, the network's big success in the mid-1950s. BBDO concurred with ABC that improving the "entertainment value" to "meet television's increasing program competition" would be wise, and at one point even suggested that Du Pont sponsor

"Disneyland" itself.[182] Every effort to change something about *Cavalcade*—whether the network, the production facilities, or the content—ran up against Du Pont's determination to maintain full rights and control.[183] BBDO characterized *Cavalcade* as "unique" in the entire mass media industry in this sense.[184] If anything, this became even truer around 1955, as the networks then began to assert greater control over programming and content, and most sponsors and their agencies disappeared from the production side of television.[185] By 1956, as BBDO sought to find a new television home for Du Pont for 1957, the agency complained that in the new "seller's market," networks could demand sponsorship of their own shows as part of any deal for airtime.[186]

BBDO still advised Du Pont to maintain full control of their television production. The other option, picking up a network show that someone else had sponsored previously, held little appeal because viewers would not identify the program very strongly with Du Pont, and, for Du Pont, there would be a "psychological drawback" in buying someone else's refuse.[187] So BBDO concentrated efforts on moving to one of the two stronger networks while leaving Du Pont in full control of its program. In the end, these dual objectives could be achieved only by abandoning the historical drama format.[188]

Conditions—in politics, in business, and in advertising—had changed considerably by the late 1950s. However, Du Pont continued to face public relations challenges, and large corporations still felt besieged by public resentment of their economic dominance. In a strange twist of fate, Bruce Barton was summoned to serve on a grand jury in 1955 that would consider another antitrust suit brought against Du Pont; he was excused.[189] A poll conducted in 1959 suggested that 38 percent of Americans thought large companies should be broken up, regardless of their value. Du Pont fared somewhat better in polls; BBDO believed this could be attributed to *Cavalcade*. Thirty-six percent of Americans said they knew the Du Pont Company "well," by far the highest percentage for any company that did not primarily sell directly to consumers. And for the most part, Americans approved of the company; only 3 percent did not—quite a change from 1935.[190] Still, Du Pont's top executives felt it would be necessary to continue an exclusive television sponsorship. Through 1961 the company sponsored the *Dupont Show of the Month* on CBS, a program that featured mostly contemporary dramas.

A few years after *Cavalcade* left the air, historian Henry Steele Commager wrote that the American national memory was a "literary and in a sense, a contrived memory." Here the "image of the past was largely the creation of the poets and the storytellers." Commager wrote of an earlier age of popular historical stories, the antebellum period, but as his own writings suggest, the interest in a usable American past was quite strong in the mid-twentieth century.[191] Through *Cavalcade*, Du Pont became one of the most successful "poets and storytellers" of the age. The ubiquitous repetition of the company's message on the air, in books, in the home, and in the classroom had no close competition. No other single source offered as much information about American history, for so long, to so many people. Finally however, even the mythologized history on *Cavalcade* succumbed to the new realities of the maturing television industry; the public, offered more choices, proved less willing to sit through propaganda disguised as historical dramatizations.

3

History, News, and *You Are There*

It's a damn good program. . . . How do you get away with it?

Edward R. Murrow, in Abraham Polonsky, *You Are There Teleplays*, 27

History served us well. We had no need to invent conflicts to serve our purpose. They were there for the taking and we happily and conscientiously took them.

Walter Bernstein, *Inside Out: A Memoir of the Blacklist*

In 1953, soon after Du Pont first aired *Cavalcade of America* on television, another historical program, CBS News's *You Are There*, also moved from radio to television. *You Are There*'s historical interpretations presented 1950s audiences with leftist political ideology almost exactly opposite Du Pont's. On this series, political dissidents extolled "resistance to tyranny," and the historical episodes included the "most shameful moments in American history" as well as a few triumphs. Themes of revolution and struggle occurred with much greater frequency than stories of bold yet responsible entrepreneurs or triumphant westward expansion. *You Are There* was also anti-exceptionalist, incorporating American history into a broader world history that linked ideas and events across cultures and time, and its interpretations anticipated future trends in the historical profession such as greater social and cultural emphases, attention to issues of class and race, and subaltern and transnational history. The series also helped to define television news in its formative years.

The defining characteristic of the series, however, was its nearly perfect chronological overlap with the blacklist in the entertainment industry. The first incarnation, *CBS Is There*, debuted on radio just months after the "Hollywood Ten" confronted the committee of Representative James Parnell Thomas in November 1947. The final television episode aired in the summer of 1957, as the blacklist era began its slow fade into history. The series had an almost symbiotic relationship with anticommunism, which provided much of the subtext of the ostensibly historical episodes, both on radio and TV. The anticommunist movement also indirectly provided much of the talent for the show—especially the writers, who, blacklisted from Hollywood, found not only work but also a medium through which they could fight back against the forces that would deny them almost everything.

You Are There featured key historical events that "alter and illuminate our time"—the telling phrase writer Abraham Polonsky had penned for the voice of anchor Walter Cronkite. By design, it possessed the same sense of immediacy as the network's newscasts, putting the viewer in the center of the action. The title of the program recognized film's power to persuade the viewer that the camera indeed captured past reality. Ironically, this very confidence followed from the same logic that imposed the contemporaneous blacklist in film, television, and radio. In the wake of the presumed successes of propaganda films during the 1930s and through World War II, belief in the potential power of media to persuade audiences increased.[1] Broadcasters, advertisers, writers, and directors with an interest in reaching a broad audience had witnessed the power of the Mercury Theatre's *War of the Worlds* broadcast and of films from Riefenstahl's *Triumph of the Will* to Capra's *Why We Fight* series, and they believed in persuasive possibilities for their art. *You Are There*'s writers, who had gone to Hollywood to make movies that were both entertaining and politically significant, thought they might achieve similar ends through the television medium once they were blacklisted from film.

At the same time, cultural critics, politicians, social scientists, and many intellectuals began to fear those possibilities and sought to eliminate opportunities for the manipulation of political thought through mass media. Some on the political right, like the publishers of *Counterattack!* and *Red Channels*, both of which sought to expose communists in the entertainment industry, became obsessed by the thought that communists were secretly brainwashing millions of unwitting Americans.[2] Despite disparate agendas, corporations, advertisers, networks, writers and other industry workers, as well as the anticommunist crusaders who successfully imposed the blacklist, all shared a belief in the power of mass media, and they all probably exaggerated the impact on viewers.

Sponsors played the crucial role in the operation of the blacklist by withdrawing advertisements from shows that employed alleged communists.[3]

You Are There's relationship with this side of the business determined the course of its history. The radio show aired unsponsored, as public affairs programming provided by CBS as a public service. On television, the Prudential Life Insurance Company, and later America's Electric, Light, and Power Companies, sponsored the show only every other week, leaving alternate weeks unsponsored. At first, the producers tried to air the more obviously controversial episodes on off weeks, but the sponsors never indicated awareness or concern. More important, the advertisers had no control over the content of the show (unlike *Cavalcade*) and apparently never knew that blacklisted writers worked on the program.[4] However, this situation left the writers without any security. When executive producer William Dozier eventually decided to fire them—to *really* fire them—they could do nothing about it. Thus, not only were their positions precarious, but their defeat, through the specific peculiarities of 1950s corporate power in the media marketplace, was perceptible even before they began to write.

Since the program left the air in 1957, nothing like it has been attempted on television; no other program has premised itself as a live news report from another time, and network news divisions have refrained from producing dramatic series. That CBS News ever considered historical dramatization a worthy pursuit for a network news division speaks to the greater role for history sought by many people at the time, both inside and outside CBS News. After cancellation, the series endured in classrooms across the country, where throughout the Cold War, millions of schoolchildren watched historical dramas written primarily by three unrepentant former communists: Arnold Manoff, Walter Bernstein, and Abraham Polonsky.

These three men channeled into the series all of their frustrations at being blacklisted, their disgust at the direction in which their country was moving, their disappointment in their fellow Americans for failing to live up to the ideals they believed inherent in the American tradition, and their astonishingly unvanquished faith in the basic goodness of their country. Two of them had served during the war; all three remained loyal despite their persecution; none chose the expatriate route; and none turned "friendly witness." They earned a very modest living while challenging the anticommunist terror more publicly and more consistently than almost anyone else at the time. As Polonsky later said, *You Are There* became "probably the only place where any guerrilla warfare was conducted against McCarthy in a public medium."[5] While this is an exaggeration, perhaps the only truly false note to this claim is the writer's failure to recognize the strong stand taken by the earlier radio version of the same program.

The series' anticommunism has been recognized by historians, but that recognition has obscured its other, broader goals and accomplishments, both as a watershed radio and television program and as an important site of historical analysis.[6] *You Are There* was also an innovative news program, from which CBS News borrowed techniques for its "real" news broadcasts. And the talent behind the writing, directing, acting, and reporting nearly boggles the mind. The search for anti-anticommunist meaning in every episode has also ignored other, likelier contemporary interpretations. Neither persecution by the state nor artistic concerns about such persecution began in 1947 with the Hollywood Ten; rather, the subjects returned to again and again by *You Are There*'s writers — Galileo, Socrates, Joan of Arc, Salem — had been used and were still being used to denounce fascism, totalitarianism, and any other political system in which artists, scientists, writers, and intellectuals were forced to conform to an obnoxious political standard. For the most part, *You Are There* more closely resembled Orwell's writings against totalitarianism than a distinctly communist critique of contemporary politics. The "radical" label describes the series' unconventional subject matter as much as its implicit anti-anticommunism. The topics included white America's perfidious treatment of Native Americans; black Haitians and southern slaves rising up to seize their freedom; Joan of Arc, Ann Hutchinson, Lucretia Mott, and other "feminists"; the "theft" of jazz music from African Americans; the uneasy relationship between art and politics; American empire; and, of course, plenty of historical trials in which unscrupulous demagogues attack the right to free speech, thought, and association. Consequently, *You Are There* can also be understood as part of the group of the programs on radio and television in the late 1940s and early 1950s within which George Lipsitz identified "sedimented" New Deal–era liberalism that presumably appealed to the still largely urban audience.[7]

To whom, though, was this program addressed? Would a mainstream audience appreciate the nuance of the historical interpretations, much less the veiled references to contemporary politics and society? In a 1952 Gallup poll, over 60 percent of respondents could not correctly identify Plato in any way, to any degree. Seventy percent could not name a single artist of the previous fifty years.[8] Yet *You Are There* seems to have assumed an audience that would appreciate shows about just such topics. The creative forces behind the series would have known that much of what they put into the show would be over the heads of many viewers, but they often had another audience in mind — or rather they wrote and produced these shows for multiple audiences, or a diverse grand audience. Many episodes contain lines obviously intended by the writers for their fellow persecuted, with others for an elite audience that might absorb the message and maybe even respond with some action. Viewers also included schoolchildren, anticommunists investigating the industry, CBS (News and Corporate), and "average" Americans. Like *Cavalcade*, an unusually high viewers-per-set figure indicates that many families watched *You Are There* together.[9] While a single program might reach the varied parts of this audience, not every-one would see the same thing. The idea, as expressed by Polonsky, was to reach as many people as possible with "some truth."[10] The show appealed to the writers for the same reason that leftist cultural workers went to Hollywood in the 1930s: it offered a way to connect with and communicate to a broad public.

CBS News also had an agenda for the series, which was at least as important as that of the writers, directors, and other contributors. During the 1930s, the decade that saw network radio come into its own, CBS lagged considerably behind NBC. Rather than spend huge sums to lure talent away from the domi-nant network, CBS invested more modest amounts in its news department, using news programs to fill airtime (after World War II, CBS president Bill Paley also decided to purchase top NBC talent). By 1940, NBC still dominated entertainment programming, but CBS had achieved supremacy in less costly and less remunerative news programming. The network's fortunes really began to change with the coming of World War II, which generated unheard of audi-ences for news.[11]

Motivated partly by a desire to use existing resources for added benefit, the news division drifted into an ambiguous area of educational entertainment with *CBS Is There*, which later became *You Are There*. Newsmen staffed the series, which CBS News produced rather than CBS Entertainment. Even more than Du Pont's series then, *You Are There*'s radio and television producers intended the program to represent documented history. Following Roy Rosenstone's designation of "history film," which he contrasted with the more clearly fiction-alized tales of the past made by Hollywood, this series might be labeled "history radio" and "history television."[12] CBS presented the news from the past through historical figures appearing "live" on radio or television while being interviewed by reporters who acted as if they reported the events of the day circa 1950. The same men trusted to provide honest reporting of key current events were likewise entrusted with recorded history. The cast included Walter Cronkite, whom executive producer William Dozier selected after watching his acclaimed coverage of the 1952 national party conventions, where he first pioneered the role of "anchorman" that he continued to develop on *You Are There*.[13] His "voice of authority . . . communicated a strong sense of authenticity for the show." When Cronkite told the audience that "all things are as they were then, except 'You Are There,'" he was convincing in a way that few other broadcast journalists could have been.[14] The reporters included John Daly, Mike Wallace, Harry Marble, Don Hollenbeck, Edward P. Morgan, Allan Jackson, Bill Leonard (later head of CBS News), Winston Burdett (until he confessed to being a Soviet spy in 1955[15]), Lou Cioffi, Charles Collingwood, and Ned Calmer. The experience and the direction these innovators of television news reporting received on *You Are There* undoubtedly influenced not only their own styles and techniques but also those of later reporters.

You Are There actually had multiple god-like authorities. More commanding than Cronkite even was the unseen, unnamed announcer who opened the show by bellowing out the appropriate date from the past and the tag line, "YOU . . . ARE . . . THERE!" The same voice closed each episode. Since the reporters stayed off camera, they also fit the definition of voice-of-god narration. They represent lesser deities, of course—the minor gods sent down from Olympus to interact with mortals—but they still stand apart from, and pass judgment on, the people of the past.[16]

The musical soundtrack also helped to set the desired tone for the series. The shows opened without any introductory notes, but the credits rolled to a varied repertoire (on television—the radio show had no music). At first the music changed each week to match the episode's content. Then Aaron Copland's *Fanfare for the Common Man* became the theme. Like series writer Walter Bernstein, Copland had been cited in the first *Red Channels* publication in June 1950. Thus, while Copland's tribute to the "common man" may have provided the sought-after tone in its own right, by using it each week *You Are There* declared itself almost openly against the blacklist. Music, like history, provided some cover for politics.

Radio: CBS Is There (and You Are There, Too)

Before *You Are There* made its mark on television, the series ran fairly successfully on radio from 1947 to 1950. CBS News reporter Goodman Ace dreamed up the idea for the radio series, and CBS president Bill Paley authorized it over subordinates' objections. In 1942 John D. Rockefeller Jr., benefactor of Colonial Williamsburg, approached Paley with the idea of "a series of historical radio programs to try to awaken in the citizens of this country a consciousness of their own traditions." Perhaps Paley initially imagined *You Are There* would be the type of program Rockefeller suggested.[17] Though the later television writers, and the still later biographers and historians, were dismissive about the radio version, many of the subversive themes celebrated by the television writers first appeared on radio. It was not, as blacklist historians Paul Buhle and Dave Wagner characterize it, "familiar facts-and-patriotism." Nor did it deal only with personalities, and not ideas, as Walter Bernstein later claimed.[18]

Robert Lewis Shayon directed radio's *CBS Is There/You Are There* and wrote or co-wrote many of the episodes. The *New York Times* called him the "most important 'new' writer on radio," but Shayon also directed and produced, and he ran CBS's Documentary Unit until he left this series and the unit in the summer of 1949.[19] One year later, in June 1950, *Red Channels* published Shayon's name and secured him a spot on the blacklist. That same month, *You Are There* disappeared from radio, possibly because of the taint of association with Shayon.[20] It is surprising that the historical discussions of the television program and its blacklisted writers have ignored this earlier chapter. Perhaps it takes away from the "revolutionary" story the television writers and their biographers prefer to remember.

In striking contrast to Du Pont/BBDO's happy, triumphant march through American history with its *Cavalcade of America* series, *You Are There* demonstrated a willingness to examine the darker side of the nation's growth. In the spring of 1948, for example, in an episode about Sitting Bull's capture, *CBS Is There* took listeners "back 67 years to one of the most shameful moments in American history." Just by covering a "shameful" episode—really, just by acknowledging the existence of such an event in the American past—*You Are There* departed from and challenged the unquestioning patriotism of *Cavalcade of America*.

Unlike the later television incarnation, *CBS Is There* opened not with an anchor in the studio but with a reporter in the field: usually John Daly. Always, as the announcer stated at the beginning of each broadcast, the reporting was "based on authentic historical fact and quotation." To further "authenticate," sound quality could be manipulated to reproduce "real-life" lower-quality connections between the news studio and reporters far afield, or could be "disrupted" during battles, shipwrecks, or natural disasters. Substantial dialogue was delivered in foreign languages before reporters translated for the audience, apparently *ex tempore*. Scripts adhered as closely as possible to CBS's descriptive news-reporting style, still under development.[21] Contemporary reviewers admired the show's realism; a *Washington Post* reviewer wrote, "Such a line as, 'And now over to Plato's home and Don Hollenbeck,' could easily be preposterous. It isn't preposterous because CBS has done exhaustive research, because the writers have blended solemnity and showmanship in about equal quantities, and because the production of each of these epics is as slick a bit of business as you'll find in radio."[22]

In "Sitting Bull," Daly reported over a "land-line quality" connection from the Dakota Territory, on an unseasonably cold and blustery July day in 1881, when locals, as Daly related, dressed in winter overcoats and chatted about the recent attempt on President Garfield's life. The episode spotlights Sitting Bull's decision to surrender to the army in exchange for a pardon, and the army's immediate betrayal; it offers a highly critical interpretation of America's frontier history. Early on, a Captain Clifford of the U.S. Army and a French trader named Jean Louis Legare converse about U.S. Indian policy. Legare insists that Sitting Bull should be considered one of the "great men of all time." White men, on the other hand, "make a treaty—they sign a piece of paper—and then they break their word—and they send soldiers to ram it down the red man's throat." The American officer replies, speciously, that the reservation system is "obviously a superior way, because we wouldn't be here if it weren't." Legare insists that the United States stole Sioux land and accuses America of reserving its vaunted "independence" for whites only. Clifford finally admits that mistakes "have been made," but "nobody—not even Sitting Bull and the whole Sioux Nation—can stop this country from pushing the frontier clean to the Pacific Ocean." The American's triumphalism sounds hollow compared to the proud, manifest destiny approach to the history of American expansion expressed on *Cavalcade of America*. The story only gets worse as Sitting Bull is deceived by the duplicitous American commander and is then captured and chained. The pitiful episode concludes with John Daly's observation that the Sioux leader seemed to be smiling ironically to himself, "almost as if he expected this to happen."[23]

By directly confronting the historical mistreatment of Native Americans, the series challenged contemporaries' collective memory. In *The End of Victory Culture*, Tom Englehardt notes that around 1950 some films in the western genre (e.g., *Broken Arrow*) began to portray Indians more favorably and described the conflict between whites and Indians as equivalent in terms of the degree of savagery practiced by both sides. But *You Are There*'s "Sitting Bull" takes things a step further. Here, whites—excluding the non-American Legare and CBS's own reporters from the future-present—act villainously, while the Sioux behave nobly to the end.[24]

Perhaps the most surprising radio episode, in its revolutionary fervor and its taboo subject matter, was "The Betrayal of Toussaint l'Ouverture." This episode was written by Shayon and Joseph Liss, who together also wrote "Sitting Bull." CBS reported from Haiti, 1802, where twelve years of fighting have finally culminated in treaty negotiations. Haitians detail countless French atrocities for CBS listeners while the French dance and gorge themselves at a lavish party. CBS listens in on a short speech against racial prejudice from Toussaint just before his betrayal by General LeClair. As in "Sitting Bull," the white imperialists have only pretended to make peace. But in "Toussaint," the Haitians fight back immediately, and the show closes with violent chaos brought on by the deceitful and racist French: a disaster that might have been avoided.[25]

As the television series would do in 1953 and 1955, Shayon's *CBS Is There* presented the "Salem Witch Trials" in 1948. Written by Sylvia Berger, this denunciation of state-sponsored persecution aired less than two months after the Thomas Committee's assault on the "Hollywood Ten." Immediately after those congressional hearings, executives from the major studios met in New York at the Waldorf Astoria and issued what became known as the Waldorf Statement on November 25, 1947. Declaring their resistance to intimidation, they nevertheless promised to rid Hollywood of communists. This marked the earliest stage in the development of a systemized blacklist.

Shayon's radio production aired a half decade before the premieres of Arthur Miller's *Crucible* and Arnold Manoff's *You Are There* teleplay "The Witch Trial at Salem." The artistic reaction in 1948 was in some ways stronger than the two later productions, reflecting the vigorous defense of free speech voiced by some Americans at the very beginning of the blacklist era. For example, in Hollywood, several prominent actors formed the Committee for the First Amendment, which protested against the hearings in Washington. Quickly however, the ranks of liberals prepared to defend their leftist friends' constitutional rights began to shrink, and such militant rebuttals as Berger's no longer suited the milieu.[26]

In a New York studio on January 4, 1948, John Daly reported from Salem, Massachusetts, June 29, 1692. The Reverend Samuel Parris, portrayed as a petty, almost base clergyman, has charged accused witch Rebecca Nourse of plotting "against the government." Furthermore, a mysterious "they" had held suspicious meetings at which they plotted to "root out the Christian religion from this country." When John Daly presses Parris about his ongoing salary dispute with his congregation (and Nourse's husband in particular), Parris stubbornly deflects, insisting, "Rebecca Nourse has been plotting the destruction of our government."[27] In this opening scene, Berger and Shayon not only establish the falseness of the charges but also discredit accusers who mask their motives by launching vague attacks on easy targets. The next report by Daly is even more to the point:

> The excitement over the witches brings to a head the anxiety and unrest which has been disturbing the people of Salem. Dissatisfaction with a succession of

governors, high taxes, a high cost of living, and lately, rumors of war—make it easy to understand why the distracted Salemites feel, as one put it to me this morning, that "Satan is loose in New England" . . . and why they are not surprised to learn that 150 of their own neighbors and even friends have been plotting with the Devil against them and their government.

Substitute "United States" for "Salem/New England" and "communism" for "Satan/Devil" (logical substitutions already made in other contexts), and Daly paints a disturbingly accurate picture of how contemporary American society's fears and concerns could foster paranoia. As the trial proceeds, the judges ask confusing and unfair questions. Instead of asking *if* she hurt the girls, the judges demand Rebecca tell them *why*; her guilt is a foregone conclusion. They say that Rebecca's only choice is full confession to the court. The seventy-one-year-old Nourse cannot hear well, but the judges refuse to repeat questions and force her to stand throughout her trial with her hands tied behind her back. Our sympathies are clearly to lie with her. Daly reassures us she is "showing extraordinary courage!"

In a final statement about the absurdity of the trial, after the jury returns a verdict of not guilty, the judges order the jurors to leave and come back only after deciding on a guilty verdict. To answer Daly's incredulousness, Nourse's son Sam explains her persecutors' motivation: "Because they've got some people in office around here, who are scared of being pushed out. There are too many people who don't like them. So they find themselves some scapegoats. They take women like my mother. They say she's a witch. They say they're trying to bewitch our children, and sink the government. All they're trying to do is save their own necks, and for that they're going to hang my mother." Before sentencing, a *faux naïf* Daly found Sam's interpretation hard to believe. Yet "everything he said was true . . . and if this is contempt of this court, let it be so." Herein lies the beauty of the historical setting, which allows Daly to risk a "contempt" charge without really risking anything.

"The Execution of Joan of Arc" made a similar statement the following month, to rave reviews from Hollywood producer Walter Wanger and from Ingrid Bergman, the star of his 1948 film *Joan of Arc*. Both were "violently enthusiastic" about the CBS production.[28] As in *Salem*, the reporters suggest that "Joan of Arc was condemned for political reasons," and her accusers here similarly refuse comment when pressed on their "underlying motives." The triumph for Joan comes in denying her judges the satisfaction of a confession and in preserving her own integrity by refusing to cooperate. "Her refusal to sign the oath of abjuration was quiet, but unequivocal. She did not seem to waver for a moment. It seemed as if all her mental torture, her long months of struggle and doubt are over, over at last."[29] Daly describes the execution as "a kind of circus," where bored people congregate to watch someone else suffer. Ken Roberts, reporting from the crowd, first interviews a French woman come "on vacation" to see an execution; then the English guard who only cares that he will get his dinner soon, whether she recants or burns; and the executioner, who receives payment only if she does not recant and who thus wants her to hold fast to her beliefs. Collectively the interviews paint a distressing picture of how ordinary people interact with state-sponsored persecutions.

Over and over the script emphasizes the base politics behind the persecution(s). For authenticity the actors speak French during most of the broadcast, and CBS's reporters apparently translate on the fly. Some speeches are left in the background, untranslated, and those brought to the listeners' attention clearly carry more weight. Daly fully translates the list of offenses read by the court, which suggests both the scope of the investigations and their true nature: wildly casting about for any nonconformist activity. In addition to witchcraft labels like "sorceress," this "disturber of the peace" is called "scandalous," "seditious," "indecent," "immodest," and "profane." Joan of course holds fast to her faith, refuses to accept the court's power over her, and burns to death accompanied by the cries of the suddenly awakened crowd calling for the execution to stop. "Even some of the men who condemned her are weeping and praying . . . they are overcome with guilt and horror." A happy ending then—in a way.[30]

Happier endings followed "The Impeachment of Andrew Johnson" and "The Impeachment Trial of Supreme Court Justice Samuel Chase," both presented as fables against overreaching congressional committees.[31] In the former, an unwitting Thaddeus Stevens gives the game away, saying, "We don't need criminal evidence to warrant conviction. . . . This isn't a criminal proceeding. This is a political action! I repeat—political action." The congressional committees investigating the entertainment industry at the time also made this same distinction and justified their oversight and their procedures, as well as the lack of due process for "witnesses," by denying they had created a criminal court in the legislative branch.[32]

A different interpretation of this period might have emphasized the good that radical Republicans hoped to achieve for ex-slaves in the South. That story would have to wait; in 1948 popular history from the left had a different and more immediate purpose—to fight for the right to exist. Similarly, "The Sentencing of Charles I" might have questioned the monarch's claim of a divine right to rule, but it did not. Instead, the sentencing hearing became another parable about unjust prosecution. As in several of the other trial histories, the court, which Charles refused to recognize, offers him a choice of repentance or death. Again the judges—"not judges in the strict sense of the word," yet granted broad extrajudicial authority by Parliament—will not let the accused read his statement, just as the Thomas committee refused such statements from the Hollywood Ten.[33] John Roberts meanwhile wandered into the marketplace to interview a fishmonger and his wife, Mary. They both object to the prosecution, but the husband is reluctant to speak up lest his business suffer, leading his wife to call his manhood into question and providing a moment loaded with interrelated postwar concerns about gender, social conformity, and politics. "He's got less spine than the fish he sells," says Mary. "Aye, if you were a man you would have been speaking your mind."[34]

Several other episodes focused on historic trials, all of which contained similar thinly veiled references to the American political scene. At her 1637 trial, Ann Hutchinson, the "first American feminist," boldly challenges the attempts of "the few to rule the minds of the many." As at Salem, CBS's reporters challenge the judges' right to preside in this matter as well as their decision to disallow legal counsel for the accused. It is also noteworthy that several times in the episode Ann's husband is referred to, not at all disparagingly, as a man willing to live in the shadow of his brilliant wife. The reporters praise her husband for his willingness to support her career.[35]

You Are There featured subjects relating to equal rights for women several times over the three-year run on radio. Somewhat fittingly then, the series finale on June 11, 1950, was "The Women's Rights Convention." This broadcast centered on the 1853 convention at Broadway Tabernacle in New York, where former slave Sojourner Truth speaks and quiets an unruly and chaotic crowd, allowing the delegates to pass their equal rights resolution. Over the course of the episode, the reporters ridicule those who argue that women must only bear children and keep house—an uncommon dissent at the dawn of the 1950s.[36]

CBS News Documents History

Television brought images of congressional hearings, nuclear tests, and other momentous happenings into the home for the first time in the 1950s, but the idea of giving the public nearly immediate facsimiles of major events dates to the earliest newsreels. Beginning with the Spanish American War, newsreel companies combined staged cinema and documentary footage into a genre that blurred the line between fact and fiction.[37] In the 1910s, labor unions produced feature-length docudramas that presented their side of the struggle against capital to the mainstream movie audience.[38] With this legacy of "realist dramatization," *You Are There* also inherited the objective of fostering a more democratic political system that functioned through the re-presentation of events directly to the public.[39] This dogma of direct appeals to the people strengthened during the 1930s, manifest in both politics and culture. In that decade, the "documentary style" of theater, film, literature, art, and music presented descriptive evidence to a broad audience with the aim of affecting political behavior.[40]

The "documentary-style" realism of CBS's radio series, particularly Daly's reporting, was most apparent during battle scenes. Many listeners in the late 1940s would have remembered Daly's war reports of just a few years before, soon to come again with the Korean War. The fictional scripts and Daly's style bore an eerie resemblance to his and other reporters' wartime broadcasts. During "The Battle of Gettysburg," Daly interviewed teenage soldiers in the midst of war:

DALY: How old are you, Private McGaw?

McGAW: Eighteen.

DALY: Will you speak a little louder, please?

McGAW: Eighteen.

DALY: Eighteen. I understand that's the average age of half the Union Army here today, Tom. Seems awfully young, doesn't it?

McGAW: I don't know.

DALY: Well, why are there so many young ones like you here?

McGAW: Well, after the Battle of Chancellorsville, most of the older fellows' time was up, so they went home.

DALY: I see. Then youngsters like you volunteered to fill the ranks?

McGAW: No sir. I was drafted.

DALY: Where are you from, Tom?

McGAW: Illinois country.

DALY: What were you doing when you were drafted?

McGAW: Working in my Dad's store.

DALY: (SYMPATHETIC—BUT NO KIDDING—STILL KEEPING TENSION) Are you married? (PAUSE) Well, what are you blushing about? Have you got a sweetheart?

McGAW: I guess so.

DALY: Does she write you?

McGAW: About every two weeks.

DALY: Who do you miss most, your mother or your sweetheart? (QUIETLY, AFTER A PAUSE) You miss'em both, don't you?

McGAW: Yes sir.

DALY: How do you like the army, Tom? Do they . . . [*interrupted by battle*].

During the battle, Daly's position is shelled, and CBS loses contact with him. Don Hollenbeck takes over, reporting from Union headquarters. The action is intense, fast-paced, and frighteningly realistic. *You Are There*'s aesthetic qualities derived mostly from radio journalism, but Daly and the other reporters also likely internalized the *You Are There* interview style and brought it with them to their news assignments. Later CBS News reports from Korea, for example, including Morrow's legendary *See It Now* broadcasts, resemble the above Gettysburg interview. Rather than suggesting that Murrow copied the historical drama series, it seems more likely that *You Are There* and *See It Now* (both produced by the News Division) followed an expected style of reporting from the front, making *You Are There* all the more believable to listeners.[41]

Werner Michel replaced Shayon as head of the Documentary Unit and as director and producer of *You Are There* in the autumn of 1949. In the spring of 1950, Michel proposed to CBS News director Sig Mickelson a television version of *You Are There*. Costs would be much higher than on radio since television required costumes, sets, and crowds of extras, but the impact of seeing history happen "live" promised to be much greater. Talent expenses would at least be moderated by the continued use of CBS newsmen, a cheaper talent pool than Hollywood actors. *You Are There* would now have to be "authentic" both "orally and pictorially," though from the earliest proposals the assumption was that reporters would not appear in historical costume.[42]

The arguments for producing this challenging program bore a striking similarity to those made on behalf of *Cavalcade of America*. First, the news directors assumed that viewing history on the television screen would have a much greater impact than listening to it over the radio, and by the time production began in late 1952 both the television audience and CBS's broadcasting responsibilities to affiliates were rapidly growing. Second, such a high-class program would give CBS, "for the first time, a great institutional program which will silence the numerous critics of present-day television." Sensitive to such attacks, and conscious of its standing as the second-place network to NBC, CBS looked to this pseudo-documentary program for prestige and status.[43]

Also in 1952, NBC premiered *Victory at Sea*, a documentary compilation film divided into twenty-six half-hour episodes. Like *You Are There*, the miniseries initially aired unsponsored on Sundays, as a public service sustained by the network. *Victory* related the naval history of World War II, combining archival footage with original narration and score to create a prestige program that aired in syndication up to twenty times in some markets. The series spawned a permanent NBC documentary unit called Project XX, which would continue to make films "of lasting value on historical topics," concentrating on the twentieth century and "illuminating the cultural heritage of modern man." The objectives seem strikingly similar to those at CBS News, and, significantly, the trajectory of the Project XX story followed a similar arc. Early productions, labeled "fact-drama" or "teledocumentary" at NBC, dealt with potential nuclear holocaust, communism, and, of course, World War II, but fears of controversy led the unit in the later 1950s to focus first on more distant early twentieth-century topics and then pre-twentieth-century subjects and profiles of national heroes and celebrities. This meant that the previously unsponsored series had by 1956 "no trouble finding sponsors."[44]

At CBS News, Mickelson explained to his department the "new meaning of news" in the television age:

> News now embraces not only 'the earthquake, fire and sword'—the *hard* news of the day's events. It also embraces the small, and, to the unaided eye or ear, often imperceptible changes in long-running and slowly-unfolding stories of social and political and economic change. More than ever before in peacetime *Americans are now seeing and hearing the real stuff of history*. This is true for all of our news media. All of our channels of communication are carrying a heavier share of what I will call, for the present, the more meaningful news. *This news is the so-called soft news, news that may have meaning only when it is shown to be a part of historical trend or development* [emphasis added].

Mickelson thought *You Are There* (and its successor, *The Twentieth Century*, as well as the closely related *Eyewitness to History*) demonstrated CBS's commitment to connecting current events with the past and thus giving them "meaning." Time-traveling reporters and interviews with people long dead comprised a sincere attempt to give the public the news, which, according to Mickelson, included the "real stuff of history" as much as the day's events. But more than that, CBS News engaged in and to some degree succeeded at the "essential process of historical review and reappraisal in meaningful terms for their very large audiences." Mickelson called this "news-in-depth," by which he meant it had depth in time. His first program to attempt this was *You Are There*.[45]

Mickelson summed up his vision with the observation that "television's greatest value lies in its ability to bring to the public an *exact portrayal of significant public events* as they occur and providing for the public the sense of intimate participation in these events" (emphasis added). This kind of "news," however, could be more artistically produced in order to gain a wider audience.[46] Then and since, many others have argued the significance of television's promise to deliver to the viewer the event itself, rather than, as in print, an indirect reporting of the event. At the dawn of the television age, CBS News sought to offer an "exact portrayal" of the past as well as the present.

Mickelson imagined these programs would position the present in the past—in the grand scheme of things, so to speak. That might have worked if the series had some order, some sense of development over the ages. But it never did. Instead the history arrived in assorted small packages, sent out each week from radically different places and times, with nothing except perhaps ideology connecting the dots from one week to the next. Rather than situating the present in the great saga of human history, the series selected stories from the past that would—it was hoped—"alter and illuminate our time."

At a 1955 CBS conference, Irving Gitlin, head of the Public Affairs subdivision, suggested that viewers did not really distinguish between dramatic series and news or public affairs programming, and so the department should not do so either. He proposed moving the division toward a narrative style of news that would deliver to the audience a complete storyline. Gitlin's new show, *Face the Nation*, borrowed some of *You Are There*'s techniques, particularly the innovation of shooting interviewees from just behind their interviewer. This brought the viewer directly into the conversation. CBS executives credited this innovation and the use of remote locations, which was another *You Are There* feature, with helping the new program beat NBC's entrenched *Meet the Press* in ratings. While presenting promising new special effects to the News Division, Gitlin showed a clip from *You Are There* that used rear projection to create the illusion of an on-location shot from Mount Everest. This was from "Mallory's Tragedy on Mt. Everest," written by Abraham Polonsky as a tale of man's "assault on the unknown," and which climber George Mallory tells us was really about "every man or woman who has struggled or perished for an ideal."[47] Whether or not CBS utilized this staging technique to enhance its straight news broadcasts, it is clear that CBS News executives understood their diverse programs as not necessarily confined to any one category; rather, they believed the new medium demanded a more flexible approach to news reporting. This, then, is the context in which *You Are There* flourished as an educational, historical dramatization reported to viewers by CBS News.[48]

The Writers and the Blacklist

CBS green-lighted the television series in 1952, and the first episode aired on February 1, 1953. The network turned to its already successful team of producer Charles Russell and director Sidney Lumet. Lumet and Russell had been making another CBS show, *Danger* (1951–54), where they had replaced director Yul Brynner and producer Martin Ritt after Ritt went to direct on Broadway and Brynner decided to try his hand at acting in *The King and I*. Before he left, Ritt hired Walter Bernstein to write for *Danger*, and Bernstein continued on with Lumet and Russell.

As CBS planned for the bigger-budget television version of *You Are There*, Hollywood remained covered by an expanding blacklist that kept hundreds of actors, writers, directors, and other industry workers unemployed. In 1950, CBS had instituted a loyalty oath and an internal security system for clearing writers and actors after J. Edgar Hoover threateningly dubbed the network the "communist broadcasting system."[49] The reputation of CBS personnel as left-wing led, ironically, to the most draconian security program in television. Bernstein found himself blacklisted from television while working at CBS on *Danger*, but in Russell and Lumet he had allies.

Lumet later became famous as the director of *Twelve Angry Men* (1957) and then a catalog of other heralded motion pictures, but at that point he was known as a former child stage actor (Broadway and Yiddish theater) who had also appeared in a few movies, including 1939's *One Third of a Nation*. Lumet later faced his own trouble from red-baiters. *Counterattack* accused him of associating with communists and performing with the Group Theatre; he had— when he was twelve. It also claimed that Lumet was a Communist Party (CP) member, citing as evidence a photograph that turned out to be somebody else, and the magazine eventually cleared him for work at CBS.[50] Charles Russell's good "taste" complimented Lumet's talent, and the producer not only allowed Bernstein to continue writing under a pseudonym but also hired two of his blacklisted friends, Abraham Polonsky and Arnold Manoff.[51]

The writers' backgrounds elucidate the historical series and thus require some brief mention. The three first converged in Hollywood, where Manoff and Bernstein met for dinners and watched prizefights at Olympic Auditorium, and Polonsky and Manoff connected through the Hollywood branch of the Communist Party. Manoff helped Polonsky get his breakthrough job as writer for the film *Body and Soul* (1947). A key moment for the future writing team occurred in 1946, when Albert Maltz—CP member, screenwriter, and soon to be distinguished as one of the Hollywood Ten—wrote an article for *New Masses* that critiqued the postwar CP's hard-line interpretation of the art-as-weapon dogma. Instead, he wrote, critical judgments should focus on a work's artistic value rather than the politics of the artist. This essay followed the critiques of others on the anti-Stalinist left, especially the group centered around *Partisan Review*, but coming from a Hollywood insider and party member, Maltz's criticism forced the issue for his comrades in the industry. The CP leadership in New York attacked Maltz in *New Masses*, in an official statement, and at branch meetings. There was, however, significant debate, even in the pages of *New Masses*, but more so within the West Coast wing of the party. Maltz eventually submitted a self-criticism that acknowledged his "error" and ended the immediate crisis, but deep divisions within the party remained.[52]

The future *You Are There* writers spoke on Maltz's behalf at branch meetings called to discuss the subject.[53] Polonsky was serving on the board of *Hollywood Quarterly*, a left-leaning journal then under investigation by state senator Jack B. Tenney's committee because of the presence of communists among its editors.[54] Though not technically in the party at this point—he never rejoined after leaving it for the war—Polonsky was a rising leadership figure in party circles and had just hosted his first CP meeting at his house in Hollywood. He, along with Arnold Manoff, John Weber, and Maltz, were the only four dissenters at a special Hollywood branch meeting that condemned Maltz's heresy. In New York, Walter Bernstein also spoke up for Maltz and the liberation of art from party dictates. The episode created yet another reason for intellectual dissatisfaction with the party after Stalin's purges and trials, his pact with Hitler, and postwar Russian expansion. It left Polonsky, Manoff, and Bernstein, among others, alienated from what had been their political home.

Communist writers in Hollywood thought of themselves as, in Polonsky's words, "more radical in the human sense" than the party leadership in New York, and many could not or would not force their work to conform to rigid conventions. Besides, as those who earned their daily bread within the studio system realized, a directive to use art as a weapon faced considerable obstacles in Hollywood.[55] Having made their stand, against party hardliners and for freedom of expression, Polonsky, Manoff, and Bernstein had unknowingly prepared themselves for later stands against HUAC. In contrast, a few friendly witnesses later justified their testimonies against the CP by referring to the criticism of Maltz—even though they had been "among the strongest attackers of Maltz and the most faithful to the Party line."[56] Some of the trio's *You Are There* episodes that focused on the political power of art also drew on Maltz's question and the ensuing controversy.[57]

Because of the blacklist, Polonsky's film career consists of two separate eras, his brief film noir period following his departure from the Office of Strategic Services at the end of the war and his reemergence as a major director in the latter half of the 1960s. In 1947, Polonsky wrote *Body and Soul*, which starred John Garfield as a pugilist who fights his way out of the slums and into great personal wealth only to find that contentment lies in reestablishing a connection to his own working class and fighting for them rather than for himself.[58] *Body and Soul*, like most of Polonsky's writing, explored the conflicts that raged within an individual at a moment of existential crisis.[59] Garfield and Polonsky both received Oscar nominations for the picture, which was later, oddly enough, made into a *DuPont Show of the Month*.[60] For the two friends it must have seemed like their stars were on the rise, when in fact both would soon see their careers, and in Garfield's case, his life, destroyed. Following the critical and commercial success of the film, Polonsky stepped up to direct his next project, *Force of Evil* (1948). Hailed by contemporary and later critics, both foreign and domestic, as one of the great postwar Hollywood film noirs, this film intertwined Wall Street with the numbers racket in a parable about the corruptions of capitalism. The Breen Office made him rewrite the script to improve the image of law enforcement, but the picture Polonsky paints is still bleak. Had his Hollywood career not been so abruptly terminated, Polonsky's use of film noir for social commentary might have taken the genre in interesting directions.[61]

Having just started writing for the *New Yorker* prior to World War II, Walter Bernstein spent his war years writing for *Yank*. He jumped with paratroopers and reported from well ahead of the front lines, especially in Yugoslavia, where he became the first Western journalist to interview Marshall Tito.[62] The *New Yorker* took him back at war's end, but Bernstein had always wanted to make movies. He moved to Hollywood in 1947 to write for Robert Rossen, who had just directed Polonsky's *Body and Soul* and was adapting Robert Penn Warren's *All the King's Men*. Bernstein wrote a little for the film; he befriended Manoff, Polonsky, and other Hollywood communists; then, after just six months, he moved back to New York and resumed writing for the *New Yorker* and a few other magazines until Marty Ritt brought him to CBS and *Danger*.[63]

Although he had been politically active for some time, even writing speeches for Henry Wallace in 1948, Bernstein pinpoints the moment he became aware of the threat to his career, his liberty, and the American way of life as he conceived of it, only in 1949, at Paul Robeson's famous Peekskill concert. Instead of casually listening to Robeson sing, Bernstein found himself locked arm in arm with friends to form a defensive barricade around the concert, blocking out his fellow veterans from the American Legion—which had recently expelled Bernstein's short-lived writer's post because it contained suspected communists—and the Veterans of Foreign Wars, who "cursed the nigger bastards and the Jew bastards," burned a cross on an overlook, and beat up Robeson's supporters. He later recalled,

> I wondered how many of them had read what I had written about in *Yank*, how many like them I had admired and written about, what we had in common now. They looked familiar, some even wore their old uniforms, but which ones

had burned the cross? What had it taken to get them to beat up women and children, a few drinks fueling the menace of Reds? They had fought and won a war against hatred and bigotry—to become this? I watched them parade, trying to match these hate-filled faces with those I had known.[64]

The Peekskill concert invigorated Bernstein's resolve to again defend his country from threatening ideological forces. In that sense, he took a stance quite similar to that taken by the less violent of his adversaries. While engaged in his anonymous work at CBS, Bernstein fought the blacklist openly as well. With his friend Sam Moore, president of the Radio Writers Guild before the blacklist, he published *Facts about the Blacklist*. Through this newsletter they attempted to reveal to the public the machinery of the thing and rally Americans to a defense of constitutional rights.[65]

After CBS declared Bernstein unemployable, "Paul Bauman," Bernstein's original pseudonym, submitted his first *Danger* script.[66] Though it was accepted, "Bauman" had just one writing credit and *Danger* could use him only sparingly without drawing attention. Russell had to lie to deflect others at the network that wanted to meet Bauman (Bauman had a rare tropical disease and was seeking treatment in Switzerland) and was under increasing pressure to present him after CBS decreed that writers must show their faces at the network's studios in order to be employed.[67] Paul Bauman's career ended (as did his fictitious life—he succumbed to that tropical disease in his Swiss hospital, though Russell had suggested he commit suicide by "jumping off an Alp") and Bernstein had to find a front if he was to continue writing for CBS.

In his memoir, Bernstein describes the surprisingly difficult task of finding someone willing to do the job. A front had to be able to act as if he or she had actually written the script, when in conference or on the set, and might have to answer questions about plot or character. Getting caught could damage the front's real career.[68] For some fronts, the "false happiness" and undeserved respect from others proved too much to bear. In Bernstein's 1976 film *The Front*, Woody Allen plays an amalgam of the trio's *You Are There* fronts, sharing with the world the absurdity and humor of an otherwise despicable situation. While revealing of their own emotions, the film distorts some of the writers who fronted for the trio, particularly Howard Rodman, who fronted for Bernstein but also wrote his own scripts for *You Are There*. In the film, the writers also have far fewer friends at the network than they did in real life. Without Russell, Lumet, and probably many others, the scheme would certainly have failed.[69]

Arnold Manoff meanwhile had left Hollywood and returned to New York, bringing his play, *All You Need Is One Good Break*, to Broadway. It had been a successful one-act play and "caused something of a furor in its Hollywood tryout [at the Actor's Laboratory Theatre] because of the application of film and theatre techniques in the staging," but it failed as a full-length production. It quickly opened and closed twice in early 1950. While working on it, Manoff was blacklisted by Hollywood, where, at any rate, he had been only very modestly successful as a screenplay writer. So he chose to stay in New York.[70]

Polonsky returned to New York by way of France, where he had gone with his family to work on a novel after finishing *Force of Evil*. While he was in France, HUAC subpoenaed him, and he chose to return and testify. Darryl Zanuck, head of Twentieth Century Fox, where Polonsky was under contract, had told him just to work from home and wait it out. But after Polonsky testified and the committee classified him as "a very dangerous citizen," Zanuck fired him, leaving him both unemployed and unemployable.[71]

After Bernstein had persuaded Russell to employ all three writers, the trio came up with guidelines to share the work and the pay. "From each according to his ability, to each according to his need," recalled Bernstein. Enjoying the "pleasure of cooperation," the trio pooled money, talent, and whatever reserves of fortitude remained, and provided for each other whenever one of them faced a particularly bad time.[72] Eventually they all found fronts, and when CBS offered Russell and Lumet the *You Are There* television series, Manoff suggested that they not only write scripts but do *all* of the writing for it. Bernstein thought the idea "had the arrogance of genius"; Russell and Lumet agreed.[73] Despite this level of control, some creative choices had been made before the writers began work on the series. When Werner Michel proposed the series in 1950, he suggested thirteen titles. Several of these titles were realized, including a few that have been characterized by historians (and remembered by Bernstein and Polonsky) as specifically leftist in subject matter. The fact that Michel (or his predecessor Shayon) came up with these ideas, and not Polonsky, Bernstein, or Manoff, complicates the interpretation somewhat.[74]

The first few episodes lacked bite while the show refrained from real political material. As the review in *Time* magazine bluntly put it, the history series "flunked its first two assignments."[75] Polonsky wrote the opener, "The Landing of the *Hindenburg*," and managed to work in a little antifascism at least, if no real drama or deep meaning. Cronkite's opening remarks about the day's other events reminded viewers of the ongoing Spanish Civil War and the persecution of Catholic priests in Nazi Germany. He also mentioned that the Hollywood studios have "again refused to agree to a closed shop."[76] After "The Death of Jesse James" and "The Capture of John Dillinger," both penned by Bernstein, Polonsky's more poignant "The Execution of Joan of Arc" made it onto the small screen.

As one of the earliest *You Are There* episodes for television, "Joan" looks very different from the later, more news-like broadcasts. The short takes and rapid-fire questions from reporters on both the radio series and subsequent television episodes are conspicuously absent. Instead, it resembles many other 1950s television plays. The long scenes contain extensive dialogue, with hardly any interruption from Don Hollenbeck and Harry Marble, the only two reporters covering the execution. The shots are filled with many actors, coming and going in a confusing mass of people that is too great for the small screen. Compared with the later crisper and newsier broadcasts, the action drags.

The dramatic format of this and other early television episodes, such as "The First Salem Witch Trials," made candid communication of political ideas difficult. Without direct conversation between historical actors and the audience, which allowed for important points to be made with clarity, the audience had to look deeper to find the writers' message. In the 1948 radio "Joan," the reportage and interviews make the case against her executioners, but in this teleplay many of the cues are visual. In 1953 the first shot of the pitiable heroine shows her lying chained and semiconscious on the ground. Polonsky and Lumet build sympathy for her with the cruel Bishop de Beauvais, who enters the chamber and yells down at the prostrate Joan for several minutes. He plays the figure, so common in the series, of the man in power who both judges and must absolutely destroy any and all opposition. To Joan he says, "You must throw yourself on the mercy of the court and the church, and you must tell who aided and abetted you in these . . . this filth of heresy, and renounce all that you have done and all that you have said and you must make yourself small and nothing."

Increasingly, toward the end of the half-hour teleplay, the camera stays close on Joan's tear-streaked face to help viewers to connect emotionally. The focus becomes her suffering, but also, implicitly, her iron-willed refusal to recant or to name those who aided her. As in the radio version, the crowd is eager to see her burn, until it actually happens, and they turn away in disgust at their own bloodlust. The story continues as Hollenbeck reports on the quick spread of the legend of Joan's death at the stake and how her courage appears to be inspiring the people—perhaps the real goal of the episode. At the anchor desk, Cronkite confirms that legend soon blended with history to create for the entire world a living memory of Joan of Arc.[77] The statement seems to acknowledge that depicting history as it actually happened is impossible, since myth or memory is bound to intrude.

Later in the first season, the trio wrote several episodes that got to the heart of their interest in individual character at moments of moral crisis— understandably important to men asked by their country to conform, to recant, and to inform on their friends. The first, Polonsky's "The Crisis of Galileo," clearly indicted McCarthyism, but CBS worried more about its negative portrayal of another powerful force of the 1950s: the Catholic Church. The Madison Avenue Archdiocese reviewed the script and censored lines that referred to church torture and other morally questionable acts. However, since Cardinal Barberini still demands Galileo's recantation in the Vatican's dungeon, with instruments of torture in full view, the episode implies that the Catholic Church used or threatened torture.[78]

Polonsky used the Galileo episode to make several important arguments. First, he attacks the climate of fear and secrecy surrounding the anticommunist witch hunt and blacklisting. Galileo's daughter, Maria, tells Bill Leonard that the charges against her father are secret, and "no one is supposed to say" what the case is about. Second, Polonsky illustrates in several scenes the impossibility of the situation for Galileo and others accused by irregular courts of subversive beliefs. Galileo's plan—to "[submit] himself to the discipline but [make] his explanations"—ends in failure. Submitting to the discipline, recognizing another's right to interrogate one's beliefs, worked no better for witnesses in the 1950s who thought they could appear before a committee but somehow answer the questions without really answering. The trio criticized this stance in other episodes, and Bernstein also sympathetically ridiculed this position in *The Front* when Woody Allen's character believes he can answer his subpoena but talk around a committee's questions to avoid naming names or invoking the Fifth Amendment. In 1953, Galileo's compromise ends with his own solitary weeping. Thus Polonsky's third point: acquiescence brings no salvation.

Polonsky's Galileo, more concerned about himself than any principle, is no saint. To a question from Harry Marble about the effect of the trial on astronomy, Galileo responds that his only concern is with the effect on himself. Before the denouement, a contemporary of Galileo's, the English physiologist William Harvey, tells Edward P. Morgan that should Galileo recant, he will "look like a fool and a coward." He further suggests that Galileo should have emigrated in order to work in a free intellectual environment—a choice taken by some Americans in the anticommunist era. As elsewhere, Polonsky explores the various issues and questions without too strongly suggesting an answer.

Galileo himself bitterly complains, both about presumptive authorities who formerly heralded his work and yet now "branded [it] as criminal," and the absurdity of their accusations: "The design engraved on the title page of my book was heretical, that the type in some places was different, and that no matter what I said, I actually meant the opposite." These lines echo the attacks made on the Hollywood Left, accused of never saying what they actually mean and yet somehow sending pro-communist messages to the public through motion pictures.[79] However, there is truth to these charges, as Galileo's *Dialogues* certainly did support the Copernican theory, even if he tried to at least superficially conceal his position on the issue by using the dialogic format.[80]

Polonsky delves into the mind of the inquisitor in the dungeon scene, where Cardinal Barberini explains the direness of the situation as "heresy has gathered millions to itself" in Europe and threatens to spread still further. For such men, who are threatened by any doctrine antithetical to their own, even torture is justified. As Polonsky wrote in his diary, "they must be right from one side of eternity to another." This meant the opposition must be "rooted out"—"a clear sign of doubt," thought the writer.[81] His Galileo calls the cardinal and his ilk "cowards, prevaricators, who will not even let a little light in for fear that it disagrees with [their own ideas]." But Galileo is destined to lose this battle and not only must renounce his work but also must convince the Catholic Church of his "willingness to submit." Again, the "guilt" of the accused is presumed; the issue is whether authority can coerce confession, submission, and humiliation. Like the friendly witnesses of the 1950s, Galileo recants while "choking on his own words" and still must read a "repudiation of his whole life" prepared for him by the committee. Finally—tragically—he promises to "denounce" any "heretic" to the authorities in "any place where I may be." He remains "free," yet weeps for what he has become.

For the script, Polonsky studied several historical works on Galileo, overall somewhat forgiving of the Inquisition.[82] From his research he concluded that surprisingly little historical work had been done on Galileo, given his significance: "Everyone takes it for granted that all is known; but all is not known." He thought that the existing historiography indulged the Church's position too much and the historians "obviously just select what they want to from the books before them." But "anyone with a reasonable amount of intelligence who reads the original (in trans[lation] even) can discern a piece of truth." What made *You Are There* so appealing to Polonsky was that it provided the opportunity to present the "original," according to him, to the viewing audience. Just as Bernard DeVoto had hoped to influence historical writing through his selection process at the History Book Club, so Polonsky saw television as a medium through which he might boldly make his own mark on popular historiography.

When he watched his Galileo episode on television, Polonsky recorded that it was "not bad," adding, "So minds are reached with some truth after all." More introspectively, he then tried to write down just what it was he was trying to do with the episode and mused about whether he really sought to change people's minds. He eventually concluded, "Anything I write is always an effort to communicate some truth. I know nothing else."[83]

Many of Polonsky's diary entries from this period of April to May 1953 referred to the decline in his mental and physical health caused by "that damned committee." Two days after the Galileo episode aired he wrote, "This is what they want, even if they don't think of it, for it enslaves our consciousness, which we are trying to free." He saw the United States transforming itself into the "Land of the Frightened Giant," persecuting dissent for essentially the same reasons as the Catholic Church of three hundred years before. Despite the trouble, he seems to have relished the feeling of camaraderie with his ancient heroes. After a visit by the FBI he noted, "I like this. In this way I join the hunted and persecuted of history, for having ideas that I really don't thoroughly accept."[84]

The better-remembered treatment of Galileo from this period is Bertolt Brecht's play *Galileo*, the American version of which premiered in Hollywood in July 1947. Brecht's earlier "Danish" version was modeled on Neils Bohr's persecution by the Nazis, but the Hollywood story used Galileo to condemn contemporary nuclear scientists' capitulation to power. In the play, not only will science be "crippled" if Galileo submits, but "if you yield to coercion your progress must be a progress away from the bulk of humanity. The gulf between you and humanity might even grow so wide that the sound of your cheering at some new achievement could be echoed by a universal howl of horror." Galileo's surrender—the surrender of science to power—was significant for Brecht because it led, in his mind, directly to the bomb.[85]

About 4,500 people attended the play in Los Angeles and perhaps 5,000 more saw it when it played in New York for a week in early December, small numbers compared to the *You Are There* audience of several million. The New York run began just weeks after Brecht testified before HUAC and then departed for East Germany. In that context, the subtleties of Brecht's exploration of the social responsibilities of science may have been lost or at least subsumed by the more obvious parallel with what many on the left were already calling an "inquisition." In fact, Fritz Lang referenced Galileo in this latter sense in the concurrent December 1947 issue of *Theatre Arts*.[86] Polonsky, at any rate, does not seem to have been particularly interested in the atomic aspect of Brecht's Galileo; his teleplay resembles the earlier anti-Nazi Danish version, with its emphasis on fascist persecution, more than it does the postwar American version. Brecht's Galileo confesses that his recantation followed from fear and weakness rather than rational strategy. Both Brecht and Polonsky emphasize that Galileo viewed his decision as a personal and professional failure, yet both also seem to accept that preserving one's freedom to continue important work has a certain benefit. Of course, Brecht suggests that ultimately this leads to an even greater defeat both for science and humankind.[87]

Manoff's "The Death of Socrates" followed two weeks after "Galileo," airing on May 3, 1953. Again, man's integrity is put to the ultimate test, but this time the man chooses to die rather than retract truth. The philosopher's demise had long been a popular subject for both artistic and philosophic exploration, as well as political comment. The episode contrasts with a 1948 *You Are There* radio broadcast and with other contemporary settings such as Maxwell Anderson's 1951 play *Barefoot in Athens* and Karl Popper's 1945 argument that totalitarianism descends from Plato, and democracy, equality, and reason from Socrates. Popper held up Socrates and the "freedom of critical thought" as a model for the postwar world. Manoff's "Socrates" and Anderson's play share that analysis, and the *You Are There* teleplay at times bears some close resemblances to Anderson's play. Both are set, as literary scholar Emily Wilson writes of Anderson, "firmly in the context of the Cold War." In *Barefoot*, Anderson elaborates on the threat to democracy from totalitarian Sparta before focusing on the contradictions within democratic society. Perhaps Manoff would have done the same if *You Are There* lasted more than twenty-eight minutes. Instead, Manoff skips lightly over the alternative to the democratic state; despite his persecution, Socrates dismisses the suggestion of exile to any other, un-democratic state. The focus is on the second part of this analysis: the ironic conclusion that such a trial could occur only in a democracy, since only in a free society would an intellectual like Socrates have first spoken out.[88]

In Manoff's teleplay, the playwright Aristophanes, played with ferocious intensity by E. G. Marshall, speaks to CBS first. Though critical of Socrates, famously satirizing the scholar in his play *The Clouds*, Aristophanes angrily attacks his persecutors. In response to Harry Marble's feigned confusion, Aristophanes explains that his criticism "was in a *play* [the appropriate place for such intellectual challenges], not a public trial." He continues, briskly, "[Socrates] has committed no crimes. Socrates has strong beliefs and opinions but so have I. So has any man of intellect. Anytus and his ignorant mob cannot silence criticism of themselves by silencing Socrates. Only stupid men would get Athens into such a monstrous predicament." Revealing an elitism born of the frustrations of the blacklist, Manoff's Aristophanes mocks "this democracy by alphabetical rotation" that gives below-average men the power to judge men of far greater intellect.

In an exposition of the informer archetype, we hear next from Melitus, the man who accused Socrates at the behest of more powerful men. Now visibly frightened by the consequences of his actions, Melitus has discovered that Athens has not embraced him as he believed or was told it would. He complains that he has been used, and he begs Aristophanes and Critus to confirm his status as pawn. They do, noting that Socrates himself thought of Melitus as "an earnest but unhappy and misled young man"—a sort of Whitaker Chambers of the ancient world. Finally, Manoff and Lumet use Socrates's famous pedagogical method to explain why he will not recant in exchange for "freedom" and why he must die. The "first master of the dialectic" questions his grieving students until they understand that his beliefs are his being. If he renounces his beliefs in exchange for life, he still dies, but he also loses his claim to truth. One must never capitulate to power by conforming to the dominant political strain, for one cannot survive self-abnegation. As in the other persecution episodes, the people eventually wake up. All Athens mourns the loss of this mighty "intellect"—even his accusers belatedly realize that men like Socrates improve society through their patriotic critiques.[89]

The 1948 radio version of "The Death of Socrates" had similarly portrayed Socrates as a "gadfly on the backs of men": no threat to the republic, but essential for keeping society awake. His accusers threatened democracy by stifling dissent and new ideas.[90] Interviewed by Don Hollenbeck, a bed-ridden Plato offers an explanation quite similar to that expressed in "The Salem Witch Trials," blaming the constant state of war, exhausting to "body and soul," for the breakdown in society that has led to the persecution of men's beliefs. "And a fever of fear runs high among us. We're confused, desperate and so we seek someone to blame and sacrifice." *You Are There* played "previously recorded" excerpts of Socrates's trial for its listeners, where he challenged his accusers to name the positive influences on youth, if he was the negative. After Melitus confirms that all the rest of society acts as a positive influence on the young, Socrates points out the absurdity of the charge that he has the power to corrupt anyone that all others are busy improving. He challenges Melitus to call forth the corrupted youth and let them accuse him. No one comes forward, of course. This mocking commentary on the persecution of the entertainment industry precedes Socrates's final declaration that he shall not recant because "truth" means more than "money" or "reputation." A friend later adds, "A man should be guided only by the knowledge that he is doing right," even if it means sacrificing his career and his family's comfort. John Daly describes for us the final moments as Socrates drinks the hemlock, reporting, "I can almost taste the poison on my own lips. And it's on the lips of all who are here . . . *and all who are listening*. It is Greece that dies, Greece that *is dying*" (emphasis added). If some of the other antipersecution episodes could be interpreted as antifascist or anti-Soviet, the Socrates episodes make it clear that the setting is the world's leading democracy.

You Are There returned to the Salem witch trials with television versions in 1953 and 1956. Arthur Miller's *Crucible* opened on Broadway just before the first of these teleplays. Miller's play centers on the adolescent girls who accused adults in their community of witchcraft. Their accusations grew out of immature feelings of rejection and jealousy. Despite the reputation of the play as anti-anticommunist, the narrow focus on the girls and their repressed sexuality actually obscures the connections with McCarthyism. Unlike *Crucible*, which contains no courtroom scene, the *You Are There* radio and television plays remain in court for almost all of the half-hour broadcasts and focus more on the trial proceedings than on the girls.

In Lumet's 1953 staging of Bernstein's teleplay, the action takes place on June 2, 1692, in a rather ornate courtroom replete with wigged judges and prosecutors. As in "Joan of Arc," Lumet often keeps the camera close in on the face of the accused, Bridget Bishop, and he comes back to her tear-filled eyes for the distressing final shot of the episode. CBS interviews Cotton Mather and suggests that he has provided the intellectual and judicial basis for this trial; he accepts credit and recommends further prosecutions. In court the girls frequently scream and writhe in apparent pain, terrifying the spectators as well as the accused. Each time their status as witch-hunters is threatened by some suggestion of doubt, they launch a new attack and accuse more people. The end of the episode brings no solace as the credits roll to the eerie sounds of Mussorgsky's "Night on Bald Mountain." The real evil—the unchecked witch hunt—continued.[91]

One of the more remarkable results of the blacklistees' use of the witch trial motif is the widespread acceptance of that historical allegory, more or less equating McCarthyism and the witch hunt at Salem. A postpurge episode from 1956 reveals the early success of that metaphor, as the same producers that rid the program of its left-leaning talent felt comfortable using the former writers' analogical-historical setting. Reporting picks up from a later point in the story than that treated by the earlier radio and television episodes. The focus also changed, from attacking the idea of the trials to ridiculing their methods and their expanding reach. Broadcasting from Salem in August 1692, Cronkite introduces the audience to the world they live in: "Nobody can guess how far it will go . . . while everybody stands in growing fear of the pointing fingers." Anne Putnam scowls directly into the camera as if on the verge of accusing the viewer. This time reporters interview Increase Mather, who weakly asserts that the court is "exercising the most exquisite precautions."[92]

Back in 1953, the writers had other ideas to explicate, often focusing on historical personages who faced a terrible moral decision of a type never very different from the choices one had to make in the McCarthy era. Nathan Hale, one of Paul Newman's first television roles, like Socrates also chose to die rather than forfeit his principles. British Captain John Montressor holds the captured

American spy in his tent while preparations for the hanging are made, which gives them time to talk about the existential issues of importance to Polonsky. Hale affirms his love of life, recounting memories of playing football and other "foolish things," but though young, he is "too old to betray what I believe is just."[93] Meanwhile, Ed Morgan and Harry Marble trace Samuel Hale, Nathan's cousin, to General Howe's headquarters, where the two reporters jointly interrogate him about the rumor that he betrayed his own cousin to the British. Though Samuel at first responds "indignantly," the two reporters eventually get him to admit to "naming names." Nathan is hanged of course, but not before delivering his line: "I only regret that I have but one life to lose for my country." In Polonsky's telling, Hale takes this from Joseph Addison's play *Cato* (1713), which he reads while waiting for death—a case of life imitating art.[94]

The relationship between art and politics was explored by Polonsky in several works, including "The Recognition of Michelangelo" and "The Vindication of Savonarola," both of which aired in the late fall of 1953. The Michelangelo story centers on the political battle over whether *David* should be displayed, and if so, where. The debate recalls the 1946 Maltz controversy over art's service to politics as much as it references the blacklist. An "art committee" must make the decision, which has nothing to do with aesthetics and everything to do with politics. There is significant political pressure to suppress Michelangelo's figure, perceived by some to symbolize the Florentines' republican challenge to the Medici, but seen as politically ambiguous by others. In the end, the committee leaves the decision to the artist, who declares without equivocation that David will stand in the most prominent position in Florence. The work might yet "awaken us": such is the power of great art. Michelangelo adds, "I care not for this republic or the Medici, but only for the spirit of man." The words flow from Polonsky's feelings about the failure of the Communist Party to be truly "radical in the human sense" at least as much as they refer to censorship in "this republic."

Ending with challenging questions rather than easy lessons was a hallmark of *You Are There*. An ambiguous "The Vindication of Savonarola" (1953) continued the story of the Italian Renaissance monk who ruled Florence after the fall of the Medici, first heard on the radio series in 1949.[95] In that earlier version, an idealistic Girolamo Savonarola is disparaged by Machiavelli and defeated by the autocratic Medici. The latter conceive of an Ordeal by Fire, which John Daly describes as "a hoax, a plot, hatched by his enemies to discredit him." In Polonsky's treatment, Savonarola is a more complicated figure; the viewer never feels very sure about rooting for him. Even at the end, Cronkite can only say that Savonarola has been "puzzling" to historians: "Did he look backward toward the intense spirituality of the medieval era, or did he look forward to the age of reform, an age which unloosed personal freedom and political democracy . . . ?" CBS reported from Florence, February 7, 1497, the date of the infamous *falò delle vanità*, or bonfire of the vanities. Young children, Cronkite tells us, "bearing olive branches and singing hymns, went from door to door collecting works of art, dresses, wigs, articles of pleasure and joy, and these are to be burnt in the great square along with books and manuscripts." These innocents are the followers of Savonarola.

What makes this episode much more complex and interesting than the radio version is the presentation of three sides rather than two. This reminds us that Polonsky's use of the past really was artistic before it was political. He frequently sought out challenging historical episodes rather than easy, binary oppositions with all-too-obvious contemporary parallels. Three factions vie for control of Florence: Savonarola's followers, known as the *Piagnoni*, Rudolfo "Doffo" Spini's *Compagnacci* ("bad companions"), and the *Bigi*, who want to restore the Medici. The latter seek "laughter and gaiety" and an age without political responsibility, surely the least possible scenario for citizens of the republic.

"Doffo" tells Harry Marble that though Savonarola "speaks against tyranny he wishes to play the tyrant." As Spini's graffiti poem says to the people of Florence, "*Tu ne vai preso alle grida, E Dietro a una guida Piena d'ipocrisia*" (You are caught up by a cry and follow a guide all full of hypocrisy). From Savonarola's side, his follower, Fra Domenico da Pescia, defends the use of children to enforce cultural censorship by declaring, "They will lead us to virtue and grace this way and grow up to be lovers of republican liberty instead of libertines." It could be the sort of lesson one might hear on *Cavalcade of America*—recall the fan letters thanking Du Pont for indoctrinating children in just this way—but here it clearly is meant to be dismissed. The children stop adults and chastise them for their sins, then rob them of their possessions so that they may add to the bonfire.[96] The scene seems to presage the Chinese Cultural Revolution, though of course viewers would have associated the bonfire of books with Nazis. And while Polonsky undoubtedly has the 1950s in mind, too, this is really his dystopian vision of where things may be headed. With Savonarola and his allies "attacking the good name and reputation of citizens" and "the word traitor on everyone's mouth," Don Hollenbeck asks if any society can long survive such modes of behavior.

In the radio version, Machiavelli is held up as the cynical antithesis to Savonarola. In the teleplay, Cesare Borgia reveals the truth about power as he sees it:

Force, courage, violence are the weapons by which quiet is imposed on states. They do not always suffice, for we cannot kill everyone. Therefore, fraud and stratagem are necessary. If the citizens are used to the words of liberty, then we embrace the word; if they despise war, we oppose war; if they like ease and contentment, we promise them both; if they cherish independence, we extol it. By such means we gain power, and although they will have lost liberty, be at war, have neither ease nor contentment, and be slaves, the citizens will think they have all.

In a 1989 interview with John Schultheiss, Polonsky clarified the link to American politics, saying, "Cesare Borgia is expressing from the most practical point of view the attitude of a true politician and how you achieve and hold power. . . . Huey Long said fascism will come to America and call itself democracy. He knew that. Savonarola knew that. And every politician knows that."[97]

When we finally meet Savonarola, Hollenbeck asks why he has the right to judge and destroy art and whether he would "reduce all men to simple obedient creatures." To Savonarola's objection that he and his followers brought the great Medici library to Florence for the people, Hollenbeck counters that he has merely preserved the classics while condemning the "artists of the present" whose works make him uncomfortable. Again Polonsky puts the issue of political censorship of contemporary art and artists on the television screen. But Polonsky also has a few words against the artists, and the ambiguity of the episode comes forth as he condemns "those men who are bought and sold in the marketplace like sheep and goats" and whose works help to prop up whatever ruler pays them. The monk's "vindication" comes later, after "Italian freedom perished in tyranny." For "artists and the ordinary man" living in an age of "plenty and the soft luxury of decay," the memory of Savonarola recalled the "hard days when life was dangerous but every man was free." So the episode concludes not with a denunciation of the philistines who would destroy art, but of the "soft luxury" that ultimately may be even more destructive, as it drains citizens of their innate desire to be free.[98]

You Are There's high intellectual caliber and willingness to embrace taboo subjects shone strongest in the episode on Sigmund Freud. The episode opens with Freud, on the second day of the year 1900, speaking in Vienna on human sexuality. He speaks uninterrupted for several minutes, explaining that "sexual impulses play a tremendous part" both in bringing about mental disorders and contributing "invaluably" to the greatest cultural achievements. Consequently:

Society can think of no more powerful menace to its existence than the liberation of sexual impulses. It looks upon sex with horror, with loathing, and with concealed passionate disinterest. As a result, the scientific laws I have discovered are branded by society as morally reprehensible, aesthetically offensive and politically dangerous. We all know it is a characteristic of human nature to regard anything disagreeable as untrue, anything critical of accepted beliefs as dangerous, and anything that violates the common prejudices as immoral. So be it. We can only follow the truth where it leads us and suffer the consequences thereof.

After interviews with some of Freud's detractors and a typical, faked time-management problem where an "unscheduled" encounter seems to force Harry Marble to abandon another interview, CBS News takes us into Freud's examination room. "By arrangement with Dr. Freud and with the consent of the patient," we get to see the doctor's famous psychoanalytic treatment in action. Maintaining the false authenticity, the patient's face is obscured to protect her privacy. Even so, "Miss X" becomes reluctant to talk about certain things once the camera is present, but we still hear a little about her recently recurring dream, which followed from a disturbing incident in which a friend of her father's tried to seduce her—atypical material for 1950s television.

Robert Northshield conducts the closing interview with Freud, which brings psychology into conflict with social consciousness. Polonsky centers the discussion on a subject he deals with at greater length in his novel *The World Above*—the question of individual versus societal ills. When Freud explains that he helps his patients adjust to the world in which they live, Northshield asks, "Suppose the world around them isn't worth adjusting to? Suppose it's unfit to live in, as in so many of the cases which you have described?" This is precisely the question that Polonsky's psychologist-protagonist, Dr. Carl Myers, must grapple with in *The World Above*. In the novel, Myers must defend not only to his profession but also to an anticommunist congressional committee his conclusion that psychology on some level has to consider social problems. The writer did not doubt the fundamental soundness of Freud's methods (that is clear enough in this episode, not to mention in the novel), but both the novel and teleplay questioned the contemporary emphasis on psychoanalysis as substitute for social reform.

You Are There treated scientists far less frequently than did *Cavalcade of America*, but occasionally a persecuted revolutionary doctor or researcher gained notoriety on CBS. In addition to Polonsky's "Freud," Bernstein (as "Howard Rodman") penned "The Tragic Hour of Dr. Semmelweis." The

Hungarian "savior of mothers" theorized that obstetricians' unwashed hands caused the high number of Puerperal or "childbed" fever cases at the Vienna hospital where he practiced. For his trouble, Semmelweis was ridiculed, charged, committed, and dead at age forty-seven in an asylum. In Bernstein's hands, Semmelweis incarnates independence of thought, pure reason, and humanism. His superiors, shown to be willful murderers of women in labor, stand for all reactionary authority. As his friend and colleague Dr. Skoda puts it, "The men who run medicine are brothers to those who run everything else. . . . When a new idea comes along, it shakes and threatens them and they want not to examine, but to kill it, quickly, before it kills them." In this climate, the two researchers "cannot even discuss without fear." Worse, as a nation, "we attack only the best minds. And if we cannot refute [them], we can always persecute them through their politics."

Bernstein lays out the possibilities for his protagonist: he can flee and hope for better luck in exile, he can capitulate and accept condemnation in exchange for the privilege of continuing his work, or he can fight. Like Galileo, Semmelweis disappoints us in the end, leading to yet another unhappy ending on *You Are There*—a sign again of the lack of sponsor oversight. He lives in exile in Hungary for the remainder of his short life, before dying, "ironically," concluded Cronkite, "of the same infection suffered by the friend whose death had given Semmelweis [his theory]." His failure to stand for truth led directly to his tragic ending.

Here again *You Are There* transmits on two frequencies. Those cooling their heels on the blacklist would have had no difficulty reading the persecution subtexts of "Semmelweis," but the play also spoke to the mainstream television audience. For this larger group, Bernstein demonstrates, in the most practical and emotional terms, why democracy is incompatible with intellectual persecution and restrictions on free speech and thought: repression leads to the deaths of young mothers.

Besides the progressive politics, *You Are There* practiced history in ways that seem admirable today. This is especially impressive given the medium and its restrictions. In its subject matter, its complexity, its focus on social and cultural history, and the largely "bottom-up" interpretation of major events, *You Are There* challenges other "history television" to treat subjects of the past with such care and perceptiveness. It would be naive to suggest that romantic history had no place on *You Are There*, but the series certainly tended to de-romanticize history. One of the titles suggested by CBS was the "Hatfield–McCoy Feud." Polonsky's approach to the subject is suggested by Cronkite's opening statement, "We are going to find out just how much is fact and how much folklore."

The episode attempts to de-romanticize the legendary feud and portray its base violence as starkly as possible. We watch as two depressed, impoverished families fight and kill each other, and destruction overwhelms Appalachia. Cronkite concludes, "there was no romance in it."[99] This stridently contrasts with the *Cavalcade of America* approach to history, which not only sought out the romance but cranked it up a notch or two. *You Are There* more often than not covered the less-than-cheery side of history; when myths were addressed, as in the "Hatfield–McCoy Feud," they were deconstructed rather than celebrated or exploited.

Several episodes covered the same events as *Cavalcade* episodes, some offering dramatic contrasts to the Du Pont presentations. For example, Bernstein's "The Louisiana Purchase" (1953) lacked a du Pont hero. Bernstein also wrote 1953's "Grant and Lee at Appomattox," the meeting dramatized on *Cavalcade* as "Sunset at Appomattox" two years later. The two versions of the day's events are not easily distinguished; both plead for tolerance, forgiveness, and reconciliation. If one really deconstructs the two episodes, it is possible to argue that the *You Are There* story is a suggestion for peaceful coexistence, either between the United States and the USSR or within the United States, while the *Cavalcade* version favors the South, but it seems extremely unlikely that the casual viewer—not to mention schoolchildren—would have seen much difference between the two or drawn such conclusions. Both series covered the death of Stonewall Jackson as well, and here a greater contrast can be made. Lying on his deathbed following the battle at Chancellorsville, *Cavalcade*'s Jackson exemplifies a righteous Christian soldier, suffering for the sins of others. Howard Rodman, who sometimes fronted for Bernstein, wrote or fronted (it is not clear which) the *You Are There* treatment of Jackson's demise. The 1955 episode opens with Cronkite reporting on the "war of the Southern Confederacy against the United States of America"; we hear of no "war between the states" or "northern aggression" here. The focus on the ordinary soldier, which in this episode consists of interviews with disheartened and starving rebels from the unit that may have accidentally shot Jackson, is vintage Bernstein—the only clue that this script did come from him. The men trade their cheap whiskey for Union soldiers' coffee and sugar, Lou Cioffi asks them about their rations, or lack thereof, and we get the standard *You Are There* look at the hard lives led by young men sent to war.[100]

Bernstein's war experience and his abiding interest in veterans' well-being permeate the somber story of "Washington's Farewell to His Officers." Writing as "Kate Nickerson," Bernstein focused on a reflective moment in the lives of the general and his top commanders. No battles, no action, no tension at all except the anxiety of wondering what Washington will say. Then he speaks, and his men begin to cry as he leads them in remembrance of the sacrifices, the pain and suffering, and loss of war, and convinces them of their obligation to assist fellow veterans.[101]

Signing his script as Leslie Slote, Bernstein wrote again of the soldier's plight in "The Gettysburg Address." As in all of his scripts, every effort is made to introduce as many issues and as much complexity as possible to an already famous historical moment. Like many *You Are There* episodes, the supposed subject—Lincoln, in this case—remains completely absent until the end. Instead, CBS reporters ask representative types what they would like to hear from the president. Hostile New Yorker John O'Connell complains that his son died fighting for the rich. He believes the government ought to worry more about his own working-class "slavery." Standing by at his army's encampment, Ray Walston's William Tecumseh Sherman hopes Lincoln will tell the South that the Union Army will show them no mercy. The reporter mentions Sherman's recent letter to Lincoln—a "footnote" that subtly and deftly reminds attentive viewers that this interview is based on a historical document. For the Southern point of view, Governor Vance of North Carolina and Jefferson Davis both insist that peace depends on Lincoln.

In the longest and most important scene, CBS interviews John Muncie Forbes, Samuel May, and William Lloyd Garrison as they plan for an anti-slavery convention. Forbes wants Lincoln to reveal to the American people the true nature of the conflict: class warfare. Garrison explains that political leaders respond to pressure from the people. As he finishes making this point about political engagement, Frederick Douglass arrives and quickly dismisses Lincoln's speech as irrelevant. "If the country is to be saved, it will not be by the captain, but by the crew." At this the four men set to work at finding ways to demonstrate the "power of the people."

The call to political participation has been seen before. This episode demonstrates how diverse that participation could be, ranging from the self-sacrifice of wartime service to unquestioning patriotism to popular movements. *You Are There*, whether in World War II Paris or Civil War New England, ancient Greece or revolutionary Boston, often argued the necessity of an active and demanding citizenry. Back at Gettysburg, Lincoln's first words of the show are the enduring "Four score and seven years ago . . ." As he reads the address in its entirety, in a voice much softer than any other in the episode thus far, the camera never moves from a close-up of the president's head and shoulders, forcing the viewer to pay attention to the text. Would those watching answer Lincoln's call for a "new birth of freedom" in America?[102]

In "The Emancipation Proclamation" episode of *You Are There*, the depiction of an African American Civil War soldier who seizes his own freedom suggests the radical nature of CBS's history. (Woodhaven Entertainment, *You Are There*, 1955.)

The remarkable episode "The Emancipation Proclamation" (1955), credited to Howard Rodman, positioned the issue of slavery at the center of the Civil War and argued, following contemporary leftist historiography, that the slaves freed themselves.[103] Rodman was certainly left-of-center politically—his *Variety* obituary even states he was blacklisted during this time. While plausible, that would have made fronting for Bernstein difficult.[104] The script for "Emancipation" resembles Bernstein's style, especially his "Gettysburg Address," but there is no evidence suggesting that Rodman was the front rather than the author of this particular script. As at Gettysburg, CBS reporters scatter in order to interview people with contrasting points of view on the subject, and again we hear from all sides before returning to Lincoln. The interviews downplay the significance of Lincoln's decision, and in the end he is a figure of surprisingly little consequence. In the opening Oval Office scene, Lincoln struggles with his choice, wondering if the middle states—and England—would openly support the Confederacy if he signs. Yet morally, "if slavery's not wrong, then nothing's wrong." In the Union Army, a Captain Canfield shares this view. Canfield addresses us while under arrest for freeing escaped slaves that had been seized by his superior officer, Colonel Neebling, for the purpose of selling them south to men who claimed, without proof, to be their owners. Most outrageous to the captain is that these fugitives provide invaluable military intelligence, yet they receive nothing but hostility and abuse from many white officers.

Next we hear from slaves themselves. In this amazing scene, we watch as slaves transform themselves into full citizens. At one of several "Negro gatherings" held in Washington to discuss and pray for Lincoln's signature, we look in on weary men and women wearing straw hats and clothing more suitable for harvesting cotton in the Deep South than for winter in the nation's capital. After they finish a somber rendition of "Let My People Go," an older man stands up to say a few words about their painful past and the promise of the future, building up to and concluding with a rousing repetition of "no more of *that!*" A reporter next interviews Private Long, of the South Carolina Volunteers, a reminder or more likely a surprise to many viewers that African Americans fought in uniform during the Civil War. School textbooks of the era left out this information, an unsurprising fact given the typical and absurd interpretation that "most of the slaves seemed happy and contented."[105] Of course, in the 1950s schoolteachers in most states had to sign loyalty oaths, and unlike television writers they could not teach pseudonymously. But on *You Are There* Private Long happily relates how ex-slaves like him volunteered to serve and work their way toward full citizenship and voting rights. Then he shrugs off the question of whether Lincoln will sign the proclamation: "Sign or no sign, sir, for me, no more of that!" The scene comes to a close as the motley chorus begins anew, now standing tall and singing proudly, "My Country 'tis of Thee." The people have seized the initiative and made the words and actions of the leader—the nominal focus of the episode—almost irrelevant. The "power of the people" is again the real lesson.[106]

African Americans also featured prominently in 1954's "The Emergence of Jazz," essentially a condensed history of how white musicians co-opted the musical form from black musicians in New Orleans. Polonsky's lines for Walter Cronkite take us back to November 12, 1917, coincidentally the same day that "Premier Kerensky announced the near collapse of the Bolshevik Revolution," "Trotsky was greeted with taunts and laughter when he came to take over the Reds," and suffragettes were arrested for picketing outside the White House. The references are again a kind of tip-of-the-hat to Polonsky's dispersed comrades rather than a serious attempt at persuasion—or some complicated Soviet method of communicating with spies! The script focused on early jazz legends King Oliver and Jelly Roll Morton, played by two younger legends, Louis Armstrong and Billy Taylor, respectively. The first scene takes place in a New York recording studio, where the successful all-white Original Dixieland Jazz Band is recording one of their hits. A black porter who happens by says, "If you like this, mister, you should hear it when it's real." The white musicians later confirm that they learned the music from "the colored," "down in Storyville," a section of New Orleans. The success of the white band contrasts with the situation in New Orleans, where the federal government has demanded the city raze Storyville to protect young white soldiers and sailors from vice. Literally then, and right before our eyes, the African American roots of jazz are destroyed, while white practitioners continue their commercial successes. Later, Armstrong's King Oliver interrupts his interview with Harry Marble with one last performance of "Saints." He marches out the door and into the street, and the customers go with him. Real jazz went with them too, says Cronkite, for the music was "merged with the popular songs and ballads, what the musicians call 'sweet and commercial.'"[107]

In Polonsky's transnational story, Ned Calmer reports from a Paris café, where war-weary Europeans embrace jazz as a message of hope. Belgian poet Robert Goffin explains that white Americans fear jazz as a "free creation of the Negro people whom they still don't recognize as free and equal." His use of "Negro" contrasts with the white American's derogatory "colored." "That is an irony isn't it, that from the slaves and the oppressed comes the only original contribution to art made by the American nation. All else is imitation." These few lines summarize Goffin's landmark work of jazz criticism, *Aux frontières du jazz*. Polonsky, who had lived in France and also wrote during the later 1950s about intellectuals of the Francophone left, had undoubtedly read Goffin and probably later French jazz critics like Boris Vian as well.[108]

Polonsky's "The Torment of Beethoven" studies the musician in society and rejects the idea that real artists can find satisfaction in this world—alienation is unavoidable and should be embraced. The "rebel" is tormented by loneliness, symbolized by his deafness, but really deriving from the natural isolation of the true artist. "I am an exile," he says, "and yet, my conception of life is heroic . . . to struggle, to seize fate by the throat and strangle it." Beethoven's music critiques "false" happiness; it is music for "this new age in which no man knows whether he will live or die from day to day." The only legitimate stance for the artist was to be, like Beethoven, a "hero."

This epitomized the divide between the CP leadership and communists like Polonsky and his colleagues of similar mind and spirit. For the party, art was a weapon in the fight against capitalism. For many artists and writers, leftist politics was a foundation, but their art would suffer from forced conformity, whether to the party line or to HUAC. Beethoven, product of the Enlightenment and the apex of musical achievement before the nationalistic strain of Romanticism came to the fore, personified the artist of radical humanism that Polonsky wanted to be. "The role of the artist is not to worry about the political sensitivities of people," he wrote two years later in a review of Simone de Beauvoir's *The New Mandarins*, "but to stimulate them into new areas of experiment and expression." Sounding very much like Dwight Macdonald, he added that works of art should not concern themselves with "practical politics" per se, as the "tendency in social commitments is uniformity," which destroys art.[109]

Intellectually, Polonsky continued to claim the mantle of Maltz's 1946 critique, but his work consistently demonstrated political and social commitment. His decision to write pseudonymously for television rather than openly for the theater or as a novelist (a decision that, in retrospect, he could not explain), indicates that he valued the potential for reaching a mass audience, by any means available, very highly.

Defining News, Shaping Memory

On television, as on radio, the technique of simulating difficult and possibly fatal reporting conditions, and including technical and sound "problems," was used again to great effect. The writers and directors also instructed CBS reporters on their delivery—when to pause for dramatic effect, when to speak with no breaks in order to enhance the intensity of an unfolding situation, when to fire questions rapidly in order to pressure someone and make them appear unsympathetic, and when to probe more softly and generate "human interest." How much of this instruction these reporters and others in the news division absorbed and then used in their "real" news broadcasts is impossible to know, yet one can easily imagine how such artistic direction helped *You Are There* veterans improve their on-air style. Certainly Cronkite's skill and reputation as a national "anchorman"—a new designation—grew because of this show.[110]

Many CBS News programs also derived style or substance from *You Are There*, illustrating the series' lasting impact on network news. In the late 1950s, for example, *You Are There* veteran reporter Clete Roberts had a show called *Clete Roberts Special Report*, which always opened with introductory remarks performed in the style of *You Are There*. In *CBS News: Eyes on the World*, a 1962 special hosted by *You Are There* veteran Charles Collingwood that overviewed the extensive News Division, Walter Cronkite introduced two programs that should be considered the series' progeny, *Twentieth Century* and *Eyewitness* (formerly *Eyewitness to History*). The latter offered an "electronic eye through which we can focus on the scenes where history is being made." In other words, it took the premise of *You Are There* and moved somewhat further in the direction of news. Cronkite even used the catchphrase, but ironically in the past tense: "And you were there—an eyewitness to an event in the history of our time." The other program, *Twentieth Century*, had succeeded *You Are There*, changing the chronological focus and, of course, the format.

You Are There itself sometimes edged closer to news, particularly in the last season (1956–57) and in several earlier episodes that covered World War II. In a 1956 special *You Are There*: "Cyprus Today," CBS dispensed with re-creations but reported the news of the previous few months from Cyprus in the show's typical format. Footage of rioting was mixed with interviews to "develop and explain the situation."[111] Soon after, a similar *You Are There* program aired from Moscow.[112] This indicates the extent to which CBS News thought of *You Are There* as one of the network's premiere public affairs programs.

These episodes were clearly "news," but what about a broadcast covering the events of a decade before? In 1955, as "Leo Davis," Polonsky wrote the script for "The Liberation of Paris." Reporting from August 25, 1944, Cronkite sets the scene by quickly explaining that the Axis powers are finally starting to "feel the return blow of the Allies." This is the "*second* front," made possible only by the great effort of the Soviets on the eastern front. "Liberation" contrasts with a later, postpurge episode, "D-Day," credited to writer Maury Stern (more on that credit later) and directed by Jack Gage. In "D-Day" the USSR is never mentioned, and the war is conceived of as a wholly American undertaking. Several times a reporter refers to the invasion at hand as "the beginnings," as if D-Day marked the start of World War II. In a way, this episode prefigures the World War II Memorial on the National Mall in that the Allies are absent and sovereign U.S. states stand almost in their stead. Rather than construct an episode or monument that demonstrated how the various Allied nations came together to defeat fascism, the structure emphasizes how the various states worked together to win the war. CBS reporters interviewed soldiers preparing for and in the midst of battle by asking about their home states, their families, and their very American hobbies and sports. Nor are we ever asked to remember fascism's atrocities, which is probably the raison d'être of Polonsky's "Liberation."

Early on in the Polonsky episode we watch in horror as "French fascists" (the narrator spits out the alliteration) shoot at "patriots." There is no dialogue at all for several minutes. The lengthy third and final scene takes place in the German's suburban prison, where the Nazi commander continues to execute French partisans even during the evacuation. He condemns one man charged with some minor offense after the prisoner gloats a little in the impending victory. First putting up a fight, the man then screams, "You are right to kill me. It is right for a Nazi to kill to the last minute. It would be wrong to spare me and let the world imagine for even one moment that you are members of the human race. Yes, kill me. Yes, kill me! So that we will never forget what you are!" Poignantly, facing the firing squad and the viewer, his last words are, "Remember. For those who forget may God curse them with wars and death 'til they and their children are no more. Vive la . . . [*gunshot*]."

To help us remember, real footage of innumerable executed faces and bodies rolls in silence for an uncomfortably long time. How different this is from America's quick postwar forgetting of German atrocities in order to bring the Federal Republic into the fight against the Soviets. Where else in 1955 could one see such a vivid denunciation of fascism with, for good measure, a reminder of the Allies' debt to the Soviets?[113]

The key issue in this episode, and the question the reporters keep coming back to, is whether it was "wise" for Parisians to revolt. Had they remained passive and waited for Allied troops to arrive in Paris, would they and their city have been better off? Integrated footage of French partisans burning a German soldier alive in the street deliberately questions claims of French moral superiority—but only to force viewers to more seriously consider how fascist crimes were essentially different. Cronkite finally explains that whatever the consequences, resistance by the citizenry was vital to the "spirit, the soul, the very honor of the French people." Like many other Cold War era scripts, this one praised the engaged citizen—the patriot. But these citizens became heroes by actively, violently opposing their own fascist-allied government. These were the last warriors of the Popular Front, cousins to the antifascist international brigades that fought Franco in Spain.

Polonsky's World War II story thus looked back to the alliances of the war and the 1930s. In contrast, "D-Day" looked ahead to the postwar era of American superpower. These two episodes have now been packaged together on one DVD. They likely would be viewed together, providing a more complete picture of the war than either would have done separately. But for the most part the D-Day story of the war won out in American memory. In popular historical imagination, World War II had little to do with an international struggle against fascism or Parisian guerrillas. But *You Are There* demonstrates that alternate histories of the war did reach a mainstream audience, at least for a while.

Several *You Are There* episodes used the framework of empire to question American expansion and, quite possibly, growing involvement in Vietnam.[114] In "The Great Adventure of Marco Polo" (1954), Kubla Khan tries to make sense of the "inscrutable and incomprehensible" Western powers. "What I find full of laughter is their words, the marvelous words of peace and piety with which they clothe their wicked acts." The "great Khan Genghis" never said, "'I come to save you' when he meant to slay."[115] The same critique of "the West" adds the most reflective layer to the already well-textured "Cortés Conquers Mexico." This first-season episode featured Eartha Kitt as Hernán Cortés's Indian interpreter and mistress. The interracial extramarital affair with Kitt's character assumes a level of cosmopolitanism not commonly associated with 1950s television. Kitt's "Marina" devises the notoriously devious scheme through which Cortés forces Montezuma to proclaim him emissary of the gods. Part threat, part promise, with his sword in Montezuma's back, Cortés demands the king speak to his people and proclaim the Spaniards heaven-sent. "Tell them and we will be brothers and we will love and protect each other. Tell them, or else you and all of them will die. Now speak." The choice of the soon to be absorbed: immediate execution or a slower demise obscured by promises of mutual benefits.[116] "The Battle of Gibraltar," credited to Howard Rodman, closely examined the consequences of two superpowers clashing over odd bits of remote foreign territory. The episode focused on the suffering of the lowest-rank soldiers (of England, France, and Spain) and the local population—who suffer most of all through starvation, rape, the destruction of their homes, and death—during this one small conflict in the global struggle between two great empires. "Half my life I've spent in these caves," complains an old woman, "while strangers fight each other on my land. Why? What right do they have?" In the end the good guys, the English, win, but at the same moment, mocking both the "victory" and the idea of an indirect war, the old woman and her husband find that their home has been completely destroyed.[117]

The final episode of the Polonsky-Bernstein-Manoff-Lumet-Russell era, "The Triumph of Alexander the Great," aired on March 27, 1955. Alexander faces a mutiny from his Macedonian troops, who object to foreigners holding prestigious positions in "their" government. This crisis sets the stage for a more significant discussion about the nature of government, empire, and world peace. Wearing Persian clothing, to express his rejection of both Macedonian provincialism and Greek ethnocentrism, this early "world federalist" insists that "all men are brothers," and "all the peoples of the earth" must be treated equally. He seeks "a world, a government, in which all nations are partners" with "all peoples equal, none subject to the other." Peace is to be achieved through world government with equal representation—no *Pax Americana* here—and an end to racial discrimination. It is a fitting finale.[118]

Several other leftist writers wrote scripts for *You Are There*. Some were produced; some were not. Paddy Chayevsky, who would soon write and gain notoriety for the Academy Award–winning *Marty*, and later *Network*, the darkly satirical study of a network news division, offered a script to *You Are There* titled "The Triangle Shirt Waist Company Fire." Though it was never produced, the script indicates that other friends of the writing trio knew that they had a possible outlet for their talent at CBS, where they could not only make some money but also offer their social or political views through historical events. It also indicates the limits of what could be done on the show, as Chayevsky's proposed scenes of scores of young women burned alive would have been shockingly gruesome.[119]

Saul Levitt, another blacklistee, also wrote scripts for *You Are There*. He submitted several scripts through a front named Maury Stern. Levitt would achieve his greatest fame through his play, and later made-for-TV movie, *The Andersonville Trial*—which Stern claimed he wrote.[120] He (or perhaps Stern?) wrote at least four scripts for *You Are There*, including "D-Day," "William Pitt's Last Speech to Parliament," "The Resolve of Patrick Henry," and "The Abdication of Napoleon." These episodes are not among the most engaging of the series, nor are they culturally, politically, or historically provocative. Like the later episodes of 1956–57, they lack tension: no unsolvable moral dilemmas, just stories about famous men in their finest hours.[121]

Endings

The decline of *You Are There* occurred in two stages. First, the network forced out Polonsky, Bernstein, and Manoff and the show left for Hollywood in the fall of 1955 without Lumet or Russell. Not surprisingly, the quality suffered. Earlier shows had confronted difficult and complex issues but the later episodes presented straightforward facts in a nearly drama-less format. Two years after the move, *Twentieth Century* replaced *You Are There*. This was 1957, the same year that Du Pont ended the *Cavalcade of America*. It may have been coincidence that the two most heralded historical dramas left the air at the same time, both replaced by more contemporary programs, but it seems more likely that something had changed.

On a practical level, the networks and sponsors decided that they could reach more people and make more money through contemporary programming. The expansive interpretation of "news" shrank to limits more recognizable to us today. And the networks increasingly replaced anthology shows with formulaic series and their regular casts of lovable or at least unobjectionable characters. Television had extended its reach into almost every part of the country by then, and its audience had grown more diverse economically as well. *You Are There*'s message no longer suited the medium. More important to our protagonists, the worst manifestations of McCarthyism were passing into history. The blacklist was losing its effectiveness. It would still be several more years before everyone tainted by "a list somewhere" could work openly, but things were starting to open up. It was therefore no longer necessary to talk only in code. Perhaps, too, the ideological battles and political trials that had begun decades before were finally over—or were at least changing form.

At the same time, the increase in television viewing choices represented a broader expanse of sources of information. Public affairs programming on the very restricted television medium of the early 1950s had in key respects descended from World War II–era propaganda and ideologically driven productions of the 1930s. These directed lessons, historical or not, were decreasingly acceptable to an audience that was growing more sophisticated and more accustomed to a wealth of choices. Moreover, television's entertainment function was emerging triumphant over both public affairs programming and highbrow anthology series—the two genres straddled by *You Are There*. By the late 1950s, Americans used the medium differently than they had earlier in the decade, actively searching for amusement on an increasing number of stations positioned across two frequency spectrums. The complicated and often-obscure historical episodes reenacted on the *You Are There* of Lumet and his writers disappeared from public view, though they persisted in classrooms as an educational tool. The attempt at popular education through the television medium again faced the problem that plagued every such effort: in short, the need to match the desires of the American consumer.

In 1957 David Susskind hired Bernstein's friend Marty Ritt to direct Sidney Poitier and John Cassavetes in *Edge of the City*. Otto Preminger openly hired Dalton Trumbo to write the screenplay for *Exodus*, after which Kirk Douglas hired him to adapt Howard Fast's *Spartacus*. Bernstein began to shake off the blacklist when Sidney Lumet was hired by Carlo Ponti to direct a movie starring Ponti's wife, Sophia Loren. Lumet hired Bernstein to write the script for *That Kind of Woman*, released in 1959. Even then, he still faced difficulties, as Paramount for a long time refused to give him a contract. While still dealing with that, Marty Ritt and Yul Brynner, the original producer-director team of *Danger*, offered him the chance to write *The Magnificent Seven*.[122] After that he revived his career completely and went on to write many acclaimed motion pictures, including 1961's *Paris Blues* (directed by Ritt and starring Paul Newman, Joanne Woodward, Sidney Poitier, and Diahann Carroll), *Fail Safe* (the 1964 and 2000 versions), *The Molly Maguires* (1970), *Yanks* (1979), and *The Front* (1977), for which he received an Oscar nomination.

Arnold Manoff's story is the saddest of the *You Are There* team. He had a difficult time getting un-blacklisted. After Lumet hired him for Ponti's film, Bernstein actually fronted for Manoff on a script he submitted to Marty Ritt. Manoff wrote a bit more for television, including the series *Naked City*, *Ivanhoe*,

Pursuit, and the *Defenders,* before he succumbed to ill health and passed away in 1965 at the age of fifty-one.[123]

Polonsky managed to contribute to a small number of films in the latter half of the 1950s. His near-break came when Harry Belafonte hired him to write *Odds against Tomorrow* (1959), a film produced by the star's new production company, Harbel, and directed by Robert Wise, best known for *The Day the Earth Stood Still* (1951). The plot of *Odds against Tomorrow* centers around three men (Belafonte, Ed Begley, and Robert Ryan) who fail in their attempt to rob a bank because of their ingrained racial mistrust. Belafonte and Ryan's characters kill each other in an explosion set off by their gunfire, leaving their bodies so unidentifiable that the authorities cannot determine which was white and which black. After *Odds,* Belafonte, Polonsky, and Sidney Poitier planned to make a whole series of films about African American life, but the financing for their very first project, a Polonsky script called "Sweetland," fell through after Paul Newman and other investors grew fearful of professional fallout and withdrew. Not until 1968's *Madigan* would Polonsky receive a writing credit for a studio motion picture. The following year he directed Robert Redford in *Tell Them Willie Boy Is Here,* twenty-one years after directing John Garfield in *Force of Evil.*[124]

You Are There lived on as films used in history classes. I learned about ancient Greece through "The Death of Socrates" in the early 1990s, forty years after the episode first aired as a response to anticommunism. Current online reviews suggest that *You Are There* continues to be seen as an accurate representation of history by fans, teachers, and homeschooling parents. One fan remembers, "Our whole family would watch this show together, and we were as I recall fascinated by it. I distinctly recall one of the shows was on the death of Socrates which even to this day must affect me in some way." Several others note the lack of comparably good historical programming today.[125] An assumption of the series' accuracy by most viewers raises troubling questions for historians, yet in many ways the series' interpretations prefigured those of the historical profession, especially in its emphasis on social history and its investigations of the relationship between politics and culture. Playing a bit fast and loose with the facts—condensing several days into one half hour, for example—might be the gravest indictment of the series.

As for the intended lessons the writers hoped would reach millions of American television viewers, any interpretation that finds radical themes throughout the course of the series needs to be tempered. Certainly the show's politics fit a liberal worldview, but the cues indicating positions from the far left often were too slight for notice by anyone not already on the left. The trio clearly wrote for at least two audiences—one that watched the program to be entertained or educated by televised history, but without having a very clear sense of the analogies being made, and another that understood the references, shared the politics of the writers, and chuckled sadly at the truth of the comparisons across time.

4

The Freedom Train's
Narrow-Gauge Iconography

More important to the world than the atom bomb, is this conception of freedom for the individual.

> Harry S. Truman, at dedication of the Freedom Train, quoted in
> H. Walton Cloke, "Truman Asks U.S. to 'Share Liberty,'"
> *New York Times*, September 17, 1947

Its abiding consequence will be to clarify the people's perceptions of the grandeur of the nation's past, the majesty of its present, and the glory of its future . . .

> William J. Peterson, "America's Freedom Train"

This is the story of an unusual form of public history, one in which the past was delivered on railcars and also through "all methods of mass persuasion."[1] From September 1947 to January 1949, a "Freedom Train" carried 126 of America's most vital historical documents to 322 towns and cities in all 48 states. More than a third of the population participated in some part of the campaign, which also included patriotic and celebratory "Rededication Weeks" at every stop. Initially conceived of by Justice Department personnel and endorsed by President Harry Truman, the newly formed American Heritage Foundation (AHF)—an association of leading advertising and business personnel sponsored by the nation's largest corporations—organized and promoted the tour. In every community touched by the "popular movement," the business and advertising leaders behind the AHF organized civic participation around the central theme of "freedom." Along the way, other groups from across the political spectrum challenged the AHF's definition of freedom. In the course of this extended conversation, postwar Americans elaborated a civil religion that was built on the foundation provided by the collected documents.

The Freedom Train traveled the country "bearing a precious freight of documents, and speeding through the land like a modern Paul Revere to arouse the people to a sense of danger while stirring their pride in the glory of the national heritage."[2] Communism was the immediate danger, but as it rumbled along its 37,000-mile journey, extolling "freedom" at every stop, this train looked to flatten all ideologies and squeeze American history into the narrowest of tracks. It demanded worship as the diesel-fueled ark of a sacred heritage and branded as heretics any who refused to join the new church of "Americanism." At the same time, as a result of the need to build unity and consensus, this dogma underwent revision. The historic freight toured the country at the moment when the United States became a real presence in nearly every corner of the globe and ceased to exist as merely a nation in and of itself. With so many people watching, both at home and abroad, the Freedom Train represented American heritage very cautiously, painting a too-rosy picture but also insisting on the practice of the principles it claimed were the fundamentals of that heritage, namely liberty and equality.

Despite organizers' efforts to control the message, the term "freedom" carried with it many different meanings, as did the documents assembled to stand for the nation's eternal values. For the most part, the campaign's activities ignored the documents themselves, except to figuratively wave them around as a rally flag. At times, however, Americans heeded the train's call to civic engagement by more actively considering the implications of free speech, the equality of all humankind, or how freedom related to their economic rights. The last of these particularly disquieted the train's corporate sponsors. Despite the AHF's rhetoric, learning from and experiencing history firsthand was less the intention than claiming the mantle of freedom for the sake of the sponsors' political and economic agendas. Ultimately, the public's failure to follow the political course suggested by the AHF halted a popular effort to launch a second tour.

Following a long tradition of mixing religion and patriotism, the Freedom Train broadened and redefined American civil religion for the postwar era. The collected documents, as well as their nearly mythic authors, functioned as the core idols of this new religion. At the celebrated stops at stations in every state, "advance agents" of the AHF instructed Americans of all backgrounds in the catechism, while the media reported the penalties, particularly ostracism, for nonparticipation. Headlines admonished readers to "Visit It!"[3] Wartime bond drives and other home front propaganda campaigns had prepared Americans for the Freedom Train. The media blitz from radio, newsreels, newspapers, and magazines made a personal interaction with the American past difficult to avoid in 1948. The act of proclaiming oneself "for freedom" joined the individual to society, reviving once more the disappearing feelings of wartime unity. "Rededication" provided a guidebook for continued patriotic service in peacetime—or rather, in the Cold War. Much of the rhetoric focused on spreading freedom abroad, while the prescribed activities helped to set the tone for increased anticommunism at home. Not everyone followed the AHF's direction, but the Freedom Train stimulated civic engagement at phenomenally high rates of participation.

A number of scholars have written about the Freedom Train and have concluded that the organizers sought to impose "consensus," a basic agreement on values and ideology, on the American people.[4] A fair conclusion, but without a careful examination of that process, including the dynamic interactions of the past and the present, the public and the documents, religion and politics, and propaganda and history, much of the story has remained invisible or obscured by this interpretation. Many people, leftists and African Americans in particular, spoke their own language of freedom that attempted to use American history just as the AHF used it to advertise its pro-business rhetoric. Yet history, whether consensus or any other kind, ironically carried very little weight aboard the Freedom Train. Rather, what began within the National Archives as a public history project instead evolved into semi-official iconography, propaganda, and civil religion appropriate for the Cold War. Along the way, "freedom" took on significance and meanings that derived less from the historic texts than from contemporary issues, both national and local. While an examination of the document selection process reveals important information, ultimately the specifics of the documents mattered little since they were treated collectively as icons rather than studied individually and historically as primary sources. This chapter begins by considering the significance of the campaign's locus and then briefly reviews the history of the Freedom Train's origins and the varied motives for participation. How the public experienced the Freedom Train often diverged from official statements of purpose, and the rest of the chapter elucidates how the train and the surrounding campaign operated, what limitations it faced, and the reasons behind its unexpected demise. The story reveals how an amazingly successful effort to engage the public with history resulted in complicated and problematic outcomes.

The Great American Railroad

Trains hold a special place in American memory. Their presence, audible and visible, stirs the collective consciousness of continental conquest and settlement—a memory regularly affirmed by Hollywood. Though the country has long since become the land of automobiles and the "freedom of the open road," historical America—and even more so the hazily remembered or mythologized old-time America—is largely a land of trains. Published in 1947, the first year of the Freedom Train, History Book Club editor Stewart Holbrook's *The Story of American Railroads* celebrated the train's special place in American memory. He wrote of steam engines, "No sight, no sound in my native land so stirs up my imagination as those do. As symbols of the United States they are better, and more accurate, than the covered wagon and the report of the homesteader's rifle. I think of them as unmistakenly American as the Stars and Stripes and the Constitution."[5]

The following summer, and again in 1949, Chicago hosted a "Railroad Fair" that marked a hundred years of trains in that city. It drew millions of Americans to the site of the 1933 Century of Progress Exhibition in Burnham Park. Made possible through the cooperation of thirty-eight independent carriers, Museum of Science and Industry president Lenox Riley Lohr organized the exhibition. Lohr had been the general manager of Chicago's Century of Progress, then became president of NBC, and finally returned to Chicago in 1940 to transform the Museum of Science and Industry into an internationally recognized institution, albeit one heavily reliant on corporate America. The fair's program claimed it allowed millions of Americans to "relive again in vivid realism those dramatic moments of the past when an infant people was fighting its way to its present position in the world."[6] The fair drew on nostalgia for then-disappearing steam trains to advertise the future of rail travel to the post-war public. It also expressed a particular historical narrative that emphasized transcontinental movement, national expansion, and progress. Walt Disney journeyed to the fair and then around the park on a model train, apparently imbibing inspiration for Disneyland. Disney's evocation of America's mythic past of railroads, western frontier, and old-time Main Street resembled the kind of history found in Chicago.[7]

Besides marking the start of the Cold War and domestic anticommunism, the late 1940s represented a last chance for American railroads. During the first half of the twentieth century, the railroad industry rose to its peak levels in the

1910s, declined during the 1920s and 1930s, revived dramatically during World War II, and then suffered a quick and likely permanent downturn after that. By the early 1960s, competition from air, road, and sea transport had decimated the nation's railroads. In the immediate wake of World War II, however, a sense of optimism pervaded the industry. Wartime profits erased much of the accumulated debt of the previous twenty years, Congress and the public were grateful for railroads' essential contributions to the war effort, and earlier investments in new technologies appeared ready to yield returns.[8] That rail travel instead came almost to its terminus was not a complete surprise, but hope glimmered in the late 1940s.

When Holbrook published his appreciation in 1947, he thought America's trains would continue to run for many decades to come.[9] Even a decade later, when an Interstate Commerce Commission official suggested that Pullman sleeper cars would disappear by 1965, and passenger coaches by 1970, "most people laughed."[10] In retrospect, the trends are more than obvious; even at the time, the kind of nostalgic history engaged in by Holbrook and the Chicago fair suggests that, his protestations to the contrary, the signs were clear enough in the late 1940s. Before the war ended, labor issues had emerged as a major challenge to the railroad industry. War increased the industry's labor force by 25 percent, to 1.4 million by war's end (out of a national labor force of about 55 million).[11] Facing rising costs due to inflation, unions demanded pay increases, and a threat to strike on December 7, 1941, eventually led to an increase in average annual salary from $2,045 in 1941 to $2,307 in 1942. But by 1943, inflation again led to dissatisfaction, and another proposed December strike caused Roosevelt to briefly take over the railroads. The action averted the strike and again won higher wages, which averaged $2,726 by 1944. However, workers' wartime victories contributed to the industry's long-term infeasibility.

During World War II, the industry worked hard to avoid a federal takeover, as had happened during World War I. The industry claimed to epitomize the tremendous value of free enterprise, and corporate America pointed to the railroads as a shining example of what less-regulated business could accomplish.[12] In spring 1946 railroad workers struck again, but President Truman resisted the unions by seizing control of the railroads and drafting workers into the army. His speech to Congress, interrupted by a message informing him of the success of his bold maneuver, described the chaos that he claimed faced the nation if the strike continued. The strike "threatens to paralyze all our industrial, agricultural, commercial, and social life." "Food, raw materials, fuel, shipping, housing, the public health, the public safety—all will be dangerously affected. *Hundreds of thousands of liberated people of Europe and Asia will die*" (emphasis added).

In an almost apocalyptic passage, Truman insisted these railroad employees were fighting against "the Government of the United States itself," and that "can never be tolerated." The escalating conflict between labor and management threatened to tear the country—and the world—apart.[13]

Planning for the Freedom Train began during the spring 1946 strike. The "disunity" exhibited in these disputes between capital and labor caused concern well beyond the railroad industry. The strikes and some election-related violence in 1946 convinced many governing and business elites that the country desperately needed some sort of unifying campaign.[14] The labor unrest also led many Americans to support the Taft-Hartley Act, passed over Truman's veto on June 23, 1947. A massive campaign by the National Association of Manufacturers had characterized the bill as, finally, "some pro-public legislation" that benefited all Americans instead of only labor unions.[15] Business framed the debate in terms of a harmful collective bargaining system versus the American system "based on the dignity and freedom of the individual."[16] The Freedom Train reaffirmed that definition of America and implicitly rejected labor's approach.

In either a highly ironic or highly suitable decision, when a "unity" campaign finally came together in 1947, the chosen location was a train. Billed as the "longest train trip in history," the Freedom Train showcased "unparalleled cooperation" by fifty-two railroad companies, proving to the public just how well private industry functioned.[17] The organizers confronted disunity on its home turf and sought to demonstrate what a powerful force consensus could be. Despite its effort, the AHF failed to fully contain the diversity of public opinion, and the train sometimes provided a very public forum for dissent.

All Aboard the "~~Civil Liberties~~ . . ." er, "Freedom Train"

On April 8, 1946, the Justice Department's William Coblenz formulated the embryonic plan for an archival exhibition train after passing a lunch hour in the National Archives rotunda. As he looked over the documents, Coblenz thought that, fragile though they were, they contained a potential energy—the power to refocus a country that seemed, to him, to be quickly fragmenting after wartime unity. He immediately took the idea to Solon J. Buck, archivist of the United States, and then to his bosses at Justice. Buck endorsed it, as did Attorney General Tom Clark shortly thereafter. In less than forty-eight hours, Coblenz drew up detailed plans for a rail-traveling "Civil Liberties Exhibit." That name too clearly recalled recent communist-led campaigns for justice, so after taking control in late 1946 the project's corporate leadership vetoed it. Coblenz also proposed contrasting America's most important texts with those of Nazi Germany, to more clearly delineate the meaning of American liberty, but this too changed. Some Americans had seen a small collection of German documents on the November–December 1945 "Victory Loan Tour," a modest rail-traveling exhibition created by the National Archives that served as a small-scale model for the Freedom Train.[18] But the final bell had sounded in the fight against fascism, and the contrasting texts would serve no immediate purpose in 1947.

Staff at the National Archives began assembling documents for the traveling "Bill of Rights Exhibit," as it was then called, and Tom Clark took over the project. Despite later corporate domination, it is important to remember that the substantial work done by federal employees made the traveling exhibit possible. Clark later explained his enthusiasm for the project to a congressional committee by noting that the train possessed "the means of aiding the country in its internal war against subversive elements" and would "improve citizenship by reawakening in our people their profound faith in the American historical heritage." Truman gave his "strongest endorsement," and noted, "We have come to a moment in the history of the world, when such an exhibition has timeliness and great educational value."[19] Presumably Truman thought the documents held some value at other times too, but his emphasis on their present utility explains the unusual enthusiasm generated by a historical exhibition. For the business leaders who would soon take over the project, the train did not possess "educational value" so much as it offered educative opportunities.

By September, Coblenz's one-car, three-month exhibition had expanded to a full train and a full year of transcontinental travel. As the venture blossomed, costs grew beyond the point where Congress would fund the project. Clark turned to the private sector, starting with his friend Edwin Weisl, a New York attorney connected to Hollywood. Weisl introduced Paramount Pictures president Barney Balaban and his assistant, Louis Novins, to the project. At Balaban's bidding, Novins quickly made the project his. Shortly thereafter, the National Archive's Elizabeth Hamer commented, "Hollywood, chiefly, is putting up the capital for the exhibit." When Coblenz and McInerny left Washington for a meeting with Balaban and Novins at Paramount's New York offices in November 1946, control of the project went with them. Thereafter, the business, advertising, and media executives determined the character, scope, and content of the Freedom Train.[20]

American business supported the train because of fears that a postwar economic slump might lead to a 1930s-style "assault" on corporations. Emphasizing the importance of unrestricted freedom, the train offered a preemptive argument against a potential second New Deal. Privatization also followed from the wish to avoid charges of propaganda, an ironic situation in light of the massive propaganda campaign soon launched by the corporate sponsors.[21] The public-private partnership represented a continuation of that which began during the war, when the cooperation of the War Advertising Council, the Office of War Information, Hollywood studios, and other corporate and advertising bodies fostered the idea that business was a willing and able ally, and not foe, of government. As Daniel Lykins has shown in his work on the Advertising Council in particular, in the years immediately following World War II, leaders in these organizations impressed upon government officials their abilities to handle precisely these types of propaganda campaigns.[22] For an administration eager to persuade Americans of the necessity of a tough stand against communism, the offer was hard to refuse.

As their first move, Novins and Balaban brought the Advertising Council and its nascent "campaign to sell America to Americans" into the mix. An effort to redefine America on terms palatable to capital and to then sell that new definition to the public, the campaign merged with the Freedom Train under the leadership of Novins and Thomas Brophy, president of the advertising agency Kenyon & Eckhardt, Inc. and a leading figure on the Advertising Council's Board of Directors.[23] Brophy and Novins assembled a group of forty leading men in business and entertainment, including the heads of the networks and Hollywood studios, and major newspaper publishers. In December 1946, they met with the government people—Buck and Hamer from the National Archives, Luther Evans from the Library of Congress, and Coblenz, McInerny, and Clark from Justice—at Clark's office in Washington.

There, Novins presented a broader proposal in which the train's historical documents served as the central focus of a wider reeducation campaign. Reading a statement prepared by Novins, Attorney General Clark stated that the end of war had brought "cynicism, disillusionment, and lawlessness." These words, which would be used often to promote the campaign, referred primarily to the public's perceived lack of faith in the system of free enterprise and labor's rebuff of assurances that what benefited business, benefited all Americans. They also tapped into public fears of a rise in juvenile delinquency and other criminal activity and into establishment concerns that in peacetime a disengaged public would fail to support an aggressively internationalist foreign policy. Novins's statement also claimed that the "indoctrination in democracy" offered by the Freedom Train was "the essential catalytic agent needed to blend our various groups into one American family. Without it, we could not sustain the continuity of our way of life."[24]

In January 1947, Brophy asked Winthrop W. Aldrich, chairman of Chase National Bank, to help get the wheels turning. They incorporated a new organization, the American Heritage Foundation, with Aldrich as chairman, Brophy as president, and Novins as the executive secretary. Aldrich's solidly Republican background effectively silenced complaints from Republicans that Truman was launching a propaganda campaign, unfounded at any rate. Echoing the words of the other prominent organizers, Aldrich announced he supported the project because "cynicism, lawlessness, and seeming disregard for American traditions of fair play and individualism" threatened America.[25]

Through the spring of 1947 Aldrich, Novins, and Clark assembled a board of trustees, carefully including a few men, at least, from beyond the advertising and business worlds. CIO leader Philip Murray and AFL head William Green joined as executive vice presidents: powerless positions, but essential for public relations. Hundreds of contemporary newspaper and magazine articles characterized the project as a government-business-labor collaboration, paid for by individual contributions. But almost all of the funding, and all of the direction, came from corporate America, with Du Pont, U.S. Steel, General Electric, and Standard Oil of New Jersey contributing at least $20,000 each.[26] Labor's role in the campaign paralleled its still prominent but increasingly constrained position within the "corporatized welfare state."[27] In an indication of how narrowly the "broad coalition" was actually construed, no African Americans served on the board. Clark nominated Walter White of the NAACP, but Aldrich and Novins declined to invite him as well as A. Philip Randolph and Lester Granger. Nevertheless, given the widespread support for the campaign, already evident in the spring of 1947, all three of these rejected men felt compelled to announce their support, and each attended a ceremony at the White House in May. White, though, spoke his mind, stating that he was not as worried about foreign ideologies as he was about American lynchings. Still, he pledged the "unqualified support of thirteen million American Negroes who desperately want to see democracy made a living reality in our country."[28]

Complex Motives, Simple Freedom

In addition to the appeal for national unity, the campaign summoned individuals to political participation. For the AHF and others concerned about "creeping socialism," a disengaged public might not worry about, or even notice, the arrival of communism: "Thinking Americans present no problem but non-thinking do—non-thinking Americans who fail to appreciate the blessings of our American Heritage and who refuse to take seriously the duties of American citizenship. These inactive citizens constitute a veritable Sixth Column that threatens the national fabric more critically than all the maneuvers and intrigues of the Fifth Column."[29]

Plenty of other Americans were similarly worried, often with more immediate considerations in mind. *Newsweek* reported in 1948 that leaders in Cowlitz

County, Washington, had written Congress to have the Freedom Train make a stop there after a straw poll found that Henry Wallace led the list of potential presidential candidates with 24 percent of the vote. "As they saw it, approximately one-fourth of Cowlitz County's population of fishermen, lumbermen, and farmers, needed an education in the fundamentals of American democracy."[30] This aspect of the program received even greater attention after Truman's 1948 reelection, when the AHF leadership decided that broadly encouraging political participation, without sufficient "education," was not a wise course for them to follow.[31]

Even among the organizers, freedom served two masters, each with a different use for the word. A perceived need to educate the public motivated the corporate sponsors. They feared that too many Americans failed to understand their "heritage of freedom" correctly—that is, understand that the preservation of freedom required full unambiguous support of free enterprise. The Truman administration shared the concern that the public needed a reminder of the necessity of protecting freedom, but for Truman and Clark, this referred not only to American freedom but also the entire "free world." And theirs was a generally positive political freedom (an assertion of rights) rather than a negative economic freedom (the absence of government regulation). In a March 1947 address to the nation, Truman set forth what became known as the Truman Doctrine. In the speech, the president described the nation's foreign policy as a global struggle for freedom. To gain the public's support, Truman characterized his anticommunist policy as the defense of freedom, proclaimed the United States the leader of the "free world," and demanded America's support for "freedom-loving peoples" all over the globe.[32]

In April 1947, Clark and Aldrich both reached out to Reinhold Niebuhr and asked him to join the board. Niebuhr, who had helped to found Americans for Democratic Action that January, was already serving on the Public Advisory Committee of the Advertising Council and had thus worked with many of the principals involved in the new AHF. Characteristically, Aldrich misled the theologian by writing that the project, including the council's reeducation campaign, was "sponsored by the United States Government." Clark's letter to Niebuhr made no mention of sponsorship but strongly encouraged Niebuhr to join "an effort that has . . . enormous potentialities of re-awakening in Americans the deep-seated reverence I know them to have for the exalted history of our country." Niebuhr hardly shared Clark or Aldrich's view of American history (entirely un-"ironic," as it were), or their understanding of the purpose of the past. In *The Irony of American History* Niebuhr responded directly to the type of assurances provided by the AHF when he wrote, "the price which American culture had paid for this amelioration of social tensions through constantly expanding production has been considerable. It has created moral illusions about the ease with which the adjustment of interests to interests can be made in human society."[33] His participation is better explained by the overlap between the AHF's rhetoric about serious civic engagement and his own interest in encouraging Americans to consider the less pleasant realities of both their own history and the eternal human condition. He may have been attracted as well by the campaign's ecumenical approach to religion, which related to the postwar interfaith movement. Novins, Balaban, and other business leaders involved with the AHF also worked for religious tolerance, and their campaign, like the interfaith movement, emphasized a Judeo-Christian tradition.[34] It also stressed strong religious faith as the best counterbalance to communism. As if to illustrate these perceived connections between a consensus religious faith, the American economic system, and anticommunism, when Will Herberg pronounced the process of unifying the American faiths complete in 1955, he also noted that "free enterprise" had formed the basis of this new "common religion."[35]

Widespread desire for a vital, anticommunist civil religion contributed to the popularity of the train. Niebuhr argued that dual dangers—communism and secularism—confronted Americans in the late 1940s, and he sought greater integration of religion into political life, though not necessarily in the celebratory form adopted by the AHF. Only through careful study of its own ethical principles, rooted in the Judeo-Christian tradition, could the United States succeed in its Cold War mission without losing its soul. Robert Bellah retrospectively characterized this particular vision of American civil religion, which sought to transform patriotic worship into a spiritual quest, as ultimately interested in transcending the nation. Instead, he thought, it ended up fostering the worship of "universal" Judeo-Christian core values that, in turn, allowed postwar Americans to see their own way of life as the global ideal.[36] Similarly, in 1945 Carl Becker described how civic celebrations and patriotic holidays reminded Americans that "their institutions and freedoms are the kind of institutions and freedoms best suited to all mankind because prescribed by the law of nature and the will of God."[37] When the Freedom Train arrived in Washington, DC, on November 27, 1947, Speaker of the House Joe Martin said, "It is a symbol of our humble faith in God, our faith in ourselves, and our heart-deep desire to help the rest of the world to see, to learn, to share, and to love the marvelous fruits of freedom as have we in the United States."[38]

In canned form, actual fruits were being collected for distribution in Italy and France by a transcontinental Friendship Train that ran contemporaneously with the Freedom Train. Newspaper articles sometimes confused or combined the two trains, partly because of their simultaneity, but the confusion also reveals more significant meaning. In different but related ways, both the Freedom and Friendship Trains symbolized, in the most positively benevolent terms, America's new Cold War roles as provider and protector. Starting with twelve boxcars in Los Angeles, the Friendship Train soon dwarfed its better-known brother, growing to hundreds of cars stocked full of flour, dried and canned produce, sugar, evaporated milk, and pasta.[39] During the Freedom Train's run, Americans also were asked to reduce their food consumption in order to "help Europe's hungry."[40] Though noble in intention, the proclaimed food emergency undoubtedly fostered a sense of crisis that made the Freedom Train's message seem more important and also offered Americans another way to show how strong Judeo-Christian values meshed with an aggressive defense of freedom.

Less theologically sophisticated public figures echoed Niebuhr's arguments for the necessity of religious engagement. John Foster Dulles, one of just four members on the Documents Committee that selected which historic texts to display on the Freedom Train, suggested that the most pressing need was to "regain confidence in our spiritual heritage."[41] Whitaker Chambers wrote in his autobiography of the need to face communism with an equally powerful faith—one that drew upon both religious and political belief. "At every point," he wrote, "religion and politics interlace, and must do so more acutely as the conflict between the two great camps of men—those who reject and those who worship God—becomes irrepressible." Chambers's words allude to the fact that the new postwar civil religion was more inclusive than the old, but also more tightly controlled and defined. Eisenhower's famous injunction that "our government makes no sense unless it is founded on a deeply held religious belief—and I don't care what it is," followed from this same sense of an urgent need for adhering to a *faith* other than communism. So did the change in the national motto from "*E Pluribus Unum*" to "In God We Trust" and the addition of the words "under God" to the Pledge of Allegiance.

Contemporary Americans also heard this theology espoused by evangelist Billy Graham. William Randolph Hearst started to "puff Graham" at about the same time that he joined with the AHF to promote the Freedom Train. The publisher's admiration for Graham's blend of "morality and fervid Americanism" underlay his support of the train as well. Graham contributed to the cause of religious unity through his "willingness to ignore doctrinal and institutional barriers in gathering his forces." And his brand of religion shared the AHF's vision of what "rededication" could accomplish—"the staying of God's wrath against all humankind," and American civilization in particular.

The same theme of civic responsibility through individual morality stressed by the AHF was apparent when Graham implored, "You say, 'But Billy, I'm only one person.' Ah, yes, but when you make your decision, it is America through you making its decision." Individual conversion, experienced by millions, would redeem the nation.[42]

The Freedom Train similarly emphasized national redemption through individual participation and conversion. The editors of *Palimpsest*, the popular history journal of the Iowa State Historical Society, noticed a "continuing pattern that shows up among these documents [that stresses] the importance of the individual human being."[43] Like the Christian fixation on individual salvation, this approach may have comforted people who felt overwhelmed by mass society and global war, and whose economic fortunes seemed to depend on forces beyond their control. Insofar as the train encouraged a belief in individual potential following the necessary conversion act of "rededication," it closely resembled Graham's crusade for individual and national salvation.

Other postwar intellectuals and public figures believed that a strong, stable society must hold and agree upon a set of sacred beliefs and symbols. Emile Durkheim formulated this theory of social cohesion in the early decades of the century, which American sociologists had by the 1940s recast in American terms. Talcott Parsons and W. Lloyd Warner in particular argued that society breaks down if shared public symbols, "invested with religious significance," cease to be worshipped in "periodic collective rites" that affirm core traditions and values.[44] The uneasy international situation of the late 1940s led many Americans to a greater sense of urgency regarding such rites of rededication.[45] J. Paul Johnson wrote in his popular postwar textbook on American religion that democracy by itself was "insufficient to carry through the crises of the coming decade." The religious fanaticism of communists had to be faced down by a similar faith in democracy as the will of God: "Democracy had to be made no less than 'an object of religious dedication.'" This required regular "ceremonial reinforcement."[46]

The Freedom Train ultimately functioned like the reinforcement for which these prescriptions called, and it helped mold American civil religion into a form fitted for the fight against communism. W. Lloyd Warner's work in the 1950s on Memorial Day parades applies almost equally well to Freedom Train ceremonies; both functioned as key civil religious rituals, and both expressed, as Warner said, the unity of the participants as a group with a nonsectarian God. The train thus demonstrated the "fluid" relationship between secular and religious ritual in the United States.[47] It demanded worship, and it became a symbol—not of historical American freedom, as the organizers claimed, but of a specific type of patriotism that the campaign helped to construct.

Defining Freedom

Is it for real—or just a show again?

Langston Hughes,
"Freedom Train"

In May 1947 the name changed finally from "Liberty Train" to "Freedom Train," and Truman hosted the launch party at the White House on May 22.[48] "All Americans," Novins explained to the assembled crowd, "meet on the common ground of their American Heritage . . . the soul of their way of life. Without our heritage of freedom, differences become subversive, personal opinions become futile, and controversy becomes anarchy." The documents on the train, he continued, would turn the ancient but abstract principles that underlay the nation's existence into "vital factors for our everyday existence." Novins laid out the three phases of the American Heritage Foundation program. First, the Freedom Train would carry the documents, "sanctified by the blood of martyrs." Second, each community visited by the train would hold a Rededication Week. Each day would have its own special designation, such as Veteran's, Labor and Industry, Women, Schools, Bench and Bar, and Freedom of Religion. Third, the Advertising Council would simultaneously coordinate a national campaign to resell "America" to Americans.[49]

Even though control of the project had passed from the public to the private sector, the original expectations of these documents remained unchanged: they would provide a unifying foundation for postwar society. The difference was in the specific results wished for by the various groups involved. The National Archives and Justice Department staff had proposed and begun to assemble an exhibit focused on civil rights. This exhibit prominently featured documentation of economic and social reforms of the twentieth century. The documents would serve as examples of effective legislation and point Americans in the direction of continued reform. The corporate sponsors and organizers envisioned a different future and thus wanted the train's documents to encourage patriotic worship of a more restrictive "freedom"—namely, free enterprise.

Some key documents had been selected, but many decisions still had to be made. Two unequal committees shared this burden. First, the Documents Advisory Committee made recommendations. This committee consisted of the librarian of Congress, Luther Evans; the archivist of the United States, Solon J. Buck (usually represented by Elizabeth Hamer); Princeton historian Julian P. Boyd; renowned collector A. S. W. Rosenbach; and several others. This panel of experts submitted their proposals to the Documents Committee, which possessed the real power and made the final decisions. This group consisted of a different sort and included John Foster Dulles, John W. Davis (Democratic nominee for the presidency in 1924, anti–New Dealer, and later defendant's counsel in *Brown vs. Board of Education*), William Aldrich, and Ed Weisl. They rejected proposals for documentation of the immigrant experience, forbade anything related to Jews because they were deemed too controversial, declined Executive Order 8802, which established the Fair Employment Practices Commission, as well as the recent Report of the President's Commission on Civil Rights, and dictated that no documents related to labor unions would be included. Elizabeth Hamer, the archivist who had first started compiling documents during the previous summer, expressed her utter disillusionment with the AHF by March 1947, calling the Documents Committee "a bunch of reactionaries."[50] The train might have carried a very different selection of texts had the organizational structure not privileged the views of the business-oriented group over those of the advisers trained in history. This again illustrates the tight control exercised by the corporate interests.

Historians have described the selected documents of the Freedom Train as representative of consensus history.[51] Without question, the AHF, as well as the Truman administration, presented the history of the United States in a manner that suggested minimal conflict among Americans and a broad unity of purpose in foreign affairs. Avoiding divisive issues such as race and economics, the committee limited the amount of internal strife to a selective reading of the history of women's suffrage — a relatively safe and contemporarily contained topic. The Civil War documents erased slavery with the Emancipation Proclamation and the Thirteenth Amendment, but the absence of the Fourteenth and Fifteenth Amendments left African American civil rights unaddressed. The highlight of the period, the Gettysburg Address, was itself a consensus-building speech and featured here in just that way — though Lincoln himself proved a contentious choice for inclusion.[52] Other wartime documents on the train yielded no hint of dissent or doubt.

However, this selection process reveals something beyond consensus. The perceived threat from the USSR motivated the drive for national unity that in turn demanded consensus history (and religion). The Truman administration involved itself in the Freedom Train project largely out of this concern. The AHF's participation was, in contrast, driven primarily by corporate fears of labor unrest and strength. Document selection was only the first step in an advertising blitz that ultimately depended on the texts less for what they said than for what they symbolized, as interpreted by the foundation. Consensus stood in front of the ultimate goal: the redefinition of America in terms of a deliberately vague, yet singular, "freedom," which meant more than anything the freedom of business to act without restriction.

For Freedom Train visitors and Rededication Week participants, freedom remained an elusive term. Mostly it escaped definition. The accompanying parade in Sioux City, Iowa, "proved," according to the city's *Journal* newspaper, that America "has freedom, appreciates that freedom and is ready, if necessary, to defend that freedom." It further demonstrated that "what we crave in this country is a FREE society." The failure to consider what freedom meant typified press coverage of the campaign. Instead, newspapers followed the AHF in celebrating a heroic conception of the "heritage of freedom." The *Des Moines Register* commented, "Documents are symbols. . . . And when you board the Freedom Train you'll believe again in all the great men who set us free. You'll believe in the reality of your American freedom. You'll realize all over again the need to . . . perpetuate the American legend."[53]

While "freedom" enjoyed widespread support, not everyone went along with the campaign's usage or heeded the call for overt displays of patriotism. Communists pointed out that the Truman administration's chant of freedom coincided with its imposition of the Loyalty Oath for federal employees, a point made also by Henry Wallace, who attacked the train as a symbol of dangerous, bipartisan Cold War consensus. Wallace had spoken of the "free world" long before Truman did, but his category included the Soviet Union and referred to a world in which the "common man" had real power.[54] Wallace also questioned the proclaimed "unity" by citing discrimination faced by African Americans, unfair persecution of Jews by "the Loyalty Order," and repression of workers under the "undemocratic" Taft-Hartley Act.[55] The Communist Party viewed the train as "democratic camouflage": a "huge propaganda cover-up for the most widespread violation of the Bill of Rights and the Constitution in our history."[56] *Pravda* labeled it "hypocrisy on wheels." "Hired radio liars, provincial Senators, and 'selfless' business men, atomic diplomats and pro-Fascist philosophers advertise freedom so hard they foam at the mouth."[57]

The critique strikes at the heart of the whole campaign: the organizers' co-optation of the word "freedom." While the Communist Party correctly identified the word's centrality and rightly questioned its usage, the critique overlooked the divisions within the campaign regarding freedom's meaning. At the christening of the train at its first stop in Philadelphia, Tom Clark explained how the United States must share its freedom with the world, else "there will soon be no freedom for anyone." "Smashing his fist on the speaker's table," Clark demanded, "All of us must be free or none of us are free."[58] The attorney general's public statements about the train always emphasized this point—freedom was an all-or-nothing proposition, at home and abroad. When not talking about exporting democracy, Clark spoke against America's "worst enemy": prejudice. "When you find a man who is prejudiced against some certain group of Americans because of color, race, or religion," he said at the Philadelphia launch, "you can set it down that he is an ignorant man." In what he saw as the train's implicit refutation of prejudice, Clark believed it would help to "put this badly torn up world back on the right track." Truman likewise stated that America's "noble heritage of freedom for the individual citizen, without distinction because of race, creed or color," offered the world the "great hope of lasting peace."[59]

The AHF's definition of freedom varied little from that of business and advertising organizations of the previous decades. Freedom was negative—the removal of all constraints on business enterprise. The only addition was the adoption of an internationalist meaning that included the promotion of free enterprise as freedom abroad. The business community's trend toward internationalism started during World War II and persisted as the desire to "continue the prosperity of war corporatism undergirded [its] support for postwar economically based internationalist policies."[60] In this significant area of overlap the Truman administration's tough anticommunist foreign policy partnered with the interests of big business.

Four months before his death in 1945, historian Carl Becker delivered a series of lectures on "Freedom and Responsibility in the American Way of Life." Contrasting Becker's lectures with the Freedom Train spotlights certain aspects of the AHF program and reveals several limitations. Like the AHF, Becker worried that Americans lacked an understanding of both their freedoms and their responsibilities as citizens. And like the Freedom Train, he illustrated his points through key documents of American history. The state and federal constitutions of the United States, he began, "disclose the annoying fact that for every right or freedom they confer they impose, implicitly if not explicitly, a corresponding obligation or responsibility." For most of America history, freedom without much responsibility had proved sufficient. In "normal times," Americans could treat "politics casually, even cynically, as a diverting game." Now, however, the situation had changed, and Becker called upon his fellow citizens to focus "far more serious and intelligent attention to public affairs."[61]

Each lecture examined a freedom that Becker said was constitutionally guaranteed in order to determine what it really meant, what aspects of that meaning were truly essential to contemporary American life, and what responsibilities were implicit in each essential freedom. What makes Becker's lectures even more interesting, in this context, is his concern about the growing influence of corporations and the advertising industry on an uninformed public. Thus, while his message appears similar to the AHF's, Becker's concern is that Americans know their rights and obligations in order to protect themselves *against* organizations like the AHF. "[T]he thinking of the average citizen and his opinion about public affairs is in very great measure shaped by . . . ideas that the selective process of private economic enterprise presents to him for consideration—information the truth of which he cannot verify; ideas formulated by persons unknown to him, and too often inspired by economic, political, religious, or other interests that are never avowed."[62]

Becker's personal campaign also differed from the AHF's in terms of which freedoms composed the American heritage. Free enterprise did not necessarily make the list. In fact, "economics and politics are not separable from ethics and morality," and "advising the people not to discuss the institution of private enterprise" is a rather devious way of concealing the "central issue" facing postwar Americans. Additionally, he criticized vague appeals to "revere the founding fathers" and their eighteenth-century solutions. Better to follow their example and "re-examin[e] the fundamental human rights and the economic and political institutions best suited to secure them." Perhaps, he provocatively suggested, a critical, collective analysis of the founding documents would reveal that the government structure created almost two hundred years before no longer suited the "complicated problems" of 1945.[63]

Historian Eric Goldman provides another example of the historical profession's attitude toward the project in his review of Frank Monaghan's *Heritage of Freedom* catalog of the Freedom Train exhibit in the *Mississippi Valley Historical Review*. Goldman points out that, without exception, "the documents do not concern social reforms of the last half century." While the wish to avoid controversy partly explains this, he suggests that the "key fact" is that the "overwhelming emphasis of the documents defines American liberty as the establishment and defense of political independence and of political and religious liberties"—which Becker referred to as negative liberty. In contrast, Goldman thinks that many Americans understand American freedom as "including opportunities for a generally better life." And from a policy standpoint, is it wise, he asks, "to offer a quasi-official conception of American liberty that has precisely the limitations which the Soviet Union gleefully assigns it?"[64]

As the train moved through each and every state, the press, engaged citizens, and political and civic leaders continued to define freedom in ways that sometimes went well beyond the AHF's construction. For example, a new and short-lived journal called *Freedom & Union: Journal of the World Republic* adopted the Freedom Train into its movement for world government. Looking at the same historical documents, the editors saw George Washington arguing for a global "Union of the Free" and the gradual creation of a universal republic. Similarly, a Baltimore attorney suggested that a peace plane modeled on the Freedom

Train should circle the globe promoting a new United Nations citizenship. Other groups and causes advertised themselves through the claim that they could best preserve the most vital ideals of the Freedom Train.[65] Even some of the official speakers at AHF events challenged the campaign's emphasis on free enterprise as the central tenet of American freedom. A Cornell College (Iowa) professor, an Austrian refugee, told an Iowa crowd, "Freedom is liberty plus groceries . . . when the stomach gets hungry our senses of liberty and freedom sometimes gets lost."[66] Labor leaders associated with the campaign also voiced dissent. At a labor-management luncheon in New York staged to demonstrate consensus, A. F. Whitney, president of the Brotherhood of Railroad Trainmen, spoke out against "industrialists who reaped millions of dollars during the two world wars." His speech celebrating labor's contributions to society contrasted sharply with Balaban's praise for business.[67]

Despite high overall participation, the public showed signs of skepticism. In some of the first cities visited, the train was preceded or soon followed by a rally of the Progressive Citizens of America (PCA). In fact, the PCA held its Philadelphia rally during the Freedom Train's inauguration there.[68] Reiterating his objections to the campaign and proclaiming the need for negotiation rather than confrontation with the USSR, an end to segregation, and protections for labor, Henry Wallace would address the crowd following entertainment provided by John Garfield and Zero Mostel. Speakers varied but included Paul Robeson, Lena Horne, and PCA vice chairman Dr. Frank Kingdon. Robeson connected with the Freedom Train in a unique way: his recording of Langston Hughes's poem "Freedom Train," sold through advertisements in the black press for one dollar, promoted Hughes's skeptical take on "our American heritage."[69] The fall 1947 PCA events were well attended. In New York Wallace drew between 20,000 and 25,000 to Madison Square Garden—at least 6,000 more than the train's highest single-day total in the New York City area, though the train stopped there for almost a week. In Providence, the Freedom Train drew about 12,000 on October 8, 1947; Wallace drew 5,000 two nights later. About 7,200 saw him in Boston and another 5,600 in Cambridge. In comparison, throughout its tour the train averaged onboard attendance of 9,000 per day. Even though that number excludes the related Rededication Week events, considering the vast gulf between the two organizations' promotional abilities, the fact that the PCA crowds were not terrifically smaller than those of the Freedom Train indicates a fair amount of public ambivalence, perhaps even discomfort, toward the AHF project. This created concern for local business associations, Elks lodges, and the like that claimed the Communist Party was engineering a secret campaign to co-opt the train's message and define freedom in more radical terms—or it at least provided a convenient motivational tool for the AHF's local supporters that they used to drum up support.[70]

Some protestors challenged the narrow definition of freedom through more overt actions. Reactions to these protests reveal how the campaign tried to control freedom's meaning. In New Orleans a group called "4 Freedoms 4 All" demanded the inclusion of the Wagner Act and FEPC Order 8802, picketing the train and presenting copies of both documents to the traveling public relations director. He did not add them to the exhibit.[71] In Philadelphia and New York, demonstrators picketed the train on behalf of conscientious objectors to World War II who remained imprisoned for exercising too much freedom. Even though New York police had earlier given protestors permission to demonstrate, the police "ripped placards from stanchions, broke the wooden standards into small bits," and silenced them by force. A photographer who captured the "herding of one group into a shoe store doorway" was himself arrested, further mocking the train's contents.[72] At other stops, "soap boxers" waited until they were inside the train to begin speaking, in which cases the marines "escorted the protesting offender, as gently as possible, to the exit."[73] Some people protested less directly. Several wrote to the *New York Times* to point out the discrepancy between rhetoric and practice mentioned above, and one reader wrote the *Hartford Courant* that the president and Congress were acting to "negate" freedom even while they celebrated it with the train. Many African Americans wrote letters to the black press that generally shared the sentiment that "this train has shown what a farce our so-called democracy is." A Marine Corps–Navy chaplain wrote the *Washington Post* that truly "free" men "do not have to sign loyalty pledges, or visit Freedom Trains, or shout 'Red, Red' in order to obtain or preserve freedom."[74] Not all Americans appreciated the call to wear one's patriotism on one's sleeve, and not all accepted the AHF's definition of freedom.

More positively, protests directed at southern segregation on the Freedom Train elicited a relatively firm stance against "the essential un-Americanism of such attitudes" from the organizers and from most of the country, though it took protests by the NAACP and the Urban League to make southern plans for segregating the train an issue.[75] If the train isolated communists who objected to its interpretation of the past, it also excluded southern segregationists from its definition of Americanism—a "moral victory with implications far beyond the immediate event," noted the *Washington Post*.[76] Indeed, the African American press seems to have understood the stance as a sea change that exposed segregationists as isolated and anachronistic racists, even if readers often expressed a more disillusioned attitude in letters and man-on-the-street interviews.[77] In effect, African American elites essentially ignored the AHF's efforts to co-opt "freedom" and instead created their own definition. The NAACP led the protests in the South and organized boycotts in case the AHF allowed the train to appear in recalcitrant locales, particularly Memphis and Birmingham. Local chapters involved themselves with the AHF's local committees and did their best to ensure a desegregated train. Some of these AHF committees contained local African American elites; Little Rock's was actually chaired by an African American doctor and political activist, J. M. Robinson.[78]

The AHF prohibited strict segregation in the train cars but quietly compromised to accommodate a few cities that wanted to maintain separate lines outside of the train. But in Birmingham, where plans called for alternating group entry so that modified segregation would exist inside the train, the local NAACP chapter refused to countenance compromise. Finally, five days before the train's scheduled appearance, Brophy cancelled the Birmingham stop.[79] In Memphis, evidently acting at the behest of the "Boss" Crump political machine, Mayor James Pleasant explained that "Negroes would be embarrassed if segregation policies were removed," and they were "satisfied with conditions" as they were. Thus, Memphis denied the Freedom Train. But other Memphis whites, led by the American Veterans Committee and supported by the state's liberal newspapers and the local Americans for Democratic Action, began a petition drive that called on the mayor to reverse his decision.[80] In a twist on the usual feel-good news stories of Americans trekking great distances to see the Freedom Train, approximately twenty thousand Memphians traveled eighty-eight miles to the train in Jackson, Tennessee, to demonstrate their spite for their mayor. In elections the following summer, Crump's candidates were soundly defeated by a coalition of Labor, African Americans, and white liberals, a result traced directly to the Freedom Train controversy.[81] For a moment at least, reality matched the rhetoric.

Other southern cities allowed entry on a first-come, first-served basis, regardless of color. In Montgomery, two African American girls boarded the train before anyone else, without incident. The experiments in integration in Little Rock, Mobile, Atlanta, and other cities also worked just fine.[82] In New Orleans, the local NAACP vigorously protested initial plans that called for segregation, and when citizens eventually boarded the train there was none.[83] However, Rededication Week events, put on by local businesses and community organizations, often remained segregated, and some African Americans declined to embrace the Freedom Train. An editor of Little Rock's *Arkansas State Press* noted that he was "already familiar with the great freedom-charged documents of English and American history and will wish to donate his space in the line to some undemocratic white person who may need to learn about them."[84]

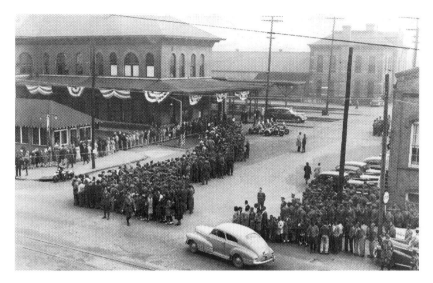

Some southern cities kept in place a system of segregation outside of the Freedom Train and acquiesced to the American Heritage Foundation's demand for desegregated train cars by alternating entry for groups of whites and blacks. While waiting to board the train on December 29, 1947, residents of Columbus, Georgia, including a large number of African American soldiers, had hours to contemplate their counterparts in the other line. (Courtesy of National Archives and Records Administration.)

The meaning of freedom here has nothing to do with free enterprise and everything to do with civil rights. African Americans defined freedom and American heritage very differently from the AHF. Rather than celebrating past achievements or recalling a common and idealized heritage, the black press viewed the train and its documents as spurs to radical change. A kind of demanding optimism pervades the hundreds of news stories mentioning the Freedom Train (far more than in white newspapers), heralding renewed hope for African Americans in the later 1940s. And it appeared segregation was suffering serious defeats, including Jackie Robinson's April 1947 debut in major league baseball, the president's Commission on Civil Rights' November 1947 report, "To Secure These Rights," and Truman's Executive Order 9981, issued in July 1948, to desegregate the armed forces. The *Chicago Defender* reviewed 1947–48 as a period of nearly innumerable victories in the war against racial prejudice, and the NAACP presented a special award to the AHF in January 1948—somewhat ironic given the early exclusion of African Americans from the national organization but indicative of how effectively black elites had rerouted the campaign. According to the *Defender*, during train visits, "friction between the races was at a standstill."[85] The South, with the exception of an apparent minority, embraced the AHF's no segregation policy. Even after the cancellations in Birmingham and Memphis, the *Chicago Defender*, Kansas City's *Plaindealer*, Little Rock's *Arkansas State Press*, and other African American newspapers celebrated the moral victory over reactionary forces as the beginning of the end of Jim Crow.

The liberal white press and the communist *Daily Worker* wrote about the apparent triumph in similar terms, and there was overlap in the papers on other issues as well. After the train's last stop, an editorial in the *Arkansas State Press* that evaluated the journey focused not on the segregation issue but on the implicit protections for labor that the documents contained. Free speech, freedom of religion, freedom from unreasonable searches, and the right to join a union to better one's economic position—these were the meaningful freedoms. Free enterprise garnered no mention.[86]

Clearly, for all its efforts, the AHF failed to sell everyone its distinct distillation of American history. As the *Chicago Defender* editorialized, "The Freedom Train may be a good idea—but we want its sponsors to understand that the Negro people know the score, know the real documents, understand the hollowness of three amendments in the Constitution—and what would happen to a labor man if he sought to quote the Declaration of Independence to certain of the sponsors of the Freedom Train." Unless the AHF could explain the gap between the language in the documents and the realities of economic and racial inequality, many Americans would take the message ironically.[87]

The segregation issue still dogged the train all over the country and was not always resolved as well as in the Deep South. The Virginia leg of the journey occurred before the AHF came up with its rules for the South, and the NAACP complained that several cities in that state practiced some degree of segregation while hosting the train. The same was true at the first stops in Georgia. In Oklahoma City one hundred members of an African American chorus quit a historical pageant after being told they would be kept out of a "'melting pot' scene" and a "statues of freedom scene" and would have to sit separately in the balcony. As with other troublesome groups along the route, the choristers' actions merited charges of communism.[88]

Outspoken women were treated to similar accusations. In an April 1948 *Washington Post* column, Malvina Lindsay connected a "below-the-belt" campaign against the Women's Action Committee for Lasting Peace to both the Freedom Train and a broader effort to intimidate women out of politics by labeling them communists. As evidence that the attacks worked, Lindsay noted that at least one town had tried to bar the local branch of the committee from participating in Freedom Train ceremonies on the grounds that they were communists.[89] Women visited the train at every stop, of course, but they also engaged with the campaign through Rededication Week "Women's Days" and were thus granted the same status as Labor and Industry, Sports, Religion, and so on.[90] Women's Days were usually devoted to the same sort of patriotic ceremony as the other days, containing little that focused on issues of particular importance to women. Many speakers and attendees were male, while honored women were often the wives of prominent men. Probably many women connected to the campaign more through retailers that used the Freedom Train logo in their sale advertisements and shop window displays. Some cities actually created a combined "Women's and Merchants' Day," further clarifying how female citizens fit in the plans.[91]

On top of the exclusion of women from the AHF's committees and board, as well as the charge of communism leveled against politically active women, the confinement of women to a single, separate day in which they were marginalized still further reflected the "disappearing" of women from the political sphere in the age of McCarthyism.[92] The special news features written and distributed for local publication by the AHF that targeted women outlined a different form of participation in the campaign than that identified in the articles written for men. These pieces encouraged engagement, asking female readers if they measured up to Abigail Adams or Lucretia Mott, and demanded that contemporary American women accept their responsibilities to preserve freedom. At the same time, however, they presented a narrower definition of political participation and condescendingly explained what freedom meant for women. American heritage means more than "a precious stone" or a family heirloom; it also refers to "the independence which was won for you." For women, unlike men, the right to vote was a "privilege" for which they should be grateful. "Liberty" might be best understood as the freedom to buy the fashions that made American women "internationally famous." One article summarized the women's rights movement, noting the "wives and mothers and sweethearts" of the nineteenth century had "asked that they be allowed" their rights, which was "our lady ancestors' way" of "arriving" on the political scene. Moreover, as was "typical of American women, they arrived with escort," meaning they were all "happily married and mothers of large broods," just like the women honored on Women's Days. The features repeatedly reminded women of their work at home, even while ostensibly defending their right to work outside the home. One article related the history of women's fight "for the right to speak on issues which mothers and wives hold dear." Another piece, titled "History Proves a Woman's Place Is in Home and Office," referred to "their heritage of a place in business and family life." Women had to do their jobs in "two spheres," both of which demanded their full dedication, and for them "freedom" clearly meant greater responsibility.[93]

Onboard

The tour began in Philadelphia on September 17, 1947, the 160th anniversary of the signing of the Constitution. "Constructed as a National Shrine," it cost $175,000 to outfit the train with steel and thick plastic display cases, close off windows with steel walls, install fluorescent lighting, and paint the interior a "subdued greenish-blue" and the exterior a solid white with red, white, and blue stripes running the length of the train. Inside, display cases lined both sides of each car in a slightly zigzagged configuration. Murals constructed of clear plastic and white outlines depicted historical themes or famous persons next to some of the exhibited documents. These consisted of a few great men and several military victories. Exemplifying this philosophy of exhibit, the mural next to the Emancipation Proclamation contained no African Americans. Instead, it depicted several stages of Abraham Lincoln's life in a fashion not unlike church murals or windows that depict scenes from the life of saints or Christ.[94]

The first car entered contained documents from the colonial era through the nineteenth century. Memorabilia and exhibits of documents connected with famous Americans lined the second. The third car held twentieth-century material, especially World War II memorabilia. Of these "most cherished documents of our American past," eleven hailed from the colonial era or earlier. This group included a copy of the Magna Carta, a letter written by Columbus that described the West Indies, the Mayflower Compact, two documents from the free speech trial of John Peter Zenger, Roger Williams's statement on religious freedom, and the first book printed in the colonies (by Stephen Daye, in 1644). Fifty-four documents represented the revolutionary generation, including what most people thought of as the highlight of the train, Jefferson's draft of the Declaration of Independence. The nineteenth-century exhibits were few in comparison, reflecting the unstated assumption that the founding—the sacred origins of the nation—required the most veneration and offered the best guidance as well. Just six documents covered the antebellum period, eight had some connection to the Civil War, and only two came from the Gilded Age, both concerning women's suffrage. Late nineteenth-century conflicts between business and labor earned no representation on the train, nor did anything related to the rise of corporations and the great captains of industry. The eight Civil War documents included an offer of elephants by the king of Siam to President Lincoln; no one seems to have asked why this should be considered as one of the most significant documents of American history. World War II dominated the twentieth-century car with almost thirty documents. This emphasis was logical given the project's goal of rekindling the wartime spirit of unity but also typified the historical imbalance. The remaining eight documents included the constitutional amendment guaranteeing women's suffrage, six documents that demonstrated the benevolence of American empire, and Woodrow Wilson's draft for a League of Nations, which was the sole reference to World War I.[95] A separate display case contained the "Bonds of Freedom," which displayed a selection of U.S. Treasury bonds from 1779 to 1947. When America really needed money, the exhibit suggested, it raised funds through bonds—not higher taxes. Moreover, the exhibit framed the bonds in the context of individual stock ownership, something that the Ad Council and the AHF's corporate sponsors pushed hard for in the years after World War II as a way of merging the interests of average Americans with big business. Through the purchase of Treasury bonds, Americans bought "shares in America" and made a tangible and personal investment in the nation.[96]

Surprisingly little explanation accompanied the documents, perhaps because any interpretation contained within it the possibility of conflict. National Archives staff delivered the documents to the train and watched to see they were correctly installed and secured in the cars that Novins designed himself, but they expressed concern about the AHF's methods of selection, preservation, and exposition.[97] Though they did not know it at the time, after the Freedom Train terminated, the exhibit cases would find their way into the National Archives, serving as the permanent and frustratingly inflexible Circular Gallery exhibition area until modest remodeling funds came available decades later.[98] The AHF's labels offered basic facts: date, author, and perhaps a sentence or two of identification. For example, Washington's copy of the Constitution "shows corrections in his large, firm handwriting," but nothing explained the significance of those corrections. The label for Edmund Randolph's speech to the Constitutional Convention on May 29, 1787, read simply: "This, the so-called 'Virginia Plan,' became the framework from which the Constitution was drafted."[99] The lack of explanation suggests again that the specifics of the documents mattered very little to the organizers as long as they contained nothing explicitly contrary to their goals. The train symbolically transported freedom—that was the important thing to know.

Millions of Americans turned out to show their support for freedom and to bask in the aura of the famous documents. Once the train arrived in each of 322 American communities, the overwhelming majority of visitors—over 90 percent in some places—never made it onboard. Of the 50 million people (one in three Americans) who participated in at least some part of the campaign, only 3.5 million actually beheld the "immortal parchments."[100] Much of the campaign focused on schools and encouraged children to attend the ceremonial events surrounding the train's arrival. Yet at many stops only two lucky children per school gained entry, unless they visited in an unofficial capacity and waited in line with everyone else. Adults often waited for a full day and in the end could be found still standing on the platform.

Other happenings kept those in line occupied. Small-time entrepreneurs hawked souvenirs at every stop, persisting despite attempts by the AHF to regulate this market. Performance artists and singers entertained crowds in exchange for tips, and children played tag and other games.[101] In the South, visitors to the train must have spent a considerable portion of their long wait contemplating the mixed crowd. In those cities that insisted on partial segregation, photographs show people standing in the two lines looking across rather intently at their opposite number.[102] Officially, queued visitors heard speeches from local dignitaries and received copies of the *Good Citizen* pamphlet and the *Reader's Digest* "Bill of Rights."[103]

For those who made it inside the "rolling treasure house," marines on duty ushered them through as quickly as possible. Early on, organizers changed the background music that played through speakers in each car to faster-paced songs that would keep people moving. Those who gained admittance "got 20 to 30 minutes of the greatest show on earth—a heart-warming, soul-stirring exhibit of the documents that made the United States free—and great."[104] In fact, over the whole tour, time spent in the train averaged just fifteen to twenty minutes, leaving just a few seconds per document.[105] The ostensible purpose for removing these priceless papers from their secure locations and taking them on the road was that people needed to read and experience these texts for themselves. But in practice the train's administrators showed very little concern for this. In New York, visitors engaged with each document for a longer period of time than anywhere else on the tour. While there, Walter O'Brien, the train's traveling director, commented, "People seem to be spending more time reading the documents. It's a good thing in a way, but it keeps other people from seeing them." To increase flow, New York City police joined with the marines to usher people through more quickly, and the background music was frequently interrupted by pleas to hurry along.[106]

Reading each document on the train was impossible; in fact, reading even one document proved to be a challenge in all but the smallest towns on the tour. Instead, "It is enough, in the short time that can logically be apportioned, to gaze with silent admiration at the matchless scene: to experience a mood of reverence; to spend an unforgettable moment among these documents of our liberties."[107] The reverence accorded the documents followed partly from their presentation, which suggested that these sheets of paper granted certain freedoms and guarantees at suitable moments in history. Or else some famous person granted it at that time. Either way, the implication was that something very significant happened because someone important wrote and signed this piece of paper. In this mode of explanation, there are no social movements, no people, and no history.

Americans had also been told, by many levels of authority, that they should be impressed by the documents in a spiritual way. Walter Benjamin's position that these originals would have possessed an aura for viewers that facsimiles could not also helps to explain why people endured such long waits for just a fleeting glimpse. More recently, Rachel Maines and James Glynn have explored the meaning of objects' "numinosity": their presumed association with somebody or something great. For many museum visitors and history buffs, society's sacred texts and objects seem to be "inhabited by a *numen* or spirit that calls forth . . . a reaction of awe or reverence."[108] Public history professionals grapple with how to balance this reverence with critical perspective, but the AHF actively encouraged the former while ignoring the latter.

Reverent observation did not necessitate careful study in the way that, for example, Becker's invitation for critical analysis would have done. The fact that most participants in the campaign never set foot in the train, and the fact that those who did see the documents were only permitted by their military custodians to quietly and quickly admire them as they passed by, indicate how organizers thought the texts should be used—*not* as subjects for historical study, but as something that they could point to while making their arguments to the crowds outside. *National Geographic* inadvertently touched on this when it noted, "Seeing history instead of reading it was a treat for schoolchildren."[109] The difference between seeing and reading is crucial since the former implies receptivity and the latter demands interactivity. Other contemporary reviews overlooked this problem, especially those that, like the *Saturday Review*, praised the train for emphasizing documents that were "capable of being read afresh and with new inspiration" through the visitor's "power of reason," over relics like the "shinbone of a saint, the ashes of great men or of martyrs."[110]

Despite the stated intentions to ground the "abstract principles" of American freedom in these texts, the way that they were hurried from town to town, allowing relatively few people a quick glance, achieved nothing close to this. Instead, not only did the principles remain abstract, but the documents, brought tantalizingly close but kept just out of reach, gained additional mystic qualities. The language used by supporters referred to the train as a site for civil religious observation rather than history, indicating to the public the proper spirit with which to approach the train's contents. Descriptions referred to it as a "traveling shrine" and "a shrine consecrated to human freedom and American liberty."[111] The official exhibition catalog, edited by Frank Monaghan, advertised itself as "the Bible of our political freedom . . . and the story of what it means today." In 1949, Rabbi Ira Eisenstein told the Rabbinical Association of America that civil holidays and "documents such as those included in the Freedom Train . . . should be made the subject of pious study and meditation."[112]

"Inside, one has the feeling he is in church," said the *New York Times*. "The only light is the soft, fluorescent glow reflected from the lighted documents. Parents shush their children and little school boys take off their caps without being told. People speak in low-guarded tones used by tourists in ancient cathedrals."[113] In Sioux City, Iowa, each of the faithful "underwent the soul-satisfying experience of communing with the great men and women who had helped discover, develop and shape the great nation." In Davenport, the city's newspaper editor wrote about the glorious opportunity to "stand humbly in the presence of documents charged with personalities of great and heroic men, and thank God for America!"[114] Director O' Brien said, "It's almost a cathedral effect. Everyone seems to become reverent and sort of quiet," but "some of the girls find it hard to keep their eyes on the documents and off the Marines in their brilliant blue uniforms." Edward R. Murrow noticed schoolchildren who entered as if headed into the circus, but exited "as though they had been to church."[115]

This sacralization, however, contrasts with frequent references to relevance and familiarity. The *Saturday Review* clarified its positive position on the documents by adding "as long as they are still relevant to our own time and situation." Only because Americans again faced a time that "tries men's souls" did Tom Paine's "Crisis" mean something.[116] Visitors approached the documents as sacred yet familiar texts that also pertained to their own lives, but not as primary sources for historical study. In Nashville, "it was not a consuming interest in history that brought the family to town. Their reverence for the Constitution was not that of historians." Rather, while visitors typically "[stood] in awe of freedom's history," they also enjoyed connecting their own lives to the documents on display.[117] African Americans connected their lives to the texts too, but often did so in order to expose incongruence.

Visitors consistently sought out the most familiar and most famous documents rather than spending their time discovering something new. When Ernest Edwards hiked forty miles to see the train at Pueblo, Colorado, he went to see "those documents that I read about in my civics class." In particular, like so many others, Edwards wanted to see the Declaration of Independence, "because I've read so much about it."[118] One reporter suggested that the "symbolism" of the key documents drew visitors to the train. Without it, "these documents would be of interest only to the historian."[119] In other words, the public came to see the most familiar symbols rather than to read or study unfamiliar texts.

In the end, many other documents could have served the same purpose as those selected for the train. Except for those that bore directly on religious and political freedom, very little connected the historical evidence with the free enterprise arguments made by the AHF. Nor did the organizers expect visitors to look that closely at the documents on display. The fact that any documents that complicated or conflicted in some way with the national celebration of individual freedom were hidden out of the public's view mattered much more.

As they disembarked from the third and final car, every visitor received a copy of the "Bill of Rights," a three-page summary printed by *Reader's Digest*. They also had the opportunity to sign the Freedom Scroll. Vague phrases supporting freedom composed most of the brief text, though the closing line may have bristled isolationists in its reference to America's global responsibilities: "This heritage of freedom I pledge to uphold, For myself and all mankind." As David Hacket Fischer argues, this pledge differed from a pledge of allegiance or a loyalty oath; it emphasized individual autonomy and the right and duty to stand for what one believes is right, and it followed from the AHF's emphasis on "individual participation in maintaining . . . liberty." Three million people signed the scroll, so half a million (20 percent) either declined or failed to sign for some other reason.[120] However, even the universal pledge could be tampered with by local authorities; the Chicago city council added a line for the train's stopover there that reflected the aspirations of black Chicagoans and attempted to solidify the gains made over the previous months in the South. It reads, "Free to work and live without discrimination."[121]

Pageantry and the Production of a "permanent residue of patriotism"

> The time for rededication has arrived!
> American Heritage Foundation,
> *Good Citizen: The Rights and Duties*
> *of an American*

Before the train arrived, the AHF required that mayors appoint committees of prominent citizens to oversee the project.[122] The committees received hundreds of pages of instructions for producing their own "Rededication Week," including articles and editorials for the local papers, announcements and stories of "American heritage" for radio stations, speeches for civil and religious leaders, and advertisements to which businesses could affix their name. The local populations "were fairly bombarded with slogans, pictures, and cartoons" created by ad agencies affiliated with the AHF.[123] As Langston Hughes wrote ironically in his poem "Freedom Train,"

> I heard on the radio about the Freedom Train.
> I seen folks talkin' about the Freedom Train.
> Lord, I been a-waitin' for the Freedom Train![124]

Although regional AHF representatives confirmed the arrangements eight weeks before arrival, event preparation was coordinated mainly through mail, telegraph, and telephone, rather than through a mobile team of professional planners. Local observances of Rededication Week varied, but every community put on a show, as mandated by the AHF. In smaller cities especially it seems likely that many people participated simply because the campaign offered large-scale entertainment. Sioux City, Iowa, began its week with Sunday church services that extolled American freedom. A concert on Monday night by the Sons of Legion musical corps (literally the sons of veterans) "left few members of the audience dry-eyed." A parade on Tuesday evening featured floats, "giant searchlights," and C-47 transport planes flying back and forth overhead. Not surprisingly, military planes performed flyovers at many other stops, too. The next day Sioux City schools showed off students' floats—something other Iowa cities could not do since those municipalities had closed schools for the Freedom Train visit. On Thursday the train "glided into Sioux City 'like a graceful swan.'" Residents started lining up at 3:30 a.m. to catch a "fleeting glimpse of the most inspiring and priceless documents ever brought to the Hawkeye State." The campaign achieved a special moment of perfection in Burlington, Iowa. When the train stopped there, "four boy scouts—a Catholic, a Protestant, a Negro, and a Jew—posted the colors at the welcoming ceremony." Later that day, the two millionth visitor climbed aboard.[125] All across the country communities planned and executed similar celebrations. A Burlington, Vermont, Rededication Week saw George Washington, Paul Revere, Betsy Ross, and other impersonations of historical celebrities "walk the streets" as part of the festivities. Some 250,000 people watched a two-hour parade in Dover, Delaware.[126]

Local businesses usually organized the events, and citizens often participated through their places of employment. Factory workers from Oak Ridge, Tennessee, to Lawrence, Massachusetts, were led outside by their managers to welcome the train and recite the Freedom Pledge.[127] In Hartford, Connecticut, downtown retail stores cooperated on the city's week-long program. Two days before the train arrived, all employees participated in "mass meetings" held in their respective stores. At these events employees heard speakers ranging from store owners to local religious and political leaders and then recited the Freedom Pledge collectively. They did not hear from labor leaders, which seems to have been true of most Labor and Industry Days across the country. Speakers representing labor generally came from state departments of labor and other agencies while industry was represented by local business owners or the heads of business associations. The prominent men who organized local activities included military leaders and educators but were mostly businessmen, often heads of chambers of commerce, some with connections to the AHF. Chicago's Rededication Week committee was chaired by Barney Balaban's brother John, who owned the Chicagoland movie theaters that showed Paramount films. In Hartford, retailers also divided responsibility for the city's Rededication Week activities, with one major store celebrating freedom of religion, another honoring labor and industry, and so on, with each store combining elaborate window displays with in-store orations and special sale pricing for consumer-citizens.[128]

Protesters questioned parts of the campaign, but the most caustic description of the rededication pageantry came from an absurdly prescient short story by James Agee, first published in *Politics* in April 1946, the same month of William Coblenz's inspired vision. And oddly, Coblenz later critiqued the hype surrounding the Freedom Train's dedication in words very similar to Agee's. He complained to Clark, "I don't care how they patch together Jimmie (Schnozzola) Durante and the rest of Hollywood with the Bill of Rights, it's extraneous, in bad taste, and awkward."[129] Agee's "Dedication Day" describes a national (via radio and television) ceremony in which Americans participate without understanding just what they are celebrating. At a new structure built halfway between the "Washington obelisk" and the Lincoln Memorial, "it was not clear either to the speakers or to the listeners precisely what or to what purpose or idea the Arch had been raised." Etched in bold above the newly lit "Eternal Fuse," the monument's inscription, kept veiled and secret until the ceremony, reads, "THIS IS IT." But the public has mobilized for the event out of an "irresistible obligation" to participate. Asked to "sign their names to the moment," Americans respond as expected, just as most would recite the vague Freedom Pledge and sign the Freedom Scroll one year later. Prefiguring the scrupulous planning of the AHF, Agee imagines the inclusion of Catholic Cardinals, "eminent Protestant clergymen," and the "most prominent and progressive of American Reformist Rabbis." Bing Crosby and the Andrews

Sisters, who actually would record and make a hit of Irving Berlin's "Freedom Train" in 1947, have already recorded, in Agee's earlier fiction, a hit hummed version of "Taps."

The point of the undertaking was the ritual itself. Disrupting the ritual, the only subversives in the story are a guilt-ridden nuclear physicist and a young soldier who distastefully kneeled and wept. His action, in a domino effect, led tourists in line behind him to kneel and disrupt the flow of pedestrian traffic—a disaster for this type of choreographed program. The physicist commits suicide while throwing the switch that lights the Eternal Fuse, hoping in this final act to give the new monument its meaning. Agee's physicist behaved much like the Communist Party when it urged "progressives" to illicitly conduct tours of the train to explain the "true meaning" of the documents. But like the Freedom Train and the campaign to resell "America," ritualized "optimism" substituted for attempts at "understanding."

Before the second printing of "Dedication Day," one month before the Freedom Train finally came to rest, another short story appeared that also commented on celebrations of American heritage. In June 1948, the *New Yorker* published Shirley Jackson's famed story "The Lottery." Generally understood as an attack on small-town America, its emergence at the midpoint of the Freedom Train's journey suggests its relevance to the twilight of the golden age of national propaganda campaigns, especially those in the form of civic celebrations that helped citizens to negotiate between heritage and modernity, and between local and national identity.[130] In its horrifying depiction of one town's ritualized, annual rededication ceremony (in which a lottery determines who will be stoned to death that year), "The Lottery" questions both the ethics of patriotic sacrifice and the worshipful respect paid to a "tradition" that clearly should be abandoned rather than celebrated. At the beginning of the AHF's campaign, New York pacifists asked, "Is our American Heritage a past to worship?"[131] Jackson's story offered a hesitant answer similar to Becker's: that heritage needed to be looked at more critically. But as with the protestors, the contemporary public generally responded to Jackson with either indifference or hostility.

If it achieved nothing else, the unity campaign succeeded in unifying capital and mass media. The AHF's communications committee included the heads of the radio and television networks as well as Eric Johnston, who as president of the Motion Pictures Association of America instituted the Hollywood blacklist during the train's first months, and the presidents of the three major newspaper-publishing associations. These men ensured that the train received far more attention than other public history projects. Hosting his first fundraising luncheon for the project, Brophy proclaimed: "Here is a great opportunity to tell the truth to the people of this country by the means we know best how to use—Motion Pictures, Radio, Newspapers, Magazines, all methods of mass persuasion developed to a high state of perfection in America by American Business."[132]

The onslaught began with news features written by the AHF and distributed nationwide. These often misled readers as much as they informed. For example, an interview with Brophy quoted him saying, "The American Heritage Foundation's program has nothing to do with our economic system." Other articles described the train or listed some of the documents, a couple related the history of American railroads, and several attempted to connect popular sports to the train's mission as a way of interesting a wider audience in definitions of Americanism. An article about basketball claimed, "It is hard to think of basketball being invented or encouraged in a totalitarian country. . . . Basketball is as American as the Declaration of Independence." The sports pages were not the only lowbrow space invaded by this disguised advertising; several comic strips, including *Li'l Abner* and *Ripley's Believe It or Not*, featured promotional stories. Joe Palooka even called off a prizefight when he learned it would conflict with the arrival of the Freedom Train.[133] A special edition *Captain America* also promoted the campaign.[134]

The coordinating efforts of Barney Balaban and other Hollywood studio executives led to a collaboratively made short film, *Our American Heritage*, which had played to audiences in 14,445 theaters across the country by November 1948.[135] RKO Pictures produced the one-reel film with the cooperation of "all the major studios." It succinctly illustrates the unifying and limiting aspects of the campaign. The film opened with a mass of uniformed men marching in lock step, cheered by crowds that lined the street. Eventually an American flag, marking the head of the marchers, comes into view. Until that point one could incorrectly assume these are Nazis, put in the film by way of contrast. The narrator explains the scene by informing viewers that this is "a time for flag-waving"; the new age demanded such patriotic displays. The "hectic" postwar world offered "new panics every 15 seconds," and people needed to grab onto something solid. "Our" history was solid.

The rest of the film defined the nation's ideological boundaries through the narrative of American history. "We fought" for independence, "we wrote" the Constitution, and "we added amendments." "We," the Americans of 1947, had done all of these important things while "this guy" (shot of malcontent) griped and pointed out various problems in society. "But while he griped for 162 years, we built for 162 years." Real Americans worked in unison; those who protested and complained about injustices or inequities did not belong to "we." Ideologically, the *volk* have little wiggle room: everyone is middle class, and if anyone suggests the existence of inequality or systemic unfairness, they are both wrong and un-American.

Our American Heritage summarized the whole campaign in less than ten minutes. Complementing the exclusion of dissent, the film explicitly included immigrants, Jews, and African Americans. A few words about freedom of religion accompanied a shot of four houses of worship: three types of churches and, most prominently, a large synagogue. A polling place scene opens as a black man submits his ballot and exits just before a white woman casts her vote. At the end of the film, as a chorus sings the "Freedom Pledge," diverse faces appear sequentially in close-ups. There are men and women, sufficiently foreign-looking immigrants, grimy laborers and dusty farmers, and the best dressed of these Americans is a black man in a sharp jacket and tie.[136]

The AHF also used radio and direct mail as part of the extensive effort to broaden support. Radio spots resulted in 130 million listener impressions (one radio message heard by one listener) per month in 1948, or 1.7 billion for the tour's first thirteen months. These consisted of short advertisements as well as information integrated into regular radio programs.[137] The corporate sponsors also pressured local stores to support the Freedom Train. An AHF "Retailers' Manual" went out to storeowners in every community touched by the campaign. Suggestions included advertising the store's support in the local press or on radio, creating window displays that use facsimiles of some of the train's documents or mannequins made to look like great Americans, posters and elevator signs, and giving their employees time off work so that they could participate in Rededication Week activities.[138] How many employers gave their workers time off is unknown, but photographs suggest that many storeowners created window displays, and contemporary newspapers contained countless advertisements from local businesses announcing their support of the campaign.[139]

In addition to the publicity coordinated by the American Heritage Foundation, some of the campaign's corporate supporters promoted the Freedom Train through their own devices. While the train hauled its "precious cargo," Du Pont offered to its *Cavalcade of America* listeners "The Man Who Took the Freedom Train." Here, the lesson reached millions of listeners at once, including many people who would be unable to see the train in person. In this episode, protagonist Eddie Bullock is a frustrated and frightened young man, prevented from achieving much of anything (even marriage) by a sort of postwar malaise. "Strikes all over the country. The cost of livin's goin' up. A depression's comin', and some folks say there'll be another war any minute. And a lion—a *lion* even escaped from the zoo!" To this list of fears, his girlfriend, Shirley, responds,

"You make me sick, Eddie Bullock. You'd think you were the only person in the world who had any worries. Well, if you think I'm going to sit around and wait for peace on earth and no more war and no more depression and inflation and deflation and what not just so you can sleep nights you're mistaken. I don't want to marry anybody with that much patience."

Eddie goes to see the train in New York, where he slips into a daydream that soon makes his experience much more interesting than that of the average visitor. During his fantastic voyage on the Freedom Train, more courageous men like Washington and Lincoln teach Eddie his duties as a citizen. In one car he encounters the Pilgrims, who seek his counsel on whether or not to persevere in their mission. To Eddie's position that it's none of his business, the Pilgrims insist, "Do not avoid the issue, Brother Bullock. Decide." At this stage, Eddie refuses to commit and flees to the next car. Two cars later, in response to Eddie's whining protestation that he does not want to ride the train to Gettysburg, Lincoln replies, "Neither do I, son." The leaders, Eddie learns, are no different— no one seeks the heavy responsibilities, but they accept them as conscientious citizens.

Eddie's brother, John, also rides this eerie train. John died a few years before, on Iwo Jima, after he too answered the call of duty. The brothers' meeting is almost too much for Eddie to bear, but in the end it helps him to accept his own responsibilities. As the train speeds ahead, Eddie eventually makes his way to the locomotive, only to find that *he* is the engineer—average, ordinary Eddie drives the train of freedom. To save his brother, Eddie initially wants to use his newfound power to stop the Freedom Train, but once again, like female leads throughout the *Cavalcade* series, Shirley appears to remind him of his duty: "If you stop the train, John won't get to Iwo, but neither will the others and we'll lose the war. Lincoln will never get to Gettysburg. Mrs. Jessup won't get to Oregon, Washington will freeze forever at Valley Forge and Columbus won't ever discover us. Don't you see, Eddie? Freedom is you and me. You're the boss. You can drive the train anyplace you want to."[140]

Finally, Eddie understands that individuals control the destiny of the republic. This conversion narrative derived from the AHF's emphasis on individual freedom and individual responsibility. Du Pont and other corporations involved themselves in this project because the lesson as they meant it referred to the eternal absence of any need for government "interference" in the lives of individuals, be they human or corporate. As they understood it, individual freedom led directly to free enterprise.

Several circumstances link Du Pont and the Freedom Train. The company contributed to the American Heritage Foundation, and Du Pont also participated in the broader campaign to resell America to Americans. But perhaps just as important, the historical consultant to *Cavalcade*, Yale history professor Frank Monaghan, served in the same capacity with the Freedom Train, advising the committee of Dulles and others. In the end, Monaghan shared the dissatisfaction voiced by Hamer and the other archivists, historians, and librarians. He advised replacing 40 percent of the chosen documents with more relevant material, which, of course, was never done.[141] Despite his long involvement with Du Pont, Monaghan failed to understand or refused to accept that the corporate sponsors' agenda depended far less on the selection of relevant historical evidence than on a facade of historical truths from behind which it could propagandize more securely.

"For everyone who really wants to be a 'Good American,'" the AHF offered the seventy-two-page booklet *Good Citizen*. "Cynicism" and "neglect" were weakening the system at home, while abroad "its flaws are being exaggerated." The booklet therefore laid out nine keys to good citizenship. These included voting, jury duty, cooperation with the law, paying taxes, serving in the armed forces when necessary, toleration of difference, support of public education, participation in one's community, and family: "the atom-that-can't-be-split of our republic." Each of these warranted from two to four pages of detailed explanations regarding how to achieve them, especially how to adequately prepare to vote.

These keys to good citizenship were unobjectionable, which was precisely the point. Following the guidelines would help to preserve the system, just as the AHF suggested. Only those people who wanted to change the system—or, as the AHF said, "those groups . . . hostile to the dignity and freedom or men"—could possibly object to the campaign.[142] One might object to propaganda that argued explicitly for fewer protections for labor or less government regulation of business, but objecting to voting and jury duty made little sense. On a subtler level, the rededication to these fundamentals implied a return to stricter constitutionalism. *Good Citizen* linked its nine keys to the Bill of Rights and a few other constitutional amendments. The parts of the American experience not directly included, some of which might not have been as pleasant, were off limits. As Eric Goldman said of the documents on the train, this narrow definition of American heritage, basically confined to the Constitution, circumscribed more troubling issues of economic rights or social justice. History—what happened in between then and now—almost disappeared, or at least it possessed no meaning beyond sacred origins. More importantly, this implied that "our American heritage" consisted solely of the negative freedoms enumerated in the Bill of Rights.

The AHF's publicity program extended into twenty-seven thousand public schools nationwide. The foundation considered this aspect of their program to be one of the most important, and it was one of the most beneficial as well. The late 1940s witnessed an upsurge in courses in American history and civics, but when the Freedom Train pulled out of Philadelphia in September 1947, the curriculum remained uncertain and uneven.[143] Few contemporary observers doubted that schools should do more to educate students for republican citizenship.[144]

The AHF prepared a thirty-two-page "study guide" for teachers of fourth through twelfth graders and distributed 135,000 copies nationwide. The guide contained lesson ideas for courses in English, U.S. history, civics, and social studies. It suggested both individual lesson plans and longer curriculum units structured around themes of rights and responsibilities, the democratic process, and key freedoms.[145] A 1948 study conducted in Louisville, Kentucky, showed that schoolchildren there engaged in a year's worth of civic education activities in preparation for the train's summertime visit. The author's suggestions for continued exploitation of the train's popularity included the creation of learning units based on particular documents borne as cargo. For example, the Bill of Rights could foster the study of contemporary civil rights and political issues, which would help students to understand the 1948 presidential campaign. And studying the trial of journalist John Peter Zenger could stimulate classroom discussions of free speech in 1948.[146]

Using the collected documents to encourage civic engagement was, of course, a primary objective of the AHF campaign, but teachers who used history to stimulate discussion about controversial political issues carried freedom's torch quite a bit beyond the boundary drawn by the AHF. How many teachers actually did this, and how many schoolchildren absorbed the lessons of active political participation, is unknown. In any event, as a result of the AHF campaign, schools emphasized citizenship and history's contributions to and demands on the present, and millions of young Americans spent more time studying the political process and their potential roles in it than they would have otherwise.

During autumn 1948, the train ran concurrently with Truman's famed whistle stop campaign across the country—another type of rail journey that would soon cease to make sense. Given the ease with which the AHF raised the necessary funding for the Freedom Train, it is notable that Truman's trip nearly ended in the middle of the country due to his campaign's lack of funds. Truman visited nineteen states, generally stopping for only minutes before heading to the next station.[147] The two trains were never in the same city at the same time, but one wonders if the Freedom Train may have provided some inspiration for the journey on which Truman forcefully denounced his former allies, the corporate sponsors behind the AHF.

The Freedom Train ended 1948 with a return trip to the East Coast, spending three weeks in the greater New York City area before heading south to its final stop in Washington, DC. The train sat in DC's Union Station during the 1949 presidential inauguration, where Tom Clark, now a U.S. Supreme Court justice, closed down the train. At the time it appeared that Congress would help fund another tour that would begin soon. But by May the appropriations bills had quietly disappeared without a vote. The rapid loss of enthusiasm confounded archivists who were preparing for a new train, and historians have been similarly flummoxed. Given that Woodrow Wilson's inaugural address had been removed from inclusion by the Documents Committee because of frequent references to "Democratic victory," Truman's surprise reelection may have caused some supporters to question the project's efficiency.[148] Perhaps his campaign's appropriation of train travel also contributed to the corporate sponsors' sense of failure. Some of the AHF trustees expressed concern that "merely getting people to vote without encouraging them to vote intelligently and on an informed basis is not necessarily a good thing."[149] On the other hand, the AHF had promoted the train as just the thing that would correctly advise the public. It simply worked out differently than they had hoped. Southern Democrats also may have decided that the train carried more baggage than they were prepared to handle.

The train that brought American history to people of every state from 1947 to 1949 would be unimaginable in little more than a decade. By then, many of the visited towns no longer had passenger rail service. Even the tracks had disappeared in some parts of the country. A tour of this kind would have to travel by bus or by airplane, neither of which offered anything like the same spirit of community manifested in the gatherings of entire towns at their rail depots. Emerging from a global war and entering into a new era of prolonged superpower conflict, the time was right for self-reflection, thoughtful consideration of what constituted American values and ideals, and a rededication to the principles found to be worth sacrificing and fighting for. In the best light, these were the goals of the organizers behind the Freedom Train. Participants would see and learn for themselves exactly what the abstract principles of freedom and liberty really meant, as illustrated by America's foundational texts.

In practice, the content of the documents mattered very little. Most visitors did not see the documents, and those who did could only admire them as relics. Few opportunities existed to discover meaning in the texts, to say nothing of considering broader historical contexts, but the AHF had already supplied the public with the "correct" interpretations anyway. As they said in their own advertising, "*we* seek to give meaning to the American heritage" (emphasis added).[150] Unless one boarded the train seeking to challenge the foundation's business-friendly interpretation of that heritage—and, of course, some did—the weeks of promotion obviated any need to actually read the documents. The men behind the vast publicity machine invoked their spiritual power and claimed to speak for the documents, but in fact the documents remained in the background, dimly lit and still inaccessible to most.

5

Building a "National Shrine" at the National Museum of American History

Today there is greater need than ever before in our history for reaching all of the people with the story of our country's heritage and the development of the American way of life. The Smithsonian Institution is especially strategic in disseminating this message.

Smithsonian Institution, internal report, 1953

Pride in the exhibit extends to the elevator girl—"At last, we've got something modern."

Matt McDade, "Smithsonian Brightens Up Ancient Hall,"
Washington Post and Times-Herald, April 18, 1954

More than ever before, Americans in the 1950s visited and learned history from museums. Dissemination increasingly supplanted preservation as the primary purpose of the museum, as curators sought new ways of reaching the public, and museums became prominent tourist attractions.[1] A "new museology" that emphasized interaction, educative functionality, and popularization swept the field. Patronage of museums increased dramatically, as did efforts to instruct the new visitors.[2] The Smithsonian Institution played a leading role in these efforts while constructing a functional American history designed to meet the propaganda needs of the Cold War. Similar to the Freedom Train, and also linked in several ways to the history presented by Du Pont, the postwar Smithsonian became the site of an intensely patriotic, pro-military, and pro-business history created through the cooperation of corporations and the state.

The Museum of American History developed out of a specific historical moment that followed the end of World War II and the beginning of the Cold War. As one would expect, a national story forged at a moment of both triumph and anxiety absorbed characteristics that would be incongruous at other times. Focusing on the origins of the museum, this chapter explains how the political concerns that motivated the postwar demand for more "history" were felt and acted upon on Capitol Hill and the National Mall. In addition to its capacity for stimulating interactions between visitors and original material from the past, the museum was valued as a bulwark against an age of reproductions and mass communication.[3] Museums contained something "real," perhaps even some fundamental truth, and during the 1950s the Smithsonian provided rapidly increasing numbers of visitors with semi-official truths of American history. The museum assumed a key role in the construction of national identity and the definition of the "American Way of Life"—not incidentally a position from which requests for funding could be more easily made. In 1957, legislation signed by President Eisenhower created the National Museum of History and Technology (MHT), later renamed the National Museum of American History (MAH). This act culminated the exhibits' modernization program that spanned the 1950s, as well as a dozen years of intensive planning and campaigning by curators and their supporters. It reflected a dramatic new appreciation of, and hope for, the invigorating role that the past could play in modern American life.

In recent years, perhaps no other site of collective memory and historical interaction has so consistently been the subject of controversy as the history museums that line the National Mall. As the publicly funded curator of America's national story, the Smithsonian's interpretation of history has come under intensive scrutiny from historians, politicians, interest groups, the media, and the general public. Several historians have devoted considerable energy to documenting and analyzing the battles over recent exhibitions, particularly the Air and Space Museum's *Enola Gay* exhibit. With reason and without exception these writers have expressed outrage at the nonhistorians who have meddled in their domain. Edward Linenthal, Paul Boyer, Tom Engelhardt, Philip Nobile, Barton Bernstein, Mike Wallace, and others have complained that at the Smithsonian historical accuracy has been forced to withdraw in the face of base

The exhibition of missiles illustrates the close relationship between the military, the corporate state, and the National Museum in the 1950s. (Courtesy of Smithsonian Institution Archives, Image 2002-12168.)

political posturing. Yet after they explain how the "inevitable" occurred—that is, how politics intrudes in this most political of locations (by law the governing board of regents must include the vice president and the chief justice of the U.S. Supreme Court)—more historical questions about the nature and purpose of this museum remain.

If we are to understand how, at this key site of historical memory, particular narratives gained in prominence while others failed, we must revisit the postwar moment when the modern Smithsonian really began to take shape. Although the MHT opened in January 1964, the new museum's contents came from exhibits refurbished or created during the late 1940s and 1950s. The museum's early history followed the patterns of postwar Americans' relationship to the past, as well as broader contemporary concerns. Existing historical treatments of the museum fail in this respect, since they fall into the same internalist trap as the curators they critique.[1] In fact, broader changes in society's requirements of public history led to the dramatic overhaul of history exhibits at the Smithsonian.

The museum's mission radically changed from its prewar role as national repository, becoming instead a sort of public-learning complex. The choice of subjects, the design of exhibits (and greater attention to how their spatial relationships produced meaning), an explosion of new outreach programs, and increased efforts to explain what exhibits meant through better labels and new media: all reflected this aspiration.[5] To some extent this shift occurred throughout the museum world in the 1950s; for example in 1958 the Southeastern Museum Conference adopted the principle that museums have the "obligation" to interpret their collections through "creative activities."[6] Although recent scholars in the fields of public history and memory have suggested that museums have evolved into sites of popular entertainment only within the past generation, the "edutainment" function of museums began to emerge at the Smithsonian just after World War II as part of a calculated plan to reach and influence new audiences.[7] Curators and designers prioritized communication with visitors, made different levels of text available, and constructed parallel galleries for those interested in learning in greater detail than the new methods of presentation in the general gallery would permit. Assuming an increased need to appeal to a broader public, they hoped the new postwar exhibits would communicate material effectively to multiple audiences across age and education levels, class lines, and regional and national boundaries.[8]

Curators recognized that the Institution's specimens held both a "historical value" and a "patriotic value," since the objects, often referred to as "relics" and "treasures," inspired patriotism and civic commitment.[9] Ivan Karp argues that museums possess a special capacity to generate, or at least revitalize, social commitments to the system, and they encourage citizens' self-regulation.[10] In other words, visitors to museums learn how to interact with the state and civil society. Much of the discussion during the extensive 1950s renovations concerned how to most effectively use the artifacts in order to achieve such ends. It is clear that, to curators and congressional supporters, the museum offered the possibility of conditioning visitors' thought and behavior, and new programs and exhibits were created with that goal in mind. Steven Conn recently questioned the Foucauldian trend in museum studies that sees only odious institutions of instruction, asking why visitors would come to "get disciplined and punished."[11] In this case, postwar Americans visited for many reasons, mostly for fun and to see enshrined patriotic objects, but once inside the Smithsonian buildings they faced many cues regarding their relationship with the state.

Museums—especially national museums—claim greater authority to bestow legitimacy than most other "institutions of memory."[12] The Smithsonian's authoritative location on the National Mall adds to this weighty quality and likely encourages visitors to presume the accuracy of the history within—provided they possess some level of trust in the system. However, not long after the Museum of History and Technology opened its doors in 1964, systemic doubt may have contributed to the significant decline in attendance at the museum during the last three years of the 1960s (though it continued to draw the largest crowds of any Smithsonian museum until 1976, when the National Air and Space Museum opened).[13] There may be a high correlation between attendance and public faith in the system during the 1950s and 1960s.

The Smithsonian constructed several historical narratives for postwar Americans. The most prominent of these were narratives of military, corporate, and technological progress, as well as the more general "rise to greatness" of the United States. No matter what the field, from medicine to military, the stories told through the new exhibits led from meager origins to postwar supremacy. In many ways, the Cold War Smithsonian functioned similarly to the United States Information Agency (USIA) and other propaganda bureaus. Just as their overseas exhibits, films, lectures, conferences, and publications presented the evidence of a vital American culture in the past and present, so the Smithsonian flaunted American accomplishments in political, cultural, and especially material life. In fact, besides "inspiring patriotism" at home, the Smithsonian also participated directly in overseas propaganda efforts.[14] Curators wrote "lectures" on topics such as "American Inventions Have Altered Our Way of Living," which were distributed to USIA Information Centers around the world. USIA also filmed some of the Smithsonian's "treasures" to show to foreign audiences, though whenever possible, foreign dignitaries were led through the museum itself on special tours.[15]

The new postwar exhibits encouraged admiration, or even worship, rather than serious investigation into the past. As a 1964 opening-day headline read, "Museum Is Shrine to Rise of U.S. as Nation."[16] In this respect the Smithsonian also resembled contemporary history textbooks, in which "America was perfect:

the greatest nation in the world, and the embodiment of democracy, freedom, and technological progress."[17] History exhibits designed for the U.S. public, foreign dignitaries, Congress, and other sensitive groups necessarily painted a rosy picture. Postwar funding depended on a positive portrayal, and curators had to exercise caution with topics that might cause controversy. Consensus defined American history, and anything that challenged that interpretation had to remain outside the museum.

Inclusion in the Smithsonian's hallowed halls certifies an object's significance. As they "objectif[y] the past and organize . . . memory around diverse artifacts," history museums rely on things to help tell a coherent story and to stimulate memories. These things have their own specific origins that cannot be ignored.[18] The routes they follow on their journeys to the exhibit hall reveal a broader set of contributors and interested parties—from railroad magnates to pharmaceutical companies—who should be considered along with the more commonly recognized creators of museum displays: the curators. Likewise, their removal from their original contexts to often decontextualized museum displays unavoidably alters, and often erases, the objects' historical meanings.[19]

To help create the new exhibits the Smithsonian turned to American businesses, which de facto meant the creation of history favorable to business interests. In the 1950s, corporations became substantially more involved with nonprofit institutions like the Smithsonian, as symbolized by the 1957 appointment of Du Pont president Crawford Greenewalt to the Smithsonian's Board of Regents, replacing famed engineer Vannevar Bush. Incidentally, in the 1960s, MHT director Frank Taylor served on the Advisory Committee of the Hagley Foundation, Du Pont's new research library and museum at the company's original Eleutherian Mills powder works.[20] The increased corporate involvement followed the landmark 1953 New Jersey State Supreme Court decision in *A.P. Smith Manufacturing Company v. Barlow, et al.* that effectively upheld the legality of corporate philanthropic donations to institutions that did not directly benefit either the corporation or its shareholders. Society now assumed, said the court, that business would support its public institutions. The assumption made in turn by business was that those institutions should reflect corporate attitudes.[21]

Museums flourished in the postwar period. Not since the closing decades of the nineteenth century was there such a widespread interest in museum building, acquisitions, exhibitions, and, especially, education. The two eras also shared a sense of historical discontinuity produced by rapid change, and Americans of both periods sought a usable past. But where the Victorian museums were, according to Neil Harris, "a corrective, an asylum, a source of transcendent values meant to restore some older rhythms of nature and history to a fast-paced, urbanizing, mechanized society," the postwar Smithsonian celebrated the journey *to* that new society, as the pinnacle of human achievement. The point of the past in most exhibits was the impressive distance traveled to the present and, by implication, the even greater potential of the future. Displays illustrated how particular trajectories through time prepared the nation for the dawning Space Age. In this way the exhibits represented a key middle ground where discourses of the past and future mingled to create usable knowledge for the present. In fact, as an institution devoted to both history and technology, the whole MHT symbolized the awkward yet vital coexistence of these two strains in contemporary society.

The postwar museum also built upon foundations laid by earlier technological museums, world's fairs, and trade shows, following in particular Chicago's 1933 "Century of Progress" and the 1939 New York World's Fair.[22] The rich literature on those fairs illustrates how the scientific community interacted uncomfortably with corporations to produce a legacy of celebratory technology exhibits that strongly influenced American museums of technology history. In some cases, fair exhibits designed to advertise particular corporations were transferred directly to museums, particularly Lenox Lohr's Museum of Science and Industry in Chicago.[23] But even later exhibits constructed at the MHT derived from the same uneven balance of corporate advertising and educational objectives. The Smithsonian's 1936 *Annual Report* remarked that the "suddenly aroused exhibits consciousness of industrialists through the country" caused by the 1933 fair had a "definite effect" on the work of the Arts and Industries department. By 1939 Smithsonian curators Frank Taylor and Carl Mitman had worked on exhibits for the New York World's Fair and the Golden Gate International Exposition in San Francisco. The experience certainly affected the postwar exhibit overhaul led by Taylor in particular.[24] Also in 1939, two renowned studies critiqued museums—especially technology museums—that failed to rise beyond the "stage of the commercial exposition" and thus presented next to nothing of the social and economic implications of the progress they celebrated. Showing the public only that which is "spectacular," museums could not but fail to relate the exhibited machines to social problems. Even before World War II then, critiques of the types of congratulatory and evolutionary technological history that the Smithsonian carried into the postwar era had appeared.[25]

Some aspects of the postwar Smithsonian can be traced further back to the influences of its remarkable late nineteenth-century director, ichthyologist George Brown Goode. Goode followed Charles Wilson Peale's emphasis on connecting scholarship and public education through the systematic display of significant objects.[26] Goode established the Smithsonian's method regarding technological and material artifacts, "situating them on a progressive continuum from rude to complex, savage to civilized." This evolutionary approach, typical of turn-of-the-century anthropology, would never really be supplanted at the Smithsonian.[27] Exhibits also reflected the fact that the collections had already outgrown available space and staff.[28] Two of Goode's subordinates epitomize the dichotomy of his neatly taxonomized yet still cluttered science and technology exhibits and the museum's shrine-like but cramped American history section. A. Howard Clark, the National Museum's history curator, conceived of the museum's role as a shrine housing important relics, where awed citizens could contemplate the great deeds of Revolutionary heroes. Clark merely expressed the prevailing attitude that preserved objects were important not for their uses but for their associations.[29] During the Cold War, arguments in favor of increased funding for the Smithsonian often expressed the same sentiments, referring to "national treasures" and the "treasure house" of the "relics of the past," indicating that this conception of the museum's function had resiliency.[30] Goode's other assistant, John Elfreth Watkins, a civil engineer with links to railroad companies, began collecting artifacts that would tell the story of American progress through developments in that industry.[31] Thus, history at the Smithsonian consisted of hagiography as well as displays of the nation's technological prowess, and the museum had already linked itself in multiple ways to capital.

Mining engineer Carl W. Mitman arrived in 1911, and in the 1920s he advocated for a separate museum for the history of technology, arguing that the United States was virtually alone among advanced nations of the world in neglecting to create a museum—a "monument"—in which to display the history of America's material progress. Only after World War II would Congress see the value of such a display.[32] From the 1920s onward, Mitman and his protégé, Frank A. Taylor, worked to create a new Smithsonian museum focused on the history of technology. Crucially, this same period witnessed the proliferation of science and technology museums, the professionalization and entrance into the middle class of engineers and scientists, and clashes between labor and capital that directly involved the industrial processes then being documented and displayed. The uneasy relationship between capital and labor in the 1910s and 1920s might have been interesting territory to explore, but curators stayed clear of the difficult issues that would have arisen from placing their prized mechanical possessions in a socioeconomic setting.[33] Frank Taylor later recalled that they sometimes discussed developing the "broad social significance" of the technologies on display, but no one had any idea of how to do that.[34] Mike Wallace argues that beyond this purported ignorance, American engineers—and the men who administered the Smithsonian—had by the 1920s rejected an earlier reformist ideology prevalent in their profession and had accepted new positions within the hierarchical corporate system. Consequently, the engineer-curators fostered the development of collections that supported that system ideologically, with a simplistic conception of history as technological progress.[35] Peter Kuznick's work on science at the 1939 World's Fair complicates this thesis somewhat by demonstrating the sharp opposition to corporate domination in the 1930s by at least a large minority in the science-technology community.[36] However, the extreme emphasis and reliance on objects—donated, of course, with public relations purposes in mind—made it unlikely that such exhibits would explore broader historical circumstances in any depth. In decontextualized settings, museum visitors become "fixated on the object." The objects become fetishized, beheld as if they produced their own meaning rather than existing as part of a more complex story that requires further analysis.[37]

Mitman and Watkins legated to the Smithsonian an ideology identifiable even in the contemporary Institution: an understanding of history as a "genealogy of invention" in which "progress automatically follows technology," a "noncontextual" or internalist approach that has generally persisted despite recent curatorial efforts to add social and cultural contexts.[38] It implied the equivalency of industrial and social progress, and with each successive machine on display, it affirmed a rigidly progressive interpretation of history.[39] The understanding of history as technological progress paralleled the ideology espoused by corporations at world's fairs and in such promotional undertakings as *Cavalcade of America*; it was also in line with Cold War–era requirements for a national museum that could advertise the material achievements of democratic capitalism.

During the 1920s and 1930s the collections stagnated as few people inside or outside the museum considered the exhibits important enough to warrant their attention, and Mitman's vision remained unrealized.[40] His protégé, Frank Taylor, would prove to be more adept at the lobbying necessary to secure funding and support on Capitol Hill. Taylor began working at the Arts and Industries Building after graduating from high school, though he eventually earned a BS at MIT and a JD at Georgetown. At Mitman's urging, during college Taylor traveled to Europe to visit and study Munich's Deutsches Museum and other institutions. When he returned to the National Museum Taylor sought to elevate it to the level of Europe's best museums.[41] During the New Deal era Taylor began to successfully promote the Smithsonian's work, increasing the staff by drawing from the Civil Works Administration and modestly improving the quality of the exhibits. He also enhanced the reputation of the Smithsonian through a radio program, *The World Is Yours*. The unsponsored show aired nationally on NBC with support from the U.S. Department of Education and the Works Progress Administration.[42] On the program, Taylor and other staff lectured on topics in history, science, and technology to millions of Americans, gaining valuable publicity for the institution. The most popular noncommercial radio program in 1940, it still lost its timeslot to World War II. Taylor later stated that the show brought the Smithsonian the "reputation of having the first of everything" (the quip "old enough to be in the Smithsonian" dates from these years) and made the museums on the Mall a favorite destination for tourists.[43]

In the years just before the war, Taylor also established new civil service specifications for positions at the Smithsonian. Through his descriptions he shaped the positions themselves, using this power to emphasize exhibit work. He dictated that, for the first time, "preparation of an exhibition done by a scientist or a historian was equivalent to a publication" in terms of evaluation for promotions. Even so, Marilyn Cohen concludes that Smithsonian exhibits "reached the nadir immediately prior to World War II." Efforts to get new buildings had failed and wages were so low that the Smithsonian's 1940 *Annual Report* begged Congress for money needed just to retain current staff.[44]

Showcase for America

During WWII, research on new materials and on strategic areas around the world gained the Smithsonian some congressional supporters. However, at war's end the exhibits remained in poor condition.[45] In the cramped quarters of the Arts and Industries Building, visitors were likely to "suffer at least a slight attack of claustrophobia," said the *Washington Star*. Single, bare light bulbs illuminated "faded" cases, and the whole place smelled of formaldehyde. It was an "attic," the "world's quaintest museum," or a "country store" stuffed full with a "confusing jumble of dusty exhibits identified by fly-specked labels printed in ancient type."[46] The thirty-five million "specimens" possessed by the Smithsonian by this period represented the "growth of objects" in contemporary museums. Collections resembled an attic full of priceless junk, much of which would remain forever hidden in warehouse crates, and on which the curators might quixotically try to impose some sense of order, more in the fashion of Walter Benjamin's collector than according to professional standards or an articulated program.[47]

The situation outside the Smithsonian's red brick walls had changed though, and soon the effects would be felt within the museum. The United States sought to show the world, Europe in particular, that its culture, technology, and history spoke well of a nation that presumed to lead the world. Competition with the

Soviet Union, especially in the hard sciences, led to increased support from Congress for other parts of the Smithsonian's mission such as applied research, but the money for exhibit modernization and, eventually, funding for the MHT building sprung from a perceived need to display the American success story to audiences both foreign and domestic.

Taylor seized the moment by calling attention to the role the Smithsonian could play in teaching Americans the "history, culture and traditions of their country" and suggested that a visit to a refurbished museum could "influence their activities and decisions as individuals and citizens." On a practical level, Taylor saw postwar exhibit renovations as a necessary first step toward gaining political support for a new building.[48] In 1948, Mitman left to plan the National Air Museum, and Taylor succeeded him as head curator of the Department of Engineering and Industries. As such, Taylor headed the project to create the History and Technology Museum and became its first director in 1958.[49] Smithsonian secretary Alexander Wetmore's reservations about the potential for embarrassment notwithstanding, he permitted Taylor to network around Washington and build support for exhibit modernization and, eventually, to form his own committee of like-minded curators to consider how it might be done.[50]

The three curators who joined Taylor on his committee shared his belief that the Smithsonian's focus should be on general education. John C. Ewers, Herbert Friedmann, and Paul Gardner had each promoted exhibit revitalization in their respective departments, though none of them had yet enjoyed much success. Ewers, who specialized in the Plains Indians within the Smithsonian's Department of Anthropology, had been particularly eager to overhaul the decades-old Native American exhibits. Friedman, who recalled that his predecessor at Natural History remembered the pre-Darwin world of zoology fondly, felt the exhibits there were likewise outdated. Gardner had a dual role on the committee, representing the Fine Arts collections and taking charge of artistic and creative planning in the years before the museum hired designers. The committee toured museums across the country in early 1950 in order to assess possible routes to modernization. Disappointed, they found that, with few exceptions, exhibits at most American museums were no better than the Smithsonian's. Hardly anyone, it seemed, had developed informative and interesting displays for the public.[51]

The committee proposed the following: first, altering the floor plans in the Arts and Industries Building and the National Museum of Natural History to make exhibits more accessible and to make visitors' routes through the museums more logical and instructive; and second, renovating several popular exhibit halls. They also proposed, under the aegis of the Department of Anthropology, a new art and cultural history exhibition, combining specimens from Ethnology and Fine Arts, that would tell the story of mankind. This would be called the Museum of Man, though significantly its central theme would be "American growth." It never came together, but years later this idea would be partly realized in the "Growth of the United States" exhibits at the MHT/MAH. Finally, the committee suggested that the renovated exhibits would be only one part of a broader program to interact with and educate the public, through lectures, popular publications, and special exhibitions. Wetmore eventually gave his reluctant approval to the plan, but the more adventurous Leonard Carmichael would soon replace him as secretary. In the meantime, even before congressional appropriations, Taylor and his allies had begun to implement their plans. Ewers started to update the Ethnological and Anthropological Halls, planning began for renovating the Main Hall and the First Ladies exhibit, and a new Naval History Hall was created.[52]

The Federal Bureau of the Budget, which Taylor had lobbied directly for years, recommended congressional approval of the Smithsonian's greatly increased proposed budget in 1952, after the Korean War had delayed plans for the request. The House Appropriations Committee approved an additional $360,000 for 1953, an increase of almost 50 percent over the previous year but insignificant in comparison to what would come. In just a few years, Congress would enthusiastically approve $650,000 annually, just for exhibit modernization.[53]

In many ways, the new exhibits' "basic script was written in the U.S. Congress."[54] Michal McMahon concluded this about the National Air and Space Museum (NASM), but it applies here as well. Supportive statements made on Capitol Hill, and the arguments made to Congress by Smithsonian administrators seeking funding, reveal the implicit philosophy behind both exhibit modernization and the emerging MHT. As Congress appropriated greater sums throughout the 1950s, the new exhibits indeed assumed the desired characteristics. The *Annual Report* of 1953 contained a seven-page "manifesto" from Taylor—the first official philosophy of exhibits since the 1890s. It demonstrated a new commitment to the history of culture and technology and a move away from natural history, which had dominated the early twentieth-century Smithsonian. New exhibits would be designed to tell a coherent story that interconnected the varied objects on display. Overarching themes would be made clear to visitors, and the exhibits would collectively "emphasize the special contribution of the United States to the improvement of man's physical and social well-being" through the display of the nation's impressive material culture.[55]

To convince Congress to fund these and grander plans, Taylor and his staff "capitalized on the mood of the United States population toward celebrating national history and technological achievements in the early 1950s." They also played upon fears that the Soviet Union better advertised its successes. As with the later Air and Space Museum, the presumed *advertising* ability of the MHT remained paramount through the years of proposals and planning.[56] Promotional material and appeals for funds were wrapped in patriotic language, sometimes emphasizing the "bargain" offered by the Smithsonian as well. According to one promotional booklet, "There is no more effective or economical way to impress the more than one million visitors from every state and foreign land who see the collection each year, with the successful working of the democratic process in America."[57] These types of arguments helped to convince conservative congressmen such as George Dondero of Michigan to prioritize museum appropriations. In the early 1950s, while railing against the "art of 'isms'" and the "communist conspiracy" then threatening both art museums and "our tradition and inheritance," Dondero contemporaneously served on the Smithsonian's Board of Regents and also chaired the House Committee on Public Buildings.[58] The support of both of these bodies was crucial to the creation of the MHT.

Other congressmen couched their support for the museum in similar expressions of patriotism and averred the need for more history exhibits that demonstrated the superiority of the American way of life. The assertions and demands made in appropriations hearings help to explain the character of the museum that they funded, including the awkward union of technology, civil, and military history within a single edifice.[59] In approving the MHT plans, House Appropriations Committee chairman Clarence Cannon of Missouri boasted that this new building would be as "imperishable as the pyramids."[60] It would be not just a shrine, but a lasting monument of American civilization. Interestingly, the plans at that point called for the demolition of the historic Arts and Industries Building and for the new "imperishable" temple to be built on the vacated site.[61] The older Smithsonian buildings were then seen as unfortunate remnants of Victorian architecture. The triumphant progress of the United States, especially its technological progress, could not be displayed in such an edifice. Since emphasizing history was in some respects merely a way of emphasizing achievement, curators and supportive congressmen campaigned for a sleek, "suitable modern building" outfitted with modernist exhibit designs. The quote from the "elevator girl" at the beginning of this chapter suggests that the attitude was broadly shared. The 1950s were a "turning point for museum architecture," and the MHT designed in 1955–57 by the firm of McKim, Mead, and White holds a significant place in this architectural history, despite its flaws.[62] The choice of architects represented a further irony in that an 1870s survey of New England's oldest buildings by the firm's three founders has been credited with sparking the late nineteenth-century historic preservation movement.[63]

In a promotional booklet that contrasted the poor state of exhibits with the plans for renovation, Taylor argued that the Smithsonian could uniquely influence the thoughts and actions of millions of Americans. Even with the current exhibits, three million people visited each year by 1950 — up from less than a million four years earlier. If the exhibits could be improved, there existed substantial potential for mass education.[64] In a foreword, Carmichael stressed the great achievements of the United States, particularly in "erect[ing] a new industrial world based on mass production" and claiming its current position of "world leadership." The time had come to "display before the world the historic material evidence of our national growth and achievement," not only fulfilling the Smithsonian's mission but also serving "other urgent national interests." This proposal laid out the necessity of funding a new museum on the Mall in language that would appeal to politicians focused on paying for the Cold War. America needed this building to demonstrate its "heritage of freedom" and to showcase the "basic elements of our way of life." The pamphlet also warned of the results of inaction: existing artifacts were so packed together that curators could not "exhibit them in a way that develops their full meaning and value as a national heritage," and "irreplaceable material records of historic events" disappeared because of lack of space.[65]

Best exemplifying this point, the Smithsonian's "greatest national treasure," the Star-Spangled Banner flown at Fort McHenry, covered two full pages of the brochure. In the first photograph, the giant flag is shown as currently exhibited, "half hidden by adjacent displays" and unable to be completely unfurled. A solitary man stands wedged against the glass case, staring ahead at the lower left corner of the immense flag, which is all he can see. Toward the end of the brochure, in a section that explained the layout of the proposed museum, another full-page picture depicts the banner as it would be displayed if Congress appropriated the money. It would be visible from all three floors, reminding all who view its "full-length display" of the "heritage of freedom from which sprang the national achievements there commemorated." In this picture, several people stand looking up at the flag, now completely exposed and positioned behind an apparent altar. The setting strongly encourages reverence. Two men appear to be in solemn conversation about this venerable object; near them, a mother instructs her child, as he stands rapt in amazement.

The scene appeals to power by suggesting how this symbol of the state would be worshipped if provided an appropriate space. The instructional element inherent in the oversized display exists as well in the open space reserved for visitors. Where museumgoers of yesteryear might have remained hidden among the cases as they studied the flag, the new arrangement would expose individuals to the scrutiny of fellow citizens: a variation on the panopticon famously analyzed by Foucault. This may not have been a consciously sought after result, but it is consistent with early Cold War demands that American citizens demonstrate their patriotism in the public sphere, whether through recitation of the Pledge of Allegiance, singing the national anthem at sporting events, signing loyalty oaths, or standing in line to board the Freedom Train and sign the Freedom Scroll.

The Star-Spangled Banner would be the "center of attention" in the new museum, but other "authentic original relics" and "heritage treasures" would of course be exhibited. Primarily these items would be those "elements of our technology and culture that characterize our way of life" (note the present tense) and "give to the problems of living today a historic perspective in the mirror of our past." In other words, rather than merely representing and elucidating an earlier historical period, the "relics" served as part of an explanation of "our" current condition. Further, they verified that 1950s America properly descended from the heritage on display. But the relics could not achieve this on their own—that was the problem with the old method of exhibition—so exhibits would lead visitors around the displays in the appropriate order, moving from one "pivotal" moment to another. Upon completion, visitors should understand the "story of our national progress from colonial settlement to world power" and experience a "deepened faith" in America's "destiny."[66]

They would also be awed by the "inspiring opportunity of beholding the . . . relics" within the "national shrine."[67] The use of the religious idiom suggests the veneration of specimens such as pieces of clothing worn by great Americans and locks of hair from every president from Washington to Pierce. Arguments against admission fees used similar language to argue that the museum must be as open as churches and schools. Admission fees "would have an adverse effect on the national interest" and conflicted with the Smithsonian's unique position as an "educational and cultural institution and also as a national shrine." The museum must be kept free "so that citizen and foreigner alike may freely inspect the material evidence of our national growth and achievement—mementos of the men and events that have made this country great." As such mementos would not, in fact, be "material evidence," this sentence again demonstrates the omnipresent tension between the museum of progress and the national shrine.[68]

Looking back from 1957, Secretary Carmichael summed up the changes from his perspective, noting that before the mid-1950s modernization the Smithsonian had been the "picture of a gaslit museum in an age where people are used to television and the newest techniques of display." But with the new exhibits, "we want to educate, inform, and at the same time interest the visitor," said Carmichael. Instead of a messy attic, the Smithsonian had become the "showcase of America—a well-lighted, logically arranged showcase."[69]

The new "logical" arrangement encouraged patriotic belief in a capitalistic, militaristic, and technologically superior America, but Smithsonian administrators continued to complain about inadequate facilities. This message now resonated in the Capitol. Senator and Smithsonian regent Clinton P. Anderson protested to his colleagues in 1957 the fact that the United States now lagged decades behind Europe in museum design.[70] House Democratic Majority Leader John W. McCormack argued the National Museum was twenty years behind "even some of the second- or third-class powers of the world"—a wholly unacceptable position for the United States. Only a few isolationists objected; for example, Charles Vursell of Illinois argued against the expenditure with the same spendthrift reasoning that he used against the Marshall Plan ten years earlier—an indication that officials on both sides of the issue possessed the same understanding of the Smithsonian's potential in foreign affairs.[71]

By 1957, most congressmen saw the need for "a greater understanding of our own culture here and abroad," as Representative Frank Thompson put it in announcing his support.[72] Congressman Cannon, a former history teacher and Smithsonian regent, championed the MHT at every step.[73] Congress, of course, approved the plans for the museum, designed for, in the words of another regent, Congressman John Vorys of Ohio, both the "diffusion of knowledge" and "inspiring patriotism."[74] The educative or propagandistic function continued to be the central theme of those who supported the MHT. At the dedication in January 1964, Senator Anderson averred it would be "not only the largest but also in some respects the most truly educational museum in the world." President Lyndon Johnson thought this would especially benefit foreign visitors:

> Why not open the historical doors and let the visitors see what kind of people we really are and what sort of people we really come from? They would instantly realize that we were not always the affluent nation, the powerful nation, the fortunate nation. From the exhibits in this Museum, they would learn that the demagogues' dingy slogans around the world have no basis in fact. . . . We would show visitors from newly emerging nations that their labors are not in vain—for the future belongs to those who worked for it. . . . If this Museum did

nothing more than illuminate our heritage so that others could see a little better our legacy, however small the glimpse, it would fulfill a noble purpose. I am glad to be here. I am always glad to be where America is.[75]

It is worth mentioning that arguments put forward by Congress in support of the National Air Museum, later the NASM, bore a striking resemblance to those above. They also referred to the vital necessity of advertising American achievement and potential through historical artifacts—in this case airplanes and spacecraft. In light of what later transpired, it is interesting that in 1970 such supporters as Congressman Frank Thompson and Senator Barry Goldwater encouraged Frank Taylor, then the NASM's acting director, to divest the Smithsonian of the *Enola Gay*, the plane that dropped the atomic bomb on Hiroshima. Goldwater thought the aircraft lacked historical significance, and Thompson agreed, suggesting that "I don't think we should be very proud of that as a nation. At least it would offend me to see it in the museum."[76] The same sentiment apparently derailed a proposed MHT exhibit on Hiroshima that same year because Americans, then at war in Vietnam, "are really a peace loving people and the Hiroshima exhibit is too gruesome for us to expose to the general public."[77] But above all, the bomber remained in storage for another two decades because it was an object that implicitly questioned the narrative of inevitably positive technological advancement, a narrative that existed at the MHT as much as at the NASM.

Design Revolution

To accompany new exhibits, curators prepared "scripts"—explanatory text about the displays—for the first time at the Smithsonian. Ewers brought that innovation with him from the National Park Service, an institution already more focused on public history; no one at the Smithsonian had bothered with such an endeavor before. Ewers would succeed Taylor as director of the MHT, but he later retreated to the Museum of Natural History, feeling more comfortable there as an ethnologist.[78] Taylor also created a new position called exhibits specialist (later chief of exhibits), which oversaw all of the exhibit makeovers. Meanwhile, a new hire, Benjamin Lawless, brought the exhibit methods of the Cranbrook Museum in Michigan—practically the only museum Taylor and Ewers had admired on their 1950 tour—to the Smithsonian. Lawless had presented himself to the personnel office after touring the First Ladies Hall, "what seemed to me to be the worst exhibition of things I had ever seen in my life."[79] Another new staff member was C. Malcolm Watkins, who arrived from Old Sturbridge Village, a living history museum in Massachusetts. As curator at

Sturbridge, Watkins developed period rooms that visitors could enter to be transported back to an earlier age. Watkins's rooms were different than earlier iterations because he cared less about aesthetics or the preservation of one family's memory, rather intending to re-create a part of the past in the present. He sought to literally reconstruct the social life of earlier Americans through the use of material evidence, correctly combined, contextualizing rather than fetishizing his specimens. When the MHT appropriated all historical exhibits from the Natural History Building and from the Anthropology Department, Watkins became curator of Cultural History.

New methods included a role for an exhibits designer responsible for the appearance of Smithsonian exhibits, while the curators determined the content of collections and scripts. Designers moved exhibits away from a standard rectangular pattern divided by precisely straight rows. Curved and angled walls, movable panels, odd-shaped rooms, and temporary floors created a more dynamic space. Staff, critics, and visitors commented on new "lighting and color effects" more than any other changes. Lack of adequate lighting had made several of the old exhibits nearly impossible to see and had also contributed to the perception of the museum as a cavernous storage room best left to some-one with appropriate expertise. The new exhibit halls appeared friendlier and protected against the public's usual "museum fatigue."[80]

Designers and curators also worked to control perspective, both visual and interpretive. New designs forced visitors to look at particular displays in a particular order by closing off access and blocking views, hopefully allowing for greater absorption of intended meaning. The new exhibits featured far fewer objects as well, because curators selected only those specimens that served the themes they tried to convey to the public. Less effective or contradictory objects were removed to storage. Scholars of science and technology museums have argued that the absence of machines that did not work, that did not fit into a linear evolutionary story, or that too obviously caused social disruption is un-fortunately typical of such institutions.[81] And understandably, corporations would be unlikely to donate their failures since those objects would send precisely the wrong message to the public. Another factor was the undeniable over-abundance of objects in the old exhibit halls. Descriptive labels also were re-moved to the exhibit panels to reduce clutter around the remaining objects on display and to integrate their descriptions into the story being told by the whole exhibit.[82] Halls were "streamlined" so that visitors would not be confused by too much information or stimuli. For example, Latin American Archeology removed hundreds of specimens, instead using just a single item to illustrate each "step" or "archeological development" in the region.[83] The Historic Americans

Hall, designed to "express forcefully, tastefully, and reverently" the connections between the displayed objects and their famous owners, similarly eliminated unnecessary clutter from the past. Curators "relegat[ed] many objects associated with minor political figures to the study collections. . . . There will be space only for the most notable figures in American life."[84]

Perhaps the most dramatic change occurred in exhibit scripts, the textual displays that attempted to bind the artifacts together in a narrative constructed by the curators. Smithsonian staff rewrote panels to erase their own doubts about whether less-educated visitors would be able to read and understand the displays correctly, "substitut[ing] plain talk for scientific jargon." Indicating the lengths to which curators went at the dawn of this new era, local laborers were brought in to see how they responded to scripts. For example, when workmen "pulled a blank" on the phrase "unstratified society," curators changed it to read, simply, "no social classes."[85] Such simplifications complemented other exhibit modernization efforts, all of which sought to increase explicatory power.

The Smithsonian's curators also began to solicit visitors' opinions in the form of questionnaires. In both language and intent they reflected the sea change that had taken place vis-à-vis the institution's purpose. Mostly these went out to visiting organizations, usually schools. The questionnaires asked if exhibits were appropriately written for the visitors, if they were dull or interesting, and if they were effective. This solicitude suggests how the Smithsonian transformed from a research institution to a patron-centered museum.[86]

In stark contrast to the old, the new exhibits were "easy" and a "fun way of absorbing knowledge," according to a *Washington Post* reporter who often covered the Smithsonian during this crucial period.[87] "Interesting and educational exhibits [were] designed to capture the imagination of young and old." Several innovations changed forever the way that museums engaged with visitors. The "Early Life in America" exhibit, opened in January 1957, featured new "step-in windows," an innovation brought by Malcolm Watkins and soon adopted for other exhibit halls, that allowed visitors to enter reproductions of rooms, cabins, and teepees.[88] To replace lengthier written labels, curators created "talking exhibits" that visitors triggered merely by walking up to a certain spot. These machines "beamed" distinct "messages" at two different heights, corresponding to those of adults and children. In some halls the displays themselves were separated into adult- and child-sized levels so that children would be spared inappropriate unpleasantness.[89]

The 1950s modernization effort lay the foundation for the campaign to obtain the ultimate goal: the MHT, which would not only provide a modern edifice to celebrate technological progress but would also revolutionize the museum experience. However, during the modernization, Smithsonian staff assumed that the new building would be open by about 1960, and that each new hall they finished before then would be "transferred intact to the new museum." Thus, preparations for the MHT and renovations of existing exhibits were generally two sides of the same coin. The planned museum's interior design prepared for multiple audiences by allowing for different levels of experience. The ten-hall (later reduced to five) "Growth of the United States" would collectively tell the story of American progress, but a "digest" would be available in just one hall for visitors with less time or less interest, which would still expose them to the essential meaning of the more extensive exhibit. The digest would also suggest "areas of further exploration" to the more scholarly inclined.[90] The layout followed Taylor's plans for parallel galleries, which he had first proposed in 1946. There were other audiences to consider too: Taylor invoked the necessity of designing a museum that would impress both "our intellectual friends and our ideological enemies throughout the world." At the height of Cold War competition, both the functionality of the building and the "philosophical soundness of its content" needed to be unimpeachable.[91]

Visiting the Museum

Museums stand conspicuously at the intersection of memory and history. Visitors' collective and individual memories come into contact with, or are "prompted" by, a more formal and visibly constructed history.[92] Much of the most recent work in the field of museum studies has concentrated on museums as sites of memory rather than history. If memory means thinking about objects or events in their absence, exhibits could be understood, according to Susan Crane, as "forms of representation that attempt to solidify memories' meanings" by providing visitors with the "real" object—proof of a certain event that they should remember. Jan Vansina argues that objects play this role in the performance of oral (or nonliterate) traditions as well. In this figuration, curators wield the power that is implicit in the ability to "solidify" particular meanings. Moreover, since the collections encourage individual recollections, what is displayed may affect visitors' "extra-institutional memory." In other words, their existing memories interact with and to some degree absorb newly acquired collective memories, which thus continue to influence how visitors think about events, people, or themes after they have left the museum. Omission from exhibits conversely encourages forgetting, or at least not actively remembering, the neglected parts of the story.[93] Barbara Misztal calls this process of learning what is memorable and what should be forgotten "mnemonic socialization."[94]

Where instinctual memory and more self-conscious history interact, as at many historical museum exhibits, the displays may awaken unconscious memory, forcing either a revision or confrontation with the newly encountered facts. Or, it may simply reinforce existing memory, especially if the design of exhibits follows, as it often does, from a desire to avoid controversy. Despite the trend to analyze museums' effects on memory, visitors undoubtedly conceive of their time in history museums as an interaction with or experience of history. Few tourists on the Mall would make Pierre Nora's distinction that "at the heart of history is a critical discourse that is antithetical to spontaneous memory."[95] Museums are sites of memory, but they also function as historical interpreters for the public.

By the later 1960s, more visitors entered the MHT than any other museum on the Mall, at a rate of 750,000 per month during peak season. Despite the modest efforts to engage visitors of all backgrounds, studies conducted at the Smithsonian in the mid to late 1960s concluded that the "average" visitor to the MHT was white, male, middle-aged, and upper middle class. He possessed an above-average education, visited for pleasure, and came with friends or family. Three-fourths of visitors came from outside the metropolitan area, mostly from the Northeast and South, with merely 11 percent from the western United States and 7 percent from foreign countries. Just over half had visited at least once before, and just under half came to see a particular exhibit, as Princess Margaret did when she came to see the locomotives in 1965. Only 15 percent visited museums more than a few times per year, which led Smithsonian researchers to conclude that since "these persons really do not know how to operate in museums," they required still more guidance.[96]

Once inside the museum, 14 percent stayed less than one half hour, 31.5 percent stayed for one hour, 19.8 percent for an hour and a half, 19 percent for two hours, and about 15 percent stayed longer than that. Regardless of their intentions, more than half of all visitors to the MHT saw the major American history exhibits (Growth of the United States was visited by 55 percent; Everyday Life in the American Past, 54 percent; Star-Spangled Banner, 53 percent; First Ladies, 55 percent; Historic Americans, 52 percent; American Costume, 55 percent; Washington Statue, 46 percent). Only 34 percent of visitors visited the Armed Forces Hall in 1967–68, though the exhibit may have been more popular when first designed in the mid-1950s. What visitors saw was also determined by their point of entry—entering from the Mall instead of from Constitution Avenue made it one-third less likely that one would see any of the first floor. However, half of all visitors managed to see at least some of all three floors.[97]

Surprisingly, only a few—3.5 percent—described their visits as "educational." The main goal was entertainment. Most visitors were well educated (only 7 percent had not finished high school, and almost half were college graduates), which belies the directors' efforts to appeal to and instruct people of all educational backgrounds. Just before this visitor study began in 1967, Frank Taylor said, "The new exhibits at the Smithsonian are based on the premise that exhibits should be didactic."[98] The survey shows that visitors approached the displays differently, looking for amusement as much as knowledge.

New guided tours also helped to explain the exhibits. Several years prior to the Smithsonian securing funding for its own tour guides, the Junior League of Washington, an organization of women volunteers interested in the improvement of their community, began docent service for the National Museum in the American Indians Hall on February 20, 1956, and in the First Ladies Hall on March 19, 1956. By May 1956, Junior League docents had served 4,491 schoolchildren, mostly fourth, fifth, and sixth graders from local school systems. Approximately four to five thousand students visited the Smithsonian with a Junior League tour each year from 1956 through 1959. The outreach program expanded rapidly, and in the first years of the new decade the figure reached over twenty thousand per year. By 1963, just before the MHT belatedly opened, the Junior League had led more than a hundred thousand students through Smithsonian exhibits, providing an effective model for the Institution's new Extension Service.[99]

Teachers could also forgo docents and instead use Teachers Guides, prepared by University of Maryland and George Washington University graduate students for the Washington Area School Study Council.[100] Graduate students submitted drafts of the guides to Smithsonian curators, who edited and gave final approval. The guides contained scripts for teachers to use during their class's visit, as well as some classroom activities, and a list of additional readings and educational films. The scripts for teachers all followed the same formula, no matter what the subject: things were a bit rough; then they got better; now they are perfect. For the "Industrial Revolution" exhibit (which could easily have been used for much different purposes, had labor been featured at all in the displays) the tour covered the "first crude machines" and then later improvements, "which finally result in our modern processes." Suggested follow-up materials included free motion pictures made by two corporations, General Electric (*A Woolen Yarn*) and General Motors (*King Cotton*).[101]

Despite the enthusiasm for the present, the scripts and exhibits revealed a tension between the desire to teach schoolchildren and other visitors about the past and the more forceful if less conscious pull to affirm the glories of the current day. For example, the "Guide to Water and Land Transportation" begins with a note to teachers explaining that the youth of today have the opposite understanding of an adult when they think of jet airplanes as normal and oxcarts as incredible. The museum fieldtrip would correct this, according to the guide, through its displays of old boats, trains, and early horseless carriages. But in fact, the focus of the guide and the exhibit is on the automobile, which made possible the "American way of life" as the young students already knew it. The guides thus confirm that the evolutionary approach still underlay the modernized exhibits.[102] The "Shelters" exhibit, which led children through time and space to, finally, a miniature American house from the second decade of the twentieth century, similarly instructed visitors that nothing surpassed the American way of life and again reinforced what they already knew.

Planning for a new Educational Service Department began in the mid-1950s, when the Smithsonian did not yet have its own docent service, nor book-shop, lectures, or tours of any kind. Outreach programs included only the occasional traveling exhibition, the publication of scientific reports, replies to specific requests for information, the sale of black-and-white photographs of specimens on display, and a few informational pamphlets. The new service would coordinate the existing limited programs, plus affiliated efforts such as the Junior League Docents and the Teachers Guides, as well as new ideas such as regular gallery tours, audio guides, classes and lectures, a bookstore, and a school loan service. By the early 1960s, the Smithsonian had broadened its field of interaction with the public considerably and functioned more or less as it does today: a full-service "edutainment" center.[103]

Docents likely followed the scripts prepared for them, and teachers may have led their pupils around according the guides. But other visitors often ignored the viewing sequence laid out for them by the curatorial staff, and even the students on field trips took away far different memories than those intended for them. One elementary school class, led through the Indian exhibits by Ewers himself, wrote him thank-you letters that reveal that they enjoyed and remembered best the weapons "they killed people with" and the scalps—not the organization of the displays. Adults often toured the exhibits backward or went straight to the parts they wanted to see, skipping the carefully planned sequence they were supposed to follow.[104] According to the 1968 survey, about one-fifth of visitors to the MHT followed a guided or self-guided tour; the rest explored without guidance. The self-guided tours were available as brochures that included routes through the displays or specimens considered most signifi-cant. Among the first of these tours were the "National Museum Discovery Tour," the "National Treasures Hunt," the largely overlapping "Famous

Americans Tour" and "American Heroes and Heroines Tour," "Machines," and "Rooms and Shops of the American Past," which led visitors through every re-created structure in the museum.[105]

The Discovery Tour was an ambitiously designed scavenger hunt for the minority of visitors who spent at least two hours in the MHT, to give a nearly complete sense of the collections. The forty-six objects selected for the tour either contributed directly to the "growth of America" or were "associated with a famous American." The idea behind the object-oriented tour was that visitors would have a "sense of purpose" that would keep them "'hunting' for the past" and lead them to make their own discoveries as well. If Smithsonian administrators accepted the earlier report that suggested MHT visitors did not know how to correctly approach museums, this tour answered with a plan to help them on their way. Fortunately the museum stopped short of the study's absurd but telling recommendation to advise people lunching in the cafeteria (a third of all visitors did this) about where to go after eating or about what they "might discuss and think about . . . while at lunch." Overall the tours were part of a generation of efforts to get more people to actually study and learn from the didactic exhibits that had been created since the late 1940s. These efforts included audio guides, increased signage, tours, more explanatory displays, and the removal of hundreds of objects from public view. Still, the public persisted in museumgoing for fun and declined most of the guidance offered.[106]

The Corporation on Display

Each of the Teachers Guides listed references, almost always major corporations or industry associations. For the "Iron and Steel" exhibit guide, for example, the American Iron and Steel Institute and U.S. Steel provided the information for teachers and students. From the guide they could learn that the iron industry made colonization of America possible, that a key motivation behind the independence movement was American resistance to an English law that prohibited new steelworks in the colonies, and that the industry then played a decisive role in the Revolutionary War. Later, foreign competition threatened, but otherwise the script remained wholly positive. Iron- and steelworkers did not appear in the script—a typical omission in the industrial exhibits.[107]

Working within modest budgets, Smithsonian curators turned to big pharmaceutical, telecommunication, automobile, and chemical companies, as well as business and industrial associations. Many of these relationships went back decades, but now these corporations became much more directly involved in Smithsonian exhibitions, advising on content and layout and sometimes even creating entire exhibits themselves. Merck and Company, the drug manufacturer, presented "Vitamins for Health, Growth, and Life," an exhibit featured in the Medical History Gallery. Visitors not only learned about vitamins generally but also discovered exactly which vitamins they should buy if they suffered from any of the symptoms described in a diagnostic display. Similarly, Ciba Pharmaceuticals donated an antihistamines display case, and the American Pharmaceutical Association; Parke, Davis & Company; Wyeth Laboratories; R. P. Scherer Corporation; Whital Tatum Company; Norwich Pharmaceutical; and several other drug companies contributed drugs, objects, and displays to the gallery.[108]

The 1939 New York World's Fair turned would-be scientific and medical exhibits into "a magnificent monument by and to American business," in the words of *Life* magazine. A "so-called Hall of Pharmacy" was billed as a "scientific exhibition, but instead we find it commercialized by hideous signs advertising proprietary products."[109] More recent institutions have also come under fire for allowing corporate sponsors to conceal their advertising within donated exhibits. "When these institutions become marketing arms of corporate America," wrote Mathew Jacobson of the Center for Science in the Public Interest, "culture all too easily succumbs to commerce." A 1979 study of several technology museums criticized the MAH, citing a "Bell Telephony" exhibit as an obvious advertisement for the monopoly.[110] But the criticism also fits the early postwar Smithsonian.

The Medical History Gallery illustrated the differences between modern, Western medicine, which was depicted as universally successful, and all other methods of healing, which the displays disparaged. As in other exhibits, the imperfect past contrasted sharply with the perfect present. The exhibit led visitors from "superstition and quackery" (charms, zodiac stones, hypnosis, etc.), through the development of "regular" Western medicine, to modern pharmaceuticals. The "objective moves with the chronology from cultural into technical history," and from "simple and gruesomely picturesque tools of the past to the reassuringly sleek and complicated paraphernalia of the present," wrote Robert Multhauf in a contemporary review.[111] Merck and Squibb donated models of old pharmacies that illustrated the evolution of successful drugs and "real" medical science. Several diseases merited detailed exploration—all of them former killers destroyed by modern vaccines or other drugs—while contemporary diseases that defied science were omitted. A section about food and drug safety also concluded in a completely safe present day. The "Surgical Dressings" exhibit donated by Johnson and Johnson explained how dressings were now produced "under rigid conditions of control" and "sterilized . . . to insure sterility"—the last step in the "evolution of the bandage."[112] Ken Arnold has argued that the history in medical history galleries is presented, "as at the

Smithsonian's medical exhibition, 'to warn the public against the perils of quackery and the faults of folk medicine.'"[113] More to the point, the exhibits set out to convince the public of the sound science behind modern health care and the benefits of newly available drugs. This also served as another reminder of the glorious future promised by American capitalism and again illustrates the conflict within exhibits, ostensibly devoted to history, between appreciating the past and exalting the present and future.

Much of the success of exhibit modernization, and later the new exhibits in the MHT, depended on corporate assistance. Indeed, Briann Greenfield recently described the MHT of this era as "dependent on the values and desires of donors."[114] The major automakers maintained their own auto specimens; machinery, from typewriters to tractors, likewise came from corporate donors. Bell Telephone helped design the "Telephony" exhibit, bestowed many of the displayed objects, and installed telephone handsets through which visitors could hear narration about what they saw in front of them.[115] The 1953 *Smith v. Barlow* ruling that increased corporate involvement with museums and public education had stressed that "there is now a widespread belief throughout the nation that free and vigorous nongovernmental institutions of learning are *vital to our democracy and the system of free enterprise* and that withdrawal of corporate authority to make such contributions within reasonable limits would seriously threaten their continuance" (emphasis added). In fact, "enlighten[ed]" corporations *should* make donations in order to "insure and strengthen the society which gives them existence," which in turn would "protect the wider corporate environment."[116]

Logically, at least, this way of thinking bears similarity to contemporary arguments for intellectuals to engage more with society and to demands for museums to consider the public first, as articulated by such prominent museologists as Theodore Low. Low wrote, "The only way to meet people is at their own level and with what they want, not with what you want to give them." He also advocated better in-museum restaurants, more kiosks, more benches, and more helpful staff—all methods adopted by the MHT.[117] These arguments cumulatively suggested that corporations, historians, intellectuals, researchers, and curators all had a responsibility to the society that produced and supported them. Part of that responsibility was giving back in the form of scholarly work intended specifically for the public and, significantly, for the support of the system itself. Corporate philanthropic donations to museums represented a calculated attempt to bolster confidence in American capitalism in particular.

Thus, while corporate influence may have declined in some ways on television, where by the late 1950s the networks relied on sponsors less than earlier in the decade, museums' very survival increasingly came to depend on corporate largess. A "marked shift in corporate contributions" followed the *Smith* decision, so that by the middle 1950s, corporations gave substantially larger sums, particularly to educational institutions. Within a few years companies had developed techniques to ensure their money went to institutions "whose objectives most closely paralleled their own." Overall corporate contributions doubled between 1950 and 1960 and doubled again from 1960 to 1970, and donations to "education" rose from 17 percent of contributions in 1950 to 35 percent by 1958. Donations to museums and other cultural institutions not engaged directly in research also doubled in this period but remained small in comparison to education—though the two fields certainly overlapped in both corporate objectives and institutional practice.[118]

In 1953 Taylor requested corporate funding for the proposed museum. Described as an immediate "national need," the museum would serve to "relate our technological progress to the freedom which encouraged it, to spark the interests of youths in fields in which we are so seriously undermanned, and to restate the debt that we owe to our inventors, scientists, engineers, and industrial venturers." The language is similar to the stated objectives of Du Pont's *Cavalcade of America*, just as the two organizations both approached the past as almost exclusively the story of individual technological and financial accomplishment. The Smithsonian's technological history "highlight[ed] the work of America's greatest inventors" just as it "illustrate[d] and commemorate[d] the lives of . . . renowned statesmen, scholars, scientists, writers, men of enterprise, and Indian leaders."[119] For those "organizations in industry" that contributed, Taylor offered an audience of eight million visitors a year. Curators were not completely unaware of the possibilities for improper advertising disguised as history, but they rationalized corporate involvement by suggesting that companies not selling directly to the public would have no ulterior motives for sponsorship.[120]

Nevertheless, exhibits offered opportunities for both institutional and direct advertising. For example, the American Petroleum Institute and other "leading concerns in the petroleum industry" coordinated with the Smithsonian on the proposed Hall of Petroleum planned for the Arts and Industries Building in 1957 with the idea that it would move, more or less intact, to the MHT once it opened.[121] This presentation of the history of the petroleum industry in America emphasized technological advancements, new oil field discoveries, and evolving distribution methods. The history of oil corporations per se did not appear except in the wholly benevolent role of developers of new technologies. Models and displays donated by oil companies specifically credited companies that sponsored the exhibit with each particular innovation that the Smithsonian verified as essential to the development of modern energy systems.[122] As at the

"Century of Progress" Fair, the models would help visitors to enjoy the "romance of oil." When it finally (re)opened in the MHT, the exhibit featured a mural of a drilling platform on which stood the "likenesses of the industry CEOs as rig workers," symbolically displacing real workers.[123] While most people un- doubtedly understood the exhibit as a straightforward presentation of advances in the technology used in the oil industry, it also effectively naturalized the role of corporations in energy. In this sense, too, the MHT exhibit echoed the 1933 and 1939 world's fairs, which sought to "provide Americans with faith in corpo- rate leadership and in scientific expertise" and to demonstrate that the celebrated "technological progress required large corporations." Corporations discovered the sources of the fossil fuel, devised the machines to obtain, refine, and distribute it, and then sold the energy to consumers for profit. Notably absent was the *history* that might have explained *how* this particular system came into existence, not to mention alternative historical possibilities. Instead, it simply was.

Technology museums often celebrate creative inventors and companies while excluding the workers whose lives were most directly affected by the machines. Workers' exclusion from the narrative effectively devalues them as human beings. "Under capitalism, this emphasis is not accidental," writes historian Lawrence Fitzgerald.[124] H. R. Rubenstein further argues that American museums have promoted the view that "business people are the movers [and] the shapers of society and that workers are no more than interchangeable cogs."[125] Or, as Mike Wallace posits, neither workers nor their employers have much of a historical role in technology exhibits, since machines that seemingly move society forward on their own supplant both.[126] At the Smithsonian, Frank Taylor suggested that through the display of "objects on which American tech- nical and economic leadership were founded," the MHT would persuade "generations of Americans" that "diligence, perseverance, . . . and scientific and technical ingenuity were the foundations of U.S. cultural heritage." And technological innovation would continue to provide an "ever-increasing stan- dard of living" for Americans, provided they continued to support the system as described.[127] In a museum thus constructed, "glorification becomes the principle business of the institution, and the public is cajoled in place of being educated," as Thomas R. Adams warned in 1939.[128]

History, American Style

The first two exhibit halls to undergo modernization, the popular American Indians and First Ladies Halls, established the priority of style over substance and provided the blueprint for future renovations. Gala events and extraordi- nary publicity also distinguished these re-openings from anything that had been done at the Smithsonian before. Suddenly, the Smithsonian became host to national and international dignitaries.

Anthropology had been at the forefront of modernization efforts under Ewers and head curator F. M. Setzler, who in 1947 submitted a request to re-design the American Indians exhibits. Renovations were finally made in the mid-1950s, following the increase in funding, but the content and organization remained substantially unchanged from the 1890s exhibits. Ewers was more concerned with the exhibits' effectiveness, and he surveyed visitors to find out how to improve the displays' communicability. In response to visitors' complaints that they could not figure out the logic or order to the Indian displays, nor gain any real sense of Indian cultures, Ewers reorganized the displays to make them chronological and added more elaborate dioramas.[129] The American Indians remained in the Museum of Natural History, though it would be wrong to read too much into this as that building housed exhibits from various fields, especially the anthropology collection but also including, at times, some of the historical and fine arts collections. The postwar proposal for a Museum of Man nearly led to the departure of not only the American Indians Hall but the entire Department of Anthropology from the Museum of Natural History. This would have led to an interesting merger of the anthropology, American history, and science and technology collections. Instead, since money for new wings to the Museum of Natural History appeared before money for the proposed Museum of Man, the anthropologists and the Indians stayed where they were.[130] As planning for the MHT went forward, no one seems to have considered making the Native American halls a part of the American history exhibits.

In retrospect, the 1950s Indian scripts seem dated and confused. "Tribes" that peacefully "settled down on a reservation" were depicted as more advanced and more successful than those that "continued their hostility against the whites" and resisted being "pacified." The "desert peoples" script describes how southwestern tribes first irrigated the arid region, building sophisticated canal systems to grow cotton, corn, beans, and squash. Yet the scene depicts a primitive-looking group of Cocopa Indians gathered around a shelter on the top of which are "a large, red jar, used for storing drinking water, and a crude basketry corn-crib." In the foreground a man teaches his young son to use a bow and arrow, and a woman "cleans grass seed for food." Thus, nothing connects the content of the written text to the diorama. The exhibit script presents a history of American Indians that avoids judgment by circumscribing and hiding the role of white Americans. For example, "Two centuries of warfare and epidemics of disease greatly reduced the populations of the Woodland tribes" of the eastern seaboard. No one bears any responsibility for the damage.

And by the mid-nineteenth century, Indians "were placed upon reservations" (were they the miniature plastic toy Indians?) to "make room" for the expanding American nation. Several scholars have recently described how museums in colonialist nations demonstrated mastery of "the Other." The enclosure of cultural difference in museum cases buttressed "claims of the capacity to know and govern" and also helped to demonstrate the technological superiority of the Western powers. The Smithsonian's postwar anthropological-historical displays' implicit claim to superiority over distant and different Indians reveals a similar essential logic, still suitable for American transcontinental and global hegemony.[131]

Visitors could also hear the Indians—a benefit of the emphasis in the 1950s on "multimedia" exhibits. For the audio tour, musical selections from Library of Congress and Folkways recordings that supported the tone and content of the new exhibit were added to enhance the experience. Curators rejected a song that sounded like the singer might be drunk because it might "encourage disparaging associations." They selected a record of an Eskimo speaking with laughter at the end to demonstrate the "Eskimos' sense of humor" and humanize the mannequins behind the glass. For the Creek they liked the Stomp Dance partly because of its "similarity to Negro Spirituals," though another, "more 'Indian-ish'" version of the Stomp Dance was also considered. First and foremost, however, the selections could not undermine the distinctiveness of Native Americans, just as they were kept apart from the MHT/MAH. Thus, a Tlingit "Paddling Song" had to be reconsidered because "it sounds too modern."

American Indians at the Smithsonian were specifically not "modern." As they had been for many decades by that point, Indians were "pacified," "removed," "long gone," and "extinct," but decidedly not contemporary.[132] And neither they nor African Americans figured in the American history exhibits. In the extensive Growth of the United States exhibit, a single glass case devoted to Indians *and* Negroes in Colonial America remained in the planning stages as late as 1966, allotted just fifty dollars in the annual budget that year. Africa's contributions to the development of the United States were written off as "hard to document."[133] This began to change only at the very end of the 1960s.

The popularity of the First Ladies Hall led Taylor to suggest it as the other first experiment in modernization. Curator Margaret Brown wrote the script and worked with Benjamin Lawless to refurbish the display cases, which until then had nothing in them except generic mannequins. When President and Mrs. Eisenhower opened the new hall on May 24, 1955, the cream of Washington society saw individualized models of first ladies set in their own contemporary White House rooms.[134] At the gala event, Secretary Carmichael declared

History got a makeover before the Eisenhowers attended the gala opening of the renovated First Ladies Hall in 1955, one of a number of contemporary Smithsonian affairs that signaled a new emphasis on the public reception of history exhibits. (Courtesy of Smithsonian Institution Archives, Image 2002-10613.)

that the exhibit "symbolizes the growth of the country step by step from General Washington to General Eisenhower."[135] While this may have been pandering in the presence of the then current president-general, the secretary's phrase encapsulated the philosophy of the refurbished American history exhibits. They linked contemporary America to its past—its mythic or heroic past—but simultaneously reaffirmed the tremendous progress that the nation had made.

The ten thousand square feet set aside for the hall in the planned MHT made it one of the larger exhibits, and it remained one of the most popular as well. But despite the rhetoric, formal dresses worn by the wives and daughters of presidents elucidate very little about the history of the United States. Yet because Americans wanted to see the gowns, this hall featured prominently in modernization plans, tours, and planning for the MHT. Thus, even at the height of creating "didactic exhibits" that would instruct as much as entertain, curators responded to public demand, in this hall at least.

The script for the "First Ladies Hall Teachers Guide" tried to emphasize the democratic nature of the American political system by characterizing the well-dressed mannequins as the "wives of planters, of farmers, lawyers, legislators, tradesmen, statesmen, frontiersman, soldiers, and of teachers—men from all walks of life who were called to act as leaders of our nation." The ornate gowns on display somehow supported common men who became great through patriotic service. Scripts focused on the president rather than the woman who wore the dress on display. The Polk script typified the method of instruction and the almost complete dismissal of the first ladies:

> The next president was James Polk. You already know something of the history of Polk's time because your friend, Davy Crockett, was going off to Congress and also becoming involved in *the war to free Texas from Mexico* [emphasis added] when he lost his life in the battle of the Alamo. Another important thing that happened while Polk was President was the discovery of gold in California. I'm sure most of you have heard about the gold rush haven't you? And the men who went out to prospect for gold called themselves the '49ers which is a great help in remembering the date of the rush and part of Tyler's administration. This blue silk dress was the dress worn by Mrs. Polk.[136]

Only in the display cases for Mrs. Hoover and Mrs. Roosevelt could one gather that the first ladies were themselves real people. The scripts praised both women for their own educational and professional accomplishments. This hall contrasts with an exhibit in the Arts and Industries Building called "Woman's Rights." Like the first ladies, Susan B. Anthony stood encased, wearing a red shawl that appeared in a photographic portrait behind her. But the display also featured her inkstand, her newspaper, gavels from several conventions, and other objects that served as evidence of her life's work. Besides their dresses, no such tools accompanied the first ladies, who remained mere mannequins even in their new surroundings. The refurbished exhibit re-created White House rooms but made no other effort to contextualize the gowns or the first ladies. This left the hall at odds with the other second-floor exhibits in the MHT, which included Everyday Life in the American Past, Historic Americans, Growth of the United States, and American Costume, which at least considered the fashions of people outside of the executive mansion.[137]

Growth of the United States would be the centerpiece of the new MHT, telling the national story through its technical and material triumphs and "graphically communicat[ing] the character and contribution of each period."[138] Beginning with the first European settlements, tracing its colonial development as both "market" and "asylum," through the "age of reason" and into the nineteenth century, objects on display ranged from Jefferson's writing desk to a John Bull locomotive, a New England bedroom, and Whitney's cotton gin. Summarizing broadly, in the planned "Growth" exhibit, and in a similar exhibit made up of much of the same material that was installed in the Arts and Industries Building in 1958, the mid-nineteenth century marked a dramatic shift from a society that fostered individual achievement to a society dominated by incorporated organizations, which were in turn dominated by an industrial elite—progress, apparently. The late nineteenth century witnessed the "mechanization of American society," the "emergence of the United States as a world power," and the "continued increase of the American democratic tradition." The recent past would depict the "full force of the scientific revolution in American life, exemplified by recent advance in electronics, atomic power, biological research, and the investigation of outer space."[139] Divided by type of industry, the exhibits again focused mainly on the technological progress of each era. For example, the "Chemical Industries" exhibit in the twentieth-century section displayed objects such as aluminum from ALCOA and several examples of nylon donated by Du Pont (the familiar story of American history told through Du Pont research and development).

If political and cultural history were not ignored, they also were not treated with much insight. The Civil War exhibit epitomized the failure to ask difficult historical questions. "Initially a conflict of governmental activities," read the script, "[the war] changed the American way of life—North and South." At the end of the war, "the United States became a nation freed of the scourge of slavery." Something cleansed the nation of its great sin, but no mention is made of responsibility or guilt, or even of victory and defeat. The exhibit might not contain much educative value, but it would at least be inoffensive. Secretary Carmichael stressed the need to "have careful regard for the sensitivity of our visitors—from schoolchildren to Congressmen," and to avoid controversial displays whenever possible. As an example of how to do this, he suggested the figures representing the Civil War era might be confined to famous congressmen.[140]

In contrast, a women's history section celebrated individuals who dedicated their lives to the cause of women's rights, demonstrating that, similar to the Freedom Train, the Smithsonian felt more comfortable with the issue of equal political rights for women than with slavery and the Civil War. Mannequins of suffragists, nurses, professionals, and athletes wore the fashions that, in this story, helped women achieve "equality." By 1945 women had "successfully competed with men in nearly every endeavor, from the factory to the military." As in the First Ladies Hall, Eleanor Roosevelt stands here as the paragon of feminine achievement, and as an elite "symbol of women's responsibility in a mechanized world."[141] Perhaps the key was that these symbols of women's equality were easily contained within the glass cases, whereas a real history of the Civil War, necessarily replete with controversy, would inevitably spill out of the museum and create a political mess. History could be used to surreptitiously deal with contemporary controversy, but historical controversy was sometimes as contentious as current politics.

Other exhibit halls dealt with American progress in a variety of different ways. "Power," suggested Frank Taylor, was the real key to American abundance and hegemony, and planning for a "Hall of Power" began in 1952. In addition to creating the "abundance of goods and the high standard of living which we enjoy," American power surpluses in the 1950s were "proving to be a solid material support for our campaign to win friends around the world." The well-known postwar power exhibit, "Atoms for Peace," also made a brief stopover at the Smithsonian in 1956. Taylor and Secretary Carmichael quietly opened the exhibit early one morning after they decided the Atomic Energy Commission's traveling exhibit did not merit the now typical gala opening.[142]

The new exhibits related American history as the story of technological progress and the growth of industry, but they also presented the nation's development through the "History of the Armed Forces."[143] Or, more accurately, the exhibit presented the history of a militarized nation. Just as corporations helped to create their relevant exhibits, the Department of the Army advised and constructed dioramas for the military history hall. This hall—at 33,000 square feet, one of the largest when it moved to the MHT in 1965—consisted of uniforms, weapons, flags, ship models, maps, and numerous personal effects of military heroes, from George Washington's epaulets to General Philip Sheridan's horse. The "main attraction," however, was the gunboat *Philadelphia*, part of the American fleet commanded by Benedict Arnold at the Battle of Valcour Island in 1776. One glass case near the boat memorialized the crew, and another remembered the battle. In spirit and substance the *Philadelphia* display resembled an older U.S.S. *Maine* display from the Naval History Hall in the Arts and Industries Building. The *Maine* was also prominently featured and framed the military adventures of the turn of the century within the contextual theme of patriotic sacrifice.

As with the petroleum industry exhibits, the Armed Forces Hall naturalized the contemporary U.S. military by creating a past in which the military always played a leading, beneficent role. After entering the hall, visitors were more or less confined to the route that led from the colonial era through the present.[144] This followed the museum-wide effort to reconfigure exhibit layouts so that visitors would "progress along a generally chronological path," rather than moving around randomly.[145] The tour through the hall offered a military explanation of American development and an education designed to help visitors "better appreciate the contribution" of the military.[146] The first panel depicted the earliest English colonists, "more than half" of whom were soldiers, who "came equipped to hold their ground against Spaniard or Indian." An illustration depicted these colonist-soldiers under attack by larger and more muscular Indians. America grew along with its armed forces, through the French and Indian and Revolutionary Wars, the "development" of the West (where the "Army took the lead in exploring" and held the new ground by force), "new frontiers" in the Philippines, Hawaii, China, and Cuba, and into the global conflicts of the twentieth century. The Wright brothers "opened a vast new horizon for military activity" just two display cases away from the mushroom cloud over Hiroshima, which was the largest photograph in the World War II display. For the armed forces, the bomb—always singular, though dropped on two different cities—marked the "completion of another phase of its continuing mission to defend the United States." Finally came contemporary "Free World Leadership," which featured a rifle next to a map of Korea of identical length, and "New Horizons," a display of the nuclear missiles currently deployed or under development. The exhibit showed how the military also controlled the nation's rivers and developed its natural resources. When Americans "needed aid or disaster struck, the Army was there to help."

The narrative emphasized that throughout American history the military had been a dynamic and essential force in the nation's development. But the exhibit ended with propaganda for the present, which threatened to make a disastrous break with the militarized past. Now the public foolishly demanded "heavy cuts," forcing the armed services to "return almost to peacetime strength with a resultant loss of combat effectiveness." This at a time when the communists had, "despite the aid we had given them during their fight with Germany and Japan," launched numerous assaults against freedom. In Korea, the U.S. military had been "rushed into the breach" to "save the free peoples of the world," but with budget cuts and an impending demilitarization of society, who knew what might happen in the future.[147] G. Kurt Piehler argues more recently that a campaign to erect a national military museum failed because of the "misgivings many public officials and much of the public had toward the large military establishment that had to be maintained during the cold war: Americans did not want to see themselves as a militaristic people."[148] While an entire edifice devoted to the military apparently repelled many people, the Smithsonian still embedded the armed forces in every phase of American history and effectively created a military museum within the MHT.

A Museum for the Age

In the early 1950s, a Smithsonian brochure described how the institution's arti-facts "enable the American people of today to study and know their country's past, to apply the experience of the past to the problems of the present, and to substantiate their thinking concerning the future with facts instead of fancies."[149] The brochure thus concisely reflected the postwar conception of public history as utilitarian. "Patriotism is a word that is sometimes misused," said Secretary Carmichael shortly thereafter, "but who can doubt that any American citizen becomes more truly patriotic when he has knowledge of the basic natural resources of his country and of how these resources have been and are now being used in the growth and maintenance of our modern life?"[150]

The fast-growing Smithsonian of the 1950s represented American history in celebratory fashion. Curators, administrators, and designers joined their political, corporate, and military liaisons in accepting the dominant ideology of postwar America. The new version of history that visitors came to see at their renovated national museum sought to legitimate a growing corporate hegemony based at least in part on the corporation's historical naturalization and benevo-lence. As Mike Wallace has written about museums in general (following Gramsci), the "unexamined assumptions undergird the legitimacy of a social system . . . far more effectively than crude ideological cudgeling."[151]

Generalizing about the role and position of museums in American society, Ivan Karp distinguishes between political society and civil society, arguing that museums are institutions of the latter. The Smithsonian, though, has a special relationship to the state, as illustrated by its patriotic, nationalistic content and its location—not to mention the high level of involvement in its affairs by Congress and other members of the political and financial elite. Thus, the Smithsonian wields more persuasive power than most other civil institutions, even if this power is confined to the realms of ideas and history. While these institutions can either "support or resist definitions imposed by the more coercive organs of the state," in the emergent Smithsonian of the 1950s, very little ambi-guity existed.[152]

Of the sources of history offered to the American public in the 1950s, the Smithsonian most clearly represents the state, its authority, and its narrowly defined interests. From the elected officials and CEOs that served on the Board of Regents to the curators linked to corporate research, many of those involved in (re)presenting the past had personal connections with the military-industrial system that the exhibits implicitly promoted. More important, the museum constructed and displayed a limited but distinctive national history for

American citizens to see and comprehend as their own unique and superior heritage. And to the rest of the world, the MHT staked the American claim to global leadership.

However, in spite of significant efforts to the contrary, visitors to museums can to some extent pick and choose what they want to see—disrupting the limited view offered to them. Curators did what they could to make visitors follow the designated routes by constructing temporary walls, offering guided and self-guided tours, and establishing information desks and signs, but no one could force visitors to stop and read every panel or see every exhibit. While to a certain extent this suggests visitors' empowerment, it also increases the museum's flexibility to disseminate ideas. When television viewers lose interest in *Cavalcade of America* or *You Are There*, they turn off the program completely, but at the museum they can turn their gaze elsewhere without exiting the building. The bored or dissatisfied visitor has several options short of rejecting the museum outright, and once they have made the decision to enter the building, visitors are unlikely to reject the exhibits completely. After all, it is the flexibility of the system that makes hegemonic power so enduring.

Conclusion

Once and Future Truths

When we venture into the past we engage in a sort of time travel. One of the sacred myths of science fiction is that time travelers can alter the course of history, in unpredictable ways. When we venture into the past through "authentic" historical dramas such as *Cavalcade of America* or visit the "real" historical objects displayed at the Museum of American History, the point is rather different. We can in these cases travel through time, but we never risk altering the apparently natural flow of American history—not because we are imperceptible, but because no alternative history seems possible. Every detail—the dress, the buttons, the clocks, the rifles—is precisely correct, leaving little space for imagining alternate pasts or interpretations. As David Lowenthal argues, the "verisimilitude" is also used to conceal "major bias."[1] In addition, unless one is willing and able to discard this past, imagining alternatives in the present becomes more difficult. From this perspective the past differs stylistically from the present, but people, institutions, and structures are fundamentally the same across the centuries, and what once was true is equally true now and forever. The supposition that key truths never change yokes popular history with its meaning; the power to define the past clearly amounts to the power to define the present because the two are portrayed as substantially analogous. Thus the need in the 1960s for a break with this limited past: a rupture from the narrowly defined heritage that excluded possibilities for institutional change.

As for "authenticity," attention to detail, and the insistence on "facts"—things that elicited critical praise for representing excellent history on *Cavalcade* and *You Are There*—in the end they are merely the means by which we see how easy it is to commune with the past. On the other hand, historical distance and contexts are extremely difficult to imagine, *especially* when our senses are confronted with "authentic" re-creations that render the foreign familiar. Dangers abound when history appears to be both obvious and authoritative.

Lack of critical distance is one kind of problem; highlighting only the events or subjects that support one's argument is another. When Howard Green critiqued the emerging field of public history for its apparent service to sponsors' interests in 1981, he made much the same point about the subordination of historical work to advertising or public relations goals.[2] Abraham Polonsky later said of his work on *You Are There*, "We were making history comprehensible in terms of what we thought was significant at that time—without distorting history to do it!" He further defended the series, explaining, "The show was deliberately political—but it was not political propaganda. . . . In propaganda you deliberately and consciously have a message that you want people to understand and for which you find illustrations. What we did was political interpretation. And in the interpretation you try to make it dramatically flow out of the natural historical conflict."[3] Likely, none of the authors of these popular histories thought of what he was doing as propaganda or as distortions of history. Yet each, in his own way, achieved both ends.

In some sense, all of the cases examined succeeded only for a limited time, which coincided with the particular relationship between midcentury Americans and the past. By the 1960s, their time had clearly passed. The Museum of American History and the History Book Club both continue to operate, but their radically changed forms support the conclusion that these specific efforts had their moment—and could only have had their moment—in the earlier period. The HBC is now part of a conglomerate of forty book clubs run by "the premier direct marketer of general interest and specialty book clubs."[4] History has been commercialized and absorbed into the mass of books and other consumer products sold by this conglomerate. Besides the discounted prices, the primary draw is the "vast selection" available to subscribers, which is hardly a benefit in a world of unlimited sources. Advertisements emphasize the diversity of subjects but feature presumably popular topics, including pseudo-historical subjects such as the "saints, scoundrels, and other characters" of the Bible, most prominently.[5] Original interpretations can be found within the cornucopia of new titles, but for the most part the selections represent an attempt to appeal to popular memory and taste. It has become, in other words, something like *American*

Heritage and its offer of a "commercial substitute for the traditional stories" that nostalgically "highlight your heritage, your sense of roots and place, your invaluable legacy"—but it fails to approach the past with the fresh, critical perspective that DeVoto and his colleagues envisioned.[6]

The MAH has sometimes balanced appeals to popular memory with scholarship. Beginning in the 1970s, the museum incorporated more critical history as well as a much broader understanding of who belongs in the national story. Exhibits reflect trends in the historical profession toward social, cultural, and subaltern history, but they also cover just enough of everything that different types of visitors would insist upon seeing. Vietnam War memorabilia, the lunch counter from the first sit-in in Greensboro, race cars, Dorothy's ruby slippers— each display is offered as a concession to a particular subset of the population. Catering to contemporary tastes for an inclusive history in which everyone can find some part of a usable past, the museum sacrificed coherent narrative to gain the approval of diverse audiences. However, exhibit halls still reflect the promotional objectives of donors. The historic Ipswich house, which has some outer walls removed so that visitors can see inside, unsubtly promotes home ownership as the most sought-after goal of all American families and implicitly advocates policies that favor cheap loans and new construction—an unsurprising message given the exhibit's underwriter: the National Association of Realtors. The renovated exhibit opened just as the U.S. housing market collapsed, which is ironic and disappointing. The agenda of General Motors' "America on the Move" exhibit, a history of American transportation, is made similarly obvious through an evolutionary framework that ends with late-model GM cars and trucks.

The Cold War–era MAH served propaganda needs and encouraged an iconographic approach to American history. As George Orwell wrote of the party's version of history, the MAH demonstrated that every American was "better off than his ancestors and that the average level of material comfort is rising."[7] And like consensus history in general, the museum's history exhibits imagined a consistency in American ideology that demonstrated infallibility— not of the party of course, but of the postwar corporate state. The renovations of 2006–8, approved and implemented in the post–September 11 age, reflect a patriotic imperative similar to that of the early Cold War. The Cold War plans moved the "greatest American treasure" from a plain glass case that allowed for only part of the Star-Spangled Banner to be displayed to the huge atrium of the new MHT/MAH. The change would purportedly allow for proper admiration and reflection—significantly, with visitors in full view of each other so that patriotism could be enforced by citizens. But that space became a busy intersection and a meeting place for tour groups. Now, where the flag once hung, a sterile metallic replica hangs in its place. Behind the replica, in a hall dark and quiet except for *pianissimo* shell explosions, the real flag lays unfurled on a slight incline behind a large window. Benches line the wall opposite, so that visitors may sit and contemplate the oversized banner; on each of my visits the ever-present guard instructed me to sit for a while. The long-desired reverent atmosphere has finally been achieved, apparently with even greater coercion.

"Tradition in America had to be labored," wrote Henry Steele Commager. Precisely because the American past "could not be absorbed from childhood on in the art and architecture of every town and village, in song and story and nursery rhyme," it had to be invented and transmitted via other, less organic means.[8] In the middle decades of the twentieth century, the American public increasingly learned history through new mass communication technologies; public history was mobile and transmittable. Even at the Smithsonian, where Frank Taylor observed that "of the many media now employed for the popular interpretation of history, science, and art, the museum remains unique in its ability to show the public actual objects illustrative of these fields," at mid-century the curators sought to "exploit the potentialities" of exciting new methods of display, especially new media.[9]

Overwhelmingly, the currents between the public and the past were regulated by the powerful and resourceful, especially corporate America. True, HBC authors wrote of corporations that "disembodied evil," but their message reached but a handful of "small-town intelligentsia" compared to the tens of millions reached by Du Pont's histories of corporations as heroes, not to mention the popular exhibitions of the Freedom Train and the Smithsonian. The effort to naturalize the corporation in American history, or perhaps to construct a *mythical* foundation for the postwar corporate state, principally succeeded. Capital's attempt to define the heritage of contemporary Americans also consisted of limiting the more democratic elements in public history. Lammot du Pont spoke frequently of a need to distinguish between "democracy," a term he disliked and thought inappropriately expansive, and "republic," which "is used in our Constitution."[10] Du Pont's *Cavalcade* reflected the family's perspective (Liberty League founder Irénée's feelings toward democracy were even more negative than his brother's[11]) that the potential force of popular movements needed to be contained, and the series' historical lessons tried to limit awareness of such disruptions to hierarchy in the past. *Cavalcade* thus disseminated pro-business messages and also attempted to limit potentially dangerous knowledge.

However, by the late 1950s American society began to move in a different direction. A significant number of people, from veteran civil rights activists to college students, actively sought to increase democratic participation. The contemporary United States needed change, not continuity. If they looked to the past at all, they looked beyond the narrowly conceived history presented by our sponsors to the mostly unexplored, usable but still untapped histories of the groups and individuals left out of the "American cavalcade"; history witnessed a "redistribution of property."[12] Only a few glimpses of this kind of history appear anywhere in these five cases. The first History Book Club board selected some neo-progressive histories that emphasized class conflict in American history, but these contained little working-class, labor, or social history of the kind that gained stature within the profession in the 1950s and even more in the 1960s. *You Are There* went a little further, occasionally covering African American history and culture, social movements, and ordinary folk in the midst of great events. Of the five cases studied, these two ventures, at least in their original forms, persisted for the shortest lengths of time. Both succumbed to commercial pressures quickly. The other three cases—Du Pont's *Cavalcade*, the Smithsonian, and the Freedom Train—made no effort to enlarge the social picture of American history, until the Smithsonian began to do so at the close of the 1960s. And then the newfound past at the museum mythologized previously forgotten Americans more than it historicized them.

Similarly, CBS brought *You Are There* back in 1971 as a more inclusive and more sentimentalized story of the American past than its first incarnation. For example, an episode on the Underground Railroad featured a saintly Harriet Tubman, accompanied by maudlin music, heroically leading slaves to freedom. Close-ups of her face freeze her expressions as if she were posing for her memorial, which in the end is exactly what the episode was. Perhaps out of a sense of nostalgic gratitude, Walter Bernstein wrote a few episodes for the series, but the shows were, in his words, "no good." The producers were "frightened at the very idea that you might deal with conflict." Bernstein thought, "The irony was that during this supposedly liberated time when they could have been more daring—they weren't. They were scared to death."[13] Perhaps the producers recognized, on some level, that the challenging subjects confronted by the original *You Are There* would be contested in the more democratic society that emerged in the 1960s—or at least they feared such reactions. In that environment, CBS risked inciting protest or losing viewers if the series contended with complex, controversial subjects and irresolvable moral dilemmas.

History seems to have been more useful as meaningful analogy during the 1950s, a period when the range of political discourse was curtailed. Later, when contemporary society opened up, it became both easier to share diverse political views and more difficult to sell the public on a particular and limited past—without risking some kind of backlash from a more vocal public. In 1969 Martin Marty argued that in contrast to earlier generations to whom the past was "obviously useful," his contemporaries felt "cut off" from history; its usefulness was not apparent to them.[14] By then, many Americans either rejected history completely or sought to rewrite it to such an extent that the old past was no longer recognizable. We still have a shared past, of course, but it is more contested and more complex—to the point that often it no longer feels like a shared past at all. Historical revisions exploded shared traditions—or ignored them while looking for usable pasts in alternative communities, among outsider groups. Despite some important differences between them, the interpretations of history expressed in this book all maintained their place in the older tradition, even while they attempted to take custody of that heritage. When, in 1995, Speaker of the House Newt Gingrich complained that from the settlement of Jamestown until 1965 "there was one continuous civilization built around a set of commonly accepted legal and cultural principles," he, in a sense, merely overstated his case about a departure from tradition.[15] Protestors challenged the official history that accompanied the Freedom Train, DeVoto's "boys" scouted for books that would make readers think critically about American history, and *You Are There* brought the sorrier aspects of the past to light, but they all worked from similar assumptions about the relevance of the nation's traditions. As Cold War aims became muddied in the 1960s, and numerous and previously submerged domestic tensions boiled to the surface, that story-line contained too many noticeable discrepancies to be left alone: progress was not even, and perfection had not been attained after all.

It may now be even more difficult to challenge popular historical memory than it was during the early postwar period—not in spite of, but because of, increased possibilities for communication. DeVoto's wonder at the great pro-liferation of history in 1947 led him into his failed effort to provide scholarly guidance. Today there are millions more sources of information and misinformation about the past, often tending toward myth, iconography, and memory rather than history. Relatively few hail from academic or other noncommercial sources. Even if something approaching formal historical scholarship makes it onto the public's radar, it is unlikely to reach more than a small fraction of the population. Moreover, such work is likely to make every effort to avoid controversy by declining to upset existing popular historical memories. The Smithsonian history exhibits certainly err on the safe side of controversy, especially after the *Enola Gay* debacle, but the best example of this might be the documentaries of Ken Burns.[16] Taking our five cases as representative of the way that history reached the public in the mid-twentieth century, and then looking at

Burns's determinedly uncontroversial films and the contemporary HBC and MAH as representative of current mediators in that relationship, it is clear that the impetus has shifted from elite direction to popular or commercial demand.

Having brushed aside the interpretive "guidance" offered by interested postwar elites, much of the public lacks both mediators and connections with the past. Despite their limitations, at least a possibility of communicating ideas to a large population existed in these enterprises, which was precisely what made them exciting to the people involved. Though flawed, they fostered a shared sense of the past within mainstream society. Some apparent interest from the public was necessary, but the various methods of communication that allowed for the promulgation of these ideas played the key role, because of their limitations as much as their capabilities. Today, just as the Freedom Train would no longer be able to visit but a small proportion of the communities where it stopped sixty years ago, so no effort to communicate ideas about history could now hope to speak to as large an audience, proportionally, as these "historians" sought to persuade—excepting the unsuccessful historians of the early HBC.

In the early 1960s, "fomented in part by the very contradiction between history portrayed and the history lived," as the Port Huron Statement put it, a new generation just coming of age still referenced Jefferson's words, but only to point out the disconnect between the nation's foundational myths and reality.[17] Perhaps, for the young children who watched *Cavalcade* on television in the 1950s and matured in the 1960s, the lessons that stressed America's promises of fairness, equality, and opportunity, along with obligations of participation and citizenship, encouraged exactly the kind of political and social disruptions Du Pont hoped to discourage. As Frances Fitzgerald argues, college students' anger at the system in the 1960s "came in part from their sense that, along with government officials, their textbooks and their teachers had concealed from them the truth about American politics and history."[18] If this was initially a rejection by the left, more recently the far right has shunned mainstream heritage, showing more interest in substituting their own story of America than in locating themselves in the prevailing narrative.[19] The Freedom Train, which historians have described as a coercive dynamo driven by right-wing corporate interests, seems quite tame—almost progressive—in comparison to contemporary conservative protests. The AHF disparaged "unfair" regulation, yet their carefully designed reeducation campaign emphasized the need for all Americans to cheerfully pay the taxes asked of them, to support the expansion of public education, and to actively appreciate the tremendous benefits that accrued from national citizenship. Here, at least, consensus was not just a willful disregard for past conflicts in American history; it also reflected widespread acceptance of the evolution of American government and society to its contemporary status, especially amongst elites.

Conversely, today's conservatives make plain their desire to destroy consensus rather than create it, and they directly challenge the AHF's coupling of freedom and broad social responsibility. Like President Herbert Hoover's definition of American individualism as inherently entwined with public service, the individualism celebrated by the train and even by Du Pont still contained an underlying element of social connectedness—rooted in American history. Historians reflexively disparage the Freedom Train's consensus history, but if history is destined to be used and distorted for political purposes, consensus and unity are not the worst objectives. And we should not trivialize the work of transporting rare documents to every state so that citizens had the opportunity to see the sources for themselves and perhaps challenge AHF's interpretation—though that was not easy to do. Claiming exclusive rights of inheritance and denying all doubters involves less effort.

In the early 1950s, Daniel Boorstin lamented Americans' apparent inability to discuss political ideas, the resulting reliance on the "Founding Fathers" for answers, and the assumption—what he called "givenness"—that their solutions are "adequate to all our future needs." Not all Americans approach the past this way, but for those who do—and I think Boorstin is right that many do—history becomes fundamentalist. In her recent book about the Tea Party and the American Revolution, Jill Lepore uses the phrase "historical fundamentalism" to describe the conflation of originalism and evangelism in the movement.[20] In looking only at the Revolutionary period, Lepore perhaps credits the far right with a more sophisticated sense of history than they have. In fact, their notion of the "founders" is far less historical and far more sacred, including biblical figures, Christian "discoverers" such as Columbus, and, of course, the Pilgrims, at least as much as the revolutionary generation itself.

This fundamentalism injures and obscures history even more than the narrow uses of the past described in this book. Not merely seeking precedent, and not merely conservative, it asks contemporary Americans to discard two centuries of history (in the truer sense of that word) in favor of rigid adherence to a mythical ideal that acts as law—divine law as much as civil—and prevents activities and speech that challenge the presumed fundamentals. With the rise of the Tea Party, with significant support from conservative media, a national political movement has made this approach to the past the central theory around which its supporters rally. Newly elected Tea Party congressmen read aloud the Constitution in January 2011 to clarify that their literalism would delimit the nation's political agenda.[21] If Boorstin's argument held water before, it has become bloated by the Tea Party's substitution of quotes from favored founders in place of reasoned argument or political theorization. Compromise has no place; discussion is pointless since the believers' truth is sacred and therefore indisputable.

Immersing the public in a form of history that confronts change, as opposed to presenting snapshots of particular events or periods, is difficult. Public and popular history excels at preserving or re-creating moments in the past, whether in the form of memorials, historic houses, or movies and television programs. Fewer projects analyze change. The examples in this study also failed— mostly—to offer citizens anything but a static view of the past. This may seem paradoxical given the imperative to link the past to present concerns, but in fact the erasure of intervening history allowed for easier comparisons across time. Du Pont, certainly, wanted the past for its useful examples, not as an explanation. The Freedom Train also failed to confront change, simply drawing straight lines from each icon to present-day rights, privileges, and duties. The Smithsonian presented change through the evolution of machines but offered little historical explication of society. The radical leftists at CBS News, rooted as they were in Marxist theory and some postwar leftist historical scholarship, sometimes tried to deal with broader and longer-term developments, and Walter Cronkite's summary at the anchor desk always linked the events portrayed with later history, but, of course, the twenty-eight-minute show had limitations. The stories themselves offered a window into one specific day in history. Really, only the History Book Club sought to provide the American people with works that dealt with change over time rather than fixed images of a fixed past, as almost all of their books took a very long view of historical development. But despite the historians' dreams of influence, books are not really public history.

When Boorstin wrote about Americans relying on partly cloudy imaginings of history instead of political theory, there was widespread, not total, agreement about the past: not necessarily "consensus history," but a shared sense of what constituted the past. The Right and Left now have very different ideas of what history is, who and what are legitimate subjects, and how critically the past should be examined. Exclusive inheritances, as opposed to a shared sense of history, make the past less useful to the whole of contemporary society. Now we may easily ignore or dismiss history that seems to have been created for another group, which often means we dismiss that group as being fundamentally different from us. Right-wing Texas School Board members have little need for a Deistic

Jefferson or confrontational minorities in their textbooks; the Left rejects the idea of a sacred story—or any other tautology—that runs from Columbus through the Pilgrims through the divinely inspired Constitution.

Universal public education may be disappearing along with a shared historical sense. Early in 2012, New Hampshire enacted a Tea Party–supported law that allows parents to challenge or opt out of any part of their children's educational curriculum that they find offensive, be that American history or biology or French.[22] Even students attending the same school may thus develop radically different notions of the past. In 2011, conservative television and radio personality Glenn Beck began to broadcast *Liberty Treehouse*, a children's television program that, like the popular DVD series *Drive thru History*, offers a sacred history of the United States. Both series are marketed to the growing population of homeschooled children and their generally conservative Christian parents. A distinct group of right-wing scholars provides the academic underpinnings for the programs and for a growing body of textbooks and other educational materials whose approach to the past bears little resemblance to contemporary mainstream American history.[23]

In a way the sacralization echoes the Freedom Train's attempt to co-opt American freedom. But the sacred texts of the Freedom Train, while not as inclusive as they might have been, did not *end* with the founding documents (as much of the new conservative popular history does)—an explicit recognition that later historical developments matter. The other cases I studied were usually more open in the sense of broadly examining history to find meaning for the present, and each sought to create "citizen's history"—useful knowledge that could be brought to bear on contemporary issues—rather than to hold up the past as an unbreakable commandment. Even Du Pont, with its overriding commitment to the positive portrayal of American business, included stories about the beatnik Johnny Appleseed, as well as John Brown and countless female doctors, scientists, and businesswomen. This seems to me a very important point. Denying all of history other than a chosen core—an origin myth—ultimately means denying the worth of other human beings. Perhaps this is what the latest conservative use of history really intends to accomplish: their stated aim, after all, is to "take back America" from those who are not a part of their version of American history.

Though only a minority of people seem to put much stock in the historical references drawn by the Tea Party, the real danger is that public discourse regarding history—especially through the mass media—gets mired in easy analogies and unfalsifiable assertions about how the founding fathers would deal with the deficit or health care, but such discourse will absolutely not explore how past policy choices led the nation into economic recession. Public discourse references the past but seldom engages in history. Even on PBS's *NewsHour*, historical analysis means asking Doris Kearns Goodwin or Michael Beschloss to comment on precedent or historic acts and to offer some variation or another on the "What would the founders do?" question. But if history has something to contribute to public discourse, surely it is the ability to confront problems with a sense of how they have developed over time.

Americans continue to connect with the past in ways that bristle historians, the past continues to serve the specific interests of those who cherry-pick examples that support their message, and history that seeks to explain complex changes over time as a way of suggesting solutions for the present and future lacks a broad audience. Historian Charles McLean Andrews noted in 1924, "A nation's attitude toward its own history is like a window into its own soul and the men and women of such a nation cannot be expected to meet the great obligations of the present if they refuse to exhibit honesty, charity, open-mindedness, and a free and growing intelligence toward the past that has made them what they are."[24] Fostering an intelligent, broadly shared, and under-stood "citizen's history" is not easy, but it may be necessary to preserve a func-tional democratic society. The five cases I have described shared this objective, though they also grew from competing motivations of less-noble birth, and ultimately they amplified the politicization of historical memory.

Abbreviations

BDV   Bernard DeVoto Collection at Stanford University Library, Palo Alto, CA

DM   Dumas Malone Papers at the University of Virginia, Charlottesville, VA

HML   Hagley Museum and Library, Wilmington, DE

LC   Library of Congress, Washington, DC

NARA   National Archives and Records Administration, College Park, MD

NYPL   New York Public Library, Performing Arts Library, Lincoln Center, New York, NY

SI   Smithsonian Institution Archives

WHS   Wisconsin Historical Society, Madison, WI

Notes

Preface

1. James C. McKinley Jr., "Texas Conservatives Win Curriculum Change," *New York Times*, March 12, 2010.

2. Gary B. Nash, Ross E. Dunn, and Charlotte A. Crabtree, *History on Trial: Culture Wars and the Teaching of the Past* (Westminster, MD: Alfred A. Knopf, 1997), 71.

Introduction

1. On the illusion of consensus, see Alan Brinkley, "The Illusion of Unity in Cold War Culture," in *Rethinking Cold War Culture*, ed. Peter J. Kuznick and James Gilbert (Washington, DC: Smithsonian Institution Press, 2001), 61–73.

2. George Orwell, *1984* (New York: Plume, 1983), 221.

3. Maurice Halbwachs, *The Collective Memory*, trans. Francis J. Ditter Jr. and Vida Yazdi Ditter (New York: Harper & Row, 1980), 24.

4. Warren Susman, *Culture as History: The Transformation of American Society in the Twentieth Century* (Washington, DC: Smithsonian Institution, 2003), 19.

5. Barbara A. Misztal, *Theories of Social Remembering* (Philadelphia: Open University Press, 2003).

6. C. Vann Woodward, *American Attitudes toward History: An Inaugural Lecture Delivered before the University of Oxford on 22 February 1955* (Oxford: Clarendon Press, 1955), 7; Daniel J. Boorstin, *The Genius of American Politics* (Chicago: University of Chicago Press, 1953), 8.

7. J. R. Pole, "The American Past: Is It Still Usable?" *Journal of American Studies* 1, no. 1 (1967): 63–78; Barry Schwartz, *Abraham Lincoln in the Post-Heroic Era: History and Memory in Late Twentieth-Century America* (Chicago: University of Chicago Press, 2008).

8. Daniel J. Boorstin, *An American Primer* (Toronto: New American Library, 1968), xiii–xiv.

9. Reinhold Niebuhr, *The Irony of American History* (New York: Scribner, 1952), 76; Eric Goldman, *The Crucial Decade—and After: America, 1945–1960* (New York: Alfred A. Knopf, 1960), 3–6; see also William Graebner, *The Age of Doubt: American Thought and Culture*

in the 1940s, ed. Lewis Perry (Boston: Twayne, 1990); and Paul S. Boyer, *By the Bomb's Early Light: American Thought and Culture at the Dawn of the Atomic Age*, 2nd ed. (Chapel Hill: University of North Carolina Press, 1994), which examines how the atomic bomb's awesome power affected social thought.

10. This point was made by C. Vann Woodward in his Oxford address, *American Attitudes toward History*.

11. Frances Fitzgerald, *America Revised: History Schoolbooks in the Twentieth Century* (Boston: Atlantic Monthly Press, 1979), 57.

12. Terrence Ball, "The Politics of Social Science in Postwar America," in *Recasting America: Culture and Politics in the Age of Cold War*, ed. Lary May (Chicago: University of Chicago Press, 1989), 77–78.

13. "Books on War and Atom Bomb Avoided by U.S. Readers, Library Survey Shows," *New York Times*, February 2, 1948.

14. Woodward, *American Attitudes toward History*, 7.

15. David Glassberg, *Sense of History: The Place of the Past in American Life* (Amherst: University of Massachusetts Press, 2001), 9; John Bodnar, *Remaking America: Public Memory, Commemoration, and Patriotism in the Twentieth Century* (Princeton, NJ: Princeton University Press, 1993), 14.

16. Michel-Rolph Trouillot, *Silencing the Past: Power and the Production of History* (Boston: Beacon Press, 1995), 19, 22.

17. For example, Emily Rosenberg incorporates popular memory into *A Date Which Will Live: Pearl Harbor in American Memory* (Durham, NC: Duke University Press, 2003). In a more thorough approach to studying memory's effects on history, James Burkhart Gilbert explicitly explores these interactions in *Whose Fair? Experience, Memory, and the History of the Great St. Louis Exposition* (Chicago: University of Chicago Press, 2009).

18. Jeremy Black, *Using History* (London: Hodder Arnold, 2005), xi. Historians often identify the usable past with nostalgia—a longing for a selective and sanitized version of history—and view its apparent growth in recent decades as problematic. In the early 1970s, David Lowenthal and Eric Hobsbawm explained nostalgia as a late- or postmodern need for some connection to the past, even (or especially) a fictitious one. More recent works in psychology, anthropology, and sociology, as well as in history, have sought to explain this need through a variety of approaches. Barbara Misztal provides a particularly useful overview of the surge of interest in memory studies in her recent work. David Lowenthal, "Past Time, Present Place: Landscape and Memory," *Geographical Review* 65 (January 1975): 1–36; E. J. Hobsbawm, "The Social Function of the Past: Some Questions," *Past and Present* 55 (May 1972): 3–17; Misztal, *Theories of Social Remembering*; see also Paul Antze and Michael Lambek, eds., *Tense Past: Cultural Essays in Trauma and Memory* (New York: Routledge, 1996).

19. The grandest attempt at a narrative of American memory is Michael Kammen's *Mystic Chords of Memory: The Transformation of Tradition in American Culture* (New York: Knopf, 1991). Kammen's last period of American memory, 1945–90, is characterized by a "sense of discontinuity" with the past. Kammen is correct in challenging the idea of a

postwar liberal consensus that was disrupted only in the 1960s (differing ideas about history competed throughout that period), but I think that the sudden break with the past he finds in 1945 was a gradual process in which Americans increasingly connected to history through the mediation of popular culture.

20. Richard Slotkin, *Gunfighter Nation: The Myth of the Frontier in Twentieth-Century America* (Norman: University of Oklahoma Press, 1998), 347.

21. Harvey J. Kaye, *The Powers of the Past: Reflections on the Crisis and the Promise of History* (Minneapolis: University of Minnesota Press, 1991), 18; Ian Tyrrell, *Historians in Public: The Practice of American History, 1890–1970* (Chicago: University of Chicago Press, 2005), 71.

22. Nash, Crabtree, and Dunn, *History on Trial*, 65.

23. Richard White, "A Commemoration and a Historical Mediation," *Journal of American History* 94, no. 4 (2008): 1077.

24. Tyrrell, *Historians in Public*, 148, 188–209.

25. Smithsonian Institution Archives (hereafter SI), RU 623, Box 7, Extension Service Folder, Extension Service Proposal (ca. 1953).

26. Thomas Doherty examines how television and McCarthyism influenced each other, in *Cold War, Cool Medium: Television, McCarthyism, and American Culture* (New York: Columbia University Press, 2005).

27. For example, business historians such as Alfred Chandler Jr. and Thomas Cochran reconceptualized the growth of corporations in the nineteenth- and twentieth-century United States as a happier story.

28. Allan Nevins quoted in Peter Novick, *That Noble Dream: The "Objectivity Question" and the American Historical Profession* (New York: Cambridge University Press, 1988), 342.

29. Daniel Horowitz, "A Southerner in Exile, the Cold War, and Social Order: David M. Potter's *People of Plenty*," in *The Anxieties of Affluence: Critiques of American Consumer Culture, 1939–1979* (Amherst: University of Massachusetts Press, 2004), 79.

30. James L. Baughman, *The Republic of Mass Culture: Journalism, Filmmaking, and Broadcasting in America since 1941* (Baltimore: Johns Hopkins University Press, 1992), 42.

31. Nash, Crabtree, and Dunn, *History on Trial*, 70; on the broader subject of textbook adoption see Frances Fitzgerald, *America Revised*.

32. Frank Monaghan, *Heritage of Freedom: The History and Significance of the Basic Documents of American Liberty* (Princeton, NJ: Princeton University Press, 1947), 145.

33. Robert F. Horowitz, "History Comes to Life and You Are There," in *American History, American Television: Interpreting the Video Past*, ed. John E. O'Connor (New York: Frederick Ungar, 1983), 80.

34. William H. McNeill, *Arnold J. Toynbee: A Life* (New York: Oxford University Press, 1989), 205.

35. Arnold Toynbee, *"Civilization on Trial" and "The World and the West"* (1948; repr., New York: Meridian Books, 1958), 37.

36. W. H. Auden, *The Age of Anxiety: A Baroque Eclogue*, ed. Alan Jacobs (Princeton, NJ: Princeton University Press, 2011), 132n48.

37. Communist historian Herbert Aptheker also criticized the book's spiritual (rather than materialist) interpretation. Herbert Aptheker, "History and Reality," in *History and Reality* (New York: Cameron Associates, 1955), 21; see also the essays by Pieter Geyl and Pitirim A. Sorokin in Pieter Geyl, Arnold J. Toynbee, and Pitirim A. Sorokin, *The Pattern of the Past: Can We Determine It?* (Boston: Beacon Press, 1949); and the collection of critical essays from twenty-nine historians in M. F. Ashley Montagu, ed., *Toynbee and History: Critical Essays and Reviews* (Boston: Porter Sargent, 1956).

38. Pieter Geyl, *Use and Abuse of History* (New Haven, CT: Yale University Press, 1955), 10.

39. Geyl, Toynbee, and Sorokin, *Pattern of the Past*, 15, 21.

40. Ibid., 75–79.

41. Herbert J. Muller, *The Uses of the Past: Profiles of Former Societies* (New York: Oxford University Press, 1952), 8–9.

42. Ibid., 22.

43. Novick, *That Noble Dream*, 324.

44. The nostalgia paradigm was offered by Richard Hofstadter in *The American Political Tradition and the Men Who Made It* (New York: Alfred A. Knopf, 1948), v; and more recently, in Kammen, *Mystic Chords of Memory*, 618.

45. While the discipline's origins lie in the 1930s, as Hennig Cohen writes, "for all practical purposes American Studies came into being shortly after World War II." Hennig Cohen, *The American Culture: Approaches to the Study of the United States* (Boston: Houghton Mifflin, 1968), v.

46. Gene Wise, "'Paradigm Dramas' in American Studies: A Cultural and Institutional History of the Movement," in *Locating American Studies: The Evolution of a Discipline*, ed. Lucy Maddox (Baltimore: Johns Hopkins University Press, 1999), 171.

47. Hennig Cohen, preface to *The American Experience: Approaches to the Study of the United States* (Boston: Houghton Mifflin, 1968), v.

48. *American Quarterly* 1, no. 1 (1949): front matter.

49. Cohen, preface, v.

50. Edwin H. Cady, "'American Studies' in the Doldrums," in *American Studies: Essays on Theory and Method*, ed. Robert Meredith (Columbus, OH: Charles E. Merrill, 1968), 37.

51. Wise, "'Paradigm Dramas' in American Studies," 179.

52. Marshall W. Fishwick, *American Studies in Transition* (Philadelphia: University of Pennsylvania Press, 1964), 12; David Riesman, "Psychological Types and National Character," *American Quarterly* 5, no. 4 (1953): 338.

53. Glassberg, *Sense of History*, 7–8.

54. Kaye explicates this phrase in *Powers of the Past*.

55. This general phenomenon is discussed in Hobsbawm, "Social Function of the Past," 4.

56. Jan Vansina, *Oral Tradition as History* (Madison: University of Wisconsin Press, 1985), 40.

57. Gilbert, *Whose Fair?*, 76.

58. Misztal, *Theories of Social Remembering*, 48.

59. David Lowenthal, *The Past Is a Foreign Country* (Cambridge: Cambridge University Press, 1985), 238.

60. Misztal, *Theories of Social Remembering*, 28.

61. Ibid., 24.

62. Ibid., 28; see also Vansina, *Oral Tradition as History*, xii, 21–25.

63. Boorstin, *Genius of American Politics*, 9.

Chapter 1. The History Book Club Offers the Past as an "Image of Ourselves"

1. Stanford University Library, Bernard DeVoto Collection (hereafter BDV), Box 3, Folder 38, DeVoto to Ray Dovell, February 4, 1947.

2. William Harlan Hale, "The Boom in American History," *Reporter* 12 (February 24, 1955): 42.

3. BDV M0001, Box 13, Folder 259, Dovell to DeVoto, September 11, 1947, with enclosed copy of *New York Herald Tribune* advertisement.

4. Tyrrell, *Historians in Public*, 69. Tyrrell's dismissal of the club as commercial and ideologically restricted misses this key difference between the founding mission and the later operative philosophy.

5. Roy Rosenzweig, "Marketing the Past: *American Heritage* and Popular History in the United States," in *Presenting the Past: Essays on History and the Public*, ed. Susan Porter Benson, Stephen Brier, and Roy Rosenzweig (Philadelphia: Temple University Press, 1986), 32, 37–38.

6. Joan Shelley Rubin, *The Making of Middlebrow Culture* (Chapel Hill: University of North Carolina Press, 1992).

7. Misztal, *Theories of Social Remembering*, 99.

8. BDV M0001, Box 3, Folder 36, DeVoto to Ray Dovell, February 28, 1946; Folder 37, DeVoto to Paul Kieffer, March 15, 1946.

9. Louis P. Mazur, "Review: Bernard DeVoto and the Making of *The Year of Decision: 1846*," Reviews in American History 18, no. 3 (1990): 436.

10. Charles P. Everitt, *The Adventures of a Treasure Hunter: A Rare Bookman in Search of American History* (Boston: Little, Brown, 1951). HBC alumnus Frank Dobie reviewed the book favorably in the *New York Herald Tribune Book Review*, December 16, 1951.

11. BDV M0001, Box 13, Folder 257, Dovell to Arthur M. Schlesinger Jr. (hereafter AMS), February 21, 1946.

12. The Book-of-the-Month Club initially required a monthly purchase, but this quickly changed to a minimum annual purchase of four books. The early history of that club is well told in Rubin's *Making of Middlebrow Culture*.

13. BDV, Box 3, Folder 36, DeVoto to Dovell, February 28, 1946.

14. BDV, Box 3, Folder 38, DeVoto to Kitty [Bowen], January 13, 1947.

15. BDV M0001, Box 6, Folder 112, Randolph G. Adams (hereafter RGA) to DeVoto, November 27, 1947.

16. BDV M0001, Box 13, Folder "Holbrook," Holbrook to DeVoto, November 7, 1946; Box 19, Folder "Schlesinger," AMS to DeVoto, March 18, 1947.

17. BDV M0001, Box 6, Folder 109, Circular No. 5 to History Book Club Judges from RGA, December 3, 1946.

18. BDV M0001, Box 13, Folder 257, Dovell to DeVoto, February 21, 1947; Dovell to DeVoto, n.d.

19. Susan Jacoby, *The Age of American Unreason* (New York: Pantheon Books, 2008), 116–17.

20. BDV M0001, Box 6, Folder 109, "Circular No. 4 to History Book Club from RGA," November 26, 1946; Rubin, *Making of Middlebrow Culture*, 99–101.

21. Novick, *That Noble Dream*, 304; Morison quoted in Novick, *That Noble Dream*, 315.

22. Schlesinger Jr. quoted in Novick, *That Noble Dream*, 356–57. Poor Nevins was attacked from the other side—the revisionists—as well. Craven thought Nevins's work lacked "objectivity and balance" and also injected northern moralism into the history of the Civil War. Schlesinger did see a difference between Nevins and Craven, but he thought both led ultimately to the same conclusion: appeasement.

23. Bernard DeVoto, "The War of the Rebellion," *Harper's*, February 1946, repr. in Bernard DeVoto, *The Easy Chair* (Boston: Houghton Mifflin, 1955), 152, 156.

24. Higham quoted in Novick, *That Noble Dream*, 357.

25. BDV, Box 13, Folder 257, Dovell to DeVoto, n.d.

26. BDV, Box 13, Folder 257, Dovell to DeVoto, September 11, 1947.

27. Rosenzweig, "Marketing the Past," 29.

28. BDV, Box 3, Folder 38, DeVoto to Dovell, February 4, 1947; Folder 50, DeVoto to Mr. Ulman, April 1947; BDV M0001, Box 6, Folder 109, Adams to DeVoto, February 6, 1947.

29. BDV, Box 3, Folder 38, BDV to Madeleine [?], January 5, 1947.

30. BDV Mi 242, Box 7, Folder 46, DeVoto to Henry Nash Smith, June 28, 1946.

31. Mazur, "Review," 440–41.

32. BDV Mi 242, Box 7, Folder 46, DeVoto to Henry Nash Smith, June 28, 1946.

33. John L. Thomas, *A Country in the Mind: Wallace Stegner, Bernard DeVoto, History, and the American Land* (New York: Rutledge, 2000), 60–63, 72–75.

34. BDV, Box 3, Folder 38, BDV to Madeleine [?], January 5, 1947.

35. Geyl, Toynbee, and Sorokin, *Pattern of the Past*, 82.

36. Bernard DeVoto, "The Easy Chair," *Harper's*, March 1948, 250; Arthur M. Schlesinger Jr., *A Life in the Twentieth Century: Innocent Beginnings, 1917–1950* (New York: Houghton Mifflin, 2000), 38.

37. BDV M0001, Box 6, Folder 109, "Circular No. 4 to History Book Club from RGA," November 26, 1946.

38. BDV, Box 3, Folder 38, Circular to Board, February 18, 1947.

39. BDV, Box 3, Folder 44, December 6, 1946, Circular to Board; DeVoto to Paul Brooks of Houghton Mifflin Co., December 1946.

40. BDV M0001, Box 3 Folder 44, DeVoto to the Board, December 16, 1946.

41. BDV M0001, Box 13, Folder 257, Dovell to DeVoto, March 10, 1947 (quoting letter from Clifford Dowdey).

42. See, for example, the reviews in *American Historical Review* and *William and Mary Quarterly*: Bruce T. McCully, "Review of *The Westward Crossings: Balboa, Mackenzie, Lewis and Clark* by Jeannette Mirsky," *William and Mary Quarterly* 4, no. 2 (1947): 247–50; Grace Lee Nute, "Review of *The Westward Crossings: Balboa, Mackenzie, Lewis and Clark* by Jeanette Mirsky," *American Historical Review* 52, no. 4 (1947): 745–46.

43. BDV, Box 6, Folder 109, "Circular No. 4 to History Book Club from RGA," November 26, 1946.

44. BDV M0001, Box 3, Folder 43, DeVoto to Board, November 4, 1946; BDV M0001, Box 6, Folder 109, "Circular No. 2 (of RGA)," November 9, 1946.

45. See James A. Hijiya, "Why the West Is Lost," *William and Mary Quarterly*, 3rd ser., 51 (1994): 276–92. Hijiya also mentions DeVoto's call fifty years earlier for more Indians in American history.

46. Jeannette Mirsky, *The Westward Crossings: Balboa, Mackenzie, Lewis and Clark* (New York, Alfred A. Knopf, 1946), xiv, 28; Novick, *That Noble Dream*, 311. See the discussion of Hijiya, "Why the West Is Lost," in "Forum: Comments on James A. Hijiya's 'Why the West Is Lost,'" *William and Mary Quarterly*, 3rd ser., 51 (1994): 717–54.

47. For example, see the story of Ojeda's demise in Mirsky, *Westward Crossings*, 22.

48. BDV M0001, Box 6, Folder 109, Adams to DeVoto, February 6, 1947; Holbrook to DeVoto and Adams, February 14, 1947.

49. BDV M0001, Box 13, Folder 263, Holbrook to DeVoto, cc Adams, January 28, 1947.

50. Townsend Scudder, *Concord: American Town* (Boston: Little, Brown, 1947), "To the Reader" and 389–90.

51. "Inside Voice of America: Fast Facts," http://www.insidevoa.com/section/voa-faqs/2317.html.

52. William Harlan Hale, *The March of Freedom: A Layman's History of the American People* (New York: Harper & Brothers, 1947).

53. Hale, *March of Freedom*, ix–x.

54. Ibid., 1, 20.

55. Ibid., x.

56. Hale, "Boom in American History," 45.

57. Hale, *March of Freedom*, 2.

58. Ibid., 10, 13.

59. Charles Beard and Mary Beard, *The Rise of American Civilization* (New York: Macmillan, 1930), 664.

60. Hale, *March of Freedom*, 15, 19, 20, 23.

61. Ibid., 49–50, 84.

62. Ibid., 99, 152–65.

63. Ibid., 274.

64. William Harlan Hale, "What Makes Wallace Run?," *Harper's*, March 1948, 241.

65. Hale, "Boom in American History," 43.

66. BDV, Box 3, Folder 48, Circular to the Board, April 11, 1947.

67. BDV, Box 6, Folder 109, Adams to DeVoto, March 14, 1947; March 17, 1947; and April 2, 1947.

68. BDV, Box 13, Folder 256, Holbrook to DeVoto, February 26, 1947; BDV, Box 3, Folder 48, DeVoto to Randolph, March 18, 1947.

69. Bernard DeVoto, "Doctors along the Boardwalk," *Harper's*, September 1947, repr. in Bernard DeVoto, *The Easy Chair* (Boston: Houghton Mifflin, 1955), 85–102.

70. Rosenzweig, "Marketing the Past," 38.

71. BDV M0001, Box 6, Folder 109, Circular No. 8 from RGA, February 18, 1947.

72. John C. Miller, *Triumph of Freedom: 1775–1783* (Boston: Little, Brown, 1948), 476–77, 687–88.

73. BDV, Box 6, Folder 110, RGA to BDV, July 26, 1947, and RGA to BDV, July 28, 1947; Howard H. Peckham, *Pontiac and the Indian Uprising* (Princeton, NJ: Princeton University Press, 1947).

74. BDV, Box 3, Folder 57, DeVoto to Dovell, September 10, 1947.

75. Thomas J. Schlereth, *Cultural History and Material Culture: Everyday Life, Landscapes, Museums* (Ann Arbor: UMI Research Press, 1990), 340.

76. Perry Miller, *Errand into the Wilderness* (Cambridge, MA: Belknap Press of Harvard University Press, 1984), 141.

77. Thomas Jefferson Wertenbaker, *The Puritan Oligarchy: The Founding of American Civilization* (New York: Charles Scribner's Sons, 1947), viii, ix, 26, 32–33.

78. Ibid., ix, 269, 345.

79. BDV Mi242, Box 6, Folder 45, DeVoto to William Sloane, May 8, 1948. DeVoto mentions in particular his effort to persuade Walter Lippman at a recent cocktail party at Elmer Davis's and his pitch to the crowd at another party, thrown by Mrs. Gifford Pinchot.

80. Richard G. Lillard, *The Great Forest* (New York: Alfred A. Knopf, 1947), 346.

81. BDV M0001, Box 13, Folder 259, Dovell to DeVoto, June 24, 1947.

82. BDV, Box 3, Folder 38, DeVoto to Frank Dobie, June 20, 1947; DeVoto to Alfred Knopf, June 30, 1947; DeVoto Circular No. 10, July 14, 1947; DeVoto to Randolph, July 21, 1947; DeVoto Circular No. 12, August 4, 1947.

83. BDV, Box 3, Folder 42, DeVoto Circular to HBC Board, December 6, 1946; DeVoto to Dovell, November 9, 1946.

84. BDV M0001, Box 13, Folder 257, Dovell to DeVoto, March 17, 1947.

85. BDV Mi242, Box 6, Folder 45, DeVoto to Holbrook, April 5, 1948.

86. BDV, Box 3, Folder 49, DeVoto to Dovell, April 17, 1947.

87. BDV, Box 3, Folder 56, DeVoto to Dovell, August 9, 1947.

88. Ibid.

89. Ibid.

90. BDV Mi 242, Box 9, Folder 47, DeVoto to Dumas Malone, July 8, 1948; DeVoto, Box 4, Folder 62, DeVoto to Randolph, December 2, 1947.

91. Ian Tyrrell suggests the same in *Historians in Public*, 70.

92. BDV Mi 242, Box 9, Folder 47, DeVoto to Dumas Malone, July 8, 1948.

93. Dumas Malone Papers at the University of Virginia (hereafter DM) 12712-b, Box 37, Folder "1954–81—'Interviews with Dumas Malone,'" "Editing the Dictionary of American Biography, Interview Conducted December 10, 1954."

94. DM 12712-b, Box 9, Folder 1969–71, Louis B. Wright to Malone, November 18, 1970; Malone to Wright, November, 1970.

95. DM 12712-b, Box 37, HBC Reviews, 1953–62.

96. DM 12712-a, Box 3, Folder "1954–1959, History Book Club," List of Books with Sales, 1955–57; Dovell to Malone, n.d. (1958).

97. DM 12712-a, Box 3, Folder "HBC 1954–1958," Malone draft for Dovell, August 1, 1956.

98. Hale, "Boom in American History," 45.

Chapter 2. Mythologizing History on Du Pont's
Cavalcade of America

1. Carl Carmer, ed., *The Cavalcade of America: The Deeds and Achievements of the Men and Women Who Made Our Country Great* (New York: Crown, 1956), viii.

2. Hagley Museum and Library, Wilmington, DE (hereafter HML), Accession 1803, Box 11, Folder 29, "Suggested Presentation on the Purpose and Objectives of the *Cavalcade of America*—For Use at Sales Meetings—Prepared Internally" (July 1950); HML, Accession 1803, Box 26, Folder 11.

3. Thurman Arnold, *The Folklore of Capitalism* (New Haven, CT: Yale University Press, 1937), 10–11. As head of the Antitrust Division of Franklin Roosevelt's Justice Department, Arnold initiated 180 antitrust cases between 1938 and 1942, about half the number prosecuted in the previous fifty years. David A. Hounshell and John Kenly Smith Jr., *Science and Corporate Strategy: Du Pont R&D, 1902–1980* (New York: Cambridge University Press, 1988), 346.

4. David Lowenthal, *The Heritage Crusade and the Spoils of History* (Cambridge: Cambridge University Press, 1998), 128. Heritage is, as Michael Kammen argues, "an alternative to history" that accentuates only the positive. Kammen, *Mystic Chords of Memory*, 626.

5. William L. Bird Jr., *"Better Living": Advertising, Media, and the New Vocabulary of Business Leadership, 1935–1955* (Evanston, IL: Northwestern University Press, 1999); Elizabeth A. Fones-Wolf, *Selling Free Enterprise: The Business Assault on Labor and Liberalism, 1945–1960* (Urbana: University of Illinois Press, 1994); Howell John Harris, *The Right to Manage: Industrial Relations Policies of American Business in the 1940s* (Madison: University of

Wisconsin Press, 1982); Roland Marchand, *Creating the Corporate Soul: The Rise of Public Relations and Corporate Imagery in American Big Business* (Berkeley: University of California Press, 1998). Marchand describes capital's efforts to link the postwar corporation with a mythological small-town past.

6. Kammen, *Mystic Chords of Memory*, 300, 410, 421, 423; Richard Pells, *Radical Visions and American Dreams: Culture and Social Thought in the Depression Years* (Urbana: University of Illinois Press, 1998), 262–68.

7. Richard Fried, *The Man Everybody Knew: Bruce Barton and the Making of Modern America* (Chicago: Ivan R. Dee, 2005), 146.

8. Bird, *"Better Living,"* 62.

9. HML, Pictorial Collections, *Cavalcade of America* Transcripts, no. 204, December 11, 1940.

10. HML, Accession 1662, Administrative Papers, Box 4, Folder "1937," Dixon Ryan Fox to Roy Durstine, n.d., probably March 1937; Bird, *"Better Living,"* 66.

11. Davis Dyer and David B. Sicilia, *Labors of a Modern Hercules: The Evolution of a Chemical Company* (Boston: Harvard Business School Press, 1990), 89.

12. Business historian Alfred Dupont Chandler argues in favor of Du Pont's claim to have profited at an insignificant rate on war production. But as Gerald Colby demonstrates, the war accounted for 85 percent of Du Pont's business. More important, despite the uncertainties, war always ushered in periods of dramatic expansion and later profit for Du Pont. Pierre managed the return to peacetime levels of production by firing 37,000 workers at Christmastime in 1918 and 70,000 more at war's end. Gerald Colby, *Du Pont Dynasty* (Secaucus, NJ: Lyle Stuart, 1984), 182–85, 195, 199–200; Alfred D. Chandler Jr. and Stephen Salsbury, *Pierre S. du Pont and the Making of the Modern Corporation* (Washington, DC: Beard Books, 2000), 393–400.

13. Colby, *Du Pont Dynasty*, 354–57.

14. Ibid., 308, 314–19.

15. Ibid., 355–57.

16. Ibid., 377. Chandler and Salsbury, in *Pierre S. du Pont*, relate how Pierre du Pont took control of General Motors at the end of World War I and connected the companies through stock ownership and board memberships. GM provided between 20 and 30 percent of Du Pont's income, and the carmaker was Du Pont's largest customer.

17. HML, Accession 1662, Administrative Papers, Box 3, Folder C24, Bruce Barton of BBDO to Lammot du Pont, president, E.I. Du Pont De Nemours & Company, Inc., May 18, 1935.

18. General Motors and Du Pont shared several board members, and the companies held close enough ties that the Justice Department brought an antitrust suit against them both in the 1950s. Interestingly, in 1932 Lammot du Pont pushed to have GM literature available in Du Pont waiting rooms and other company areas, hoping that Du Pont employees and customers would get the message that they would "do well to use General Motors' cars." HML, Accession 1662, Administrative Papers, Box 3, Folder C24, Lammot du Pont to William A. Hart, advertising director, Du Pont de Nemours &

Company, Inc., September 27, 1932; Bruce Barton of BBDO to Lammot du Pont, May 18, 1935.

19. HML, Accession 1803, Box 11, Folder 42, BBDO-written history of *Cavalcade of America* for article in *Sponsor*; HML, Accession 1662, Administrative Papers, Box 3, Folder "Advertising Dept, July 1932–Dec. 1935," Barton to Lammot du Pont, May 18, 1935; Bird, *"Better Living,"* 68.

20. HML, Accession 1662, Administrative Papers, Box 4, Folder "1938," Lammot du Pont to Lawrence K. Watrous, February 18, 1938. Watrous had written to du Pont on February 11, 1938, to suggest a new radio program (based on *Cavalcade*) that would relate the life stories of famous businessmen (and to *equate* the situation of Jews in Germany to that of business in FDR's America). Lammot du Pont to W. H. Logan, July 27, 1938; Accession 1662, Administrative Papers, Box 4, Folder "January 1941 to July 1952," Lammot du Pont to R. R. Deupree, president, Procter and Gamble Company, September 16, 1946; Mabel Randolph Brooks to Lammot du Pont, April 1944; Lammot du Pont to Brooks, June 7, 1944; B. E. Hutchinson, chairman of the Finance Committee, Chrysler Corporation, to Lammot du Pont, February 4, 1946; Lammot du Pont to Hutchinson, February 13, 1946.

21. HML, Accession 1662, Administrative Papers, Box 4, Folder "1938," Hart to Lammot du Pont, July 26, 1938.

22. HML, Accession 1803, Box 12, Folder 3, Lyman Dewey introduction to the preview of the first television *Cavalcade*, September 12, 1952.

23. HML, Accession 1803, Box 11, Folder 42, BBDO history of *Cavalcade* for *Sponsor* magazine.

24. High quoted in Bird, *"Better Living,"* 84; Franklin Delano Roosevelt, speech to Democratic National Convention, June 27, 1936, available at http://millercenter.org/scripps/archive/speeches/detail/3305.

25. Bird, *"Better Living,"* 62–66. Durstine explained that CBS offered better terms, allowing BBDO control of the program and greater coverage through affiliates. Barton convinced the executive committee of the soundness of the program over Lammot's initial objections.

26. Wisconsin Historical Society (hereafter WHS), National Broadcasting Company Records, Correspondence, 1921–42, Box 67, Folder 81, "Du Pont's *Cavalcade of America*," Stanley High to John Royal, October 10, 1935; Bertha Brainard to Royal, October 11, 1935.

27. HML, Accession 1803, Box 11, Robb M. De Graff to Wayne Tiss of BBDO, August 22, 1955.

28. HML, Accession 1803, Box 5, Folder 16, clipping from *Variety*, October 22, 1953.

29. Fried, *Man Everybody Knew*, 31, 65.

30. Bird, *"Better Living,"* 72, 75, 81.

31. Dixon Ryan Fox, preface to *Cavalcade of America*, ed. Dixon Ryan Fox and Arthur M. Schlesinger (Springfield, MA: Milton Bradley, 1937), vii. The politics behind the

history never received much attention from the historians beyond generalities about the "patriotic faith" that motivated both the historical research and the series. This echoes what Ian Tyrrell found in the 1940s and 1950s with historians who embraced an alliance with the state in order to secure support for history education. Like Fox, Carmer edited a book version of the series, published with full-color illustrations in 1956. Carmer's association with the program is easy to understand given his own work collecting and telling stories that explain and define America, especially the 1939 classic *Listen for the Lonesome Drum*.

32. Monaghan and Schlesinger Sr. quoted in Bird, *"Better Living,"* 72–73.

33. Bird, *"Better Living,"* 72–73.

34. Martin Grams Jr., *The History of the Cavalcade of America* (Kearney, NE: Morris, 1998), 7; Tyrrell, *Historians in Public*, 56.

35. HML, Accession 1803, Box 7, Folder 5, "American History to Take to the Air," *Long Island Press*, May 26, 1954. Ian Tyrrell relates several other such efforts by academic historians in "Historians in Public in the Early Televisual Age: Academics, Film, and the Rise of Television in the 1950s and 1960s," *Maryland Historian* 30, no. 1 (2006): 41–60.

36. HML, Accession 1662, Box 2, Folder "Addresses, Lammot du Pont, Chairman of the Board," "National Association of Manufacturers' Educational Work," March 19, 1941.

37. HML, Accession 1662, Box 4, Folder "1937," Dixon Ryan Fox to Lammot du Pont, April 3, 1937.

38. HML, Accession 1662, Box 4, Folder "1938," Advertising Federation of America, "Facts You Should Know about Anti-Advertising Propaganda in School Textbooks" (Advertising Federation of America, New York, 1939); Box 2, Folder "NAM," Speech in Atlanta, GA, by Lammot du Pont about NAM Educational Work, March 19, 1941.

39. HML, Accession 1662, Box 54, Folder "NAM Educational Cooperation Committee, 12/39–12/40," "Official Draft of a Memorandum of Industry's Recommendations for the Improvement of American Educational Methods in the Preparing of Students for Citizenship in a Republic," June 28, 1939.

40. Nash, Crabtree, and Dunn, *History on Trial*, 66; HML, Accession 1662, Box 54, Folder "NAM Educational Cooperation Committee, 12/39–12/40," "History of the Activities of the National Association of Manufacturer's Committee on Educational Cooperation" (n.d., ca. 1940); "What Does Capital Want for Itself and America? An Address by Charles R. Hook, Chairman, National Association of Manufacturers, before the Annual Convention of the Missouri State Teachers Association, St. Louis, Missouri, November 16, 1939."

41. HML, Accession 1803, Box 29, Folder 17, "College Campaign—Surveys 1948, 1954."

42. HML, Accession 1803, Box 29, Folder 24.

43. Fones-Wolf, *Selling Free Enterprise*, 196–97, 204.

44. HML, Accession 1410, Du Pont Public Affairs, Box 39, Folder "Hagley Museum," Dedication of the Hagley Museum by Emile F. du Pont, May 24, 1957.

45. Bird, *"Better Living,"* 110, 114–15. Orson Welles starred in "The Great Man Votes" in December 1941. Carl Sandburg read his own poems on "Native Land," which also starred Burgess Meredith as the young Sandburg.

46. Bird, *"Better Living,"* 72.

47. HML, Pictorial Collections, *Cavalcade of America* Transcripts, no. 3; HML, Accession 1803, Box 11, Folder 42, BBDO history of *Cavalcade of America* for *Sponsor.*

48. HML, Accession 1803, Box 8, untitled folder containing television advertisement scripts, 1954–55.

49. Colby, *Du Pont Dynasty*, 344–45.

50. HML, Pictorial Collections, *Cavalcade of America* Transcripts, no. 4.

51. HML, Pictorial Collections, *Cavalcade of America* Transcripts, no. 8.

52. HML, Pictorial Collections, *Cavalcade of America* Transcripts, no. 13, emphasis added.

53. HML, Pictorial Collections, *Cavalcade of America* Transcripts, no. 7.

54. HML, Pictorial Collections, *Cavalcade of America* Transcripts, no. 6.

55. It is not clear whether any unions voiced similar protests over episode number 152 in 1939's "Allen Pinkerton." This was the story of "patriots" "who devoted their lives—and are doing so today—to enforcing the guarantee of justice to our citizens."

56. HML, Pictorial Collections, *Cavalcade of America* Transcripts, no. 224. There were other newspaperwoman stories, including no. 175 about Anne Newport Royall.

57. Winthrop also accuses her of luring the people in with gifts of food (welfare), "which the Lord had denied them for their sins." He believes she "used her good works to incite the people to rebellion." Perhaps this is an unsubtle attack on Roosevelt, but the announcer clarifies that the main point is the continuing need to fight for "our democracy and its traditions." Like other 1941 episodes, this seems to be preparing citizens for war.

58. HML, Accession 1803, Box 3, "Cavalcade Publicity," "Abigail Opens the White House," February 24, 1947.

59. See, for example, the episodes on Anna Zenger, supportive wife of John Peter Zenger. No. 500, "Mother of Freedom," in 1946, and no. 626, "Remember Anna Zenger," in 1949. In 1947's "Builder of the 'Soo,'" no. 507, "Charles Harvey's determined efforts, backed by a woman's faith in his unproven ability, opened the way for the industrial development of a whole new section of America." HML, Pictorial Collections, *Cavalcade of America* Transcripts.

60. HML, Accession 1803, Box B-3, "Radio version of *Cavalcade*," Program no. 192.

61. See the television episodes "Petticoat Doctor" and "A Medal for Miss Walker," available at the Library of Congress (LC), Motion Picture, Broadcasting, and Recorded Sound Division (MPBRSD). "A Medal for Miss Walker," written by future *Rambo: First Blood* writer William Sackheim, starred the beautiful Maura Murphy as the indefatigable

Dr. Mary Walker, the first woman to receive the Congressional Medal of Honor. In an episode that also featured future stars Dennis Hopper and DeForest Kelley, Abraham Lincoln grants Dr. Walker's request to serve the Union Army (as a contract surgeon, not a commissioned officer). She then must fight against sexism in both armies. In "Petticoat Doctor," Dr. Elizabeth Blackwell (Betty Caulfield, who also brought glamour to her character) fights both gender discrimination in the medical profession and ignorance among the masses in order to begin her medical practice and dispense drugs to an un-educated population. Jack Bennet, who wrote the teleplay, also wrote two late *You Are There* episodes, 1957's "The End of the Dalton Gang," and 1956's "Hitler Invades Poland."

62. HML, Accession 1803, Box 4, Folder 50, John Dollard Report on "Mr. Peale's Dinosaur."

63. HML, Accession 1803, Box 4, Folder 48, John Dollard Reports. Similarly, in "The Proud Way" (1948), seventeen-year-old Varina Howell "risked her happiness and even her life to meet the challenge of rebuilding a man's broken spirit. She fought to bring Jeff Davis back from his past . . . to meet his destiny."

64. HML, Pictorial Collections, *Cavalcade of America* Transcripts, no. 32; no. 241.

65. Eric Barnouw, *A History of Broadcasting in the United States*, vol. 2, *The Golden Web* (New York: Oxford University Press, 1968), 269.

66. Hounshell and Smith, *Science and Corporate Strategy*, 332–33. In *Pierre du Pont*, Chandler and Salsbury also claim Du Pont resisted both world wars.

67. Colby, *Du Pont Dynasty*, 385–86. Colby even suggests Du Pont's complicity in Hitler's "final solution" based on price fixing and trade agreements signed between the company and I. G. Farben as late as 1939, when I. G. was Hitler's largest financial backer and supplier of poison gas to the concentration camps.

68. HML, Pictorial Collections, *Cavalcade of America* Transcripts, "Geronimo," no. 243.

69. HML, Pictorial Collections, *Cavalcade of America* Transcripts, nos. 252 and 253.

70. Tom Engelhardt, *The End of Victory Culture: Cold War America and the Disillusioning of a Generation* (New York: Basic Books, 1995), 39–40.

71. In October, Paul Muni starred as "Bolivar the Liberator," "a man who foresaw the need for free men to unite against the forces of tyranny and oppression abroad in the world. Later that month, Claude Rains appeared, to celebrate the life of John Paul Jones and the greatness of the U.S. Navy. *Cavalcade* also aired several programs on the "un-defended border" and stalwart friendship between the United States and Canada before, during, and after the war.

72. Hounshell and Smith, *Science and Corporate Strategy*, 332.

73. Colby, *Du Pont Dynasty*, 387–89.

74. Ibid., 399; Hounshell and Smith, *Science and Corporate Strategy*, 345.

75. HML, Pictorial Collections, *Cavalcade of America* Transcripts, no. 262.

76. HML, Pictorial Collections, *Cavalcade of America* audiocassette recordings, "Benedict Arnold."

77. Flora Rheta Schreiber, "Cavalcade from the Control Room," *Film and Radio Discussion Guide* 9, no. 8 (1943); Daniel L. Lykins, *From Total War to Total Diplomacy: The Advertising Council and the Construction of the Cold War Consensus* (Westport, CT: Praeger, 2003), 30.

78. Kammen, *Mystic Chords of Memory*, 583–87.

79. HML, Pictorial Collections, *Cavalcade of America* Transcripts, "The Common Glory," no. 574, June 28, 1948.

80. HML, Accession 1803, Box 4, Folder 19.

81. LC, MPBRSD, "Ordeal in Burma" and "The Gentle Conqueror."

82. HML, Pictorial Collections, *Cavalcade of America* Transcripts, no. 225, "The Trials and Triumphs of Horatio Alger."

83. HML, Accession 1803, Box 3, "Cavalcade Publicity," "The Peanut Vendor," April 14, 1947.

84. HML, Accession 1803, Box 3, "Cavalcade Publicity," no. 681, "An American From France" (January 2, 1951), starring Joseph Cotton as Eleuthere Irénée du Pont; no. 167, "E. I. du Pont: Founder of the Du Pont Company" (May 29, 1939).

85. Some farming stories never mention Du Pont, instead merely mentioning the benefits of someone using nitrate powder on their fields in one historical context or another. Later, during the advertisement, this would be linked with the specific Du Pont product.

86. HML, Pictorial Collections, *Cavalcade of America* Transcripts, no. 167, "E. I. du Pont: Founder of the Du Pont Company," May 29, 1939.

87. Colby, *Du Pont Dynasty*, 802–3.

88. For example, HML, Accession 1803, Box 24, Opinion Research Corporation Survey, n.d.; Box 7, Folder 6, BBDO Report on Public Opinion Survey, April 5, 1956.

89. HML, Pictorial Collections, *Cavalcade of America* Transcripts, no. 781, "A Time to Grow." The 1953 television treatment was also titled "A Time to Grow," starring Stacey Keach as Pierre Samuel.

90. LC, MPBRSD, no. 69, "The Forge," television broadcast October 26, 1954.

91. Roland Marchand suggests that Du Pont's public relations and advertising shifted from a mostly defensive posture to an offensive approach after 1940, when Walter S. Carpenter became president of the company. Marchand, *Creating the Corporate Soul*, 221.

92. HML, Accession 1410, Du Pont Public Affairs, Box 37, Folder "Du Pont Story," William A. Hart, F. C. Evans, Harold Brayman, from the Motion Picture Film Steering Committee (V. L. Simpson, Advertising Department, William S. Dutton, Public relations Department, E. F. Du Pont, Service Department), February 27, 1947.

93. Barnouw, *History of Broadcasting*, 298–99.

94. HML, Accession 1410, Du Pont Public Affairs, Box 36, Folder "*Cavalcade* of America," undated news release from 1946; HML, Accession 1410, Du Pont Public Affairs, Box 27, Folder "Exhibit 'H': Scenario for theatrical film based on Du Pont history."

95. HML, Accession 1803, Box 8, Folder 1, Nielsen Presentation to Du Pont Advertising Department, January 18, 1955. *See It Now*'s ratings numbers were less than half those of *Cavalcade*.

96. HML, Accession 1803, Box 22, Folder 23, BBDO report for Du Pont, "Du Pont Company Advertising: A Glance Backward . . . A Long Look Ahead," November 1952.

97. Ibid; HML, Accession 1803, Box 1, Folder 2, "Digest of Talks Given at Du Pont Advertising Department Clinic," May 28, 1953.

98. HML, Accession 1803, Box 11, Letter from Robb M. De Graff to Wayne Tiss of BBDO, August 22, 1955.

99. HML, Accession 1803, Box 13, Folder 7, "Quarterly reports 1954–57"; Box 22, Folder 23, "Du Pont Company Advertising"; Box 7, Folder 6, BBDO Report on Public Opinion Survey, April 5, 1956.

100. HML, Accession 1803, Box 5, Folder 29, BBDO report, *"Cavalcade of America* Audience Composition by Groups, 2/2/55." The report showed *Cavalcade* drew more viewers per set than other programs at that time slot (7:30–8:00 p.m.), 2.65 to 2.40, and much more even distribution: 1.64 children (versus 0.55 for average evening program), 0.88 women (vs. 1.11 average), 0.73 men (vs. 0.74 average).

101. HML, Accession 1803, Box 7, Folder 5, correspondence from fans; Folder 6, *Looking in on "Cavalcade"* 1, no. 2, March, 1953.

102. HML, Accession 1803, Box 7, Folder 6, *Looking in on "Cavalcade."*

103. HML, Accession 1803, Box 5, Folder 10, BBDO report, "Cavalcade of America Studies on General Public, Teen-Age School Children, Public School Teachers," March 1953; Box 7, Folder 5, Du Pont Advertising Department, "Meeting to discuss measurements of 'Cavalcade's' effectiveness," June 20, 1955; Box 29, Folder 23, Study for Du Pont Motion Picture Personnel, "To Promote the Study of Science and Engineering among High School Students," 1957.

104. HML, Accession 1803, Box 7, Folder 5.

105. Alice P. Sterner, "We Help Create a New Drama," *English Journal* 43, no. 8 (1954): 451–52; Helen P. Graham, "A Plan for Teaching the Biography," *English Journal* 30, no. 3 (1941): 238–41; Ollie Stratton, "Techniques for Literate Listening," *The English Journal* 37, no. 10 (1948): 542–44; Dana W. Niswender, "Divided We Fall," *The English Journal* 36, no. 6 (1947): 309.

106. HML, Accession 1803, Box 5, Folder 15, "Promotion—Publicity Report on Cavalcade of America 9/29/53–12/1/53."

107. HML, Accession 1803, Box 5, Folder 5, "A Proposed Publicity Plan for 'Cavalcade of America' Television Program, September 1952," and "A Campaign Directed toward Grade and High Schools"; Box 5, Folder 15, BBDO report on Promotional Activities for "Breakfast at Nancy's."

108. HML, Accession 1803, Box 22, Folder 18, BBDO "'Total Exploitation' for Television Programs of BBDO Clients," May 1956; Box 5, Folder 21, Promotional activities of local television stations; Box 5, Folder 41, Report on Publicity and Promotional Activities, October 1955; Box 7, Folder 5, letters to Du Pont Advertising Department, 1956.

109. HML, Accession 1803, Box 5, Folder 5, BBDO memo dated September 2, 1952, laid out this plan.

110. HML, Accession 1803, Box 5, Folder 15, "Promotion—Publicity Report on Cavalcade of America 9/29/53–12/1/53."

111. The Remington Arms and AT&T linkages are discussed in a fall 1954 promotional activity report from BBDO, HML, Accession 1803, Box 5, Folder 23.

112. HML, Accession 1803, Box 5, Folder 28.

113. HML Accession 1803, Box 5, Folders 14 and 28.

114. HML, Accession 1662, Box 4, Folder "1939–1940," James Roland Angell, NBC educational counselor, to Lammot du Pont, January 11, 1940.

115. HML, Accession 1803, Box 5, Folders 15, 16, 24, 31, Promotion and Publicity Reports on *Cavalcade of America*, documenting BBDO and ABC efforts.

116. HML, Accession 1803, Box 4, Folder 50, John Dollard Reports; Accession 1814, Papers of Crawford Hallock Greenewalt, Box 4, Folder "Advertising Department, 1953–56," letter from Edward A. Hogan Jr., University of California Hastings College of Law, to President Crawford H. Greenewalt, October 25, 1955.

117. Bird, *"Better Living,"* 99.

118. HML, Accession 1662, Box 4, Folder "1938," "Test-Tube Study of the Influence of 'Cavalcade of America' on Attitudes toward the Du Pont Company," August 16, 1939.

119. HML, Accession 1803, Box 7, Folder 5, "Meeting to Discuss Measurements of 'Cavalcade's' Effectiveness, June 20, 1955," June 22, 1955.

120. HML, Accession 1803, Box 4, "Wave 1 and 2 Reports," by the Psychological Corporation.

121. HML, Accession 1803, Box 7, Folder 5, letters to Du Pont Advertising Department, 1956.

122. Glassberg, *Sense of History*, 122.

123. HML, Accession 1803, Box 11, Folder 32, letter from Francis Ronalds (curator of historic sites for the United States Park Service, trustee of the American Scenic and Historic Preservation Society, and historical consultant for the *Cavalcade* of America) to Harold Blackburn of BBDO, July 10, 1951; Box 11, *Du Pont Magazine*, October–November 1951.

124. In the first fifteen years on the radio, *Cavalcade* brought Du Pont over forty awards for "educational value" or "patriotic service." The "Golden Mike" was presented "for patriotic dramatic programs of highest inspirational, educational and entertainment appeal . . . as determined by a nation-wide poll of American Legion Auxiliary members." Award mentions can be found in HML, Accession 1803, Box 5, Folder 25; Box 8, Folder 36, Clipping from *Du Pont* Magazine, October–November 1950; Pictorial Collections, *Cavalcade of America* Transcripts, no. 167; Accession 1803, Box 5, Folder 31, ABC advertisement.

125. HML, Accession 1803, Box 7, Folder 5, clippings from fan letters, 1953–55.

126. Ibid.

127. Ibid.

128. Ibid.

129. Ibid.

130. Ibid.

131. HML, Accession 1803, Box 5, Folder 3, BBDO Research Report on the commercial aired at the end of "The New Salem Story" in March 1952; Box 12, Folder 3, Lyman Dewey's introduction to the preview of the first television *Cavalcade*, September 12, 1952; Pictorial Collections, *Cavalcade of America* Transcripts, no. 683, "There Stands Jackson!" January 16, 1951.

132. HML, Accession 1814, Box 4, Folder 52, Irving Olds to Crawford Greenewalt, September 6, 1950.

133. HML, Accession 1814, Advertising Department, Box 4, Folder 52, Robert Brown to Greenewalt, December 26, 1951.

134. HML, Accession 1814, Advertising Department, Box 4, Folder 52, H. E. Dennison to Greenewalt, November 9, 1950.

135. HML, Accession 1814, Advertising Department, Box 4, Folder 52, Eddie Rickenbacker to Greenewalt, June 1, 1951.

136. HML, Pictorial Collections, *Cavalcade of America* Transcripts, no. 181, "A Continental Uniform: The Story of General Benedict Arnold," April 2, 1940.

137. HML, Accession 1803, Box 4, Folder 46, Dollard Report, "A Man's Home," May 6, 1955.

138. HML, Accession 1803, Box 4, Folder 20, John Dollard Report, "Breakfast at Nancy's" and "Mr. Peale's Dinosaur."

139. LC, MPBRSD, "Betrayal," 1953.

140. In addition to the spy stories mentioned above, see also no. 151 on Nathan Hale, no. 146 on John Honeyman, and no. 176 on Enoch Crosby.

141. HML, Accession 1803, Box 7, Folder 5, letter from Philip A. Ridgely of Upper Marlborough, MD, 1953.

142. HML, Accession 1803, Box 5, Folder 16, undated clipping from unknown Virginia newspaper.

143. HML, Accession 1803, Box 3, Folder "*Cavalcade of America* Programs," no. 184, "Robert E. Lee," April 23, 1940.

144. HML, Accession 1803, Box 3, Folder "*Cavalcade of America* Programs," no. 179, "On Jordan's Banks."

145. HML, Pictorial Collections, *Cavalcade of America* Transcripts, no. 683, "There Stands Jackson!"

146. HML, Pictorial Collections, *Cavalcade of America* Transcripts, no. 680, "A Mockingbird Sang."

147. HML, Accession 1803, Box 6, Folder 27, John Dollard Report, "The Man Who Took a Chance," which told the story of Eli Whitney's contribution to the mass production of guns.

148. HML, Accession 1803, Box 6, Folder 23, "G for Goldberger."

149. HML, Accession 1803, Box 5, Folder 28, Oil Progress Week News Release by American Petroleum Institute, September 24, 1954.

150. HML, Accession 1803, Box 6, Folder 46, John Dollard Report, "A Man's Home" and the commercial accompanying "Letter to a Child"; Folder 48, Dollard Report, "Toward Tomorrow."

151. HML, Accession 1803, Box 4, Folder 25, John Dollard Report, "Crazy Judah."

152. HML, Accession 1803, Box 6, Folder 29, John Dollard Report, "New Salem Story."

153. HML, Accession 1803, Box 6, Folder 26, John Dollard Report, "John Yankee."

154. LC, MPBRSD, "One Nation Indivisible"; HML, Accession 1803, Box 6, Folder 31, John Dollard Report, "One Nation Indivisible."

155. HML, Accession 1803, Box 6, Folder 24, John Dollard Report, "Gunfight at the OK Corral."

156. WSHS, Bruce Barton Papers, Box 76, Client Correspondence, Du Pont Folder, Barton to William Hart, July 13, 1949.

157. Roland Marchand quotes General Electric president Charles E. Wilson and a Psychological Corporation survey of American businessmen in *Creating the Corporate Soul*, 317–18. Other historians have said much the same thing about corporate America's fears in the 1940s; for example, Howell John Harris, *Right to Manage*, 6.

158. HML, Accession 1662, Box 3, Folder C24 "Advertising Department July 1932–December 1935," William H. Hart to Bernard Kilgore, president, *Wall Street Journal*, December 22, 1948; Paul Palmer, editor, *American Mercury*, to Irénée du Pont, August 27, 1936.

159. HML, Accession 1662, Box 4, Folder "1938," Lammot du Pont to Pierre S. du Pont, November 21, 1938.

160. HML, Accession 1803, Box 1, Folder 2, "Digest of Talks Given at Du Pont Advertising Department Clinic, May 28, 1953."

161. HML, Accession 1803, Box 1, Folder 1, J. W. McCoy Advertising Clinic, August 2, 1945; Colby, *Du Pont Dynasty*, 208.

162. HML, Accession 1662, Box 3, Folder C24, Walker B. Weisenburger, vice president, NAM, to Lammot du Pont, October 9, 1936; Accession 1411, Records of the NAM, Box 157, Folder "Radio, Industry on Parade, 1957," G. W. (Johnny) Johnson, director of radio and television public relations, NAM, and creator of *Industry on Parade*, to "All Concerned" regarding "Operational Information re NAM's weekly TV series 'Industry on Parade,'" July 13, 1953; "Fact Sheet" from April 1, 1955; letter from Frank Nelson, field secretary, Utah Association of Manufacturers, to Roger Young Jr., producer, Radio and TV Department, NAM, August 15, 1957; Associated Industries of Alabama distributed the program to nearly 100 percent of Alabama high schools according to a "Fact Sheet" dated April 1, 1955; "Reaction to Industry on Parade by schools in New England receiving films on a continuing basis," 1953; undated NAM press release from 1958; HML, Accession 1662, Box 4, Folder "January 1941–July 1952," William A. Hart to Lammot du Pont, June 11, 1946; letter from Lammot du Pont to Herman W. Steinkraus, president, Bridgeport Brass Company, June 13, 1946.

163. HML, Accession 1814, Box 4, Folder "1957–58," Advertising and Public Relations Departments directors F. A. C. Wardenburg and Harold Brayman to Greenewalt,

January 22, 1958; Brayman to Greenewalt, John Daley, and F. A. C. Wardenburg, July 15, 1958.

164. HML, Accession 1814, Box 4, Folder "1957–58," press release from the Southern States Industrial Council, July 13, 1958.

165. HML, Accession 1814, Box 4, Folder "1957–58," memorandum from Advertising and Public Relations Departments directors (Wardenburg and Brayman) to Greenewalt, January 22, 1958.

166. WHS, Bruce Barton Papers, Box 75, Client Correspondence, Maurice Collette to Bruce Barton, August 31, 1949; HML, Accession 1410, Box 36, Folder "Big and Little Business," "Is Big Business Useful: An Interview with Crawford H. Greenewalt," *U.S. News and World Report* (September 16, 1949); "Companies: Du Pont and the New Sin of Size," *Newsweek* (May 2, 1949); undated and untitled "News Release" about a Du Pont–sponsored study on interrelatedness of big and small businesses.

167. HML, Accession 1814, Box 4, Folder 56.

168. Ibid.

169. HML, Accession 1410, Box 36, Folder "Frontiers Unlimited," Script for *Frontiers Unlimited* (later *The Du Pont Story*).

170. HML, Accession 1410, Box 37, Folder "Dupont Story," "CHR" and "Memorandum on 'The Du Pont Story' for Use at Stockholders Meeting, April 9, 1951"; F. G. Hess, secretary, executive committee to executive committee members, April 19, 1949.

171. HML, Accession 1410, Box 37, Folder "Du Pont Films," U.S. Chamber of Commerce news release, February 2, 1955; Du Pont public relations release, May 12, 1953; memorandum to William Hart, F. C. Evans, and Harold Brayman, from the Motion Picture Film Steering Committee (V. L. Simpson, Advertising Department, William S. Dutton, Public Relations Department, E. F. du Pont, Service Department), February 27, 1947.

172. HML, Accession 1410, Box 31, Folder "150th Anniversary," Memo to J. W. McCoy from Public Relations Department," January 19, 1950; "A Checklist of Ideas for Tying in Sales and Advertising Activity with Du Pont 150th Anniversary."

173. Marchand, *Creating the Corporate Soul*, 322.

174. HML, Accession 1410, Box 31, Folder "150th Anniversary," 150th Anniversary Ceremonies program.

175. HML, Accession 1814, Box 4, Folder "Advertising Department, 1953–56," R. M. De Graff, Advertising Department, September 13, 1954; Greenewalt to Frank Stanton, president, CBS, April 1, 1957.

176. HML, Accession 1803, Box 6, Folder 40, John Dollard Report on "Smyrna Incident."

177. HML, Accession 1814, Box 4, Folder 1953–56, Greenewalt to Barton, September 28, 1954; BBDO report on television outlook for Du Pont, 1955.

178. HML, Accession 1803, Box 23, Folder 6, BBDO, "An Examination of TV for Du Pont Company Advertising," August 1952. Statistics varied considerably depending

on the city, the time slot, and the researcher, but Nielson gave Du Pont a 16 percent "average share" in 1952–53, a 22 percent share in 1953–54, and 26 percent in 1954–55.

179. HML, Accession 1803, Box 5, Folder 32, BBDO Ratings Report Comparing 1952–53 and 1953–54 seasons; Box 8, Folder 1, Neilson Report, January 18, 1955; Box 23, Folder 1, "United States Television Households by Region, State, and County," Advertising Research Foundation, June 1955. Television ownership was spread evenly between groups of all educational levels, and income level did not really affect television ownership either except for the bottom quarter of Americans, who owned far fewer televisions in the mid-1950s.

180. HML, Accession 1803, Box 5, Folder 32, BBDO report on television for Du Pont, 1955.

181. HML, Accession 1803, Box 22, Folder 19, BBDO report on audience composition, August 31, 1956.

182. HML, Accession 1803, Box 5, Folder 32, BBDO report on television prepared for Du Pont, 1955; Box 11, Folder 42, "Functions of BBDO in Servicing the Du Pont *Cavalcade* Program on Television," July 23, 1954.

183. HML, Accession 1803, Box 22, Folder 7, BBDO report, "Du Pont Company Advertising: A Glance Backward, November 1952.

184. HML, Accession 1803, Box 11, Folder 42, BBDO report, "Functions of BBDO in Servicing the Du Pont *Cavalcade of America* Program on Television," July 23, 1954.

185. William Boddy, *Fifties Television: The Industry and Its Critics* (Urbana: University of Illinois Press, 1992), 160–71.

186. HML, Accession 1803, Box 22, Folder 19, BBDO analysis of audience composition, August 31, 1956; Fried, *Man Everybody Knew*, 200.

187. HML, Accession 1803, Box 27, Folder 27, "Brainstorming Problem #13— Television Programs Attract/ Be Compatible With Institutional Advertising," 1956.

188. HML, Accession 1803, Box 22, Folder 23, BBDO, "Recommendations for Du Pont's Continued Use of Television," December 6, 1956.

189. HML, Accession 1814, Box 4, Folder 56, Bruce Barton to Crawford Greenewalt, February 7, 1955.

190. HML, Accession 1803, Box 24, Folder 16, BBDO report on public opinion toward corporations; Colby, *Du Pont Dynasty*, 420.

191. Henry Steele Commager, "The Search for a Usable Past," in *The Search for a Usable Past, and Other Essays in Historiography* (New York: Alfred A. Knopf, 1967), 25.

Chapter 3. History, News, and *You Are There*

1. Doherty, *Cold War, Cool Medium*, 10.

2. HML, Accession 1814, Box 4, Memo to William Hart, forwarded to Crawford Greenewalt January 17, 1955; ratings for *You Are There* in fall 1954 are 14.7, compared to 11.8 for *See It Now*, 17.8 for *Cavalcade of America*. The series reached about three million households per episode in 1953 and four million in 1954.

3. Ibid.; Ronald Radosh and Allis Radosh, *Red Star over Hollywood: The Film Colony's Long Romance with the Left* (San Francisco: Encounter Books, 2005), 168; David Everitt, *A Shadow of Red: Communism and the Blacklist in Radio and Television* (Chicago: Ivan R. Dee, 2007), 51, 59.

4. Paul Buhle and Dave Wagner, *Hide in Plain Sight: The Hollywood Blacklistees in Film and Television, 1950–2002* (New York: Palgrave Macmillan, 2003), 20; John Schultheiss, "A Season of Fear: Abraham Polonsky, *You Are There,* and the Blacklist," in Abraham Polonsky, *You Are There Teleplays: The Critical Edition,* ed. John Schultheiss and Mark Schaubert (Northridge, CA: Center for Telecommunication Studies, California State University, 1997), 9, 17.

5. Schultheiss, "A Season of Fear," 12.

6. The treatments discussed in this chapter by John Schultheiss, Thomas Doherty, Paul Buhle, and Dave Wagner, as well as Brenda Murphy, *The Congressional Theatre: Dramatizing McCarthyism on Stage, Film, and Television* (Cambridge: Cambridge University Press, 1999), recall the series as anticommunist (and very little else), but focusing on only a few episodes has partly misrepresented the series.

7. George Lipsitz, *Time Passages: Collective Memory and American Popular Culture* (Minneapolis: University of Minnesota Press, 1990), 62.

8. Gallup Poll #486 of February 9–February 16, 1952, http://institution.gallup .com.proxy-um.researchport.umd.edu/documents/questionnaire.aspx?STUDY =AIPoo486K.

9. HML, Accession 1803, Box 22, Folder 19, BBDO report on audience composition, August 31, 1956.

10. WHS, Abraham Polonsky Collection, Box 11, Diaries, Diary 29, April 22, 1953.

11. Baughman, *Republic of Mass Culture,* 19.

12. Roy Rosenstone, *Revisioning History: Film and the Construction of a New Past* (Princeton, NJ: Princeton University Press, 1995), 3, 4.

13. Just before the conventions, blurring any distinction between reality and television's version of it, Cronkite and William Wood oversaw a free CBS course in effective use of television for the two presidential candidates and thirty-four senators up for reelection in 1952. Cabell Phillips, "Learning How to Act Like a Senator," *New York Times,* May 25, 1952.

14. Robert F. Horowitz, "History Comes to Life," 83.

15. Eric Pace, "Winston Burdett Is Dead at 79: Covered World and War for CBS," *New York Times,* May 21, 1993. Burdett confessed to being a spy for the USSR in June 1955 and gave a Senate committee the names of other communists in broadcasting. Edward R. Murrow arranged for his reassignment to Rome, where he continued reporting for CBS into the 1970s.

16. On narration in historical film, see William Guynn, *Writing History in Film* (New York: Routledge, 2006), 60–80.

17. Robert F. Horowitz, "History Comes to Life," 80; Kammen, *Mystic Chords of Memory,* 581.

18. Paul Buhle and Dave Wagner, *A Very Dangerous Citizen: Abraham Polonsky and the Hollywood Left* (Berkeley: University of California Press, 2001), 174.

19. Jack Gould, "The Eagles Brood: CBS Documentary Deals With Delinquency," *New York Times*, March 9, 1947; Jack Gould, "The Honor Roll," *New York Times*, December 28, 1947; "WNYC to Open 'Masters' Concert Series—CBS to Offer Historical Program," *New York Times*, July 7, 1947; Robert F. Horowitz, "History Comes to Life," 80, 83; Schultheiss, "A Season of Fear," 11, 31.

20. Sig Mickelson notes that Shayon no longer worked for CBS when his name appeared in *Red Channels*, so he paid the matter little attention. However, he also says that the Documentary Unit was viewed with suspicion after *Red Channels* appeared, and certain programs were cut (he does not mention specific titles). Mickelson never mentions *You Are There* in his memoir, *The Decade That Shaped Television News* (Westport, CT: Praeger, 1998), though he alludes to that *kind* of program several times to say he objected to anything that was not straight documentary. The evidence suggests the opposite was true, as Mickelson spoke favorably on many occasions about the mix of dramatization and documentation. I suspect that as he later reflected on his role in pioneering network television news, he no longer considered *You Are There* to be a serious enough program and thus deleted it from his history. None of the other historical work on CBS in this period pays much attention to the series; historians of television news draw a line between real news and re-creations, even if their subjects did not. Most recently, a 2008 biography of *You Are There* veteran Don Hollenbeck mentions the series but clearly does not consider the possibility that the reporter's years on the show (his first few years on television) might have been significant: Loren Ghiglione, *CBS's Don Hollenbeck: An Honest Reporter in the Age of McCarthyism* (New York: Columbia University Press, 2008).

21. "Columbus Discovers America," available online at the Internet Archive, http://www.archive.org, exemplified the authenticating techniques. At the opening we learn that Daly has been cut off for three days, but then Don Hollenbeck at CBS London reestablishes contact with him during the broadcast after several failed "live" attempts. During the second attempt, Hollenbeck explains over the static that "the signal is not of broadcast quality. That sound of voices may be what the technicians call ghost voices— weird patterns of static that sound like people talking." The technical jargon helps to authenticate. Again they fail to reach Daly, so they replay his last report before losing contact.

22. John Crosby, "CBS Is There Has Fine Balance," *Washington Post*, April 25, 1948.

23. WHS, John Daly Papers, Box 5, Folder 7, "The Surrender of Sitting Bull."

24. Engelhardt, *End of Victory Culture*, 101.

25. "The Betrayal of Toussaint L'Ouverture," written by Robert Lewis Shayon and Joseph Liss, airdate May 30, 1948, available online at www.archive.org.

26. Doherty, *Cold War, Cool Medium*, 23. Many detailed histories of the blacklist are available. While most histories argue or assume that the blacklistees were unjustly persecuted, they also claim (often implicitly) that many writers in particular managed to continue to disseminate leftist messages through the use of fronts and pseudonyms. They

claim, in other words, that anticommunists were paranoid, and then, crediting their subjects with subversion, suggest the paranoia may have been justified. This chapter demonstrates that at least these three writers did try to get some of their political philosophy into network television broadcasts, but it also shows that the ideology was not so much party-line communism as it was broadly liberal.

Written during the period, Murray Kempton's *Part of Our Time: Some Ruins and Monuments of the Thirties* (1955; repr., New York: Meridian Books, 1958) remains enjoyable. Stefan Kanfer, *A Journal of the Plague Years* (New York: Atheneum, 1973); Larry Ceplair and Steven Englund, *The Inquisition in Hollywood: Politics in the Film Community, 1930–1960* (Berkeley: University of California Press, 1983); and Victor S. Navasky, *Naming Names* (New York: Penguin Books, 1981), are classic histories of the era and later works draw on their pro-blacklistee interpretations. For informative oral histories see Patrick McGilligan and Paul Buhle, *Tender Comrades: A Backstory of the Hollywood Blacklist* (New York: St. Martin's Press, 1997). Buhle and Wagner's *Hide in Plain Sight* argues that blacklistees had an unrecognized impact on film both during and after McCarthyism. Thomas Doherty's *Cold War, Cool Medium* offers a concise account of blacklist machinery. Recent books that challenge the pro-blacklistee consensus are Everitt, *Shadow of Red*, and Radosh and Radosh, *Red Star over Hollywood*. Both works question earlier historiography that uncritically accepted the blacklistees' memories of the 1950s. Everitt argues that the publishers of *Counterattack* and *Red Channels* were not paranoid fanatics but rather well-meaning and fairly moderate concerned citizens (with allies that tended toward excess). The 2007 edited volume of essays *"Un-American" Hollywood: Politics and Film in the Blacklist Era*, edited by Frank Krutnik, Steve Neale, Brian Neve, and Peter Stanfield (New Brunswick, NJ: Rutgers University Press), challenges the blacklist historiography from another perspective. The contributing authors question many of the presuppositions of earlier historians of the blacklist, including the presumed ability of anyone, blacklisted or not, to effectively disseminate ideology through film or television, as well as the earlier historians' inclinations to find anti-anticommunism in every film made by someone on the left during these years.

27. The emphasis on Parris's financial dispute and socioeconomic divisions within the Salem community is a prominent theme in later histories, in particular, Paul Boyer and Stephen Nissenbaum's *Salem Possessed: The Social Origins of Witchcraft* (Cambridge, MA: Harvard University Press, 1974).

28. WHS, Daly Papers, Box 5, Folder 5, "The Execution of Joan of Arc." The German-born Wanger had produced *Blockade*, Hollywood's only Spanish Civil War movie, in 1940 and would later produce *Invasion of the Body Snatchers*, the 1956 motion picture portrayal of a nation of mindless conformists. Anderson wrote several other historical dramas, including one about Socrates and another about Washington at Valley Forge (two oft-used historical episodes in the 1940s and 1950s).

29. Ibid.

30. Ibid.

31. Prolific radio and television writer Irve Tunick wrote both of these impeachment episodes. He served as president of the Eastern Region of the Television Writers of America in the 1950s. New York Public Library (hereafter NYPL), Billy Rose Theatre

Collection, Card Catalog File for Irve Tunick, clipping from the *New York Times*, January 14, 1954.

32. Navasky, *Naming Names*, 284; WHS, John Daly Papers, Box 5, Folder 8, "The Impeachment of Andrew Jackson" and "The Impeachment Trial of Supreme Court Justice Samuel Chase."

33. Navasky, *Naming Names*, 82. Only Albert Maltz was permitted to read his statement into the record.

34. WHS, Daly Papers, Box 6, Folder 8, "The Sentencing of Charles I, King of England."

35. "The Trial of Ann Hutchinson," written by Henry Walsh and Robert Lewis Shayon. Another episode of this type, "The Trial of John Peter Zenger," highlights the brave citizens who serve as jurors. Both episodes are online at www.archive.org.

36. "The Women's Rights Convention," directed by Mitchell Grayson and produced by Sam Abelo, online at www.archive.org.

37. Saverio Giovacchini, "Did Private Nolan Get His Glory? Movies, Press and Audience during the Spanish-American War," *Columbia Journal of American Studies* 3, no. 1 (1998): 141–58.

38. Stephen J. Ross, "Struggles for the Screen: Workers, Radicals, and the Political Uses of Silent Film," *American Historical Review* 96, no. 2 (1991): 342–45.

39. Bill Nichols, "Documentary Reenactment and the Fantasmatic Subject," *Critical Inquiry* 35, no. 1 (2008): 84. "Realist dramatization" attempts to erase distinctions between the real events it reenacts and follows conventional dramatic format. Nichols refers to the opposite approach as "Brechtian distanciation." *You Are There* did give listeners and viewers the sense of looking in on a play (or participating in it), but every attempt was made to conceal the inherent falseness of a faked newscast.

40. Richard Pells, "Documentaries, Fiction, and the Depression," in *Radical Visions and American Dreams*, 194–251.

41. WHS, Daly Papers, Box 5, Folder 4, "The Battle of Gettysburg."

42. WHS, Sig Mickelson Papers, Box 1, Folder "Programs: You Are There," Office Communication from Werner Michel to Mickelson, May 8, 1950.

43. Ibid.

44. Vance Kepley Jr., "The Origins of NBC's Project XX in Compilation Documentaries," *Journalism Quarterly* 61, no. 1 (1984): 20, 22–25.

45. WHS, Mickelson Papers, Box 1, Folder "CBS News—Miscellaneous Data—1955–1960," Draft of Speech given as president of CBS News entitled "The New Meaning of News," n.d.

46. WHS, Mickelson Papers, Box 1, Folder: Educational Television (1952), Mickelson to Siepmann, draft reply to letter of March 13, 1952.

47. "Mallory's Tragedy on Mt. Everest," written by Abraham Polonsky (as "Jeremy Daniel"), in Polonsky, *You Are There Teleplays*, 227.

48. WHS, Mickelson Papers, Box 1, Folder "CBS News—CBS News Clinic 1955," CBS News Clinic, January 3–4, 1955, 91–101.

49. Robert F. Horowitz, "History Comes to Life," 84.

50. Ibid., 213.

51. Walter Bernstein, *Inside Out: A Memoir of the Blacklist* (New York: Da Capo Press, 2000), 22.

52. Saverio Giovacchini, *Hollywood Modernism: Film and Politics in the Age of the New Deal* (Philadelphia: Temple University Press, 2001), 179–81; Radosh and Radosh, *Red Star over Hollywood*, 130; Buhle and Wagner, *Very Dangerous Citizen*, 92.

53. Buhle and Wagner, *Very Dangerous Citizen*, 92; Bernstein, *Inside Out*, 138–39.

54. Buhle and Wagner, *Very Dangerous Citizen*, 88. Polonsky replaced CP Hollywood branch leader John Howard Lawson, the director of *Blockade* (1938) and the classic World War II film *Sahara* (1943), and an easy and prominent target for Tenney. Tenney was a former Popular Fronter before losing his bid to become a union president and then abruptly changing his politics.

55. Ibid., 90–94; Bernstein, *Inside Out*, 7.

56. McGilligan and Buhle, *Tender Comrades*, 46.

57. Bernstein, *Inside Out*, 93.

58. See the discussion of the feature film in Buhle and Wagner, *Very Dangerous Citizen*, 112.

59. John Schultheiss, preface to "The Fate of Nathan Hale," in Polonsky, *You Are There Teleplays*, 101. Schultheiss refers specifically to the Nathan Hale episode but also suggests that this theme permeates most of Polonsky's work.

60. For the *DuPont Show of the Month* version, Du Pont/BBDO initially hoped Sidney Lumet would direct. For the lead roles, producer David Susskind tried to get Paul Newman, Lee Remick, Rod Steiger, and Sidney Poitier. Susskind wrote, "Their idea is to take out the money drive and portray the lead as a man who simply wants to fight for power and glory." The film was made, but not with any of the talent mentioned. WHS, David Susskind Papers, Box 11, Folder "DuPont Show of the Month," memo to Harold Blackburn at Du Pont from Herb West at BBDO.

61. Buhle and Wagner, *Very Dangerous Citizen*, 109, 118–22.

62. Walter Bernstein relates his wartime reporting adventures in *Keep Your Head Down* (New York: Book Find Club, 1945).

63. Bernstein, *Inside Out*, 8–21.

64. Ibid., 146–48.

65. Ibid., 202.

66. Ibid., 24–26, 151.

67. Ibid., 156.

68. Ibid., 157–58, 168. While waiting for "this elusive individual," Bernstein got jobs under his real name at *Life*, *Argosy*, and *Sports Illustrated*, and then did a three-part piece for *Collier's* on Rocky Graziano that helped the boxer get reinstated.

69. Ibid., 154–55, 216.

70. Ibid., 208; NYPL, Billy Rose Theatre Collection, Card Catalog File for Walter Bernstein, clippings from the *New York Times*, February 11, 1950, and March 18, 1950.

71. Buhle and Wagner, *Very Dangerous Citizen*, 145.

72. Bernstein, *Inside Out*, 173, 215.

73. Ibid., 216.

74. WHS, Mickelson Papers, Box 1, Folder "Programs: You Are There," Office Communication from Michel to Mickelson, May 8, 1950.

75. "The New Shows," *Time*, February 23, 1953, http://www.time.com/time/magazine/article/0,9171,936389,00.html. These two episodes were similarly "far from satisfactory" for the *Washington Post*. See John Crosby, "Here's a Show Taking That Long Step Backward," *Washington Post*, February 10, 1953, 29.

76. Buhle and Wagner, *Very Dangerous Citizen*, 175.

77. "You Are There: Joan of Arc," film available at the Paley Center for Media, New York.

78. Polonsky, *You Are There Teleplays*, 72–73.

79. For example, this accusation was made in the Motion Picture Alliance for the Preservation of American Ideals' "Screen Guide for Americans," written in 1947, purportedly by Ayn Rand.

80. J. J. Fahie, *Galileo: His Life and Work* (London: J. Murray, 1903), 245.

81. WHS, Polonsky Collection, Box 10, Diaries, April 12, 1953.

82. These included Fahie, *Galileo*; Mary Allan-Olney, *The Private Life of Galileo* (London: Macmillan, 1870); F. R. Wegg-Prosser, *Galileo and His Judges* (London: Chapman and Hall, 1889); David Brewster, *Martyrs of Science: Galileo, Tycho Brahe, and Kepler* (London: Chatto and Windus, 1874); and Peter Cooper, *Galileo's Roman Inquisition* (Cincinnati: Montfort and Conahans, 1844). Polonsky's script mostly followed Fahie's work, which treated the Catholic Church unsympathetically. It also contained long translated passages from the inquisition and from correspondence, which seem to have been the basis for Polonsky's work. The words from his diary are very similar to the text of Fahie, *Galileo*, 265.

83. WHS, Polonsky Collection, Box 11, Diaries, Diary 29, April 22, 1953.

84. WHS, Polonsky Collection, Box 11, Diaries, Diary 30, October 21, 1953. The remark about ideas he did not "thoroughly accept" probably meant that he did not always follow the Communist Party line.

85. Ehrhard Bahr, *Weimar on the Pacific: German Exile Culture in Los Angeles and the Crisis of Modernism* (Berkeley: University of California Press, 2007), 115–18.

86. Giovacchini, *Hollywood Modernism*, 207.

87. John Schultheiss, "The Crisis of Galileo," in Polonsky, *You Are There Teleplays*, 70–71.

88. Emily Wilson, *The Death of Socrates* (Cambridge, MA: Harvard University Press, 2007), 18, 202. Wilson engagingly traces the story of Socrates's final moments from the first contemporary accounts through the present. She finds the most dramatic change occurred with the Enlightenment, when the story shifted to the "solitude of the intellectual who resists social conformity." This interpretation becomes increasingly prevalent during the twentieth century.

89. "The Death of Socrates," 1953, available at the Museum of Broadcast Communications, Chicago, and online at www.museum.tv. Others have claimed some additional historical significance for this episode as Paul Newman's first appearance on television,

but he does not appear in any scene and is not listed in the credits. The claim about Newman is made by John Schultheiss in Polonsky, *You Are There Teleplays*, 101, and by Frank R. Cunningham in *Sidney Lumet: Film and Literary Vision* (Lexington: University Press of Kentucky, 2001), 19–20. Unfortunately, neither author cites a source. This was live television, so perhaps Newman appeared in a different broadcast based on the same script.

90. "The Death of Socrates," March 1948, available at the Museum of Broadcast Communication, Chicago, and online at www.museum.tv; Wilson, *Death of Socrates*, 3, 99–103.

91. "The First Salem Witch Trials" (1953), film available at the Paley Center for Media, New York.

92. "The Salem Witch Trials" (1956), written by Milton Geiger, directed by William D. Russell, and produced by James Fonda, available at LC, Motion Picture, Broadcasting, and Recorded Sound Division (MPBRSD).

93. Hale's journal confirms he played football, checkers, and other games. See M. William Phelps, *Nathan Hale: The Life and Death of America's First Spy* (New York: Thomas Dunne Books, 2008), 100.

94. John Schultheiss, preface to "The Fate of Nathan Hale," in Polonsky, *You Are There Teleplays*, 100.

95. WHS, Daly Papers, Box 5, Folder 9, "The Fall of Savonarola," Sunday, February 20, 1949, written by Robert Lewis Shayon and Henry Walsh. John Daly, Clete Roberts, and Quincy Howe reported from Florence, Italy, April 7, 1498. Roberts "translated" from the Italian dialogue. The play centers on the "struggle for power between the great Christian apostle of popular government—and his bitter enemies—the Medici—symbol of medieval autocracy." Howe interviews Niccolo Machiavelli, aged twenty-nine, who complains that Savonarola is "an impractical dreamer." "Man, by his very nature, is evil, fickle, false, cowardly and covetous . . . fear is all that controls his evil passions." Sadly, Machiavelli seems to be right in this case at least, as Savonarola is deposed by his enemies' tricks, and the crowd stones our hero.

96. Polonsky, *You Are There Teleplays*, 192.

97. Ibid., 186.

98. Ibid., 188–209.

99. LC, MPBRSD, "The Hatfield–McCoy Feud" (1955).

100. WHS, Howard Rodman Papers, Script for "The Death of Stonewall Jackson" (1955).

101. "Washington's Farewell to His Officers" (1955), available on DVD (Woodhaven Entertainment).

102. "The Gettysburg Address" (1953), available on DVD (Woodhaven Entertainment).

103. See, in particular, two of Herbert Aptheker's works, *The Negro in the Civil War* (New York: International, 1938) and *American Negro Slave Revolts* (New York: Columbia University Press, 1943).

104. *Variety*, December 11, 1985, 150.

105. Nash, Crabtree, and Dunn, *History on Trial*, 60–61.

106. "The Emancipation Proclamation" (1955), written by Howard Rodman, online at www.museum.tv.

107. Polonsky, *You Are There Teleplays*, 241–56.

108. Jeffrey H. Jackson, *Making Jazz French: Music and Modern Life in Interwar Paris* (Durham, NC: Duke University Press, 2003) 92–93.

109. Timon (Abraham Polonsky), "The Troubled Mandarins," *Masses and Mainstream* 9 (August 1956): 35n, cited in Buhle and Wagner, *Very Dangerous Citizen*, 170–71.

110. Mickelson, *Decade That Shaped Television News*, 81.

111. NYPL, Billy Rose Theatre Collection, "You Are There," B File, Photograph and press release from *You Are There*: "Cyprus Today," Sunday, July 1, 1956.

112. WHS, Mickelson Collection, Box 1, Folder "Programs—You Are There," Memorandum from H. L. McClinton, president of Calkins & Holden, Inc. (advertising agency) to Robert Livingston of CBS, December 20, 1956.

113. Available on DVD (Woodhaven Entertainment).

114. WHS, Polonsky Collection, Box 11, Diaries, April 7, 1954: Polonsky wrote of his anger and dismay at Eisenhower for dragging the country into war in French Indochina.

115. Buhle and Wagner, *Very Dangerous Citizen*, 176.

116. Polonsky, "Cortés Conquers Mexico," in *You Are There Teleplays*. On May 1, 1949, the radio series aired "The Death of Montezuma," written by Michael Sklar and Robert Lewis Shayon. The radio play focused on the Aztec response to Montezuma's "cowardice," as the high council strips the emperor of his title and he is murdered by his former subjects.

117. WHS, John Frankenheimer Papers, Box 6, *You Are There*: "The Battle of Gibraltar" (December 5, 1954).

118. The radio series covered this subject in "Mutiny in India" (March 20, 1949), by Michael Sklar. The two episodes bear no resemblance.

119. WHS, Paddy Chayevsky Papers, Box 11, Folder 9, "Triangle Shirtwaist Company Fire." Chayevsky framed the episode as a CBS News feature on the "problems of women in industry" ("live" from March 25, 1911). The script is dense and heavy-handed, which perhaps explains why the episode never made it on air. Of course, the horror of the climax is extreme, as the main characters, now afire, die screaming as they jump down the elevator shaft or out a window. Even a CBS reporter was to burn to death in this story! The last shot was to focus on "Naomi": "Bodies on floor. . . . Slumped over a sewing machine is a skeleton in a skirt and blouse, once Naomi Wiener, who had a big date at the Hippodrome." The proposed images of charred young women pushed too far.

120. Polonsky, *You Are There Teleplays*, 323n. As remembered by Russell, Levitt was cleared and able to write using his own name by 1955. Russell specifically mentions "D-Day" as an episode credited to Levitt, but that program, now available on DVD (Woodhaven Entertainment), gives Stern credit as the writer at the end of the film. So it

is difficult to know whether Levitt and Russell accurately remembered Levitt as the author of all scripts bearing Stern's name, or if Stern wrote one or more of them himself.

121. The theme of resistance did find its way into Levitt's "The Resolve of Patrick Henry" (1956). Levitt may have been blacklisted, but the fact that he had been cleared by early 1955 suggests his politics were of a less active (or less left) variety than our trio's, a conclusion supported by the content of the episodes he wrote. As mentioned, "D-Day" contained nothing but the most nationalistic, uncritically patriotic and celebratory history, and none of these scripts tread too deeply into perilous political waters. "Patrick Henry" is available on film at the LC, MPBRSD.

122. Bernstein, *Inside Out*, 259–77.

123. Buhle and Wagner, *Very Dangerous Citizen*, 250.

124. Ibid., 179–92.

125. The quote is from fan reviews at Internet Movie Database, www.imdb.com. Most radio shows are also available online, and twelve television films are available on DVD (Woodhaven Entertainment). Customer reviews at Amazon.com suggest its popularity for homeschooling. One mother-teacher showed the Socrates and Alexander episodes (on one DVD) to her five- and seven-year-olds. Both children "liked it a lot," perhaps because "it brought to life stuff they'd read." She calls the series a "great and thoughtful production, nice and simple from the 50s." A teacher who uses the shows in his classroom wrote, "Walter Cronkite and his news staff deliver great coverage of historic events 'as they happen.'" More excitedly, one fan points out, "They used actors playing real people, but they are interview[ed] by real CBS News reporters!" What made the series work for him more than anything else was the innovative shooting angle: "the actors talked to you and answered your questions" as if "you were there in person, seeing history in the making." Reviews submitted by listeners to archive.org, a site featuring older radio programs, reveal how fans appreciate the radio series. A home-schooler says, "This is a wonderful gateway to history topics and more indepth study. An imdb.com reviewer noted, "I cannot compare the effort to penetrate historical events with anything currently on commercial broadcast network TV."

Chapter 4. The Freedom Train's Narrow-Gauge Iconography

1. Wendy Wall, *Inventing the American Way: The Politics of Consensus from the New Deal to the Civil Rights Movement* (Oxford: Oxford University Press, 2008), 206.

2. William J. Peterson, "America's Freedom Train," *Palimpsest* 29, no. 9 (1948): 258.

3. "Freedom Train Goes on Exhibition Today from 10 a.m. to 10 p.m.: Visit It!," *Hartford (CT) Courant*, October 4, 1947.

4. Wall, *Inventing the American Way*, 5–12; Richard M. Fried, "Precious Freight: The Freedom Train," in Fried, *The Russians Are Coming! The Russians Are Coming! Pageantry and Patriotism in Cold-War America* (New York: Oxford University Press, 1998); Stuart J. Little,

"The Freedom Train and the Formation of National Political Culture, 1946–1949" (MA thesis, University of Kansas, 1989).

5. A storyteller, Holbrook filled this book with tall tales and anecdotes that, combined with some history, instruct as well as entertain. One chapter celebrates Pullman porters: their numerous feats of heroism, the quality and consistency of their work, and their leadership in the black community. It also derides those passengers who whistle for them "as if for a dog" or otherwise disrespect the men who made rail travel feel luxurious. Stewart Holbrook, *The Story of American Railroads* (New York: Crown, 1947), 451.

6. "Guide to the Chicago Railroad Fair, 1949," available at Richard Leonard's Rail Archive, www.railarchive.net.

7. Mike Wallace, *Mickey Mouse History and Other Essays on American Memory* (Philadelphia: Temple University Press, 1996), 135–38.

8. John F. Stover, *The Life and Decline of the American Railroad* (New York: Oxford University Press, 1970), 442.

9. Holbrook, *Story of American Railroads*, 443.

10. Stover, *Life and Decline*, 192.

11. Wilbert Ellis Moore, *Industrial Relations and the Social Order* (Manchester, NH: Ayer Books, 1977), 458; Stover, *Life and Decline*, 186.

12. Stover, *Life and Decline*, 189.

13. Harry S. Truman, "Special Message to the Congress Urging Legislation for Industrial Peace, May 25, 1946," in Truman, *Public Papers of the President of the United States: Harry S. Truman, Containing the Public Messages, Speeches, and Statements of the President, January 1 to December 31, 1946* (Washington: U.S. Government Printing Office, 1962), 277–80.

14. Bird, *"Better Living,"* 162; Wall, *Inventing the American Way*, 171.

15. Bird, *"Better Living,"* 162.

16. National Archives and Records Administration (hereafter NARA), RG 64, Box 6, Folder 5, *Good Citizen: The Rights and Duties of an American* (Official Freedom Train Publication, 1948), 1.

17. NARA, RG 64, Box 5, Folder 7, "The Freedom Train," *Atlantic Coast Line News* 28, no. 12 (1947).

18. Little, "Freedom Train and the Formation," 10.

19. James Gregory Bradsher, "Taking America's Heritage to the People: The Freedom Train Story," *Prologue* 17, no. 4 (1985): 229.

20. Little, "Freedom Train and the Formation," 12.

21. Wall, *Inventing the American Way*, 207; Eric Foner, *The Story of American Freedom* (New York: W. W. Norton, 1998), 249.

22. Lykins, *From Total War*.

23. Ibid., 9; Bradsher, "Taking America's Heritage," 230; Little, "Freedom Train and the Formation," 13.

24. Bradsher, "Taking America's Heritage," 231; Little, "Freedom Train and the Formation," 21.

25. Little, "Freedom Train and the Formation," 27; Bradsher, "Taking America's Heritage," 232–33.

26. Wall, *Inventing the American Way*, 207.

27. Nelson Lichtenstein, *State of the Union: A Century of American Labor* (Princeton, NJ: Princeton University Press, 2002), 130.

28. NARA, RG 200 AHF, Box 198, Folder "White House Conference," "Conference at the White House for the Purpose of Organizing the American Heritage Program and Inaugurating the Freedom Train, May 22, 1947"; Little, "Freedom Train and the Formation," 29, 36.

29. NARA, RG 64, Box 7, "The Mid-Century Manual of the American Heritage Foundation Proposing Rededication to Our American Heritage."

30. "Paging Freedom Train," *Newsweek*, March 29, 1948, 18.

31. Fried, *Russians Are Coming!*, 47.

32. Foner, *Story of American Freedom*, 252.

33. LC, Reinhold Niebuhr Collection, Box 1, Letter from Winthrop W. Aldrich to Reinhold Niebuhr, May 2, 1947; Box 3, Letter from Tom Clark to Niebuhr, April 14, 1947; Niebuhr, *Irony of American History*, 57.

34. Wall, *Inventing the American Way*, 225.

35. Will Herberg, *Protestant-Catholic-Jew* (Garden City, NY: Doubleday, 1955), 46–49, 88–93.

36. Michael W. Hughey, *Civil Religion and Moral Order: Theoretical and Historical Dimensions* (Westport, CT: Greenwood Press, 1983), 162.

37. Carl Lotus Becker, *Freedom and Responsibility in the American Way of Life: Five Lectures Delivered at the University of Michigan, December 1944* (New York: Alfred A. Knopf, 1945), 13.

38. Sam Stavisky, "Exhibit to Be Open for Second Day at D.C.'s Union Station," *Washington Post*, November 28, 1947.

39. "City to Welcome Food Train Today," *New York Times*, November 18, 1947; "Where Freedom Train Food Was Destroyed," *New York Times*, February 2, 1948; "Freedom Train Collects Food for Europe in Lincoln's Name," *Washington Post*, February 13, 1948.

40. Banner of the *Providence (RI) Journal*, October 9, 1947.

41. Mark Silk, *Spiritual Politics: Religion and America since World War II* (New York: Simon & Schuster, 1988), 94.

42. Ibid., 55, 67.

43. Peterson, "America's Freedom Train," 276.

44. Hughey, *Civil Religion and Moral Order*, xiii, 21, 25.

45. Explored by Richard M. Fried in *The Russians Are Coming!*

46. Silk, *Spiritual Politics*, 94.

47. Ray B. Browne, *Rituals and Ceremonies in Popular Culture* (Bowling Green, OH: Bowling Green University Popular Press, 1980), 22.

48. Little, "Freedom Train and the Formation," 30.

49. Ibid., 34–35; Fried, *Russians Are Coming!*, 34.

50. Little, "Freedom Train and the Formation," 56–57.

51. Stuart Little describes the train as corporate hegemony put into practice, with the imposition of consensus onto the American public. Richard Fried says the train held "the conflicting forces and languages within the political culture that were attempting to define citizenship and Americanism" (Fried, *Russians Are Coming!*, 33). Wendy Wall describes the train as part of the invention of "the American Way," a process that begins in the 1930s and lasts through the 1950s. Wall's more expansive language comes closest to the truth, but even hers seems too limiting to me. The cultural impact, especially in the contexts of civil religion and public history, is not sufficiently addressed.

52. James Douglass Anderson argued that putting Lincoln on the train was absurd. In his view—an unreconstructed Southern one—Lincoln was a tyrant who went well beyond King George III in destroying civil liberties. James Douglass Anderson, "Washington and Lincoln: Two Ill Mated Spirits of the 'Freedom' Train," *Tyler's Quarterly Historical and Genealogical Magazine* 30, no. 1 (1948): 5–19.

53. Peterson, "America's Freedom Train," 275, quoting the *Sioux City (IA) Journal* and the *Des Moines Register*.

54. Foner, *Story of American Freedom*, 232.

55. James A. Hagerty, "Wallace Warns of Wall St. 'Rule,'" *New York Times*, September 12, 1947.

56. "Communists Hit Freedom Train Tour," *Washington Post*, September 13, 1947.

57. "Pravda Assails Freedom Train," *New York Times*, December 5, 1947.

58. "Freedom Train Is Christened at Philadelphia, Reds Assailed," *Washington Post*, September 18, 1947.

59. H. Walton Cloke, "Truman Asks U.S. to 'Share Liberty,'" *New York Times*, September 17, 1947, 23.

60. Lykins, *From Total War*, 30.

61. Becker, *Freedom and Responsibility*, 2, 19, 21.

62. Ibid., 40.

63. Ibid., 39, 78.

64. Eric Goldman, review of *Heritage of Freedom: The History and Significance of the Basic Documents of American Liberty*, by Frank Monagham, *Mississippi Valley Historical Review* 35, no. 1 (1948): 107–8.

65. *Freedom & Union* 1, no. 1 (1946): 1–2; *Freedom & Union* 2, no. 4 (1947): 1; *Freedom & Union* 2, no. 11 (1947): 19; "Baltimorean Urges a U.N. 'Citizenship,'" *Washington Post*, December 14, 1947; Sound National Policy Association advertisement, *New York Times*, October 27, 1947.

66. Peterson, "America's Freedom Train," 277.

67. Wall, *Inventing the American Way*, 226–27.

68. "Wallace Lists 10 Talks," *New York Times*, September 6, 1947.

69. Display advertisement, *Chicago Defender*, April 17, 1948.

70. "'Communists Aim to Exploit Freedom Train,' Walton," *Providence (RI) Journal*, October 5, 1947; Frank L. Kluckhohn, "Wallace in New England Gets a Careful

Hearing," *New York Times*, October 5, 1947; "Wallace Raps Jim Crow: 25,000 Hear Wallace Demand Laws Ending Jim Crow," *Plaindealer* (Kansas City, KS), September 19, 1947.

71. "New Orleans Citizens Want FEPC, Wagner Act in Freedom Train Cargo," *Arkansas State Press* (Little Rock), January 23, 1948.

72. "Conscientious Objection Demonstrators Clash with Police Near Freedom Train," *New York Times*, September 26, 1947.

73. David A. Stein, "The Freedom Train Nears Last Siding," *Washington Post*, December 19, 1948.

74. George E. Clemence, "Arresting of Pickets Protested, *New York Times*, October 11, 1947; Connecticut Yankee, "Freedom of Speech," *Hartford (CT) Courant*, October 23, 1947; Mrs. Vivian L. McMillan, "Freedom Train," *Chicago Defender*, February 14, 1948; Joseph A. Rabun, "Loyalty and Conformity," *Washington Post*, December 5, 1947.

75. Robert Durr, "Speaking Out from the New South," *Chicago Defender*, August 23, 1947; "Aboard the Freedom Train," *New York Times*, December 26, 1947; "NAACP Probes Rumor of Freedom Train Jim Crow," *Arkansas State Press* (Little Rock), October 24, 1947.

76. "Freedom Train," *Washington Post*, January 16, 1949.

77. Meredith Johns and Herman Rhoden, "John Q. Public Doubts this Freedom Train," *Chicago Defender*, July 10, 1948.

78. "No Segregation in Atlanta When Freedom Train Comes," *Plaindealer* (Kansas City, KS), November 28, 1947; "Insist on No Jim Crow on Freedom Train," *Negro Star* (Wichita, KS), November 7, 1947; "Freedom Train Omits Birmingham Schedule," *Plaindealer* (Kansas City, KS), January 2, 1948; "Dr. J. M. Robinson Appointed Chairman to Freedom Train Committee," *Arkansas State Press* (Little Rock), November 21, 1947.

79. "To Skip Birmingham," *Chicago Defender*, December 20, 1947; Wall, *Inventing the American Way*, 238.

80. "Freedom Train says No to Jim Crow Memphis Tennessee," *Plaindealer* (Kansas City, KS), November 21, 1947; White Citizens of Memphis Say Officials Stand Alone," *Plaindealer* (Kansas City, KS), November 28, 1947.

81. John LeFlore, "Memphis in Hike to Freedom Train," *Chicago Defender*, January 17, 1948; "What Other Papers Say," *Plaindealer* (Kansas City, KS), August 20, 1948.

82. "Two Negroes First On Freedom Train," *Arkansas State Press* (Little Rock), January 1, 1948; "When the Freedom Train Comes to Little Rock Democracy Goes into Action," *Arkansas State Press* (Little Rock), January 23, 1948.

83. "New Orleans Changes Freedom Train Plans," *Arkansas State Press* (Little Rock), January 16, 1948.

84. Samuel S. Taylor, "Freedom Train Visit Brings Loss of Freedom in New Orleans," *Arkansas State Press* (Little Rock), January 16, 1948.

85. Albert Barnett, "Global News Digest," *Chicago Defender*, July 17, 1948; "Cameraman Gives Pictorial Highlights of 1948," *Chicago Defender*, January 1, 1949; "Freedom Train Gets NAACP Award," *Chicago Defender*, January 1, 1949.

86. "The Common Defense: Our American Heritage," *Arkansas State Press* (Little Rock), January 14, 1949.

87. "The Freedom Train," *Chicago Defender*, September 20, 1947.

88. "Virginia Makes Farce out of Freedom Train," *Chicago Defender*, December 20, 1947; "Jim Crow at Freedom Train," *Chicago Defender*, January 3, 1948; "Negroes Boycott 'Freedom Train' Welcome in Okla.," *Washington Post*, January 26, 1948.

89. Malvina Lindsay, "Cowardly Campaigning: Intimidating Women," *Washington Post*, April 15, 1948.

90. "Rededication Program by Women Today," *Washington Post*, November 24, 1947.

91. "Rededication Week Will Precede Arrival of Freedom Train July 5," *Chicago Defender*, July 3, 1948.

92. Landon R. Y. Storrs, "Red Scare Politics and the Suppression of Popular Front Feminism: The Loyalty Investigation of Mary Dublin Keyserling," *Journal of American History* 90, no. 2 (2003): 494–95, 519–21.

93. NARA, RG 64, Box 3, Folder 4, "American Heritage Program for Your Community," Women's Features, 18–19. On women's double duty in this period, see Elaine Tyler May, *Homeward Bound: American Families in the Cold War* (New York: Basic Books, 1988), 65–78.

94. NARA, Still Photographs Division, RG 200 AHF, Box 1, Photograph of the Emancipation Proclamation display; Little, "Freedom Train and the Formation," 67; American Heritage Foundation Communications Committee, "Information for Press and Radio on the American Heritage Program and the Freedom Train," American Heritage Foundation, New York, 1947.

95. Frank Monaghan cataloged the collection in *Heritage of Freedom*.

96. Wall, *Inventing the American Way*, 214.

97. Ibid., 240.

98. Frank G. Burke, "Innovation at the Archives—The Departure of the Freedom Train," *Curator: The Museum Journal* 16, no. 4 (1973): 333–34.

99. NARA, Still Photographs, RG 200 AHF, Box 1, Folder C-13 and D-30.

100. Peterson, "America's Freedom Train," 265; Fried, *Russians Are Coming!*, 40. In Los Angeles, 400,000 people turned out and 30,000 saw the documents. In Charlotte, 8,416 out of 100,000 viewed them. Most cities had similar ratios.

101. NARA, RG 200, AHF, Gilbert Bailey, "Why They Throng to the Freedom Train," *New York Times Magazine*, January 25, 1948, SM 18.

102. NARA, Still Photographs Division, RG 200, American Heritage Foundation, Box 1, Freedom Train.

103. NARA, RG 64, Box 6, Freedom Train Scrapbook and Related Materials, "Music, Documents, Postcards, Editorials" Folder, "Highlights of the First Year of the American Heritage Foundation," Interim Report of Thomas D'Arch Brophy, president, to the Board of Trustees, American Heritage Foundation, November 4, 1948.

104. Sam Stavisky, "Exhibit to Be Open for Second Day at D.C.'s Union Station," *Washington Post*, November 28, 1947.

105. Little, "Freedom Train and the Formation," 69.

106. "Slow Pace Jams Freedom Train," *New York Times*, September 27, 1947; NARA, RG 64, Box 5, Folder 7, Magazine Articles, *Collector: A Magazine for Autograph and Historical Collectors* 60, no. 11, November 1947.

107. Peterson, "America's Freedom Train," 266.

108. Rachel P. Maines and James J. Glynn, "Numinous Objects," *Public Historian* 15, no. 1 (1993): 9–10.

109. "Freedom Train Tours America," *National Geographic Magazine*, October 1949, 542.

110. "America's Ambulatory Museum," *Saturday Review* 31, no. 10 (1948): 23.

111. Peterson, "America's Freedom Train," 265; NARA, News Features, p. 10, Order NF962.

112. Irving Spiegel, "Common Religion Urged for the U.S.," *New York Times*, June 22, 1949.

113. Bailey, "Why They Throng," SM 18.

114. Peterson, "America's Freedom Train," 265.

115. Fried, *Russians Are Coming!*, 41.

116. Ibid.

117. Bailey, "Why They Throng," SM 18.

118. "Hikes to See the Freedom Train," *Washington Post*, July 11, 1948.

119. "Freedom Train," *Washington Post*, November 30, 1947.

120. Kelly Cocanougher, "Freedom Train Visits Bluefield," *Bluefield (WV) Daily Telegraph*, September 29, 1948; David Hackett Fischer, *Liberty and Freedom: A Visual History of America's Founding Ideas* (New York: Oxford University Press, 2005), 537.

121. "Strengthen Pledge," *Chicago Defender*, July 10, 1948.

122. "Permanent residue of patriotism" is from Peterson, "America's Freedom Train," 268.

123. NARA, RG 64, Box 6, "Highlights of the First Year of the American Heritage Foundation"; Peterson, "America's Freedom Train," 269; Wall, *Inventing the American Way*, 222.

124. Langston Hughes, "Freedom Train," *New Republic* 117, no. 11 (1947): 27.

125. Peterson, "America's Freedom Train," 270.

126. "Freedom Train Tours America," 539.

127. "Oak Ridge to See Freedom Train Sunday," *Y-12 Bulletin* (Oak Ridge, TN), September 28, 1948, accessed at http://www.y12.doe.gov/library/pdf/about/history/y12bulletins/Vo2N39_19480928.pdf; Wall, *Inventing the American Way*, 220.

128. "Rededication Events Open September 28th," *Hartford (CT) Courant*, September 22, 1947; Brown-Thomas Advertisement, *Hartford (CT) Courant*, September 24, 1947; "Retail Stores Plan Freedom Ceremonies," *Hartford (CT) Courant*, September 26, 1947; Freedom Train Advertisement, *Providence (RI) Journal*, October 2, 1947; "Baltimore Ops Hail Freedom Train Visit," *Billboard*, November 22, 1947.

129. Stuart J. Little, "The Freedom Train: Citizenship and Postwar Political Culture, 1946–1949," *American Studies* 34, no. 1 (Spring 1993): 50.

130. David Glassberg, *American Historical Pageantry: The Uses of Tradition in the Early Twentieth Century* (Chapel Hill: University of North Carolina Press, 1990), 285.

131. Wall, *Inventing the American Way*, 217.

132. Ibid., 206.

133. NARA, RG 64, Box 3, Folder 4, "American Heritage Program for Your Community," News Features, 14, 32.

134. Fried, *Russians Are Coming!*, 42.

135. NARA, RG 64, Box 6, "Highlights of the First Year of the American Heritage Foundation."

136. NARA, RG 342 USAF, *Our American Heritage*.

137. NARA, RG 64, Box 6, "Highlights of the First Year of the American Heritage Foundation."

138. NARA, RG 64, Box 3, Folder 12, "Retailers' Manual, American Heritage Foundation," 1947.

139. NARA, RG 200, Photographs of the Freedom Train, Boxes 1 and 2.

140. HML, Pictorial Collections, *Cavalcade of America* Transcripts, no. 563.

141. Wall, *Inventing the American Way*, 216.

142. American Heritage Foundation, *Good Citizen*, inside cover.

143. Tyrrell, *Historians in Public*, 111–12.

144. NARA, RG 64, Box 3, Folder 4, "The American Heritage Program for Your Community," 43.

145. NARA, RG 64, Box 6, "Highlights of the First Year of the American Heritage Foundation."

146. Mildred Tibbits, *Suggestions for Junior High School Teachers in Utilizing the Visit of the Freedom Train as an Experience in Teaching Social Studies* (Louisville: University of Louisville, 1948) 12, 17.

147. John E. Heaney, "Why Truman's Campaign Train Lingered in Oklahoma City," *New York Times*, October 25, 1992; see also Harry S. Truman Library and Museum, http://www.trumanlibrary.org/whistlestop/TruWhisTour/coverpge.htm.

148. Wall, *Inventing the American Way*, 214.

149. Fried, *Russians Are Coming!*, 47.

150. NARA, RG 64, Box 3, "Information for Press and Radio on the American Heritage Program and the Freedom Train," August 1947.

Chapter 5. Building a "National Shrine" at the National Museum of American History

1. Gordon Fyfe, "Sociology and the Social Aspects of Museums," in *A Companion to Museum Studies*, ed. Sharon Macdonald (Oxford: Blackwell, 2006), 39.

2. Smithsonian Institution Archives (SI), RU 623, Box 8, John C. Ewers's copy of *Museologist* 58 (March 1956), Rochester Museum of Arts and Sciences. The "new museology" of the 1950s differs from the eponymous 1980s movement that suggested a need to interrogate the essential purposes of museums. The earlier movement referred

to renewed emphasis on exhibit effectiveness and establishing an "integral contact" between visitors and objects on display. This is now referred to as "museography."

3. Daniel Catton Rich, "Museums at the Crossroads," *Museum News*, March 1961, 36–38.

4. Marilyn Sara Cohen, "American Civilization in Three Dimensions: The Evolution of the Museum of History and Technology of the Smithsonian Institution" (PhD diss., George Washington University, 1980); Arthur P. Molella, "The Museum That Might Have Been: The Smithsonian's National Museum of Engineering and Industry," *Technology and Culture* 32, no. 2 (1991): 237–63.

5. Henrietta Lidchi distinguishes between the "poetics" (the production of meaning through the construction of the exhibit) and the "politics" (the broader role of museums in the production and spread of knowledge) of exhibits. At the Smithsonian, both politics and poetics changed during this period. The "political" changes prefigured the alterations in display, but much of what was exhibited (and continues to be exhibited) remained as holdovers from earlier periods. Thus, the poetics of the postwar exhibits reflected both new thinking about communicating ideas to the public and the older imperative to retain countless specimens for specialists. Henrietta Lidchi, "The Poetics and Politics of Exhibiting Other Cultures," in *Representation: Cultural Representations and Signifying Practices*, ed. Stuart Hall (London: Sage, 1997), 151–222, cited in Rhiannon Mason, "Cultural Theory and Museum Studies," in *A Companion to Museum Studies*, ed. Sharon Macdonald (Oxford: Blackwell, 2006), 20.

6. SI, RU623, Box 8, Folder "Museum Philosophy"; *Museologist*, a publication of the Rochester Museum of Arts and Sciences that was read by Ewers, Taylor, and other Smithsonian curators, editorialized throughout the decade about the need for contemporary museums to minimize exhibited items and present key themes to the public in an educational and interesting way.

7. Misztal, *Theories of Social Remembering*, 19–21.

8. Marilyn Sara Cohen, "American Civilization in Three Dimensions," 218.

9. SI, Accession T90006, Box 8, Folder "SI—Description of Exhibits, 1947, 1950, 1951," "The Smithsonian Institution: A Description of Its Work," January 1947.

10. Ivan Karp, "Museums and Communities: The Politics of Public Culture," in *Museums and Communities*, ed. Ivan Karp, Christine Mullen Kreamer, and Steven D. Lavine (Washington, DC: Smithsonian Institution Press, 1992), 5. Eilean Hooper-Greenhill, Tony Bennett, and Stuart Hall have led the Foucauldian analysis of museums. See Tony Bennett, *The Birth of the Museum: History, Theory, Politics* (London: Routledge, 1995); Stuart Hall, "Un-Settling 'The Heritage': Re-imagining the Post-Nation," in *Whose Heritage? The Impact of Cultural Diversity on Britain's Living Heritage* (London: Arts Council of England, 1999), 26–58.

11. Steven Conn, *Do Museums Still Need Objects?* (Philadelphia: University of Pennsylvania Press, 2009), 2–3.

12. Gaynor Kavanaugh, *Making Histories in Museums*, 26, uses the phrase "legitimizing institutions."

13. SI, RU 99, Box 297, Folder "Visitor Surveys," contains attendance figures for the 1960s.

14. 101 Cong. Rec. 7909–7912, 84th Cong., 1st Sess. (June 8, 1955; statement by Rep. John Vorhys).

15. SI, Accession T-90006, Box 11, USIA, 1960–65.

16. "Museum Is Shrine to Rise of U.S. as Nation: Old Steam Locomotive, Period Rooms Appeal, Washington in His Toga," *Washington Post,* January 23, 1964.

17. Frances Fitzgerald, *America Revised*, 10.

18. Misztal, *Theories of Social Remembering*, 21; Gaynor Kavanaugh, "Making Histories, Making Memories," in *Making Histories in Museums*, ed. Gaynor Kavanaugh (New York: Leicester University Press, 1996), 8.

19. Lawrence Fitzgerald, "Hard Men, Hard Facts and Heavy Metal: Making Histories of Technology," in *Making Histories in Museums*, ed. Gaynor Kavanaugh (New York: Leicester University Press, 1996), 118.

20. "Smithsonian Nominees Get Nod," *Washington Post and Times-Herald*, March 20, 1956; SI, RU 190, Box 56, Folder "Hagley Foundation, Inc."

21. Richard Eells, *Corporation Giving in a Free Society* (New York: Harper & Brothers, 1956).

22. Neil Harris, *Cultural Excursions: Marketing Appetites and Cultural Tastes in Modern America* (Chicago: University of Chicago Press, 1990), 137.

23. Cheryl R. Ganz, *The 1933 Chicago World's Fair: A Century of Progress* (Urbana: University of Illinois Press, 2008), 153–55.

24. Marilyn Sara Cohen, "American Civilization," 50–51.

25. Michal McMahon, "The Romance of Technological Progress: A Critical Review of the National Air and Space Museum," *Technology and Culture* 22, no. 2 (1981): 284.

26. Gary Kulik, "Designing the Past: History-Museum Exhibitions from Peale to the Present," in *History Museums in the United States: A Critical Assessment*, ed. Warren Leon and Roy Rosenzweig (Urbana: University of Illinois Press, 1989), 6–7; Marilyn Sara Cohen, "American Civilization," 14, 274.

27. Wallace, "Progress Talk: Museums of Science, Technology and Industry," in *Mickey Mouse History*, 78.

28. Marilyn Sara Cohen, "American Civilization," 6, 17; Kulik, "Designing the Past," 9–10; Arthur P. Molella, "The Museum That Might Have Been: The Smithsonian's National Museum of Engineering and Industry," *Technology and Culture* 32, no. 2, part 1 (1991): 240.

29. Kulik, "Designing the Past," 9; Briann G. Greenfield, *Out of the Attic: Inventing Antiques in Twentieth-Century New England* (Amherst: University of Massachusetts Press, 2009), 175.

30. 101 Cong. Rec. 7911, 84th Cong., 1st Sess. (June 8, 1955); President Lyndon Johnson's remarks at the dedication of the Smithsonian Institution's Museum of History and Technology, January 22, 1964, in SI, Accession T90006, Box 4, Folder "MHT Opening—1961–64."

31. Molella, "Museum That Might Have Been," 242; Marilyn Sara Cohen, "American Civilization," 275.

32. Molella, "Museum That Might Have Been," 250.

33. Wallace, *Mickey Mouse History*, 79–82.

34. Molella, "Museum That Might Have Been," 257.

35. Ibid., 247, 260; Wallace, *Mickey Mouse History*, 80.

36. Peter J. Kuznick, "Losing the World of Tomorrow: The Battle over the Presentation of Science at the 1939 New York World's Fair," *American Quarterly* 46, no. 3 (1994): 341–73.

37. Michael Taussig, *My Cocaine Museum* (Chicago: University of Chicago Press, 2004), xii. Taussig's alternative to the museum's fetishization of objects traces objects' histories to discover hidden meanings.

38. Molella, "Museum That Might Have Been," 260–62; Joseph J. Corn, "Tools, Technologies, and Contexts," in *History Museums in the United States: A Critical Assessment*, ed. Warren Leon and Roy Rosenzweig (Urbana: University of Illinois Press, 1989), 239–47.

39. Molella, "Museum That Might Have Been," 262; Marcel C. La Follette, Lisa M. Buchholz, John Zilber, "Science and Technology Museums as Policy Tools—An Overview of the Issues," *Science, Technology, and Human Values* 8, no. 3 (1983): 46.

40. Marilyn Sara Cohen, "American Civilization," 20.

41. Pamela M. Henson, "'Objects of Curious Research': The History of Science and Technology at the Smithsonian," *Isis* 90, Supplement, Catching Up with the Vision: Essays on the Occasion of the 75th Anniversary of the Founding of the History of Science Society (1999), S250.

42. Paul H. Oehser, *The Smithsonian Institution* (New York: Praeger, 1970), 170.

43. Marilyn Sara Cohen, "American Civilization," 46–48.

44. Ibid., 52.

45. Ibid., 25; SI, RU 190, Box 89, Folder "Exhibits Modernization—1948," Preliminary Report of the Subcommittee on Exhibits, October 12, 1948.

46. Paul Sampson, "Smithsonian Turning 'Attic into Showcase,'" *Washington Post and Times-Herald*, May 12, 1957; Matt McDade, "Smithsonian Brightens Up Ancient Hall: Dramatic Lighting, New Fixtures Grace Latin American Lore," *Washington Post and Times-Herald*, April 18, 1954; Marilyn Sara Cohen, "American Civilization," 59–63.

47. Neil Harris, *Cultural Excursions*, 139–41; Walter Benjamin, "Unpacking My Library: A Talk about Book Collecting" (1931), in *Illuminations: Essays and Reflections*, ed. Hannah Arendt, trans. Harry Zohn (New York: Schocken, 1968), 60.

48. Marilyn Sara Cohen, "American Civilization," 64–66.

49. Ibid., 67, 300–301.

50. Ibid., 70.

51. Ibid., 74–78.

52. Ibid., 72, 83; SI, RU 190, Box 89, U.S. National Museum Office of the Director, Exhibits Modernization, Report on the Committee of Exhibits, March 31, 1950;

Memorandum from F. M. Setzler, Head Curator of Anthropology to John C. Ewers, Associate Curator of Ethnology, March 9, 1953, "Comments on memorandum on the Museum of Man (proposed)."

53. Marilyn Sara Cohen, "American Civilization," 86–87, 294.

54. McMahon, "Romance of Technological Progress," 291.

55. Ibid., 87–88.

56. Ibid., 296.

57. SI, RU 276, Box 44, promotional booklet, ca. 1953.

58. Marilyn Sara Cohen, "American Civilization," 132, 134.

59. Henson, "'Objects of Curious Research,'" 262.

60. 101 Cong. Rec., 7909–7911, 84th Cong., 1st Sess. (June 8, 1955; statement by Clarence Cannon); Jeanne Rogers, "New Museum Indorsed for Smithsonian: Rep. Cannon, Head of Appropriations, Backs Building," *Washington Post and Times-Herald*, April 30, 1955.

61. SI, RU 190, Box 89, United States National Museum, Office of the Director, Folder "Exhibits Modernization (1950)," Report of the Committee on Exhibits.

62. Smithsonian Institution, *Annual Report of the Smithsonian Institution for 1956* (Washington: Smithsonian Institution Press, 1956), 2; Marilyn Sara Cohen, "American Civilization," 206–8.

63. William J. Murtagh, *Keeping Time: The History and Theory of Preservation in America* (Hoboken, NJ: John Wiley, 2006), 18.

64. Marilyn Sara Cohen, "American Civilization," 169.

65. SI, RU 623, Box 1, History of the SI Exhibits Program, "A New Museum of History and Technology to Tell the Story of the United States."

66. Ibid.

67. Ibid.

68. SI, Accession T-90006, Box 3, General Admission Charge Study 1954, "A Report by the Smithsonian Institution at the Request of the House Committee on Appropriations, Subcommittee on Independent Offices, Relative to Paying Admission to Smithsonian Buildings on the Mall."

69. Paul Sampson, "Smithsonian Institution Expands Its Display of Indian Lore," *Washington Post and Times-Herald*, June 2, 1955, 18.

70. 103 Cong. Rec. 10085, 85th Cong., 1st Sess. (June 21, 1957; statement by Clinton P. Anderson).

71. Ibid.

72. 101 Cong. Rec. 7909, 84th Cong., 1st Sess. (June 8, 1955; statement by Rep. Frank Thompson of New Jersey).

73. Henson, "'Objects of Curious Research,'" S262.

74. 101 Cong. Rec. 7909–7912, 84th Cong., 1st Sess. (June 8, 1955).

75. SI, Accession T90006, Box 4, MHT Opening—1961–64, "Dedication of the Museum of History and Technology of the Smithsonian Institution, January 22, 1964."

76. McMahon, "Romance of Technological Progress," 294.

77. SI, RU 276, Box 44, Political History (1959–60, 1964, 1968–70), Ladd E. Hamilton to Lloyd E. Herman, April 16, 1970.

78. Marilyn Sara Cohen, "American Civilization," 90–92; Henson, "'Objects of Curious Research,'" S262.

79. Marilyn Sara Cohen, "American Civilization," 96.

80. Sampson, "Smithsonian Institution Expands."

81. McMahon, "Romance of Technological Progress," 285–86; Henson, "'Objects of Curious Research,'" S250.

82. Marilyn Sara Cohen, "American Civilization," 97–98, 106.

83. McDade, "Smithsonian Brightens Up Ancient Hall."

84. SI, RU 551, Box 5, Historic Americans Hall: General Information 1960–71, "General Statement to Accompany Script for a Hall of Political History," n.d. (ca. 1960).

85. McDade, "Smithsonian Brightens Up Ancient Hall."

86. SI, RU 279, AEC Exhibit Folder, Questionnaires.

87. McDade, "Smithsonian Brightens Up Ancient Hall."

88. "Exhibit Depicts Early America," *Washington Post and Times-Herald,* January 20, 1957.

89. Sampson, "Smithsonian Institution Expands."

90. Sampson, "Smithsonian Turning 'Attic into Showcase.'"

91. Marilyn Sara Cohen, "American Civilization," 226.

92. Kavanaugh, *Making Histories in Museums,* xii–xiii, 1.

93. Susan A. Crane, introduction to *Museums and Memory,* ed. Susan A. Crane (Stanford, CA: Stanford University Press, 2000), 1–2; Vansina, *Oral Tradition as History,* 44.

94. Misztal, *Theories of Social Remembering,* 12, 15.

95. Pierre Nora, "Between Memory and History: Les Lieux de Memoire," trans. Marc Roudebush, *Representations* 26 (Spring 1989): 9.

96. SI, RU 99, Box 297, Visitors/Surveys, Folder "1969," Attendance Figures; Box 383, Folder "Visitor Surveys, 1968–69," Survey Results; RU 157, Box 13, Record of Visitors during Fiscal Year 1955; RU 334, Box 8, Folder "Visitor Survey Committee," 1969 Visitor Survey.

97. SI, RU 584, Box 32, "Facility Use and Visitor Needs in the National Museum of History and Technology: A Preliminary Study," by Marilyn S. Cohen, Department of Psychological and Sociological Studies, Office of Museum Programs, Smithsonian Institution, November 1973.

98. SI, RU 190, Box 29, "Experiment on Exhibits," Lecture by Frank Taylor, March 13, 1967.

99. SI, RU 623, Box 1, Docent Service, G. Carroll Lindsay to John C. Ewers, June 22, 1959; Report of Junior League Docent Activities, 1958–59; *Annual Report of 1960–61*; *Annual Report of 1961–62*; "100,000th Visitor at Museum," *Washington Post,* October 10, 1963.

100. The council comprised eight local school systems that worked cooperatively on issues of interest to all parties, with sponsorship from the two universities' schools of education. SI, RU 623, Box 1, Teachers Guides.

101. Ibid.

102. Ibid.

103. SI, RU 623, Box 7, Extension Service Folder, undated proposal for schools (ca. 1960).

104. SI, RU 190, Box 89, U.S. National Museum Office of the Director, Exhibits Modernization, Report on the Committee of Exhibits, March 31, 1950; RU 99, Box 481, Visitors to SI Buildings, results of survey conducted by Caroline Wells, 1968–69.

105. SI, RU 551, Box 1, Folder "MHT Tours 1970"; Folder "MHT Signage 1969–70"; Folder "Tours 1970." "Machines" led visitors to the "most important" American machines. "Treasures" included the flag, First Ladies' gowns, Whitney's cotton gin, Greenbough's statues of Washington, Washington's field tent and camp chest, Jefferson's portable desk, John Jay's robe, and American coins and stamps. "American Heroes and Heroines" were mostly U.S. presidents and first ladies, with a few inventors and two artists (George Catlin and John James Audubon). "Famous Americans" offered a slightly more diverse group, including one African American, George Washington Carver (on a postage stamp).

106. SI, RU 584, Box 32, "Facility Use and Visitor Needs in the National Museum of History and Technology: A Preliminary Study," by Marilyn S. Cohen, Department of Psychological and Sociological Studies, Office of Museum Programs, Smithsonian Institution, November 1973.

107. SI, RU 623, Box 1, Teachers Guides.

108. Smithsonian Institution, *Annual Report, 1956*, 38.

109. Kuznick, "Losing the World of Tomorrow," 363.

110. Michael Jacobson, "Museums That Put Corporations on Display," *Business and Society Review* 86 (Fall 1993): 27.

111. Robert P. Multhauf, "A Museum Case History: The Department of Science and Technology of the United States Museum of History and Technology," in "Museums of Technology," special issue, *Technology and Culture* 6, no. 1 (1965): 58.

112. SI, RU 623, Box 5, Hall of Pharmaceutical History exhibit scripts.

113. Ken Arnold, "Time Heals: Making History in Medical Museums," in Kavanaugh, *Making Histories in Museums*, 21.

114. Greenfield, *Out of the Attic*, 170.

115. Smithsonian Institution, *Annual Report of the Smithsonian Institution, 1957* (Washington, DC: Smithsonian Institution Press), 18, 27, 34.

116. Sophia A. Muirhead, *Corporate Contributions: The View from 50 Years* (New York: Conference Board, 1999), 13–15.

117. Theodore Low, *The Museum as Social Instrument* (New York: Metropolitan Museum of Art, 1942), 29, 32, 37–46; Marilyn Sara Cohen, "American Civilization," 370.

118. Muirhead, *Corporate Contributions*, 17, 20; Eells, *Corporation Giving*, 27–29; Marion R. Fremont-Smith, *Philanthropy and the Business Corporation* (New York: Russell Sage Foundation, 1973), 10–11, 34–35, 51–52.

119. SI, RU 551, Box 1, Folder "MHT Preview of Exhibit Halls (1964)."

120. SI, RU 276, Box 42, Folder 6, Manufacturing-Petroleum Exhibits, P. W. Bishop to Frank Taylor, October 8, 1957.

121. Smithsonian Institution, *Annual Report of the Smithsonian Institution, 1959* (Washington, DC: Smithsonian Institution Press, 1959); SI, RU 276, Box 42, Folder 6, Manufacturing-Petroleum Exhibits, Frank Taylor to P. W. Bishop, July 21, 1959.

122. SI, RU 623, Box 4, Folder Petroleum Hall; RU 276, Box 40, Growth of the United States, Petrol Drilling Hall; Smithsonian Institution, *Annual Report, 1959*, 49.

123. Robert Rydell, "The Fan Dance of Science: American World's Fairs in the Great Depression," *Isis* 76, no. 4 (1985): 533; Henson, "'Objects of Curious Research,'" S263.

124. Lawrence Fitzgerald, "Hard Men, Hard Facts," 120.

125. H. R. Rubenstein, "Welcoming Workers," *Museum News*, November 1990, 39.

126. Wallace, *Mickey Mouse History*, 79–80.

127. Marilyn Sara Cohen, "American Civilization," 330–31.

128. McMahon, "Romance of Technological Progress," 285.

129. Marilyn Sara Cohen, "American Civilization," 104–5.

130. Ibid., 128–29.

131. Sharon J. Macdonald, "Museums, National, Postnational and Transcultural Identities," *Museum and Society* 1, no. 1 (2003): 3; Lidchi, "Poetics and Politics," cited in Mason, "Cultural Theory and Museum Studies," 20; David Jenkins, "Object Lessons and Ethnographic Displays: Museum Exhibitions and the Making of American Anthropology," *Journal for the Comparative Study of Society and History* 36, no. 2 (1994): 242–70.

132. SI, RU 623, Box 1, Folder "Audio Tours—Scripts and Development," Indians of the Americas, Hall 11, audio tour script.

133. SI, RU 623, Box 7, Arts and Industries North Hall exhibits modernization.

134. Marilyn Sara Cohen, "American Civilization," 93–94.

135. Ruth Shumaker, "First Ladies on View at Smithsonian: Mrs. Eisenhower Launches Historic Exhibit of Gowns," *Washington Post and Times-Herald*, May 25, 1955.

136. SI, RU 623, Box 1, Docent Service 1955–56, docent tour scripts.

137. SI, RU 190, Box 21, United States National Museum, Office of the Director, National Museum of History and Technology, Building Plans, 1965–67.

138. Marilyn Sara Cohen, "American Civilization," 221, 284–85.

139. SI, RU 623, Box 8, Arts and Industries North Hall, Script for North Hall; Box 7, no folder, Growth of the United States scripts; Box 1, Photographs of Exhibits—Lists MHT, Peter C. Welsh to Frank Taylor, September 13, 1962.

140. SI, RU 623, Box 8, Historic Americans Hall, Memorandum by John C. Ewers, June 6, 1958.

141. SI, RU 279, Box 6, Folder 7, Teachers' Aids, Women's History Hall.

142. SI, RU 623, Box 7, no folder, Frank Taylor to Dr. Herbert Freidmann, December 18, 1952, Re: Exhibits Modernization, with attached "justification" for Power Exhibit Hall.

143. SI, RU 623, Military History, News Release, undated, announcing the exhibit opening on June 12, 1958.

144. SI, RU 276, Box 86, Folder 7, Hall of Armed Forces—General—1958–66, "Working Floor Plan"; RU 190, Box 21, Outline of Requirements—MHT, March 1958.

145. SI, RU 276, Box 40, Everyday Life in the American Past, 1965–73, conceptual script for the exhibit.

146. SI, RU 276, Box 86, Folder 7, Hall of Armed Forces—General, 1958–66, "Preliminary Statement."

147. SI, RU 623, Box 3, Folder "Armed Forces history."

148. G. Kurt Piehler, *Remembering War the American Way* (Washington, DC: Smithsonian Institution Press, 1995), 163.

149. SI, Accession T90006, Box 8, SI—Description of Its Work, 1947, 1950, 1951, "The Smithsonian Institution: A Description of Its Work," January 1951.

150. RU 623, Box 1, MHT, News Release, October 11, 1961.

151. Wallace, *Mickey Mouse History*, 83.

152. Karp, "Museums and Communities," 4–5.

Conclusion

1. Lowenthal, *Heritage Crusade*, 102.

2. Howard Green, "A Critique of the Professional Public History Movement," *Radical History Review* 25 (1981), repr. in *Public History Readings*, ed. Phyllis K. Lefler and Joseph Brent (Malabar, FL: R. E. Krieger, 1992), 121–26.

3. Abraham Polonsky, quoted in Schultheiss, "Season of Fear," 13.

4. History Book Club, http://www.historybookclub.com/pages/help/negOp TopicDetail.jsp?faqId=10171214234203636&topicTitle=General+Questions& topicId=10161214233453558.

5. History Book Club advertising catalog no. HBC08100W-01 (Indianapolis: Direct Brands, 2008).

6. Rosenzweig, "Marketing the Past," 33.

7. Orwell, *1984*, 189.

8. Commager, "The Search for a Usable Past," 23.

9. SI, RU 623, Box 8, Folder "Museum Philosophy," Frank Taylor to John C. Ewers, "Thoughts regarding Museum Standards," April 5, 1958.

10. HML, Accession 1662, Box 54, Folder "NAM 6/40–12/40," Lammot du Pont to H. W. Prentis Jr., president of the National Association of Manufacturers, September 24, 1940.

11. Colby, *Du Pont Dynasty*, 344–45.

12. Nash, Crabtree, and Dunn, *History on Trial*, 23.

13. Walter Bernstein, quoted in Schultheiss, "Season of Fear," 34n.

14. Martin E. Marty, *The Search for a Usable Future* (New York: Harper & Row, 1969), 12.

15. Mary Caputi, *A Kinder, Gentler America: Melancholia and the Mythical 1950s* (Minneapolis: University of Minnesota Press, 2005), 8.

16. Glassberg, *Sense of History*, 108; Gary Edgerton, "Mediating Thomas Jefferson: Ken Burns as Popular Historian," in *Television Histories: Shaping Collective Memory in the Media Age*, ed. Gary R. Edgerton and Peter C. Rollins (Lexington: University Press of Kentucky, 2001), 171.

17. Harvey J. Kaye, *Why Do Ruling Classes Fear History? And Other Questions* (New York: St. Martin's Press, 1997), 20; Students for a Democratic Society, "Port Huron Statement," June 15, 1962.

18. Frances Fitzgerald, *America Revised*, 178.

19. In this sense, the changing relationship that Americans have to history resembles the rift described by Gary Gerstle in which late-1960s Black Power adherents were the first citizens to reject the long-sought-after promise of becoming American, as defined by the dominant group. Gary Gerstle, *American Crucible: Race and Nation in the Twentieth Century* (Princeton, NJ: Princeton University Press, 2001), 342.

20. Jill Lepore, *The Whites of Their Eyes: The Tea Party's Revolution and the Battle over American History* (Princeton, NJ: Princeton University Press, 2010), 16.

21. Dahlia Lithwick, "Read It and Weep: How the Tea Party's Fetish for the Constitution as Written May Get It in Trouble," *Slate*, January 4, 2011, http://www.slate.com/articles/news_and_politics/jurisprudence/2011/01/read_it_and_weep.html.

22. John Celock, "New Hampshire Lawmakers Pass Law Allowing Parental Objections to Curriculum," *Huffington Post*, January 4, 2012, http://www.huffingtonpost.com/2012/01/04/new-hampshire-legislature-curriculum-objection-law_n_1184476.html.

23. Religion scholar Julie Ingersoll has written extensively about this. See, for example, Julie Ingersoll, "The Constitution, the Bible and the Fundamentalist-Modernist Divide," http://www.religiondispatches.org/dispatches/julieingersoll/4005/the_.

24. Charles McLean Andrews, *The Colonial Background of the American Revolution* (1924; rev ed., New Haven, CT: Yale University Press, 1961), 220.

Bibliography

Allan-Olney, Mary. *The Private Life of Galileo*. London: Macmillan, 1870.

Anderson, James Douglass. "Washington and Lincoln: Two Ill Mated Spirits of the 'Freedom' Train." *Tyler's Quarterly Historical and Genealogical Magazine* 30, no. 1 (1948): 5–19.

Anderson, Steve. "History TV and Popular Memory." In *Television Histories: Shaping Collective Memory in the Media Age*, edited by Gary R. Edgerton and Peter C. Rollins, 19–36. Lexington: University Press of Kentucky, 2001.

Andrews, Charles McLean. *The Colonial Background of the American Revolution*. 1924. Rev. ed., New Haven, CT: Yale University Press, 1961.

Antze, Paul, and Michael Lambek, eds. *Tense Past: Cultural Essays in Trauma and Memory*. New York: Routledge, 1996.

Aptheker, Herbert. *American Negro Slave Revolts*. New York: Columbia University Press, 1943.

———. *History and Reality*. New York: Cameron Associates, 1955.

———. *The Negro in the Civil War*. New York: International, 1938.

Arnold, Ken. "Time Heals: Making History in Medical Museums." In *Making Histories in Museums*, edited by Gaynor Kavanaugh, 15–29. New York: Leicester University Press, 1996.

Arnold, Thurman. *The Folklore of Capitalism*. New Haven, CT: Yale University Press, 1937.

Auden, W. H. *The Age of Anxiety: A Baroque Eclogue*. Edited by Alan Jacobs. Princeton, NJ: Princeton University Press, 2011.

Bahr, Ehrhard. *Weimar on the Pacific: German Exile Culture in Los Angeles and the Crisis of Modernism*. Berkeley: University of California Press, 2007.

Ball, Terrence. "The Politics of Social Science in Postwar America." In *Recasting America: Culture and Politics in the Age of Cold War*, edited by Lary May, 76–92. Chicago: University of Chicago Press, 1989.

Barnouw, Erik. *A History of Broadcasting in the United States*. Vol. 2, *The Golden Web—1933–1953*. New York: Oxford University Press, 1968.

Baughman, James L. *The Republic of Mass Culture: Journalism, Filmmaking, and Broadcasting in America since 1941*. Baltimore: Johns Hopkins University Press, 1992.

Baxter, Maurice G., Robert H. Ferrell, and John E. Wiltz. *The Teaching of American History in High Schools*. Bloomington: Indiana University Press, 1964.

Beard, Charles, and Mary Beard. *The Rise of American Civilization*. New York: Macmillan, 1930.

Becker, Carl Lotus. *Freedom and Responsibility in the American Way of Life: Five Lectures Delivered at the University of Michigan, December 1944*. New York: Alfred A. Knopf, 1945.

Bennett, Tony. *The Birth of the Museum: History, Theory, Politics*. London: Routledge, 1995.

Benjamin, Walter. "Unpacking My Library: A Talk about Book Collecting" (1931). In *Illuminations: Essays and Reflections*, edited by Hannah Arendt, 59–68. Translated by Harry Zohn. New York: Schocken, 1968.

Bernstein, Walter. *Inside Out: A Memoir of the Blacklist*. New York: Da Capo Press, 2000.

———. *Keep Your Head Down*. New York: Book Find Club, 1945.

Bird, William L., Jr. *"Better Living": Advertising, Media, and the New Vocabulary of Business Leadership, 1935–1955*. Edited by James Schwoch and Mimi White. Media Topographies. Evanston, IL: Northwestern University Press, 1999.

Black, Jeremy. *Using History*. London: Hodder Arnold, 2005.

Blight, David. *Race and Reunion: The Civil War in American Memory*. Cambridge, MA: Belknap Press of Harvard University Press, 2001.

Boddy, William. *Fifties Television: The Industry and Its Critics*. Urbana: University of Illinois Press, 1992.

Bodnar, John. *Remaking America: Public Memory, Commemoration, and Patriotism in the Twentieth Century*. Princeton, NJ: Princeton University Press, 1992.

Boorstin, Daniel J. *An American Primer*. Toronto: New American Library, 1968.

———. *The Genius of American Politics*. Chicago: University of Chicago Press, 1953.

Boyer, Paul S. *By the Bomb's Early Light: American Thought and Culture at the Dawn of the Atomic Age*. 2nd ed. Chapel Hill: University of North Carolina Press, 1994.

Boyer, Paul, and Stephen Nissenbaum. *Salem Possessed: The Social Origins of Witchcraft*. Cambridge, MA: Harvard University Press, 1974.

Bradsher, James Gregory. "Taking America's Heritage to the People: The Freedom Train Story." *Prologue* 17, no. 4 (1985): 228–45.

Brewster, David. *Martyrs of Science: Galileo, Tycho Brahe, and Kepler*. London: Chatto and Windus, 1874.

Brinkley, Alan. "The Illusion of Unity in Cold War Culture." In *Rethinking Cold War Culture*, edited by Peter J. Kuznick and James Gilbert, 61–73. Washington, DC: Smithsonian Institution Press, 2001.

Browne, Ray B. *Rituals and Ceremonies in Popular Culture*. Bowling Green, OH: Bowling Green University Popular Press, 1980.

Buhle, Paul. "Abraham Lincoln Polonsky's America." *American Quarterly* 49, no. 4 (1997): 874–81.

Buhle, Paul, and Dave Wagner. *Hide in Plain Sight: The Hollywood Blacklistees in Film and Television, 1950-2002.* New York: Palgrave Macmillan, 2003.

———. *A Very Dangerous Citizen: Abraham Polonsky and the Hollywood Left.* Berkeley: University of California Press, 2001.

Burke, Frank G. "Innovation at the Archives—The Departure of the Freedom Train." *Curator: The Museum Journal* 16, no. 4 (1973): 333–41.

Cady, Edwin H. "'American Studies' in the Doldrums." In *American Studies: Essays on Theory and Method,* edited by Robert Meredith. Columbus, OH: Charles E. Merrill, 1968.

Cameron, Kenneth M. *America on Film: Hollywood and American History.* New York: Continuum, 1997.

Caputi, Mary. *A Kinder, Gentler America: Melancholia and the Mythical 1950s.* Minneapolis: University of Minnesota Press, 2005.

Carmer, Carl. *Cavalcade of America: The Deeds and Achievements of the Men and Women Who Made Our Country Great.* New York: Crown, 1956.

Ceplair, Larry, and Steven Englund. *The Inquisition in Hollywood: Politics in the Film Community, 1930-1960.* Berkeley: University of California Press, 1983.

Chafe, William H. *The Unfinished Journey: America since World War II.* 2nd ed. New York: Oxford University Press, 1991.

Chandler, Alfred D., Jr., and Stephen Salsbury. *Pierre S. du Pont and the Making of the Modern Corporation.* Washington, DC: Beard Books, 2000.

Cohen, Hennig, ed. *The American Culture: Approaches to the Study of the United States.* Boston: Houghton Mifflin, 1968.

———, ed. *The American Experience: Approaches to the Study of the United States.* Boston: Houghton Mifflin, 1968.

Cohen, Marilyn Sara. "American Civilization in Three Dimensions: The Evolution of the Museum of History and Technology of the Smithsonian Institution." PhD diss., George Washington University, 1980.

Colby, Gerald. *Du Pont Dynasty.* Secaucus, NJ: Lyle Stuart, 1984.

Commager, Henry Steele. "The Search for a Usable Past." In *The Search for a Usable Past, and Other Essays in Historiography,* 3–27. New York: Alfred A. Knopf, 1967.

Conn, Steven. *Do Museums Still Need Objects?* Philadelphia: University of Pennsylvania Press, 2009.

Cooper, Peter. *Galileo's Roman Inquisition.* Cincinnati: Montfort and Conahans, 1844.

Corn, Joseph J. "Tools, Technologies, and Contexts: Interpreting the History of American Technics." In *History Museums in the United States: A Critical Assessment,* edited by Warren Leon and Roy Rosenzweig, 237–61. Urbana: University of Illinois Press, 1989.

Crane, Susan A., ed. *Museums and Memory.* Stanford, CA: Stanford University Press, 2000.

Cunningham, Frank R. *Sidney Lumet: Film and Literary Vision.* Lexington: University Press of Kentucky, 2001.

DeVoto, Bernard. "Doctors along the Boardwalk." *Harper's*, September 1947. Reprinted in Bernard DeVoto, *The Easy Chair*, 85–102. Boston: Houghton Mifflin, 1955.

———. "The Easy Chair." *Harper's*, March 1948, 250–53.

———. *The Easy Chair*. Boston: Houghton Mifflin, 1955.

———. "Notes on the American Way." *Harper's*, May 1938, 669–71.

———. "The War of the Rebellion." *Harper's*, February 1946. Reprinted in Bernard DeVoto, *The Easy Chair*, 151–58. Boston: Houghton Mifflin, 1955.

Diggins, John Patrick. *The Proud Decades: America in War and Peace, 1941–1960*. New York: W. W. Norton, 1988.

Doherty, Thomas. *Cold War, Cool Medium: Television, McCarthyism, and American Culture*. New York: Columbia University Press, 2003.

Dowdey, Clifford. *Experiment in Rebellion*. Garden City, NY: Doubleday, 1946.

Dyer, Davis, and David B. Sicilia. *Labors of a Modern Hercules: The Evolution of a Chemical Company*. Boston: Harvard Business School Press, 1990.

Eells, Richard. *Corporation Giving in a Free Society*. New York: Harper & Brothers, 1956.

Edgerton, Gary. "Mediating Thomas Jefferson: Ken Burns as Popular Historian." In *Television Histories: Shaping Collective Memory in the Media Age*, edited by Gary R. Edgerton and Peter C. Rollins, 169–90. Lexington: University Press of Kentucky, 2001.

Engelhardt, Tom. *The End of Victory Culture: Cold War America and the Disillusioning of a Generation*. New York: Basic Books, 1995.

Everitt, Charles P. *The Adventures of a Treasure Hunter: A Rare Bookman in Search of American History*. Boston: Little, Brown, 1951.

Everitt, David. *A Shadow of Red: Communism and the Blacklist in Radio and Television*. Chicago: Ivan R. Dee, 2007.

Fahie, J. J. *Galileo: His Life and Work*. London: J. Murray, 1903.

Ferro, Marc. *The Use and Abuse of History; or, How the Past Is Taught to Children*. New York: Routledge Classics, 2003.

Fischer, David Hackett. *Liberty and Freedom: A Visual History of America's Founding Ideas*. New York: Oxford University Press, 2005.

Fishwick, Marshall W. *American Studies in Transition*. Philadelphia: University of Pennsylvania Press, 1964.

Fitzgerald, Frances. *America Revised: History Schoolbooks in the Twentieth Century*. Boston: Atlantic Monthly Press, 1979.

Fitzgerald, Lawrence. "Hard Men, Hard Facts and Heavy Metal: Making Histories of Technology." In *Making Histories in Museums*, edited by Gaynor Kavanaugh, 116–30. New York: Leicester University Press, 1996.

Foner, Eric. *The Story of American Freedom*. New York: W. W. Norton, 1998.

Fones-Wolf, Elizabeth A. "Creating a Favorable Business Climate: Corporations and Radio Broadcasting, 1934 to 1954." *Business History Review* 73, no. 2 (1999): 221–55.

———. *Selling Free Enterprise: The Business Assault on Labor and Liberalism, 1945–1960*. Urbana: University of Illinois Press, 1994.

"Forum: Comments on James A. Hijiya's 'Why the West Is Lost.'" *William and Mary Quarterly*, 3rd ser., 51 (1994): 717–54.

Fox, Dixon Ryan, and Arthur M. Schlesinger, eds. *Cavalcade of America*. Springfield, MA: Milton Bradley, 1937.

Fox, Richard W. *Reinhold Niebuhr: A Biography*. New York: Pantheon, 1985.

"Freedom Train Tours America." *National Geographic Magazine* 96 (October 1949): 542.

Fremont-Smith, Marion R. *Philanthropy and the Business Corporation*. New York: Russell Sage Foundation, 1972.

Fried, Richard M. *The Man Everybody Knew: Bruce Barton and the Making of Modern America*. Chicago: Ivan R. Dee, 2005.

———. *The Russians Are Coming! The Russians Are Coming! Pageantry and Patriotism in Cold-War America*. New York: Oxford University Press, 1998.

Fyfe, Gordon. "Sociology and the Social Aspects of Museums." In *A Companion to Museum Studies*, edited by Sharon Macdonald, 33–49. Oxford: Blackwell, 2006.

Ganz, Cheryl R. *The 1933 Chicago World's Fair: A Century of Progress*. Urbana: University of Illinois Press, 2008.

Gerstle, Gary. *American Crucible: Race and Nation in the Twentieth Century*. Princeton, NJ: Princeton University Press, 2001.

Geyl, Pieter. *Use and Abuse of History*. New Haven, CT: Yale University Press, 1955.

Geyl, Pieter, Arnold J. Toynbee, and Pitirim A. Sorokin. *The Pattern of the Past: Can We Determine It?* Boston: Beacon Press, 1949.

Ghiglione, Loren. *CBS's Don Hollenbeck: An Honest Reporter in the Age of McCarthyism*. New York: Columbia University Press, 2008.

Gilbert, James Burkhart. *Whose Fair? Experience, Memory, and the History of the Great St. Louis Exposition*. Chicago: University of Chicago Press, 2009.

Giovacchini, Saverio. "Did Private Nolan Get His Glory? Movies, Press and Audience during the Spanish-American War." *Columbia Journal of American Studies* 3, no. 1 (1998): 141–58.

———. *Hollywood Modernism: Film and Politics in the Age of the New Deal*. Philadelphia: Temple University Press, 2001.

Glassberg, David. *American Historical Pageantry: The Uses of Tradition in the Early Twentieth Century*. Chapel Hill: University of North Carolina Press, 1990.

———. *Sense of History: The Place of the Past in American Life*. Amherst: University of Massachusetts Press, 2001.

Goldman, Eric F. *The Crucial Decade—and After: America, 1945–1960*. New York: Alfred A. Knopf, 1960.

Graebner, William. *The Age of Doubt: American Thought and Culture in the 1940s*. Edited by Lewis Perry. Twayne's American Thought and Culture Series. Boston: Twayne, 1990.

Graham, Gordon. *The Shape of the Past*. New York: Oxford University Press, 1997.

Graham, Helen P. "A Plan for Teaching the Biography." *English Journal* 30, no. 3 (1941): 238–41.

Grams, Martin, Jr. *History of the Cavalcade of America*. Kearney, NE: Morris, 1998.

Green, Howard. "A Critique of the Professional History Movement." *Radical History Review* 25 (1981). Reprinted in *Public History Readings*, edited by Phyllis K. Lefler and Joseph Brent, 121–26. Malabar, FL: R. E. Krieger, 1992.

Greenfield, Briann G. *Out of the Attic: Inventing Antiques in Twentieth-Century New England.* Amherst: University of Massachusetts Press, 2009.

Grimsted, David. "Dueling Ideas of History: Public, People's, Popular, and Academic— and Henry Adams's Surprising Failures." *Maryland Historian* 30, no. 1 (2006): 11–40.

Grindon, Leger. *Shadows on the Past: Studies in the Historical Fiction Film.* Philadelphia: Temple University Press, 1994.

Guynn, William. *Writing History in Film.* New York: Routledge, 2006.

Halberstam, David. *The Powers That Be.* New York: Knopf, 1975.

Halbwachs, Maurice. *The Collective Memory.* Translated by Francis J. Ditter Jr. and Vida Yazdi Ditter. New York: Harper & Row, 1980.

Hale, William Harlan. "The Boom in American History." *Reporter* 12 (February 24, 1955): 42.

———. *The March of Freedom: A Layman's History of the American People.* New York: Harper & Brothers, 1947.

———. "What Makes Wallace Run?" *Harper's*, March 1948, 241–48.

Hall, Stuart. "Un-Settling 'The Heritage': Re-imagining the Post-Nation." In *Whose Heritage? The Impact of Cultural Diversity on Britain's Living Heritage*, 26–58. London: Arts Council of England, 1999.

Halliwell, Martin. *The Constant Dialogue: Reinhold Niebuhr and American Culture.* New York: Rowman and Littlefield, 2005.

Harris, Howell John. *The Right to Manage: Industrial Relations Policies of American Business in the 1940s.* Madison: University of Wisconsin Press, 1982.

Harris, Neil. *Cultural Excursions: Marketing Appetites and Cultural Tastes in Modern America.* Chicago: University of Chicago Press, 1990.

Henson, Pamela M. "'Objects of Curious Research': The History of Science and Technology at the Smithsonian." *Isis* 90, Supplement, Catching Up with the Vision: Essays on the Occasion of the 75th Anniversary of the Founding of the History of Science Society (1999): S249–S269.

Herberg, Will. *Protestant-Catholic-Jew.* Garden City, NY: Doubleday, 1955.

Hijiya, James A. "Why the West Is Lost." *William and Mary Quarterly*, 3rd ser., 51, no. 2 (1994): 276–92.

Hobsbawm, E. J. "The Social Function of the Past: Some Questions." *Past and Present* 55 (May 1972): 3–17.

Hofstadter, Richard. *The American Political Tradition and the Men Who Made It.* New York: Alfred A. Knopf, 1948.

Holbrook, Stewart. *The Story of American Railroads.* New York: Crown, 1947.

Horowitz, Daniel. "A Southerner in Exile, the Cold War, and Social Order: David M. Potter's *People of Plenty.*" In *The Anxieties of Affluence: Critiques of American Consumer Culture, 1939–1979*, 79–100. Amherst: University of Massachusetts Press, 2004.

Horowitz, Robert F. "History Comes to Life and You Are There." In *American History, American Television: Interpreting the Video Past*, edited by John E. O'Connor, 79–94. New York: Frederick Ungar, 1983.

Hosmer, Charles B., Jr. *Preservation Comes of Age: From Williamsburg to the National Trust, 1926–1949*. Charlottesville: University of Virginia Press, 1981.

Hounshell, David A., and John Kenly Smith Jr. *Science and Corporate Strategy: Du Pont R&D, 1902–1980*. New York: Cambridge University Press, 1988.

Hughes, Langston. "Freedom Train." *New Republic* 117, no. 11 (1947): 27.

Hughey, Michael W. *Civil Religion and Moral Order: Theoretical and Historical Dimensions*. Westport, CT: Greenwood Press, 1983.

Jackson, Jeffrey H. *Making Jazz French: Music and Modern Life in Interwar Paris*. Durham, NC: Duke University Press, 2003.

Jacobson, Michael. "Museums That Put Corporations on Display." *Business and Society Review* 86 (Fall 1993): 24–27.

Jacoby, Susan. *The Age of American Unreason*. New York: Pantheon Books, 2008.

Jenkins, David. "Object Lessons and Ethnographic Displays: Museum Exhibitions and the Making of American Anthropology." *Journal for the Comparative Study of Society and History* 36, no. 2 (1994): 242–70.

Kammen, Michael. *Mystic Chords of Memory: The Transformation of Tradition in American Culture*. New York: Alfred A. Knopf, 1991.

Kanfer, Stefan. *A Journal of the Plague Years*. New York: Atheneum, 1973.

Karp, Ivan. "Museums and Communities: The Politics of Public Culture." In *Museums and Communities*, edited by Ivan Karp, Christine Mullen Kreamer, and Steven D. Lavine, 1–17. Washington, DC: Smithsonian Institution Press, 1992.

Kavanaugh, Gaynor, ed. *Making Histories in Museums*. New York: Leicester University Press, 1996.

———. "Making Histories, Making Memories." In *Making Histories in Museums*, edited by Gaynor Kavanaugh, 1–14. New York: Leicester University Press, 1996.

Kaye, Harvey J. *The Powers of the Past: Reflections on the Crisis and the Promise of History*. Minneapolis: University of Minnesota Press, 1991.

———. *Why Do Ruling Classes Fear History? And Other Questions*. New York: St. Martin's Press, 1997.

Kempton, Murray. *Part of Our Time: Some Ruins and Monuments of the Thirties*. 1955. Reprint, New York: New York Review of Books, 1998.

Kepley, Vance, Jr. "The Origins of NBC's Project XX in Compilation Documentaries." *Journalism Quarterly* 61, no. 1 (1984): 20–26.

Krutnik, Frank, Steve Neale, Brian Neve, and Peter Stanfield, eds. *"Un-American" Hollywood: Politics and Film in the Blacklist Era*. New Brunswick, NJ: Rutgers University Press, 2007.

Kulik, Gary. "Designing the Past: History-Museum Exhibitions from Peale to the Present." In *History Museums in the United States: A Critical Assessment*, edited by Warren Leon and Roy Rosenzweig, 3–37. Urbana: University of Illinois Press, 1989.

Kuznick, Peter J. "Losing the World of Tomorrow: The Battle over the Presentation of Science at the 1939 New York World's Fair." *American Quarterly* 46, no. 3 (1994): 341–73.

Kuznick, Peter J., and James Gilbert, eds. *Rethinking Cold War Culture*. Washington, DC: Smithsonian Institution Press, 2001.

La Follette, Marcel C., Lisa M. Buchholz, and John Zilber. "Science and Technology Museums as Policy Tools—An Overview of the Issues." *Science, Technology, and Human Values* 8, no. 3 (1983): 41–46.

Leon, Warren, and Roy Rosenzweig, eds. *History Museums in the United States: A Critical Assessment*. Urbana: University of Illinois Press, 1989.

Lepore, Jill. *The Whites of Their Eyes: The Tea Party's Revolution and the Battle over American History*. Princeton, NJ: Princeton University Press, 2010.

Lichtenstein, Nelson. *State of the Union: A Century of American Labor*. Princeton, NJ: Princeton University Press, 2002.

Lillard, Richard G. *The Great Forest*. New York: Alfred A. Knopf, 1947.

Linenthal, Edward T. *Sacred Ground: Americans and Their Battlefields*. Urbana: University of Illinois Press, 1991.

Linenthal, Edward T., and Tom Engelhardt, eds. *History Wars: The Enola Gay and Other Battles for the American Past*. New York: Henry Holt, 1996.

Lipsitz, George. *Time Passages: Collective Memory and American Popular Culture*. Minneapolis: University of Minnesota Press, 1990.

Little, Stuart J. "The Freedom Train: Citizenship and Postwar Political Culture, 1946–1949." *American Studies* 34, no. 1 (1993): 35–67.

———. "The Freedom Train and the Formation of National Political Culture, 1946–1949." MA thesis, University of Kansas, 1989.

Low, Theodore. *The Museum as Social Instrument*. New York: Metropolitan Museum of Art, 1942.

Lowenthal, David. *The Heritage Crusade and the Spoils of History*. Cambridge: Cambridge University Press, 1998.

———. *The Past Is a Foreign Country*. Cambridge: Cambridge University Press, 1985.

———. "Past Time, Present Place: Landscape and Memory." *Geographical Review* 65 (January 1975): 1–36.

———. *Possessed by the Past*. New York: Free Press, 1996.

Lykins, Daniel L. *From Total War to Total Diplomacy: The Advertising Council and the Construction of the Cold War Consensus*. Westport, CT: Praeger, 2003.

Macdonald, Sharon J., ed. *A Companion to Museum Studies*. Oxford: Blackwell, 2006.

———. "Museums, National, Postnational and Transcultural Identities." *Museum and Society* 1, no. 1 (2003): 1–16.

Maines, Rachel P., and James J. Glynn. "Numinous Objects." *Public Historian* 15, no. 1 (1993): 9–24.

Marchand, Roland. *Creating the Corporate Soul: The Rise of Public Relations and Corporate Imagery in American Big Business*. Berkeley: University of California Press, 1998.

Marcus, Daniel. "NBC's 'Project XX': Television and American History at the End of Ideology." *Historical Journal of Film, Radio, and Television* 17, no. 3 (1997): 347–66.

Marty, Martin E. *The Search for a Usable Future.* New York: Harper & Row, 1969.

Mason, Rhiannon. "Cultural Theory and Museum Studies." In *A Companion to Museum Studies*, edited by Sharon J. Macdonald, 17–32. Oxford: Blackwell, 2006.

May, Elaine Tyler. *Homeward Bound: American Families in the Cold War Era.* New York: Basic Books, 1988.

May, Lary, ed. *Recasting America: Culture and Politics in the Age of Cold War.* Chicago: University of Chicago Press, 1989.

Mazur, Louis P. "Review: Bernard DeVoto and the Making of *The Year of Decision: 1846.*" *Reviews in American History* 18, no. 3 (1990): 436–51.

McCully, Bruce T. "Review of *The Westward Crossings: Balboa, Mackenzie, Lewis and Clark* by Jeannette Mirsky." *William and Mary Quarterly* 4, no. 2 (1947): 247–50.

McGilligan, Patrick, and Paul Buhle. *Tender Comrades: A Backstory of the Hollywood Blacklist.* New York: St. Martin's Press, 1997.

McMahon, Michal. "The Romance of Technological Progress: A Critical Review of the National Air and Space Museum." *Technology and Culture* 22, no. 2 (1981): 281–96.

McNeill, William H. *Arnold J. Toynbee: A Life.* New York: Oxford University Press, 1989.

Mickelson, Sig. *The Decade That Shaped Television News.* Westport, CT: Praeger, 1998.

Miller, John C. *Triumph of Freedom: 1775–1783.* Boston: Little, Brown, 1948.

Miller, Perry. *Errand into the Wilderness.* Cambridge, MA: Belknap Press of Harvard University Press, 1984.

Mirsky, Jeannette. *The Westward Crossings: Balboa, Mackenzie, Lewis and Clark.* New York: Alfred A. Knopf, 1946.

Misztal, Barbara A. *Theories of Social Remembering.* Philadelphia: Open University Press, 2003.

Molella, Arthur P. "The Museum That Might Have Been: The Smithsonian's National Museum of Engineering and Industry." *Technology and Culture* 32, no. 2 (1991): 237–63.

Monaghan, Frank. *Heritage of Freedom: The History and Significance of the Basic Documents of American Liberty.* Princeton, NJ: Princeton University Press, 1947.

Montagu, M. F. Ashley, ed. *Toynbee and History: Critical Essays and Reviews.* Boston: Porter Sargent, 1956.

Moore, Wilbert Ellis. *Industrial Relations and the Social Order.* Manchester, NH: Ayer Books, 1977.

Muirhead, Sophia A. *Corporate Contributions: The View from 50 Years.* New York: Conference Board, 1999.

Muller, Herbert J. *The Uses of the Past: Profiles of Former Societies.* New York: Oxford University Press, 1952.

Multhauf, Robert P. "A Museum Case History: The Department of Science and Technology of the United States Museum of History and Technology." "Museums of Technology," special issue, *Technology and Culture* 6, no. 1 (1965): 47–58.

Murphy, Brenda. *The Congressional Theatre: Dramatizing McCarthyism on Stage, Film, and Television.* Cambridge: Cambridge University Press, 1999.

Murtagh, William J. *Keeping Time: The History and Theory of Preservation in America.* Hoboken, NJ: John Wiley, 2006.

Nash, Gary B., Charlotte A. Crabtree, and Ross E. Dunn. *History on Trial: Culture Wars and the Teaching of the Past.* New York: Alfred A. Knopf, 1997.

Navasky, Victor S. *Naming Names.* New York: Penguin Books, 1981.

Neiheisel, Steven. *Corporate Strategy and the Politics of Goodwill: A Political Analysis of Corporate Philanthropy in America.* New York: Peter Lang, 1994.

Nevins, Allan, and Louis M. Hacker, eds. *The United States and Its Place in World Affairs, 1918–1943.* Boston: D.C. Heath, 1943.

Nichols, Bill. "Documentary Reenactment and the Fantasmatic Subject." *Critical Inquiry* 35, no. 1 (2008): 72–89.

Niebuhr, Reinhold. *The Irony of American History.* New York: Scribner, 1952.

———. *The Self and the Dramas of History.* New York: Scribner, 1955.

Niswender, Dana W. "Divided We Fall." *English Journal* 36, no. 6 (1947): 309.

Nobile, Philip, ed. *Judgment at the Smithsonian: The Bombing of Hiroshima and Nagasaki.* New York: Marlowe, 1995.

Nora, Pierre. "Between Memory and History: Les Lieux de Memoire." Translated by Marc Roudebush. *Representations* 26 (Spring 1989): 7–24.

Novick, Peter. *That Noble Dream: The "Objectivity Question" and the American Historical Profession.* New York: Cambridge University Press, 1988.

Nute, Grace Lee. "Review of *The Westward Crossings: Balboa, Mackenzie, Lewis and Clark* by Jeanette Mirsky." *American Historical Review* 52, no. 4 (1947): 745–46.

Oehser, Paul H. *The Smithsonian Institution.* New York: Praeger, 1970.

Orwell, George. *1984.* New York: Plume, 1983.

Peckham, Howard H. *Pontiac and the Indian Uprising.* Princeton, NJ: Princeton University Press, 1947.

Pells, Richard. *The Liberal Mind in a Conservative Age: American Intellectuals in the 1940s and 1950s.* New York: Harper & Row, 1985.

———. *Radical Visions and American Dreams: Culture and Social Thought in the Depression Years.* Urbana: University of Illinois Press, 1998.

Peterson, William J. "America's Freedom Train." *Palimpsest* 29, no. 9 (1948): 257–81.

Phelps, M. William. *Nathan Hale: The Life and Death of America's First Spy.* New York: Thomas Dunne Books, 2008.

Piehler, G. Kurt. *Remembering War the American Way.* Washington, DC: Smithsonian Institution Press, 1995.

Pole, J. R. "The American Past: Is it Still Usable?" *Journal of American Studies* 1, no. 1 (1967): 63–78.

Polonsky, Abraham. *You Are There Teleplays: The Critical Edition.* Edited by John Schultheiss and Mark Schaubert. Northridge: Center for Telecommunication Studies, California State University, 1997.

Potter, David M. *People of Plenty: Economic Abundance and the American Character*. Chicago: University of Chicago Press, 1954.

Radosh, Ronald, and Allis Radosh. *Red Star over Hollywood: The Film Colony's Long Romance with the Left*. San Francisco: Encounter Books, 2005.

Rectanus, Mark W. *Culture Incorporated: Museums, Artists, and Corporate Sponsorships*. Minneapolis: University of Minnesota Press, 2002.

Rich, Daniel Catton. "Museums at the Crossroads." *Museum News*, March 1961, 36–38.

Riesman, David. "Psychological Types and National Character." *American Quarterly* 5, no. 4 (1953): 325–43.

Rosenberg, Emily. *A Date Which Will Live: Pearl Harbor in American Memory*. Durham, NC: Duke University Press, 2003.

Rosenstone, Roy. *Revisioning History: Film and the Construction of a New Past*. Princeton, NJ: Princeton University Press, 1995.

Rosenzweig, Roy. "Marketing the Past: *American Heritage* and Popular History in the United States." In *Presenting the Past: Essays on History and the Public*, edited by Susan Porter Benson, Stephen Brier, and Roy Rosenzweig, 21–52. Philadelphia: Temple University Press, 1986.

Rosenzweig, Roy, and David Thelen, eds. *The Presence of the Past: Popular Uses of History in American Life*. New York: Columbia University Press, 1998.

Ross, Stephen J. "Struggles for the Screen: Workers, Radicals, and the Political Uses of Silent Film." *American Historical Review* 96, no. 2 (1991): 333–68.

Rubenstein, H. R. "Welcoming Workers." *Museum News*, November 1990, 39–41.

Rubin, Joan Shelley. *The Making of Middlebrow Culture*. Chapel Hill: University of North Carolina Press, 1992.

Rydell, Robert. "The Fan Dance of Science: American World's Fairs in the Great Depression." *Isis* 76, no. 4 (1985): 525–42.

Samuel, Lawrence R. *Brought to You By: Postwar Television Advertising and the American Dream*. Austin: University of Texas Press, 2001.

Schiller, Herbert I. *Culture, Inc.: The Public Takeover of Public Expression*. New York: Oxford University Press, 1989.

Schlereth, Thomas J. *Cultural History and Material Culture: Everyday Life, Landscapes, Museums*. Ann Arbor: UMI Research Press, 1990.

Schlesinger, Arthur M., Jr. *A Life in the Twentieth Century: Innocent Beginnings, 1917–1950*. New York: Houghton Mifflin, 2000.

Schultheiss, John. "The Crisis of Galileo." In Abraham Polonsky, *You Are There Teleplays: The Critical Edition*, 67–73, edited by John Schultheiss and Mark Schaubert. Northridge: Center for Telecommunication Studies, California State University, 1997.

———. "A Season of Fear: Abraham Polonsky, *You Are There*, and the Blacklist." In Abraham Polonsky, *You Are There Teleplays: The Critical Edition*, 11–39, edited by John Schultheiss and Mark Schaubert. Northridge: Center for Telecommunication Studies, California State University, 1997.

Schwartz, Barry. *Abraham Lincoln in the Post-Heroic Era: History and Memory in Late Twentieth-Century America*. Chicago: University of Chicago Press, 2008.

Scudder, Townsend. *Concord: American Town*. Boston: Little, Brown, 1947.

Silk, Mark. *Spiritual Politics: Religion and America since World War II*. New York: Simon & Schuster, 1988.

Slotkin, Richard. *Gunfighter Nation: The Myth of the Frontier in Twentieth-Century America*. Norman: University of Oklahoma Press, 1998.

Smithsonian Institution. *Annual Report of the Smithsonian Institution*. Washington, DC: Smithsonian Institution Press, 1945–69.

Stegner, Wallace. *The Uneasy Chair: A Biography of Bernard DeVoto*. Garden City, NY: Doubleday, 1973.

Sterner, Alice P. "We Help Create a New Drama." *English Journal* 43, no. 8 (1954): 451–52.

Storrs, Landon R. Y. "Red Scare Politics and the Suppression of Popular Front Feminism: The Loyalty Investigation of Mary Dublin Keyserling." *Journal of American History* 90, no. 2 (2003): 491–524.

Stover, John F. *The Life and Decline of the American Railroad*. New York: Oxford, 1970.

Stratton, Ollie. "Techniques for Literate Listening." *English Journal* 37, no. 10 (1948): 542–44.

Susman, Warren. *Culture as History: The Transformation of American Society in the Twentieth Century*. Washington, DC: Smithsonian Institution Press, 2003.

Taussig, Michael. *My Cocaine Museum*. Chicago: University of Chicago Press, 2004.

Thomas, John L. *A Country in the Mind: Wallace Stegner, Bernard DeVoto, History and the American Land*. New York: Routledge, 2000.

Tibbits, Mildred. *Suggestions for Junior High School Teachers in Utilizing the Visit of the Freedom Train as an Experience in Teaching Social Studies*. Louisville: University of Louisville, 1948.

Toynbee, Arnold. *"Civilization on Trial" and "The World and the West."* 1948. Reprint, New York: Meridian Books, 1958.

Trouillot, Michel-Rolph. *Silencing the Past: Power and the Production of History*. Boston: Beacon Press, 1995.

Truman, Harry S. Public Papers of the President of the United States: Harry S. Truman, Containing the Public Messages, Speeches, and Statements of the President, January 1 to December 31, 1946. Washington, DC: U.S. Government Printing Office, 1962.

Tyrrell, Ian. *Historians in Public: The Practice of American History, 1890–1970*. Chicago: University of Chicago Press, 2005.

———. "Historians in Public in the Early Televisual Age: Academics, Film, and the Rise of Television in the 1950s and 1960s." *Maryland Historian* 30, no. 1 (2006): 41–60.

Vansina, Jan. *Oral Tradition as History*. Madison: University of Wisconsin Press, 1985.

Wall, Wendy. *Inventing the American Way: The Politics of Consensus from the New Deal to the Civil Rights Movement*. Oxford: Oxford University Press, 2008.

Wallace, Mike. *Mickey Mouse History and Other Essays on American Memory.* Philadelphia: Temple University Press, 1996.

Wegg-Prosser, F. R. *Galileo and His Judges.* London: Chapman and Hall, 1889.

Wertenbaker, Thomas Jefferson. *The Puritan Oligarchy: The Founding of American Civilization.* New York: Charles Scribner's Sons, 1947.

White, Richard. "A Commemoration and a Historical Mediation." *Journal of American History* 94, no. 4 (2008): 1073–81.

Whitfield, Stephen J. *The Culture of the Cold War.* Baltimore: Johns Hopkins University Press, 1996.

Wilson, Emily. *The Death of Socrates.* Cambridge, MA: Harvard University Press, 2007.

Wise, Gene. "'Paradigm Dramas' in American Studies: A Cultural and Institutional History of the Movement." In *Locating American Studies: The Evolution of a Discipline,* edited by Lucy Maddox, 166–214. Baltimore: Johns Hopkins University Press, 1999.

Woodward, C. Vann. *American Attitudes toward History: An Inaugural Lecture Delivered before the University of Oxford on 22 February 1955.* Oxford: Clarendon Press, 1955.

Zenderland, Leila, ed. *Recycling the Past: Popular Uses of American History.* Philadelphia: University of Pennsylvania Press, 1978.

Index

Note: Page numbers in italics refer to illustrations.

STUDIES IN AMERICAN THOUGHT
AND CULTURE